Jozef Banáš
PREBIJEM SA! ŠTEFÁNIK Muž železnej vôle

Jozef Banáš
Milan Rastislav Štefánik: A Man of Iron Will

Text © 2018 by Jozef Banáš
Foreword © 2018 by Miroslav Musil, Pavol Kanis
Translation © 2019 by James Sutherland-Smith
Jacket design © 2019 by Juraj Šramko
First English edition © 2019 published by IKAR, a.s.

Second English Edition © 2020 published by Hybrid Global Publishing, 301 E 57th Street, 4th Fl, New York , NY 10022 USA and co-published by Global Slovakia, Bratislava Slovakia
Second English Edition Foreword © 2020 by Zuzana Palovic & Gabriela Bereghazyova, Kevin McNamara, Michael J. Kopanic, Jr., Miroslav Musil, Pavol Kanis

No part of this book may be reproduced or transmitted in any form or by any means electronic or mechanical, including photocopying, recording or by any information storage and retrieval system, without permission in writing form **from the publishers. Jozef banas has asserted the right to be identified as the author of this work.**

Manufactured in the United States of America, or in the United Kingdom when distributed elsewhere

All rights reserved

Library of congress cataloging-in-publication data available upon request

ISBN 978-1-951943-17-2
ISBN 978-1-951943-16-5

WWW.GLOBALSLOVAKIA.COM

Jozef Banáš is one of the best-selling and most translated Slovak writers of the last decade. He is the winner of several national and international literary awards and his 32 books (15 in Slovakia, 17 abroad) have sold a total number of almost 320,000 copies. His work on Milan Rastislav Štefánik has been translated into several languages and 'Jubilation Zone' has been published in eleven countries. Dan Brown has described him as a seeker of truth, and the Dalai Lama blessed his efforts to bring people together.

More about Jozef Banáš at
www.jozefbanas.sk
www.jozefbanas.com

The measure of a man is the measure of his sacrifice.
Milan Rúfus

I dedicate this to all who love their homeland.

ZUZANA PALOVIC & GABRIELA BEREGHAZYOVA
The Man Who Made Us Proud to Be Slovak

Slovakia and Slovaks would have no country to call their own without the courage, grit, skill and divine belief of the remarkable, mysterious and tenacious Milan Rastislav Štefánik. How much this man did for our nation!

For a large part of the 20th century Štefánik's legacy was denied to the public. The memory of his heroism, his personality and achievements were suppressed and hidden from the eyes and ears of the very people he liberated. The communist regime denied anything or anyone that was not of the Party. However, Slovaks never forgot Milan Rastislav. They carried the remembrance in their hearts and passed it on through their blood.

Children who grew up in a totalitarian regime implicitly 'knew' Štefánik. And stored his story in the far recesses of their memory, far away from the grip of the heartless system and the cowardly grey men who administered it. Dreams cannot be stolen.

When communism collapsed and the vault of history opened again, Štefánik's long suppressed flame sprung forth. Streets were named to commemorate his mission, busks and statues were erected all over the freshly independent Slovakia in his honor.

The joy for the man who belonged to the world and was also one of us is contagious. The grief for his untimely loss is bottomless. The investigations and speculations into why and how he was taken from us continue to nag at our hearts and minds. Was there a sinister plot? Or was it an act of God's will?

Whatever the story, one thing is certain Milan Rastislav Štefánik made us proud to be Slovak. What he achieved for Slovakia and the Slovaks was nothing short of a miracle.

"Veriť, milovať, pracovať/ Believe, love, work"

This was Štefánik's motto and a mantra that we also draw on for inspiration in times of duress as well as elation. For what is more holy in life then "to believe, to love and to work". His message rings as a reminder for our young country even today.

Centuries of hardship and oppression at the hands of greater powers have created a population that still suffers from nihilism. This is why Jozef Banas's beautifully written documentary novel, which truly brings to light the Štefánik saga is so timely and important. Not only does it boost morale, it also proves to us that our dreams are possible - when we are brave enough to surrender to their higher call.

Štefánik is a man who walked the line and lived in harmony with the universe. In turn, the stars he gazed upon so lovingly, returned his devotion and guided his way to unimaginable heights.

Thank you Milan! You are a world class hero that continues to prove to us that:

"Obstacles must be shattered not succumbed to / Prekážky treba prekonávať, a nie sa im poddávať"

Zuzana Palovic, PhD & Gabriela Bereghazyova, PhD
Founder and Director of Global Slovakia
Authors of *'Slovakia: The Legend of the Linden'*; *'Czechoslovakia: Behind the Iron Curtain'*; *'The Great Return'*

KEVIN J. McNAMARA
A Slovak Unbound - The Global Impact of Štefánik's Brief Life

The brief but dramatic life of Milan Rastislav Štefánik invites a superlative tone, perhaps even demands it. Indeed, it would take a perverse kind of skill to make the man seem ordinary. That is what makes this historical novel by Jozef Banáš so perfect for its subject, whose life seems to have been shot into the sky like a rocket.

Born on July 21st, 1880, under multiple layers of historical obscurity, Štefánik was born a Slovak, an invisible people lost in the rural northwest corner of the Kingdom of Hungary, a restive appendage of the multinational Austro-Hungarian Empire, which disappeared from the face of the Earth in 1918 – with Štefánik's help. His father was a Lutheran pastor among a majority-Catholic people. His mother's two brothers were killed in the Slovak uprisings against Hungary in 1848.

As a child, his favorite pastime was to climb a nearby mountain to gaze at the stars through a paper telescope. Small, frail, and with a congenital heart defect, he compensated for his physical shortcomings with relentless energy, wanderlust, and determination. He journeyed to Prague to study astronomy at Charles University, where one of his professors was Tomáš G. Masaryk, later to become the first president of the Czecho-Slovak Republic. After earning his doctorate in 1904, he ventured to Paris, where he launched a career as an astronomer, explorer, and meteorologist, planting the French flag and swelling French pride during his travels as a "French" representative across Africa, Asia, Europe, and North America – including expeditions to Tahiti, Tunisia, and Turkistan. In 1912 he became a French citizen and two years later was inducted into the Legion of Honor. As a result, the Slovak had high-level connections among French politicians.

In January 1915, Štefánik volunteered for the embryonic French Air Force in the Great War. He fought on the Western Front before being transferred to the Eastern Front and Allied Serbia, where he took on diplomatic assignments. Seriously injured in the crash of his aircraft in Albania, by December 1915, he barely reached Paris, where he underwent a major operation that saved his life, if not his health.

Aware that Masaryk was now working from exile to undermine Austria-Hungary and gain independence for the Czechs and Slovaks, 2nd Lt. Štefánik got word to him that he had "powerful political connections in France." The professor quickly arrived in Paris on January 28th, 1916. Looking for his former student, Masaryk said, "I found him lying in a Paris hospital after a severe operation."

The injured aviator, diplomat, and Allied officer was the only Slovak of stature who was able and willing to help the independence movement, lending it credibility as a genuine "Czecho-Slovak" effort. Beneš was wholly Czech while Masaryk was half-Slovak, half-Czech; critics might have doubted their credibility as spokesmen for the Slovaks. Slovak leaders inside Hungary were beyond Masaryk's reach, as his treasonous activities made him a fugitive from Austro-Hungarian justice. As it turned out, Štefánik played as much of a role in the founding of Czecho-Slovakia as did Beneš, who years later would succeed Masaryk as its president. Too few people are aware of this largely due to Štefánik's early and sudden death.

In addition to lending a prominent Slovak name to the independence movement, Štefánik made five other significant contributions to its success. From his hospital bed, for instance, Štefánik arranged Masaryk's first meeting with the leader of a major Allied country, Aristide Briand, the Prime Minister and Foreign Minister of France. And Briand made a powerful public statement on February 3rd, 1916, after meeting with Masaryk:

"We French have always entertained keen sympathies for the Czech nation, and these sympathies have been strengthened by the war. I assure you that France will not forget your aspirations, which we share, and we shall do everything in order that the Czechs may obtain their independence. We will not speak about the details now, but as far as the chief point of your claim is concerned, we are in agreement."

This was the first public Allied expression of support for the aspirations of the Czechs and Slovaks. Moreover, Briand later inserted into a unified Allied statement of war aims a demand for "the liberation" of the Czecho-Slovaks. The Briand meeting opened another door for Masaryk, prompting the Director of British military intelligence, General George McDonogh, to see him. McDonogh asked Masaryk to share any French intelligence that Paris might not otherwise share with London. Thus was Masaryk now able to gain the tacit support of both London and Paris.

Štefánik was next dispatched to resolve a crisis in Russia, where his third achievement was to single-handedly convince a sharply divided Czech and Slovak émigré community to support Masaryk's Western-oriented independence movement over rival efforts to align the movement with Slavic Russia and its Tsarist regime.

A pro-Russian Czech politician, Josef Dürich, made his way to St. Petersburg to seek the support of Tsar Nicholas II's ministers and of Czech and Slovak émigrés in Russia, who made up the second-largest émigré community in the world, behind the American Czecho-Slovak community. Like many Czechs and Slovaks, Dürich yearned for Russia to liberate them, and he began working with the Tsar's ministers to wrench the émigrés away from Masaryk – despite the fact that Dürich was a member of Masaryk's Czecho-Slovak National Council in Paris. Dürich created a rival organization that served as a virtual arm of the Tsarist government; its official business was conducted in Russian and it was funded with Russian rubles.

Close on Dürich's heels, Štefánik arrived in Russia in July 1916. As an experienced military officer, unlike Dürich, Štefánik won the support of Russia's generals. As a representative of France, an Allied nation, unlike Dürich, he secured an audience with the Tsar. Štefánik was also authorized by Paris to negotiate for the transfer to the Western Front of Czech and Slovak troops serving in the Česká Družina, a special unit of the Russian Imperial Army. This effort would later be expanded on by Masaryk to create the legendary Czecho-Slovak Legion.

Štefánik presented documents to a confidential meeting of the émigrés that exposed Dürich as an agent of Russia intent on undermining Masaryk. The émigré leaders withdrew their support of Dürich, who was subsequently expelled from the Paris-based National Council, and Štefánik replaced him as Vice President of the Council.

Masaryk then dispatched Štefánik to the United States to recruit volunteers for a Czecho-Slovak unit in France and secure support from the Wilson Administration. After he arrived on U.S. soil on June 18th, 1917, Štefánik struggled to recruit Czech and Slovak volunteers for the French Army since the U.S. declaration of war in April 1917 gave the U.S. Army priority in drafting Americans, and it limited Štefánik to volunteers who were outside U.S. eligibility criteria. Yet he was much more successful in gaining political support, his fourth major contribution to independence as the only non-American, other than Masaryk, to conduct significant work for the movement in the United States.

Štefánik was the first of the exiled trio of Czecho-Slovak leaders to meet with any high-level U.S. official, meeting twice in July 1917 with U.S. State Department Counselor Frank L. Polk, who was then acting secretary of state. Disillusioned with what he perceived as a lack of support from Wilson's Democrats, however, Štefánik called upon Wilson's abiding enemy, former U.S. President Theodore (Teddy) Roosevelt, in August 1917, and Teddy was won over.

A hero of the Spanish-American War, former U.S. president, winner of the Nobel Prize for peace, survivor of an assassin's bullet, frequent speaker, and prolific writer, Roosevelt was a hard man to ignore, and he had from the start of the Great War urged Wilson to join the Allied war effort in an escalating series of public criticisms. After listening to Štefánik's appeal, Roosevelt became the first prominent American to endorse the Czecho-Slovak demand for independence. Paraphrasing one of Wilson's best-known lines, Roosevelt taunted Wilson – "before the world could be made safe for democracy, the Habsburgs had to go."

The fifth of Štefánik's contributions to Czecho-Slovak independence was his successful effort to convince Italy to support the movement. Rome hosted a "Congress of Oppressed Nationalities" in April 1918, where Czech, Slovaks, Poles, Romanians, Serbs, Croats, Slovenes, and Italians pledged to oppose Austria-Hungary, and each agreed to seek "complete liberation and complete national unity." With Masaryk recruiting POWs in Russia for the Czecho-Slovak Legion, the Czechs and Slovaks were represented in Rome by Beneš and Štefánik.

Another factor encouraging Rome to oppose Austria-Hungary was that Czech soldiers were defecting from the Austro-Hungarian Army to the Italian front, which was made easier by Štefánik, who had visited Italy in late 1917 to persuade Rome to create Czecho-Slovak units in the Italian Army. After the Congress, Štefánik negotiated the final accord to create these Allied Czecho-Slovak units.

On April 21st, 1918, Štefánik and the Italians announced the agreement, which gave the Czecho-Slovak National Council *de facto* diplomatic recognition. At a ceremony for the new unit on May 24th, 1918, Italian Prime Minister Vittorio Orlando declared, "Long live free Bohemia!" U.S. Ambassador Thomas Nelson Page likewise made enthusiastic remarks that sounded as if Washington recognized independence – it didn't, yet – but Georges Clemenceau, the new French prime minister, publicly welcomed a delegation from the Congress and privately indicated on April 20th that he was preparing to recognize the Czecho-Slovak National Council.

Following the Rome Congress, President Wilson also took a step closer to supporting independence on May 29th, 1918, when he had his Secretary of State, Robert Lansing, say, "The Secretary of State desires to announce that the proceedings of the Congress of Oppressed Races of Austria-Hungary, which was held in Rome in April, have been followed with great interest by the Government of the United States, and that the nationalistic aspirations of the Czecho-Slovaks and Yugoslavs for freedom have the earnest sympathy of this Government."

The Czech and Slovak legionnaires in Russia became deeply demoralized after Czecho-Slovak independence was declared October 28th, 1918, and the war was ended on November 11th. Worse, a coup installed Russian Admiral Alexandre Kolchak as the Supreme Ruler of Russia that same November. Having helped to topple a dictatorial Austrian monarch, the legionnaires now found themselves serving a Russian dictator.

This led to Štefánik's sixth contribution to Czecho-Slovak independence. On November 17th, 1918, he arrived at Vladivostok with French General Maurice Janin, under whom the legionnaires served. While Janin remained behind, Štefánik traveled deeply into Siberia to talk to legionnaires at the Red Army front. Reaching Yekaterinburg, he encountered many demoralized soldiers, many of whom refused to fight or move to the front. Still battling his own injuries, Štefánik was thin, pale, and sickly; someone else was asked to read his welcoming remarks.

On December 11th he ventured closer to the front and met legionnaires in small groups and spoke with them for hours. "All that time," legionnaire Frantisek Koci said, "Štefánik talked to them like a brother, like a soldier, like a minister and politician; he talked to them for four hours, ignoring his fatigue, often fainting from exhaustion. He was pleading, begging, demanding, and appealing to the feelings of the soldiers so much that some apparently began to cry."

Washington's refusal to support an all-out war against the Bolshevik regime, together with a shortage of Allied shipping, trapped the legionnaires in Siberia. "You must hold out here in Siberia until the end, until the victory is won," said Štefánik. "And this you must do relying only upon your own strength, for I can tell you authoritatively that no help from the Allies will come to this front. It is useless our discussing the rights and wrongs of the case. The fact of importance is that help will not come."

Štefánik was under no illusion his words were persuasive or soothing. As a result, he and General Janin issued orders in January 1919 officially withdrawing the legionnaires from combat. The Legion instead agreed to guard the Trans-Siberian Railway from the Ural Mountains to Irkutsk, where one year later the Legion reached an agreement with the advancing Red Army to exit Russia.

The Slovak was set to perform another service to his new nation when the end came. While the Czechs were celebrating independence, Hungarian troops at first resisted surrendering the Slovak territory. Stefanik secured a biplane in Rome and, with an Italian crew, headed home. As they approached an airfield near Pressberg (now Bratislava), the plane suddenly lost altitude and crashed on May 4th, 1919, killing all aboard. The rocket had fallen to earth. Štefánik was not yet 40 years old.

The Slovak's elaborate funeral was one of the first major ceremonies of the new republic of Czecho-Slovakia. A monument worthy of an Egyptian Pharaoh surrounds his mountain-top gravesite in Slovakia. The Slovak Republic's main airport at Bratislava is also named for the aviator, and Slovakia's version of Air Force One (an Airbus A319) is emblazoned with his larger-than-life image. Superlative, indeed.

Kevin J. McNamara

Associate Scholar of the Foreign Policy Research Institute, Philadelphia, PA, Author of *'Dreams of a Great Small Nation: The Mutinous Army that Threatened a Revolution, Destroyed an Empire, Founded a Republic, and Remade the Map of Europe'*

MICHAEL J. KOPANIC, JR.
A Tragic End to a Storied Life

In a 2019 contest in Slovakia to determine the greatest Slovak personality in history, General Milan Rastislav Štefánik's name made it to the very top of the list. When the polling ended, Štefánik triumphed. It was symbolic that this honor came in the year of the centennial anniversary of his death. Many communities across Slovakia were preparing commemoration ceremonies, and articles about Štefánik flooded the newspapers, radio talk shows, and TV commentaries. Today one would be hard pressed to even find a school child who has not heard about this famous Slovak patriot.

On the other hand, most readers of the English-speaking world have never heard of Štefánik or, indeed, Slovakia, a small and young state of 5.4 million people in the heart of Central Europe. Jozef Banáš's historical novel has the potential to alter those numbers. He has composed an historical novel which is a tour de force, a splendidly written tribute to a man of action of humble origins. Štefánik made and shaped history by his indomitable iron will to overcome seemingly insurmountable obstacles and focus on his long-term goals – a career in astronomy and the liberation of his homeland of Slovakia. Though continually hampered by a chronic stomach ailment and scraping to get by in his early penurious years, he pressed on and surmounted hurdles which most would not dare to leap over.

I might add that James Sutherland-Smith's translation itself is also a work of art. It reads smoothly and with vivid expression; one would hardly know it is a translation. A self-described poet and a lecturer at Prešov University in eastern Slovakia, his rendition of Banáš's masterpiece flows like poetry in motion.

It is appropriate that Banáš begins and ends the book with the event that shocked the newly born Czecho-Slovak state - Štefánik's tragic end in an airplane crash as he was finally returning to his beloved homeland of Slovakia. On May 4, 1919, his dramatic death thrust his name on a Slovak public who before 1918 had known little to nothing about the man who was engineering Slovakia's place in the newborn country of Czecho-Slovakia (The new state was named Czecho-Slovakia in all official documents, including the Versailles Treaty, until the centralist 1920 constitution eliminated the hyphen.). Censorship in Austria-Hungary had concealed his deeds abroad on behalf of his homeland. At the time of his passing, The Great Powers were negotiating treaties in Paris and Czecho-Slovakia still did not have formally defined borders. Nothing was set in stone. Moreover, Czecho-Slovakia was challenged by a Hungarian Bolshevik Army eager to retake what had belonged to the former Kingdom of Hungary for a millennium.

While the Czechs could boast an array of national leaders at home and abroad, Slovakia was in dire need of firm and experienced leadership. Slovaks longed for someone to look up to. A man of vision, Štefánik could fill those shoes. As a general with a track record of instilling discipline, organization, and high morale among the Czecho-Slovak Legion, he possessed the ability to command and inspire. Having only dealt with his legions abroad, his stepping on Slovak soil would have marked a new phase in his career. Prior to his return to Slovakia, his global reputation had preceded him and the population awaited his arrival in Bratislava with great expectations. But fate had it otherwise. His sudden and shocking demise would turn him into an instant legend.

Štefánik's grand funeral, so vividly described by Banáš, was the first state funeral in the new Czecho-Slovak state. Thousands lined the streets of Bratislava, and thousands more attended the second ceremony in his home village. For perspective, one might compare the depth and the sadness of the parade to the 1963 funeral after the assassination of American President John F. Kennedy. The new nation of Czecho-Slovakia was in mourning.

Among the mourning was Štefánik's fiancée, Baroness Giuliana Benzoni, even though she could not attend his funeral. His tragic death had abruptly shattered their plans to marry in June and start a family. Joining the ranks of many who had lost their spouses or intended spouses in Europe as a result of the Great War, Benzoni subsequently never married, and devoted the rest of her life to fighting fascism. Still, she never forgot her fiancé, loved him eternally, and even visited Štefánik's tomb in Slovakia on two occasions, in 1930, and yet again in 1968.

Almost immediately after Štefánik's funeral, many tributes and laudatory books mourned his loss and extolled his virtues. As early as 1919, the Bratislava Sokol organization started plans for the building of an elaborate burial mound on Bradlo, the hill above Košariská with an awesome vista. On February 28, 1920, Dr. Emil Stodola headed a newly formed Association for the Construction of the Mound, which raised money for a grand project. Slovaks, Czechs, and even Carpatho-Rusyns founded local branches which collected many small donations to fund the effort.

In 1927, construction began based on the design of the renowned Slovak architect, Dušan Jurkovič, who had originally suggested Bradlo as the most suitable site. Constructed of white travertine from the Spiš region, the monument consisted of two terraces, with sloping sides and built with thick and heavy rectangular bricks.

Finally, on Sunday, September 23, 1928, the mound was unveiled at a grand ceremony attended by a huge number of people and soldiers. They loyally came to pay homage to their hero despite a heavy downpour and a fierce wind.

What is befuddling to this day is why President Masaryk did not attend Štefánik's funeral. Granted, there were pressing affairs of state in 1919, but this was a close colleague who had perished in a tragic accident.

Also, President Masaryk did not attend the 1928 unveiling ceremony of the Burial Mound Monument on Bradlo. Beneš not attending is understandable, since Štefánik engaged in a heated argument with him and had also threatened to take him to a National Court for allegedly embezzling funds, donated by Slovak-Americans. But Masaryk was a lifelong friend and there is no evidence that their relationship had deteriorated. At the time of the dedication, Masaryk was even in Slovakia at his summer estate in Topoľčianky, and since 1921 he had also served as the honorary chairman of the association which organized the building of the monument. His non-attendance is all the more perplexing because he was listed on the official program as an attendee.

According to an article in *Slovenské národné noviny* (November 5, 2013), Masaryk used the excuse that he had never received an official invitation and was not prepare to present a speech. Masaryk visited Bradlo several weeks later and laid a wreath at Bradlo, but it was not the equivalent of being present for the grand ceremony. The mystery remains.

I first visited Štefánik at Bradlo in 1983, only to experience a terrible shock. Knowing Štefánik had denounced the Bolsheviks after his Russian experiences, the communist regime had neglected any upkeep and hoped his memory would just fade into oblivion. The site was covered in weeds and was badly in need of repair. Of course, after the Velvet Revolution of 1989, the Slovak government restored the monument to its intended glorious state. Today it is a frequently visited tourist site with ample nearby trails for hiking and enjoyment.

Interestingly, the first place to erect a lasting monument to Štefánik was Cleveland, Ohio. Even though Štefánik had never visited the city, he had inspired its large Slovak-American community. A local publisher and leader, Ján Pankuch, spearheaded and organized a national fund drive in cooperation with the Slovak League of America. In 1922, they hired the Slovak sculptor Frico Motoška to create a 10-foot-tall Štefánik statue, which was dedicated at a prominent place in Wade Park in 1924. It remained there until 2013, when it was moved to the Slovak Cultural Gardens in nearby Rockefeller Park. In the East Village of New York City, there is a little-known bronze memorial plaque dedicated in 1942 to

General Štefánik at St. Mark's Place.

Numerous other monuments and statues honoring Štefánik exist in Slovakia and beyond. A huge statue has stood since 2009 in front of the new Slovak National Theater on the embankment of the Danube. It is a replica of the 1938 sculpture crafted by Czech artist, Bohumil Kafka, an old friend of Štefánik from his Paris days. The original statue was pulled down by the Communists in 1954. There is also a similar statue of Štefánik in southern France in Paulhan, and in Paris, a memorial plaque lies at a square called "Place du Général-Stefanik". A memorial to Štefánik also adorns the grounds of the observatory in Meudon, France.

When most of us think of legendary national leaders, we think of tall, strong and handsome men with an affluent background. Štefánik was just the opposite; he was short (5.38 feet. or 1.64 meters), had a pockmarked face from a severe case of small pox as a child, and started becoming bald early on. That is also why we usually see him portrayed wearing a cap in a smartly attractive French army uniform! He obviously compensated what he lacked in looks with a sparkling personality and social skills that enabled him to overcome his physical shortcomings.

Recent studies have shed some new light on the character of Milan Rastislav. In addition to being a great leader, a tireless worker, and a man who knew how to make connections with people in the upper echelons of society, Štefánik was also almost always in debt in his early life and was somewhat stubborn and intolerant of what he viewed as ignorant and/or dishonest people. His heated conflicts with Beneš and his own father attest to these flaws. Yet he did have the skill and the tact to know when to compromise, and his love of his homeland was unquestionable. Milan possessed a personal magnetism which is hard to put to the pen.

For sure, Štefánik exuded a charisma which enchanted those whom he encountered, from fellow scientists to diplomats and his many female friends. There is no film footage with sound.

We will never be able to hear his words, but Banáš's book takes a step toward comprehending Štefánik as a person in a way that most academic histories cannot.

One can only say, bravo pán Banáš, you have opened the world to read about Štefánik, Slovakia's beloved hero.

Professor Michael J. Kopanic, Jr.
University of Maryland Global Campus

MIROSLAV MUSIL
Enjoy!

When a creator embarks upon a new piece of work, he is projected, perhaps unwittingly, into the skin of his protagonist. What more exemplary model could the eccentric world traveller, Jozef Banáš, choose from our domestic historical scene, than Štefánik? Perhaps Beňovský (but I pipped him to the post there). When Banáš falls in love with any subject, he bites into it like a bulldog and doesn't release it until the work is done. I've been involved with Štefánik for years as the founder of the Diplomatic Museum section in the Ministry of Foreign Affairs, but I don't know anyone who could have given this personality force so thoroughly and many-sidedly as the author. Not least he has consistently chased down the historical sources hither and thither in the world. Moreover, the author has brought to bear the perspective of the novelist. It is as if when writing he has been constantly transfused by his character. Thus, with the irresistible Štefánik charm, holding to the tactics of "Cherchez la femme", and in this spirit, engaging in seductive dialogues with a love ending (discreetly indicated between the lines) that you would not discover in any archive. The queen of the Parisian salons, Claire Bois de Jouvenel, and the renowned pioneer of feminism, Louise Weiss, not to mention his eternal fiancée, the Marchesa Giuliana Benzoni, cannot resist him.

Naturally, along with the protagonist he scours continents and oceans. Banáš, like Štefánik, immediately gains the sympathy of local people because he evokes the feeling that he's one of them. For us, the image of Štefánik as a General in uniform has prevailed. Yet, the book also introduces him in a ragged piece of cloth in Tahiti in a circle of natives. He introduces us to the backstory of his first secret mission in the service of the French government to Ecuador, which presaged his dizzying rise. The author then portrays his hero as a brilliant diplomat and strategist, often behind the fan of enchanting ladies, persuading even seemingly indomitable political and military leaders in France, Italy, Russia and the USA... And all this to the limit of his physical and mental forces.

Štefánik has a number of memorials in various countries, I have also contributed to a number of them – in Tahiti, Tonga and at the Altar of the Fatherland in Rome, where he triumphantly placed the flag of the Czecho-Slovak legions. But this book is the most wonderful memorial to him because every one of you, dear readers, can take it with you and enjoy it with an intimate sense of well-being.

Miroslav Musil
Slovak Diplomat, Historian, Explorer

PAVOL KANIS
Combining Fact and Fiction

Jozef Banáš is a man of experience who knows the complexity of historical personalities and events, the strength of higher interests and goals and the twist and turns that exist in the routes to achieving them. Therefore, as a practising writer, he searches for conflicting themes from the past and the present. Such a theme is the life of the first modern Slovak in politics, Milan Rastislav Štefánik. Given the wealth of Czecho-Slovak writing on Štefánik, it is necessary today for everyone writing something new about Štefánik to have a deep understanding of the contemporary context, empathy for the national hero and no little personal courage.

The author has divided the hero's dramatic life into 79 chapters. As a result, the novel creates a similar impression to that of Breughel's paintings. Only when you look in detail can you marvel at how much about the life of a particular time is captured in each square centimetre of information. When you turn to any of the 79 chapters, you'll find something interesting to note, consider and maybe remember. Of course, this is not only due to the structure of the novel, but also, and more importantly, to the author's probe into Štefánik's extraordinary life, the sea of his dreams, plans, actions, problems and personal torments within his contemporary context.

The time span of Štefánik's life is known to many readers. The author has used this as his starting point, respected the essential facts and not completely shifted his original search for the truth about Štefánik into the sphere of his own imagination. The documentary style fuses the author's creativity with real events telling a successful story whose main motive is the liberation of the nation. Given the number of academic and popular-history books, studies, diverse memories and newspaper articles about Štefánik, it is quite surprising that Banáš's novel is, in fact, only the second project of this kind over the last century. And this comes a full ninety years after the release of L. N. Zvěřina's novel, *Milan Rastislav Štefánik. A novel of a Czechoslovak Hero.*

And the story of the hero?

It ends as in an ancient drama. The hero did what he had to do. He gained the freedom of the nation and its state. And when he is to be rewarded and glorified, he dies tragically.

Banáš's documentary novel is a tour of the ridge of mountain summits. He often balances between documentary and fabulation as he resolves the contradictions between historical reality and artistic creativity. So readers may wonder. "How was it actually? Did what the author writes really happen? Or is it just a product of his imagination? Which is which?"

But is the aim of a novel to make this distinction absolutely clear? Isn't the best communication link between readers and a national hero a certain uncertainty and the possibility to question? Perhaps this is where the author's hidden desire lies. Perhaps his primary wish is to contrast historical documentary and his creativity in stimulating the readers' interest in getting to know Milan Rastislav Štefánik, as well as his struggle for our national existence.

Pavol Kanis
Former Slovak Minister of Defense

PART 1

peace

CHAPTER 1
If I'm Killed...

On 26th April, 1919, Milan Rastislav Štefánik in Rome said farewell to the Marchesa Giuliana Benzoni and with the chief of the Czecho-Slovak military mission to Italy, Major Jan Šeba, went by train north to Padua. The headquarters of the Italian Supreme Command were located there, having moved from Udine in October 1917 after the defeat of the Italians at Caporetto. He negotiated with General Badogli on the completion of the arming of our troops. From there he continued by car to the General Staff of his own troops. On 27th April, in Gallarate at Lago Maggiore, the headquarters of the main command of the second Czecho-Slovak army and on the Golasecca training ground, he carried out an inspection of the militia battalions. He was pleasantly surprised by the discipline and military skill of the soldiers and could not hide his enthusiasm when the 50th Battalion, composed exclusively of a thousand "vigorous Slovak sons", as he himself termed them, offered military honours. From Gallarate, they returned to Padua through Milan. Along the way, he eagerly laid out plans for the period following the return of the legions from Russia, explaining to Major Šeba his ideas of the division of labor between him and the Minister of National Defense, Klofáč. He was also passionate about plans unrelated to the army. He carried in his head an idea for creating a ministry of tourism, thinking aloud about many measures concerning the organization of the new republic related to the position of Slovakia.

    He certainly didn't act like a man reconciled to preparing for his resignation. It was wonderful spring weather. The General was delighted to see magnolias, cherries and apricots in blossom outlined against a snowy backdrop of the Southern Alps. He followed the route with a map on his knee and was upset when he found the driver not going the shortest way. In vain was it that the driver explained that he knew the route by heart; that didn't count with the general. His mathematical thinking didn't permit him to deviate from a plan, so he was tense when it happened. If stomach pains were added to this, drivers were usually given a hard time. In the town of San Martino he unexpectedly asked the driver to turn north towards Lake Garda. In the village of Colombare, on the delightful peninsula of Sirmione, he got out and, charmed by the glories of nature, walked along the shore of the lake for a while. His mood improved, and with Šeba, he ordered a glass of red wine at the local tavern. They were silent for a moment. It was easy to see that many thoughts were flying round in the General's head.

"Beneš and Klofáč don't understand the army and they have nothing to say to me about its formation. I'm the Minister of War! It's necessary to organize the regiments and brigades!" he suddenly blurted out.

"Brother Minister, I'd argue that Minister Klofáč is trying to bring the army home with as few foreign officers as possible. Retaining foreign soldiers is very expensive and officers cannot communicate with ranks in speech that they understand. But we can only rely on our own forces up to a certain level, to the rank of captain and major. You say our army must have a national spirit and that foreign officers don't."

"They don't," Štefánik agreed, then paused.

Šeba took advantage of his consent and continued with a subject that was slowly but surely troubling the General. "I don't want to be intrusive, but ambulance train 103 leaves Foligno for Prague on 30th April."

"No, I have to go home as soon and as quickly as possible. Šrobár has written that a Hungarian Bolshevik invasion is imminent any day in Slovakia. We have to prepare for it and deal with the Hungarians, I'll go to Prague and then return to Siberia for our boys."

"Brother Minister, consider the dangers of flying over the Alps in an unreliable machine to an uninspected airport in Bratislava. You'll be going over enemy positions from which you can be shot down at any time..."

"Brother Major, if man is destined to die, a brick may fall on his head in the street..." Štefánik laughed. "Look, how wonderful, a fairy tale landscape! I'd love to live here. And maybe I will. After a certain serious change in my personal life, which we are planning for the beginning of June, I might even build a villa here. Look at the splendour, the endless vineyards. Many of them belong to our beloved princess, Venosa... hm, beauty..."

"Giuliana?" Šeba leaned towards him slyly. An approving smile at once shone on Štefánik's face. "An excellent idea. Ask our friend Jurkovič to design a villa for you. Our construction team, under the command of Major Vydra, has completed their work and we are considering dissolving it. However, I can easily imagine your building a lovely red brick villa in this place that would blend in with the surrounding countryside..."

"That's not a bad idea at all," Štefánik smiled mysteriously. His gaze caressed the peaks of the mountains, reflected on the surface of the lake.

Šeba hadn't seen him in such a good mood for a long time. They finished their wine, gazed at the white peaks for a while and then continued on their journey eastwards to Padua. During dinner together at the hotel, Šeba brought his minister a telegram from a friend, Vavro Šrobár. The Slovak politician was urging him again to come to Bratislava as soon as possible. Štefánik read the telegram several times. Then he shook his head.

"I know Vavro very well. It must be tough there if he's insisting."

"Brother General, I've received a telegram ordering me to return to Rome immediately," Šeba informed him carefully.

Štefánik didn't protest. On the contrary, to the major's surprise, it seemed as if this news pleased him.

"When are you leaving?"

"With your permission, tomorrow after breakfast."

"All right, we'll meet at breakfast."

Šeba had no idea that the General was unable to sleep for a long time after Šrobár's telegram. His mind couldn't get over his incomprehensible appointment *in absentia* as Minister of the Military at the time when the war was over and in icular following his recent interview with Jozef Škultéty in Paris. The experienced politician was right: the war wasn't over yet. The coup d'état in Bohemia had ended on 28th October, but in Slovakia it had just started. He who saved Slovakia would also save Czecho-Slovakia. He would be a real hero, he would lay down conditions.

There was silence between the two soldiers at breakfast, which was firmly interrupted by the General.

"I've decided. As soon as it's possible I'll fly home. To Bratislava! They need me there!"

"You wanted to go to Prague to the President," Šeba tried to break in once more.

"I can't go to Prague, it's out of range of the plane and…"

"The train has been prepared…"

"I won't enter enemy territory. And first, I'll sort out what needs to be done in Slovakia before going to Prague."

"I don't know… um… whether you've heard about the tragic accidents of Captain Palli, de Bosiss and others. They all crashed in a Caproni."

"I won't be alone. I've no doubt that my Italian friends will give me both experienced pilots and mechanics, but I know a little about flying. I flew as a military observer in a Caproni."

"Engineer Caproni himself, who was the designer, doesn't recommend flying longer routes on machines built during the war; they were made in the rush of war from poor quality materials. And the distance from Padua airport to Bratislava is at the very limit of its range," Šeba argued.

"Brother Major, I thought you knew me better. I'll fly!"

"Brother Minister, in Slovakia and especially in Bratislava there is still actually war. In the middle of March, Šrobár announced mobilization; only in Prague do they think that the whole republic is going wild with enthusiasm. Bratislava and its surroundings are still almost wholly Hungarian. Nor can we really talk about Bratislava, for most of its inhabitants it is still Pozsonyi or Pressburg. They want to win people over and seek a referendum. If I were to use strong words, politically incorrect, but real, you would actually fly to Czecho-Slovakia only on paper; according to the mood of the people, it's still Hungary! You'd be going into enemy territory. If we telephone the time of your arrival home in advance, we run the risk that interested Hungarian parties will know about it before our own. Although. Šrobár has brought with him Czech and Slovak officials, so far they only occupy a few posts, as many places in his office are still held by Hungarians and these "Madarons" who, were willing to swear loyalty to the Czech Republic. But no-one knows how it really is. Can they be trusted? Espionage is often done by cleaning staff or maintenance workers. And what do you think the Hungarian Red Guards will do when they see an enemy bomber flying over them? The entire right bank of the Danube is occupied by Hungarian Bolshevik bands. Two weeks ago, the Kun gang announced a general mobilization and young workers and peasants are enthusiastically joining up. Béla Kun has told them that, as in Russia, they're fighting against the bourgeoisie for the nationalization of land and factories. Moreover, they're supported by Russian Bolsheviks and keep them as military advisers. In Slovakia, "nemzeti tanács", national councils according to the Bolshevik Corps, appear subordinate to Budapest. Their influence is growing."

"How many troops do they have?"

"The Commissar for War, Landler, has got a hundred and twenty thousand men, of which forty were deployed against the Romanians and eighty thousand against us. But as the Romanians have signed a ceasefire with Kun, they've given the Hungarians the chance to move their divisions against us!"

"And us?"

"General Piccione has barely 54 battalions with a strength of two hundred to two hundred and fifty men each. That's not even fourteen thousand men altogether. The entire border line, as defined by Pichon, is protected by the 31st and 32nd regiments of the Sixth Division, a couple of hundred volunteers, Sokol and the Guard of Freedom. It's not enough. We don't have any more yet, even though our muster is rapidly filling up. Yet worst of all, not only Šrobár, but unfortunately the soldiers don't trust their Italian officers."

"Yes, I've heard that they pass secretly at night over the Ligetfal, Petržalka bridge, to go to Hungarian casinos and play cards with Hungarian officers."

"We, the godless Czechs are probably more unacceptable to Italian Catholics than the Hungarian Calvinists, even though they are Bolsheviks..." Šeba added bitterly.

Štefánik breathed heavily, tightening his jaw.

"It is necessary to accelerate the strengthening of our muster. The Kun gang is preparing a general offensive. According to information from the Italian General Staff, their intelligence from Bratislava reports that they could start it any day, no later than 20th May!"

"Damn it, we have sixty thousand fit fighting men in Russia and we can't get them home! The Bolsheviks obviously stick to what Károlyi said before them: we'll never give up Pozsonyi. But we aren't sissies! It seems that the separation of Slovakia from Hungary will only be possible by force. So we'll fight! We'll drive our enemies out of Slovakia and then I'll go on for an interview with Masaryk about other services to the republic!"

"As if that wasn't enough, there is a continual controversy between the Italian Piccione, who is in command of West Slovakia and the French Hennocque, who is in charge of the East," said Šebo. He lit a cigarette in his agitation. "Hennocque was ordered by Klofáč to expel the Romanians from Carpathian Ruthenia and occupy the territory."

"Klofáč... what's that clerk who's never held a rifle in his life doing in charge of this? He's the Defence Minister, and we're still in the war. And the Minister of War is me! This is what I'm going to debate in Prague – though only once I've brought order to Slovakia. In Paris, the bureaucrats tremble over a diplomatic solution..." Štefánik shook his head. "Piccione complains about the lack of a fighting spirit in our troops. He, who was the chief commander for Slovakia safely lodged in Kroměříž! Only when Šrobár began to bang the table did he kindly move his butt and came to Bratislava with his cow, because his stomach is most important, and he must have fresh milk every day. Damn it, if he'd been to Siberia for five minutes, his delicate stomach would have enjoyed itself. It is clear why Vavro needs me in Slovakia as soon as possible! General Lelovský hasn't been a brilliant success with the Škoda factory in Plzeň, they're said to have not enough copper and are unable to produce ammunition. We must gain Petržalka, otherwise the port of Bratislava is in serious danger, the only connection between our country and the sea and the Southern Slavs."

However, despite his words, Šeba continued to urge him.

"Piccione reports that the entire southern border on the right side of the Danube is occupied by the Hungarian Guards all the way to Devín. In Bratislava, they've fortified the Franz Joseph Bridge with iron barriers and barbed wire. In its centre motorboats with machine guns patrol the Danube, Hungarian and Czecho-Slovak soldiers, equipped with machine guns, are in close proximity to each other. The bridge pillars are mined, one or the other side can blow up the bridge if necessary. The Hungarian artillery menaces the government building from the right bank of the Danube, where their megaphones blast calls to refuse cooperation with the new government while threatening to hang all those working with the new authorities. The frontline between the Czecho-Slovak and Hungarian republics leads through the centre of the Danube literally under the windows of the government building. Hungarian Bolsheviks have begun to paint their air force's coat of arms over the Hungarian tricolor with a red star. But who knows if they've managed all the planes in that short time? The Hungarian tricolor is similar to the Italian: white-green-red. Any soldier can confuse it through sheer bafflement... In Slovakia, martial law applies."

"So Vavro has introduced martial law already. Good."

"Brother General... it is obvious that landing in this situation in Bratislava is extremely risky... Please consider our proposal and travel to Prague by the legionnaire ambulance train! You don't have to get out of it at any point on the way. They want to welcome you at home dearly, they're waiting for you, your mother and family..."

"So they can wait. I've already told you that I'd only go by train in the event of extreme bad weather. And I don't enjoy formal greetings. Even in Siberia, they got on my nerves. How many times have you reported to them that I'm flying?"

"Twice."

Štefánik nodded thoughtfully. They had tea together. Before saying goodbye to the General, Šeba tried once more to talk him out of the flight.

"Dear Major, you keep trying to persuade me, but needlessly. So I'll tell you directly once more. Tomorrow morning I'm going straight to Portogruara Airport."

"Is that your final decision?" Šeba stared at him.

"Friend, you keep telling me that the situation in Bratislava is extremely dangerous, so it's clear that my journey must be kept secret until the last minute. Do you think that if a minister went by train through Vienna, he wouldn't be welcomed by representatives of the Italian mission at Vienna railway station and probably by many other useless people? And in Vienna, I'd have to switch to the cross-country route that runs through Petržalka. It's still in Hungarian territory. Perhaps I'd only be accompanied by Hungarian

Bolshevik soldiers from Petržalka to Bratislava," he laughed heartily. "I want to be home as quickly as possible. We mustn't waste time... And..." His voice faltered, a lump in his throat. "You can't imagine my desire to see my mother, my brothers and sisters, my friends, my Kopanice... My God, Janko, I'm going home... You know? I have a homeland..."

"Here, lad, stay healthy." Much moved he approached the Major and hugged him unexpectedly. "If I'm killed on this journey, tell them at home that I loved our nation, our country very much."

Šeba couldn't say a word, nodding only, embracing the General and stepping into his car.

"Don't dissolve the building platoon just yet." Štefánik smiled and lifted his finger in farewell.

In the afternoon, the chauffeur drove him to the Italian headquarters, where the Chief of Staff of the Italian Army, a friend, General Armando Diaz, was awaiting him. He explained the difficult situation in Bratislava, about which the General was surprisingly well informed. It wasn't necessary to persuade him to inform Bratislava of his departure at the last minute. From now on, the flight, the airmen, the mechanics, and the aircraft itself were under the strictest secrecy.

In the evening he returned to the hotel. In Paris he'd agreed with Lieutenant Daniel Lévis and Major Gaston Fournier that Bratislava would receive an encrypted telegram just before his arrival. They'd choose the landing location and send him its coordinates in advance. Only a small circle of trusted persons would be informed about the arrival of the aircraft, including his friend, Count Hanuš Kolowrat, who'd be waiting for him at the airport with a cameraman from where they'd travel to Skalica. Štefánik ordered the chauffeur to head towards Campoformido, an airport near Udine. He didn't go to Portogruaro Airport, as he'd told Major Šeba. From 30th April to the day of his departure, he was lost for three days, probably spent in Padua with Giuliana.

CHAPTER 2
The Bell of Freedom Strikes

For a few days, clouds moved over the Kopanice region, as if they, too, wanted to express their understanding of the Slovaks being ruthlessly repressed by the Hungarian hand of the Prime Minister, Koloman Tisza. On Sunday, 18th October 1885, after the service, the sun briefly shone over Košariská, which gave the pastor, Pavel Štefánik, hope that it would come out, and that the following day's wild boar hunt would be an experience not only for him, but also for his brother-in-law, a lawyer from Senica, Štefan Fajnor, baptismal godfather to his children. He was particularly pleased that the godfather for his confirmation, Jozef Miloslav Hurban, the first President of the Slovak National Council, who was already in his seventies and enjoyed an old age in the manse in Hlboké, had announced his visit after a long time.

In front of the Košariská church stood groups of churchgoers who sat on hay wagons and set out for Priepasné, Dlhý vŕšok, Hrajnohovci, Trvajovci, Blatniakovci, Bachárovci, Markovci and other settlements scattered under the massive Bradlo, belonging to the Košariská-Priepasné parish. The priest looked up, his eyes settled for a moment on the storm clouds over the mountains. It was a few metres from the church to the manse, but he was still in a hurry. Thirteen-year-old Ľudovíta and twelve-year-old Igor were walking along with ten-year-old Oľga behind their father. Behind them was his wife, Albertína, with a hymn book in her hand, holding eight-year-old Pavel by one hand, who was leading seven-year-old Eleonóra with the five-year-old Milanko on the other side, responsibly overseeing his brother, three-year-old Fedorko. Mária Želmíra, their disabled daughter, was lying in bed at home. When the tall, muscular father Pavel, whose long side whiskers and serious face enhanced an impression of sternness, walked up to the gathered people, they stood, took off their caps, politely bowed to the "Lord" and greeted him. He was obviously delighted by the respect and honour rendered to him. He was not only a parish priest, but also a general authority who, from time to time, also dealt with neighbours' disputes and his word had weight even with the Brezová mayor. As Hurban's student, he was a worshipper of the principles that his great teacher had engraved into him: honesty, honour, truthfulness and courage. A great help in dealing with official affairs was the priest's wife, who came from an educated family and herself had graduated from the German Protestant Grammar School in Prešporok. Leading people to a national and Christian ideal felt like a mission to him. His parishioners knew that his beloved Albertína, who couldn't be angry with anyone or even look sternly at them, advised her husband, and hoped that their worries would reach their pastor's ears through her.

Pavel Štefánik was the first priest whom the people from Horné and Dolné Košariská, Dlhý Vŕšok, Trvajová, Priepasné, Mlynárovej, Šindelákov and Mosnákov had elected as parish priest after they decided not to contribute to the costly town church in Brezová and separated from the evangelical congregation there. They themselves built a dignified temple with a high tower on the meadow below Plačkéch Úboč then a widely-dispersed parish, to which the new Košariská-Priepasné priest brought his young, 18-year-old wife, Albertína, whom a Myjava native, the parish priest, Ján Trokan and senior pastor, had married to him in Myjava on 4th July, 1871. It was a wedding that had no equal. After the ceremony, the wedding procession went to Košariská and the Myjava congregation accompanied them to Polianka, where they were handed over to the people of Košariská and Priepasné, whose parish priest, Pavel Štefánik brought home his bride.

Seven years after the marriage, on the twenty-second Sunday after the Holy Trinity, on 17th November, 1878, God's Tabernacle was opened in Košariská. Ján Trokan, Senior Pastor of Nitra, consecrated it and Ján Leška, his co-senior in the Church, declared the word of God and the inauguration of the first word of the Divine Preacher of the Košariská-Priepasné Church congregation was carried out by Jozef Miloslav Hurban himself. After finishing the manse parishioners collected money for a wonderful organ made by the Brezová organ master, Martin Šaško.

The new priest enjoyed a respect from his parishioners bordering on devotion. He understood their tough situation very well having been an orphan from the age of seventeen. They liked him for his strong Slovak consciousness which had cost him a lot in his secondary school studies, when he went to Banská Bystrica together with Štefan Fajnor, Ján Mocko and the writer, Pavel Beblavý, to protest the exclusion of students from the Prešporok Lyceum. He matriculated in Banská Bystrica and thanks to Hurban, was able to study theology in Vienna and Rostock. The more educated parishioners would come and borrow the newspapers and journals *Slovenské pohľady, Kvety, Slovenský týždenník, Národnie noviny, Cirkevné listy, Slovenský denník* or family calendars, which their parish priest had ordered.

Pavel was in a hurry and his wife barely managed to keep up with him. Thoughts whirled in his head on events in Upper Hungary and in the Balkans. He was curious about what Hurban's view would be. He assumed that Hurban would not be well disposed to these not only because the leadership of the Prešporok theological academy was threatening to exclude his youngest son and other Slovak students, but also because the authorities had begun unprecedented persecutions of Boženka and Vendo Kutlík, the protectors of Slovak students in Prešporok.

In the Štefánik manse courtyard there was a welcoming whinnying of horses, who had just been taken care of by Štefan Žídek the noisy family coachman.

Štefánik came to life: "I guess our beloved brother, Janko Leška, has also come?"

"Exactly so. They're both sitting inside the manse. Granny Kubovička has already primed them with plum brandy," Žídek smiled slyly.

With joy the master of the house entered the manse followed by his wife.

"Honoured brothers, you are our guests. Most dear to me," he first embraced Jozef Miloslav, who paternally greeted Albertína, then gripped his hand as did Senior Leška. Albertína disappeared quietly. Two rooms of the at the front of the manse were reserved for pastor's guests. His wife and children could only enter here in exceptional cases. Here the priest was in charge. The second room was connected to a bedroom with a large door that was almost always closed. In the large bedroom, the smallest Milanko and Fedorko and the ailing Mária Želmíra lived together with their parents. The other children had beds in the kitchen behind the hall and in the smaller room between the kitchen and the store room.

In a moment Albertína knocked on the priest's door, waited for her husband to let her in and brought to the table fresh-smelling *lokše* with duck liver, *pagáče* and thinly sliced bacon. "Here's something to revive you after your journey. Lunch will be in about an hour," she bowed and walked to the door.

"I hope you will prepare us that delicious Košariská chicken with apple and honey, the last thing I ate at your place," Hurban raised a good-natured finger.

"As if it would be anything else, uncle," she smiled, and went out. As soon as the lady of the house had closed the door behind her, his face became more serious.

"Gentlemen let's rid ourselves of sombre thoughts," Leška tried lift the gloom. "Let's drink to the liberation of Eastern Rumelia, to the reunification of our Bulgarian Slavic brothers, led by the hand of God in liberation from the Ottoman yoke," he lifted his glass.

"Quite so. To the health of Tsar Alexander II the unifier, who did it despite the opposition of other powers," Štefánik added.

"There are rumours that the Serbs are gathering troops, want to use the Bulgarian fears of the Turks in the east and are ready to strike at Slivnica, Vidin and Sofia. And our Austrian and Hungarian power leaders are stirring up this fratricidal Slavic conflict."

"Today we prayed together that our Bulgarian and Serbian brothers wouldn't kill each other..." Štefánik said.

At that moment, the door flew open, and a whining Milanko and Fedorko ran into the room, firmly holding each other by the hand. "Papa, papa, Paľko wants to be Hurban, otherwise he doesn't want to play with us. But I want to be Hurban, and Fedorko is my aide. Let him be Kossuth!"

"Boys, boys, have some *pagáče* and stop whining. Captain Hurban never cried." His father cooled them down and winked at Hurban, sitting opposite.

"Even when they put him in jail?"

At that moment, a firm hand took Milanko and Fedorko by the shoulders. "Not even then, boy, not even then."

"Oh, uncle Hurban. Papa, it's Hurban. Our captain!" exclaimed Milan, plunging into the old man's arms with such force that he almost flipped him over in his chair. He turned to Leška and told him enthusiastically: "When the Hungarian guardsmen surrounded him in Hlboké, the farmers brought him out of the village in a wagon with manure – they'd hidden him under a trough. And uncle wasn't afraid!"

"And from where do you know that?" Hurban chuckled.

"Papa told us. Were you really not afraid?"

"Really."

"I will be like you!"

"Then they issued an arrest warrant for Štúr, Hodža and me. To this day, I remember that in it was a reward of a hundred zlatky in silver for the one who brought me to the appropriate authority. They hid me in the crypt of the church. When they were looking for me among the living, I was among the dead, and when they were looking for me among the dead, I was among the living... Oh I was at my wits' end. When they built a gallows in front of the manse and brought a mutilated man to the front of the Hlboké manse and planned to hang him in front of my Anička, saying it was me, it was terrible."

"So they didn't hang you, did they?"

"As you can see, no. But then they transferred the gallows to the Surovinovské field, where as a warning to all they hanged the Mayor of Čáčov, Martin Bartoň, with three others just because they found leaflets of the Slovak National Council calling for battle."

"And did they catch you?" Milan jumped in.

"No! We beat them so hard, the dust flew out of their pants... First, volunteers commanded by your grandfather Samko Jurenka routed the Hungarian guard at Jablonec. That was your mother's father. You can be proud of him!" He tenderly stroked the boy's head. "Then, in Myjava, eight thousand men gathered, and in September, at Brezová, we scattered the Kossuth guard with only a few rifles, flails, shovels, axes, forks. They ran in the direction of Vrbové..." Hurban smiled.

"Unfortunately, for your great-uncles, my uncles on my mother's side, Vilko and Ľudko Šulek, matters turned out badly." The boys' father took the arms of both of them and sat them on his knees. "Tomorrow will be thirty-eight years since Vilko was executed at Hlohovec for participating in our revolution. The cross we have in the parish is made from the crosspiece, from which your great-grandfather, Vilko was taken down... And for Ľudko, too, it went badly. In June of forty-nine, he died in Komárno, a fortress of cholera..."

"I will avenge them! When Fedorko and I grow up, we'll kill the evil Hungarians!" The tiny boy roared, jumped from his father's lap and slashed with a wooden sword.

"Not the Hungarians, boy," Leška objected. "The Hungarian masters and especially the Magyars must be beaten. Ordinary Hungarian people suffer just as we Slovaks, Croats, Romanians or Ruthenians."

"So we will beat the Hungarian masters," he thrust forward with his sword.

"I have a sword, too," said Fedorko beside his brother. "We'll beat them like at Világoš!" and he threatened invisible enemies.

The men laughed.

"It's a great pity that Kossuth was unable to talk to non-Hungarian nations. The Hungarian Revolution might have turned out differently..." Leška sighed. "Since the settlement of '67 and the Emperor's National Law a year later, when the idea of a unified Hungarian political nation began to be promoted, all other nationalities have been squeezed out. First they closed Slovak grammar schools, then put a police guard on *Matica slovenská*. It is quite possible that we are now being spied on... In the purely Slovak villages they are setting up Hungarian kindergartens, handing out Hungarian newspapers free of charge, and worst of all taking children from poor families to Hungarian families in the lowlands, officially to learn the language. If that were the case, I wouldn't mind, but they are literally Magyarizing them, making them forget their language and teaching them hatred for their ancestors. However, many Slovaks have guessed their intentions and are sending their children to Slovak families instead."

At that moment, the door opened and the eldest son, Igor, burst into the room.

"Bohuško is here!" he announced in a joyful voice. As soon as he had said it, a skinny young man with sunken eyes entered the room, but he held himself proudly and put on a happy and confident appearance.

"The Lord God grant us a good day," he said unusually loudly.

"The Lord God will hear," they replied.

"You're kind of late, son," Hurban said in a good-natured way.

The young man stood awkwardly and looked for a place to sit.

"The train from Prešporok was delayed, so uncle Kornel had to detain the carriage a little in Piešťany... I'm sorry."

"You're just in time for lunch," Štefan said calmly and pointed to an empty chair. Bohuslav folded his canvas bag and wiped the sweat from his brow. The men stared at him in silence, and even Milanko and Fedorko, with whom Igor was now sitting on the bench, waited for what would come next. Štefánik surprisingly didn't send them away. On the contrary, he winked encouragingly at the boys.

"We are all anxiously waiting for your explanation," said his father. "All sorts of rumours have come out of Prešporok. And your letters aren't the most cheerful."

"Well, it's not simple, but perhaps you don't have to be so glum," he said, trying to bring a smile to his father's face.

"Oh, son, I don't know how you can improve the mood of a man slowly approaching seventy and still under police supervision," Hurban smiled bitterly.

"Papa, what are you saying?" Bohuslav accused his father. "I won't even live to such an age."

"Enough of such gloomy talk," Štefánik shook his head. "Let's enjoy this great plum brandy instead. To us," he smiled wryly, and poured a dram for the men. Bohuslav drank only a drop and wiped his lips with the end of his sleeve.

"And nothing for us?" Milanko laughed.

"Aha, you young rascal," threatened Leška good-naturedly. Milanko and Fedorko giggled. The men drank and a heavy silence descended again, broken finally by a calm question from Hurban. "So, son, what's happening in Prešporok? Since the beginning of the month, we have been following only one topic in the newspapers, the Kutlik affair. And is the threat of expulsion, as you write, real?" Bohuslav's face was serious.

"It's said that they just want to scare you," said Leška.

These views were aimed at Bohuslav, who at twenty-three appeared tired and seemed to Štefánik to have aged since he'd last seen him nearly a year before. "Well, here's the newspaper," he said and placed *Pozsonyvidéki Lapok* on the table.

"We aren't interested in what this chauvinist rag writes. You tell us what's what," said his father.

"Well, on 3rd October we met up at *Iritzer* at Blumentál from eight o'clock to celebrate the name day of the lady Boženka, the wife of our good-hearted protector, the lawyer, Venda Kutlík. Vesel, Kmety, the lawyer, the theologians Roháček, Mičátek, Kuchta, Kostolný, Cablk, Baltík and other members of the Lyceum were all there. We enjoyed ourselves as in the past and, Mr. Kutlík paid the tab. It started to go wrong when we began singing our songs, *Hej, Slováci, Kopala studienku, Nitra, milá Nitra, Hore Váhom, dolu Váhom* and *Na Dunaji voda tečie*. When we shouted to the glory of the *Matica*, the cops suddenly burst in. It is alleged that Hungarian students put them up to it. Poniczky, Pálovics, Hornyánszky, Chriasztely, Holéczi, Kolpaszky and others."

"Probably Magyarized," Leška interrupted in disgust. "They're Hungarian Slovaks, because they all have adapted Slovak names."

"After the Turks worse than the Turks. God damn them to perdition!" Hurban vented his feelings.

"They also wrote a letter to the professor's council. They demanded our expulsion..."

"You don't say!" Štefánik jumped in.

"They called us agitators trying to herd congregations of evangelical theology and the evangelical Lyceum into pan-Slavic spheres of interest. We were also told that we read the *Národnie noviny*. Kutlík, the lawyer, also spoke at the celebration and praised Štúr, Hodža and you, papa. He urged us not to sell out our nation and remain true Slavic intelligentsia. They summoned me with Roháček, Veselý and Mičát for interrogation, where they called me a Hungarian. I argued that I was a Hungarian Slovak, and told them that the state was only harassing us because we were Slovaks. When they gave me a document to sign, I signed it with my full name and after it I wrote in Slovak – theology student. That really annoyed them!"

"You did well by them, son," said his father. "Ah, we must join the Lutherans and the Catholics of Slovakia, otherwise it's all up with us. Connect in words, in learning, in spirit, but there will still be victims... ah, there will be..."

"The bell of freedom is ringing, listen to it nations. Who doesn't listen will regret it. We were in it, we were like caged birds, but now we've found our feet, Slovaks," deacon Leška recited and turned to Hurban. "You wrote it beautifully. Yes, there will be sacrifices, but that is the price to pay."

"On your feet, Slovaks," Milanko and Fedorko jumped up with them, waving their sabres and lightening the serious atmosphere for a moment.

"What's the verdict?" Hurban asked with concern in his voice.

Bohuslav slowly removed the envelope from his pocket, pulled out a ragged document and, hesitating for a moment, handed it to his father.

"I can't read it! You read," he handed the letter to Pavel.

"Minutes of the Professorial Conference," Pavel read in a trembling voice, "The Evangelical Theological Academy on this day 15th October, 1885. Present: Samuel Csecsetka, Director, Francis Trsztyénsky, Andrej Masznyik, Bela Pukanszky, Julius Vassko..."

"Don't read the names of those Hungarian renegades, get to the facts," Leška snapped.

"As the congregation of the theological academy is subordinate to the provincial laws and administrative authorities, they have been guilty of violating the order of the Minister of Culture and Education of 1st August, 1883, number 1319... through singing and speaking they demonstrated against the Hungarian homeland, nationality and state, thereby also violating the laws of the Evangelical Theological Academy and Disciplinary Regulations at point 153. Considering that Bohuslav Hurban, Štefan Roháček and Ján Vesel were the initiators, leaders and instigators, from the minutes of the investigation and other writings, it has been proven that, the initiator of the disruption and seducer of the Lyceum students was Bohuslav Hurban..."

"Enough!" Hurban stopped him. "Tell us the sentence!"

Štefánik took a breath and grimaced: "Bohuslav Hurban, Štefan Roháček, Ján Vesel, students of theological academy, according to point 157 f, are punished by expulsion from the Theological Academy and from all Hungarian Evangelical institutes..."

There was a long, heavy silence. "So you have been expelled just like me, Štefan Fajnor and Paľo Beblavý once were. Don't worry, we'll get over this somehow," said Štefánik.

"You'll go to the Czech brothers in Prague. No argument!" Hurban decided firmly.

The mournful atmosphere was interrupted by the voice of Albertína inviting everyone to the kitchen table. "We have prepared caraway bread and there will be a chicken with honey," she enticed the men. But seeing their sombre faces, she immediately realized that this Sunday lunch would be difficult to eat. After lunch they stayed at the table for a while, but nobody talked. Finally, old Hurban rose.

"It would be fine to get home by dark."

They said their farewells and went to the gate. A hackney carriage was waiting in front of the parish which both the Hurbans and Deacon Leška boarded. The coachman, Štefan, shook the reins and his repeated "hijó" spread through in the village. Pavel Štefánik looked at the departing carriage disappearing at Pod Bradlom, as it turned towards Brezová. He little knew that it would be the last visit of his beloved Hurban at the Košariská manse.

CHAPTER 3
Spread the Glory of Your Nation

Between the conical hills of Úboč and Kopec, a beautiful valley of Lopušná with three mineral water springs, a twenty-minute walk from the manse, stretched southwards. Košariská children would go to the water and on a stream under the shade of tall oaks, they floated paper boats on which they wrote 'to America'. When the boys climbed up Kopec, they came upon a magnificent view of the Bradlo massif opposite. Milanko liked working in the garden from an early age and never refused to play with his sisters. They made clothes for wooden dolls out of horseradish leaves. Under the roof of the outhouse they hung wickerwork "mines" for pigeons, which Milanenko – as his mother called him – liked to watch. He racked his childish brains by thinking about how these creatures could fly. He longed to imitate them, so he brought branches from the forest, trimmed them and twisted them together. Then he attached the diapers of his younger brother, Lacko, and imagined having wings. Boldly he jumped from the table and smacked his forehead. As he later recalled jokingly, it was his first air crash.

He liked to go with the boys to the majestic Bradlo, from which there was a magnificent view of the Kopanice region. In the time after the battle of the White Mountain, many Czech and Moravian exiles had settled here, bringing with them the learning and rebellious thoughts of Ján Hus. A large image of the master hung along with images of Luther and Krman in his father's office, with its large library. German, French, Czech, Slovak and Hungarian books were available not only to the family but to anyone who showed an interest in education. Milan's older siblings; Ľudevíta Albertína, Igor Branko, Oľga Ľudevíta, Pavel Svätopluk and Elena Antónia, were among the better pupils of the Košariská school. On Sunday, after holy services, his father received visitors from churchgoers in the parish offices. He comforteded them, encouraged them, advised them, lent books, calendars, *Cirkevné listy* and *Slovenský týždenník*. At the time of elections, coaches waited in front of the Košariská manse, where voters with Slovak flags above their heads went to vote for a Slovak deputy.

From the spring of 1880, a falcon family had settled in one of the niches of the Košariská church. That year, on 21st July, a strong wind blew up in the middle of Košariská. The parish priest was getting ready for urgent business in Brezová with his colleague Leška. He was in a hurry because his wife was ready to give birth at any moment. He went to the carriage, where Štefan Žídek was already sitting, watching the bird hanging in the air high above the manse.

"God bless you, Pastor. I've been watching that falcon for a while. A strange bird, it can fly at the same speed as the wind against it, so it can stop in the air and lurk for its prey."

"Let's get going so we can be back as soon as possible," Štefánik said. They were back in an hour and the attentive Žídek raised his eyes.

"Oddly enough, the falcon is still there, as if waiting. Probably another son," he laughed.

Indeed, a newborn baby was crying from the manse room by late in the evening. At that time, no one could know that a boy was born who, one day, would become an adornment not only of the Kopanice region but also of his, the Czech and the French nations. The ruler of his birth was the planet Mars, which gives a newborn child power and courage, but also passion, indefatigability and explosiveness. The conjunction of Saturn in the Aries sign gave him ambition, organizational skills, authority, precision, tact, but also anger and jealousy. Saturn's square with the Sun weakened his health, and the square with Venus foreshadowed misfortune in love. His godparents were his father's brother-in-law, Štefan Fajnor and his wife Emília, but Antónia Vanai, his father's sister, carried him to baptism, as the official godmother was expecting. Fajnor, the godfather, was not only a lawyer but also an excellent national revivalist, composer and church senior supervisor. At his father's wish, Milan also received the second name, Rastislav, on his baptismal document, just as he had added Branko to Igor and Svätopluk to Pavel. Albertína also brought into the world Fedor Bohuslav, Marienka Želmír, Ladislav Dušan, Mojmír Alexander, Jaroslav Sergej and Kazimír Konštantín, though Fedorko, Mojmír and Jaroslav didn't live to see adulthood.

Despite his slight figure, Milan gained respect for his courage and vigour among the Košariská children. He was always the bandit captain in games of "outlaws and constables" and when they played Napoleon, he was never other than the Emperor. He had to be doctor in playing doctor, and when somebody played school, everyone knew in advance that Milan would be the teacher. Even though he was tiny, he reliably fulfilled the role of protector of his younger brother, Fedorko. They went out together with a sidesman from the church on trips to Ševcova skala, and even Klenová. Most of all they enjoyed the moments when men moved felled and trimmed trees from the forest. With the men, they sat on the long trunks, mounted on the front and rear wheels of the ox-drawn wagons, which were attended by the loggers so they wouldn't slip when they jolted over the ground. In the garden behind the house, they used children's spades and hoes to weed and clean the potatoes, cabbage, peas, beans, onions, and other vegetables. Once in May, he and Fedorko wanted to surprise their mama and hoe the potato patch. They'd already done a good job so their mamušenka, as they affectionately called her, sent them to Juhasz with jugs for milk. By the time they were back, Ľudka and Igor had finished hoeing the patch. There was an outcry and a rumpus as Milan had wanted to finish the bed by himself. Mama couldn't do anything else, but give him a new piece of land, where he and Fedorko could plant their own potatoes, which they then took good care of.

In the evenings he would sit by an upstairs window and watch the stars. When it was warmer, he would also go with Fedorko to Úboč above the manse and count the falling meteorites. In a clearing in the woods above the cemetery, they built an observation tower from rocks and branches, which they called the observatory. From a cloth merchant from Brezová, they plundered a metre-long hollow tube of cardboard, which served as a telescope. Nobody knew about their secret hideout. It became a refuge, a place where only their faithful loyal dog, Nero, would go with them. One early evening at the end of an unusually warm May 1886 they went up to below the mountain. "Will there be some falling stars? And shall we count them?" Fedorko couldn't wait.

"They aren't falling yet, not until August," said Milan. Enchanted, they gazed long into the sky and the better not to hurt their necks they lay back on the ground.

"That's the most beautiful one, the brightest," Fedorko pointed to a bright star just above them.

"Stars have names. You discovered that one, it'll be named after you. Fedorko's Star. What do you say?" Milan asked.

"Okay, but you found a star, too," urged Fedorko.

"I've discovered them all... We'll wait until August when they fall. When stars fall you have to wish for something and then it'll come true," Milanko explained. "What would you like?" He turned to his brother.

"I'd like us always to be together."

"We are."

"But always! When we are grown up, we won't be."

"How do you know?"

"Granny Kubovička said that when people grow up, everyone goes their own way."

Milan didn't answer, just grabbed his brother's hand and held it tight.

"Don't be afraid, we'll be together forever because we now swear it. Like uncle Hurban's fighters swore that they would always be united. You swear?"

"I swear."

"So do I," Milan confirmed, raising his hand solemnly. His brother repeated the gesture.

Fedorko lay down again, warmed by the May sun and stared up at the sky. "Where are the stars during the day?"

"They are still in the sky, only we don't see them because the sun has illuminated them."

"How do you know?"

"Papa said."

For a while the brothers watched the sky gently lit by the sun setting behind Bradlo. "You have a hot arm," Fedorko said quietly. "And you're shivering all over. Are you cold?" Milanko didn't answer. Fedorko leaned toward him and nudged him. "Don't go to sleep. Let's go home. It's getting dark."

"My God, boy, look at you!" Mama wrung her hands as she stared at Milanko. "You've got a temperature," she put a hand on his burning forehead. "That comes from lying on cold ground," she said to him.

"We were wandering among the stars," Fedorko declared importantly.

"That was your idea again. What are you going to be when you grow up?" his worried mama observed Milan's unusual silence.

"We will be astronomers. I already have my star. And when you find yours as well, we'll name it after you. It'll be called Mamušenka," said Fedorko.

A bowl of steaming soup waited in the kitchen table. "Perhaps, but first you must eat!" she ladled soup into the boys' plates.

"And where are the mushrooms?" Fedorko dipped his spoon in his plate, but all he found were potatoes.

"While you were roaming under the stars, the others ate them. At least you will now know to be at the table on time. Here we all eat together," said his father, who'd just entered the kitchen and didn't pass up the chance to admonish them. Fedorko began on his soup, but Milanko stared silently in front of himself. His mama watched him anxiously.

"My God, and what's this?" She walked over to the boy and examined some faint red spots that had been revealed by the light of the kerosene lamp on his face. She pulled off his shirt. "Bring the lamp closer," she ordered her husband, who held the kerosene lamp to Milan's body. It was covered with red spots which had changed in some places to blisters. The boy began to sway drowsily and coughed.

"It's chickenpox," his mother shook her head worriedly.

"Chickenpox? Where could he have caught it?" his father tried to calm his wife. "Well by the hand of the Lord God, at least he'll be done with it. He'll be going to school in the autumn, so he can now get over it. I'll send Kubovička for the wisewoman."

"We'll have to put him in the back room by the storeroom. He can't be with the other children. I'll make him up a bed right there. Send Ľudka or Igor to the wisewoman. And Fedorko is to wash right now. Kubovička should come immediately to heat up the water. Don't let anyone go near him!"

The old wisewoman from the Holotas ordered the boy's nails to be trimmed so that he wouldn't scratch his blisters, which would otherwise turn into scabs. Those on the cheeks were especially dangerous because they could disfigure his whole face. She ordered drinking plenty of water and especially camomile and agrimony tea. Only his parents and grandma Kubovička had access to Milan's room. Although the children were strictly forbidden to enter, Fedorko ducked in for an occasional, unguarded moment, under the arch below which the logs were stacked for the winter, secretly bringing freshly picked strawberries from the forest. He'd heard how the wisewoman from the Holotas in the kitchen had recommended to his mama these forest berries, which perfectly disinfect and cleanse the blood.

His father used to seclude himself in the back parlour room when he wanted to have space from the children to prepare his sermons, funeral or wedding addresses or when a visitor came to him. And they often came to see the enlightened master of the manse. One of his favourite guests was the thinker, preacher and writer Ján Pravoslav Leška, who had been the pastor of Brezová for five years, having come there from Bzince. Though there was a thirteen-year difference between the two men, they had a very friendly relationship. They both tried to dampen hostility between the people of Brezová and Košariská, caused, among other things, by the strong craftsmanship roots of the Brezovans, who, it was claimed looked down on the peasants and shepherds from Košariská. But when the two priests became friends, relations between church congregations settled down. Together they read *Národnie noviny, Cirkevné listy* or *Černokňažník* and discussed the latest events. One of their most burning topics was the report on the expulsion of Vavro Šrobár, Michal Radlinský, Jozef Hajduk and nine other pupils at the Royal Catholic Grammar School in Levoča from all schools in Hungary. In nationally conscious Slovak families, it created a wave of ill-will. Leška and the master of the house had to contain their annoyance so as not to wake Milanko, who was sleeping in the next room.

"This is how they threw out young Hurban and his comrades last year. They claim it's because of their pan-Slavic affections. At that time they were our Lutherans, now they are Catholics. Oh, it was good what uncle Hurban said at the time that we had to be united, regardless of religion. They also criticized Šrobár for disseminating the books of the Evangelical Hurban," Štefánik sighed.

"It's particularly cruel in the case of Šrobár. He was expelled from the eighth grade when he had already passed the written exam. He was one of the best students and needed only to pass his oral exams. He was blamed for having collaborated with Hajduk, who said that the closing of *Matica slovenská* was theft. But wasn't it?" Štefánik was offended.

"When asked by Director Halász whether he was a Slovak, he replied that he was and that he must belong to some nation. And imagine, my reverend brother," Leška said heatedly. "This Halász yelled at him and said he should know there were no Slovaks, but only asses. He then asked how can he be other than Slovak when his family, the Liptaks, don't know any other language than Slovak. And imagine this Halász is a native of Skalica and his father's name was Michalík. These latter-day Turks! Oh… Goddamn them!" he didn't know how to contain himself in his distress.

"I will be like Šrobár, too," said little Milanko suddenly in front of them in his nightshirt. The men hadn't even noticed in the heat of their debate that the door had been ajar all the time.

His father sat him on his knees.

"The Lord knows if you will meet the same fate. He is older than you as the reverend here is older than me and see, what friends we are," his father smiled at Leška. He looked closely at the boy and found with satisfaction that his temperature had passed and a bright cheerfulness was warming his pale blue eyes.

On the tenth day after the boy's isolation his blisters began to turn into scabs that gradually peeled off. Grandma of Holotas was full of praise at how quickly Milanko returned to mischief. When the boy looked into the mirror after his illness at his scarred face, he exclaimed in shock: "Mama, how ugly I am! I'll never find a wife."

As soon as they let him rejoin his brothers and sisters, the Štefániks once more had to call the Holotas wisewoman. On Fedorko's tiny slim body, mama found the same red spots that Milanko had had shortly before. "Well, we have it again," she announced bitterly to the family. But she didn't complain and, as in Milan's case, set up an improvised isolation room in the storeroom.

"Mama, Fedorko got it from me, didn't he?" Milan asked his mother guiltily.

"Milanko, he could've got it from you or from anyone. Well, at least we know now what to do to get rid of it quickly."

"I'll go to the forest to collect strawberries."

"Only with Ľudka or Igor. You can't go into the woods alone. You promise?" Milanko nodded unconvinced. So he went for strawberries not only with Ľudka, but also Igor, Oľga, Paľko and Norika. And though more and more strawberries came from the forest, Fedorko's condition didn't improve. Doctor Július Markovič was visibly ill at ease, fearful for the worst, unable to give advice on the disease. Fedorko's temperature didn't fall, he trembled with feverish chills, blisters and scabs burned him, the boy cried constantly from pain, not even trimming his nails helped. Later on, both his hands were wrapped in a soft, silky cloth to keep them from scratching his scabs. In addition, painful boils also developed in his mouth and he could barely swallow soup. Holotová, the wisewoman, brushed the blisters with an ointment from chickweed and bathed him daily in warm water with bicarbonate of soda, agrimony and oatmeal. After the bath, his little vest was coated with camomile tea to ease the itching. It didn't help either, so they put Fedorko in pyjamas soaked in camomile for the night. To relieve his chills, they put hot bricks wrapped in jute bags at his feet. But Fedorko's blisters did not dry out even after ten days, when almost all Milan's scabs had peeled off. Pavel was all the more troubled by having to bury four of Fedorko's peers that month. Kostelný the teacher mentioned that Dr. Erdély, an expert in skin diseases, was working in the Piešťany spa. His father instantly wrote an urgent letter to the doctor asking him to come to Košariská, sending a side of bacon, a bottle of liquor and saying he'd pay whatever money was needed. Kostelný offered to go with the coachman, Žídek, to Piešťany and bring the doctor to the sick boy. But it was too late. Fedorko was tossing and turning in pain in the back room, his mother wiping the sweat from his hot brow, talking to him, but it seemed that the boy no longer heeded her.

At that moment, Kubovička ran into the kitchen.

"Reverend sir, Reverend lady, come to Fedorko, he's babbling something asking for Milanko."

His parents hurried into the room. They could see Fedorko whispering something in an audible voice. There was no need for his parents, granny Holotová, the teacher or Kubovička to say anything. They knew that the boy's last moment had come.

"Teacher, please, take Milanko with you. If it comes to the worst, it mustn't be known that Fedorko..." she said. Tears poured down her face, her husband hugged her tightly, his hands shaking. The teacher nodded and disappeared. Fedorko looked at his parents and said in a surprisingly clear voice: "Mamuška, tell Milanko that in the garden under the jasmine bush I have a beetle in a box. Ask him to take care of it. He should feed him grass and the box should not be closed completely, the beetle could suffocate." The boy spoke only with great effort. He closed his eyes, breathing hard, twitching, clenching his fists for a moment, then opening them. Finally, on his face there was a heavenly peace and a mysterious, angelic smile. He died on 9th June, 1886, a month and four days after his fourth birthday. It was the first death in the family, and in particular the mother, who was in the fifth month of another pregnancy, was long unable to reconcile herself to the departure of her youngest son.

They tried to keep his beloved brother's death from Milan, not even taking him to Fedorko's funeral. Finally, his father decided to tell the boy about it.

"As is written, we don't know the day or even the hour," he told him. "That's why, lad, you have to live every day as if it were your last. To live to the fullest, not to kill time in idleness; to be grateful to the Lord for every moment he has given us. Every day, every hour, even second, is God's call for self-improvement and for yourself and the world. Our Fedorko went to a heaven where we shall all go and meet again. The Lord is sending us a brother or a sister who will be born in the autumn. It'll be when you go to school. In memory of our beloved Fedorko, promise me that you will learn well and spread the glory and honour of your nation and the Štefánik family. So that Fedorko can be proud of you up there." His father held out his hand and stared into the boy's face, pockmarked by the scars that remained after his recent illness. Milan stood up, put his hand into his father's open palm and gripped so hard that his father stared in surprise.

CHAPTER 4
Neither Obstacle Nor Illness Will Overcome Me

On 9th May, 1840, the foundation stone of the Košariská Church school was consecrated.

A year later the school was officially opened by Jozef Miloslav Hurban. Thirty years later, the same year the people of Košariská elected as their pastor, Pavel Štefánik, Martin Kostelný, one of the first graduates of the Evangelical Teaching Institute in Revúca, became a general teacher and organist. The subjects were determined by the Nitra seniorate and young Milan, together with his classmates, was taught Luther's Short Catechism, Leška's Catechism, Church and Biblical History, Geography, Husbandry, Agriculture (Forestry), Memorizing Songs, Arithmetic, Reading and Writing. The school year started in November and ended in March or April. The teaching day was from nine to twelve and in the afternoon from one to three. The young teacher was an exemplary model for the children with his impeccable life, beautiful family, sobriety and understanding.

Unlike other churchmen's families, the Štefánik family decided not to provide Milan with individual study but have him educated with other Košariská children. On the day of enrollment, eager first-time pupils waited in front of the school from seven in the morning, although the sign on the school gate declared that enrollment was from eight. Martinko Fajnor, Ďurko Repta, Zuzka Gábrišová, Martinko Plačko with his brother Štefan and many other children played hide and seek in front of the school. Shortly before eight, the Rector and his daughter Emilka personally opened the school gate, inviting the children inside. She and Milanko had got to know each other in games in the manse garden and in the meadows above the church. Several times he'd accompanied one of his older siblings to school, which they attended together with more than a hundred and twenty children. Since the teacher occasionally came to the Štefániks to talk about the progress of his siblings, he took Milan as an old friend. Therefore, his parents were surprised when the first-year pupil came from school after a week in tears.

"I didn't understand anything, the schoolmaster said something about the Emperor and King Franz Joseph, and that our village belongs to the county of Nitra and I don't know who the Emperor is or in which county he lives..."

"Oh, my brother, the teacher wasn't teaching the first years, but the older ones. You newbies were supposed to count your fingers on your hands. In the first year you'll be glad if you learn to count to twenty, read something and write a few words," Igor laughed.

"But I can count to a hundred," exclaimed Milan, and quickly rattled off one to a hundred in front of both surprised parents and his siblings.

"Since you're so smart, tell us how many boys are in the first level," said Pavel.

"Seventeen. Belko is first in alphabetical order, then Fajnor, Gábriš, Kopas, Kopecký, Nešpor..." Milan remembered the names of his classmates, whom he listed without hesitation in alphabetical order. "Finally, Repta, Ševčík, Štefánik, Šlahor... no... wait... T is after L, so I'm the last one."

"And who are you sitting next to?" his father asked, pleasantly surprised.

"Martinko Plačko... And the teacher calls the Plačkos the three kings, because Martin, Matej and Štefan come to school with one spelling book," he laughed heartily as did his mama, papa and siblings.

Milan embarked on learning with gusto, craving knowledge and brought joy not only to his parents but also to his teacher, Kostelný. Apart from Physical Education at which he didn't excel, he was among the best pupils in all subjects. It often happened that he calculated the examples the teacher had given them, and then through boredom corrected the mistakes of his senior classmates. After finishing his second year, Kostelný went to Štefánik and they considered how to deal with the talented boy.

"In good conscience, about Milanko I can only give you the best report out of all the children I've taught at the Košariská school so far. I'd have given him more of the curriculum, but although he is the best, I mustn't make exceptions. He stands out especially in arithmetic and it would be good if he continued to pursue mathematical sciences at high school," Kostelný said.

"Oh dear. Milanko has siblings and we can't afford expensive private schools. Since the abolition of the three Slovak grammar schools, there are only Hungarian grammar schools in the whole of Hungary, so the boy has to learn Hungarian. To put it better, to learn it because all he knows is 'nemértem' (I don't understand) and 'jona pot' (Hallo, good day)," Štefánik expostulated. "The alternative is to put the boy in a Hungarian environment and let him practise the language. I've already spoken to a friend, the lawyer Šidó in Šomorja, sorry, Šamorín, that Milanko will be taken for a term and they'll send us their daughter, Margitka for improvement in Slovak. After completing the four grades of folk school, he'll follow his brothers, Igor and Pavel, to the Lyceum in Prešporok," his father stated clearly. Nobody dared challenge his decision, but in the end the relatively cheap Prešporok Lyceum was the only education solution for many educated Lutheran families.

No sooner had he settled at the Šidós' place in Šamorín than he started to go to school. He had to concentrate very much on understanding all the instructions and commands of a strict teacher who sorted pupils by size and placed them at their desks from the tallest in the back rows to the smallest at the front. Milan sat at the first desk. The teacher then gradually reseated them. The best were at the front and the weaker ones were moved to the back benches. The worst completely sat in the back on the dunces' bench. Milan had some work to do not to be moved there. He knew almost no Hungarian, so he had to write his letters in Hungarian to his father as proof of his progress in this subject. As a result, old Štefánik learned that the teacher preferred pupils whose fathers were craftsmen, butchers, vegetable farmers, cobblers or did other useful professions. The children of pastors, coachmen and other unproductive jobs had worse marks than the parents of the children from whom the teacher profited. The rebellious Milan noticed this and protested strongly. Finally, the teacher, for fear of problems, gave up his unusual criteria for pupil assessment, but he did not forgive Milan and cursed him cruelly: "Belőled fiam nem lesz semmi, még a saját apád sem fog eltemetni, mert akasztófán fogod végezni." (Nothing will come of you, your own father won't even bury you because you will end up on the gallows.) The boy listened calmly to the teacher's words and even smiled at the bawling teacher. *Teacher, if you knew how wrong you were. I will be somebody. It's completely certain. Neither obstacle nor illness can overcome me. I'll be famous, I must be famous.*

After six months in Šamorín he returned to finish the fourth year of elementary school at Košariská. His childhood was coming to an end. Summer games of tag in the meadows under Úboč, competing to be the best at cracking whips or sliding on the frozen stream at Fošková meadow, drowning Morena, the straw doll at Beltane, driving sheep from Priepasné, grazing cows and catching trout from the stream had gone forever. The only thing left for him and which always remained was observing the stars. The cardboard telescope had collapsed from rain and snow over time, but memories of his children's observatory and his beloved brother, Fedor, were stored in his heart forever.

On 3rd September, 1890, the moment came that both Milanko feared his mama, Albertína, were dreading: the time to pack and leave the house. Forever. The ten-year-old boy found it hard to hide his unwillingness and sorrow. In vain did his father explain to him that he was going to gain an education at a nearly three-hundred-year old institution that would make him a wise man. Milanko also saw how his father struggled to control himself and maintain his dignity. The little boy walked to the end of the garden to cry alone and refused to leave his home. Nor did the persuasion of his brothers Igor and Pavel, who had already studied at Prešporok, help. Now, only the girls and four-year-old Dušan would be staying at home and so, although he was angry, he also realized that there was no other way of studying for a boy from a poor family. Moreover, when he was told that uncle Hurban, Milan's godfather, Štefan Fajnor, a celebrated Brezová pastor and frequent guest in their house, Ján Leška, the famous poets Janko Kráľ, Andrej Sládkovič, and Ľudovít Štúr himself and also a special hero of the boy, great-uncle Vilko Šulek – when he learnt that they had all studied at the school, then the ten-year-old Milan decided. His ambition and desire to excel persuaded him. On the evening before his departure day, Milan's father counselled him.

"Milan you feel pain that you're leaving home, and your mama, I and your sisters are sad. I understand you, but we have to overcome pain, because that is what makes a man. No wailing, no bowing, but a firm, proud attitude. You have experienced brothers in Prešporok and they will help you in moments of trouble. Keep to your way of speaking in Prešporok, for your mother tongue is the utterance of the spirit and the heart. But be respectful to different languages. Learn

Hungarian and German diligently and don't forget the mightiest language of our Slavic brothers, Russian. The professors are held in respect, in no wise irritate them. You know who your father is and who you are. Always be a good Slovak in your heart and don't be ashamed of your speech. If I discover that any of you are ashamed of us, don't dare to come home again. You are Štefánik, a descendant of the revolutionaries, and I know that you will withstand even the most difficult storms. God keep you. Just as when your brothers left home for the first time, you will promise me now that you will be my pride, and will uphold the honour of the Štefánik family."

"I promise, papa. I know I'm a Štefánik."

In the morning, his father clasped his son firmly to his chest, making the sign of the cross on his forehead. Mama kissed his hair, "Most of all, Milan, work hard, believe and desire and everything will be granted to you."

Then he and his brothers and uncle Žídek, who helped the lads load the trunks on the cart, headed for the station to Piešťany and from there into the arms of a great, strange world which one day he would surely conquer.

CHAPTER 5
A Defiance That Moves Mountains

The famous Evangelical (Lutheran) Lyceum was founded in 1606 and had been an elite Hungarian school for nearly three hundred years. In 1714, the polymath, Matej Bel, a great figure in the history of Hungary, became its rector. In 1778 a new Lyceum building on Konventná Street was erected near the Great Evangelical Church. In 1803, the famous department of Czechoslovak rhetoric and literature was founded in the Lyceum and led by Jur Palkovič. From 1855, the school was housed in a new building at Konventná 13. At that time, Wilhelm Michaelis, the director of the Lyceum when Štefánik arrived, had come there as a young teacher. The languages used at the school were German, Hungarian, and Latin, and it was a disgrace to speak Slovak there. Slovak was taught only as an optional subject. In Milan's class, more than half of the students were Slovaks, but almost all were nationalized as Hungarians. When the spontaneous Košariská boy occasionally forgot and spoke to his classmate in Slovak during the break, the teacher would notice, reprimand him in front of the whole class and make him pay a fine. If he repeated the offence, he could expect an offender's detention.

"This is not an ordinary Lyceum, but a school for elites," the professor of Hungarian History, Mátyás Lajos, instructed Milan in front of his classmates. "The best sons of the nation studied here. And do you know who they were?"

"Kollár, Palacký, Chalupka, Štúr, Hurban, my great-uncle Vilko Šulek..."

"What Štúr?! Šulek? The one they hanged for anti-state activities. If you continue like this, one day you'll end up the same way!" Lajos gasped furiously.

"Professor, please excuse me, but I just answered your question," Milan hadn't understood.

"A huge variety of boys have studied here, Croats, lads from Transylvania, Slavonia. Mór Jókai, which are his most important works?"

"Az aranyi ember (Golden Man), Egy magyar nábob (The Hungarian Nabob), Szeretve mind and vérpadig (Beloved Unto Execution) ó a legjob Jókai regény and Lőcsei fehér assony (Jókai's best novel The White Lady of Levoča)," Štefánik answered readily in perfect Hungarian.

"Nagyszer, gratulla!" exclaimed the professor. "Hát látod fiam hogy mikor kel akkor tudsz vállaszolni. A Sztúr bisstossan csak valami félreértés volt." (Great, congratulations, lad. So you see, if you can, you can answer correctly. We'll take it as just a misunderstanding over Štúr). The professor smiled happily.

"Excuse me, Professor, it wasn't a misunderstanding, Ľudovít Štúr was the leader of the Slovak revolution," Štefánik hastened to correct him.

"I will give you such a leader of the revolution you will forget your name. Štúr was a rabble rouser and a rebel, an anti-state element. Okay, we know that he withdrew obedience to our government and fought against our hero, Lajos Kossuth. He was and until now is the most important student of this lyceum. If you mention Štúr's name again on this ground, you will fly from here like dirty laundry! I hope you know Talpra Magyar!"

"A poem of Sándor Petőfi, a great poet, his native name was Petrovič and he studied together with Andrej Sládkovič at the Evangelical Lyceum in Banská Štiavnica. In 1843, both poets came to Bratislava, where Sládkovič studied at our lyceum and Petőfi was a correspondent of the Assembly."

"All right, all right, stop the tittle-tattle and recite!"

Milan stood to attention and proudly recited: "Talpra magyar, hi and haza! Itt az idő, most vagy soha! Rabok legyünk, vagy szabadok?..."

"What did the poet mean by that?" Lajos asked sternly.

"Is it a wonderful poem about freedom – the time has come to ask, do we want to be slaves or free? We swear to God that we will no longer be more slaves!"

"Well, on the whole good, you just weren't accurate. The poet says: A Magyarok istenére esküszünk, which means that we swear to the Hungarian God!"

"Excuse me, Professor sir, but in Religion with Professor Kvačala, we have learned that there is just one God for everybody..."

"I don't know what nonsense Kvačala is teaching you... What did our enlightened Prime Minister Kálmán Tisza say about this? Well, students, who knows?"

Július Čičvár, renamed Gyula Csicsvár as soon as he arrived at the Lyceum, raised an eager hand. "Please, Honourable kormányelnök sir, Tisza Kálmán said in 1866 that there is no Slovak nation in Hungary, there is only a single and indivisible Hungarian nation."

"Kitünő (great), Csicsvár," said Lajos. "Take that as an example, Štefánik!"

"Excuse me, Professor, but according to the Hungarian census of 1870, our country, Hungary, has 13,219,350 inhabitants, of whom 46.9 percent are Magyar, 13.8 percent are Slovaks, 13.7 percent are Germans, 3.4 percent Ruthenians... So the official Hungarian sources confirm that we Slovaks exist. I myself am a Slovak, for my father and my mother are Slovaks, so what else can I be? That doesn't mean I don't love my Hungarian brothers."

"That's enough, stop! There are no Hungarians or Slovaks, they are just Hungarians. These are all residents of the countries of the St. Stephen's Crown, end of story. I warn you if you don't look to yourself, you'll have big problems at this school!"

The professor shot out of the classroom and slammed the door.

The slight Košariská student stood still, looking at the door slamming and a defiance entered his mind that would move mountains.

CHAPTER 6

We Have Entered the Service of the Soul

After the unpleasant incident with Professor Lajos, Milan was careful not to get into a similar situation again. When the professor of religion and optional Slovak, an important expert on Comenius, Ján Kvačala, explained to the boys how to behave and how to keep certain opinions to themselves, he became more cautious. He would never forget a meeting of a group of students with their favorite professor in the back room of the Blumental inn, *U Iritzera*, where Slovak students would traditionally meet.

"Sadly, lads," said Kvačala, "we live in a country whose authority has not recognized our existence since 28th July 1867, when the Emperor signed Law No. 12 of the Hungarian Parliament on the Austro-Hungarian State Settlement concluding the end of the Austrian Empire and the birth of Austria-Hungary. The National Law of 6th December 1868 is just a massive hypocrisy. Indeed the letter of the law states that in the communication, the mother tongues of other nationalities may also be used in offices and that municipalities or churches may establish schools with a non-Magyar language of instruction. But this law is only to pull the wool over the eyes of a foreign country. And while the Hungarians sternly reject the demands of the Croats, Serbs or Romanians, they don't take us into consideration at all. We simply don't exist for them. After all, Lajos told you. They call our mother-tongue ridiculous, suitable only for wagon drivers, tinkers or shepherds. Moreover, since the settlement, the Hungarians don't have to be afraid of the intervention of Vienna because the national question is fully in the competence of Budapest. Since 1875, when they closed the gymnaziums in Veľká Revúca, Kláštor pod Znievom and later Turčiansky Svätý Martin, it has been forbidden to speak in Slovak in schools; since 1879 Magyar has been the compulsory language in all elementary schools. And this is why people pay with their own money for many elementary schools. It's bad, truly bad," Professor Kvačala couldn't contain himself. The boys were silent.

"How will it turn out, Professor?" Milan asked.

"Differently. The truth will be revealed sooner or later – it always is. No oppression has lasted forever. For the fate of each nation, it's been essential that daredevils find the courage to go against the tide, risk their freedom and often their lives. We must direct our attention more to our Slavic brothers. But we must behave with sense and diplomacy, not showing what we think, with whom we are friends and what we carry in our hearts. Our time will surely come. We aren't alone. There are also ordinary Hungarians with us, who have been fleeced just like we hvae. Remember, the Hungarian nobility for a thousand years has despised the Hungarian people as well as Slovaks. Either the Hungarian gentry will come to their senses or perish in their own pride."

Štefánik made up for the absence of Slovak in the school at the lodgings where he was with Igor and Pavel at the tailor Papánek's on the ground floor in Veterná Street No. 11. They shared Slovak books together, most of them brought from their father's library. Their father was generally known in the Lyceum as a Slovak nationalist and had had problems with his school years before. Lajos was lauded for having hammered hundreds of Slovak pan-Slavic into forged Hungarians. However, he hadn't succeeded with the Štefánik brothers and so was determined to drive out the pan-Slavic idea from the slim blonde Milan. And if not, then at least he would make life at the Lyceum unpleasant to the point where he would voluntarily leave.

Milan closely followed the situation, didn't act impulsively, but instead was level-headed and endeavoured to settle disputes. Slovak students who weren't pro-Magyar interpreted the formal vow "I will be a faithful son of the homeland", which they had to declare at the beginning of their studies, as a promise of loyalty to the Slovak homeland, and so they behaved.

Professor Lajos was a notorious re-educator of the Slovaks at the Prešporok lyceum. In the second year, when Milan was housed with a friend called Bálent at the Suché Mýto at the place of a retired servant of the Archduke Bedrich, a Czech called Daněk, Professor Lajos decided, with the consent of the director of the Lyceum, to go on a personal inspection of Milan's apartment. But he didn't find the boy at home. He was as usual in the late afternoon and evening tutoring his classmates in mathematics thus improving his financial situation. Or he was spending time in the attic where he watched the stars through the roof and dreamed. He felt there was something more spectacular than this real world, a spiritual world extending inside and beyond the universe. Looking at the stars, he ceased to be afraid; on the contrary, a strange feeling of joy, all-embracing love, self-confidence, courage, hope and faith that he'd do great things entered his soul. In the stars he searched for the coordinates of his soul and was engrossed in imagining infinity, a concept which baffled him. It all went back to when he had visited his uncle in Myjava, the priest Vanai, who'd given him a pair of binoculars. He'd carried this treasure with him everywhere to watch the stars.

He was also pleased with the binoculars because he could watch game better with his father when hunting. Since he'd become a grammar school student, the Košariská priest, a renowned hunter, had taken him hunting to the forest during his long summer break. With binoculars, it was a different experience from before. In winter he couldn't wait for the spring break when his father took him to the woods to hunt woodcock. As soon as it began to darken and the first stars appeared in the sky, low over the clearings at the edge of the forest, they began to draw in the male birds. When they heard their croaking and whistling mating calls his father would point his shotgun and fire with a sure aim. His lively setter, Nero, would joyfully run to the shot birds and bring them to his master. Milan was a great admirer of his father's shooting prowess. Once he dared ask if he could shoot. His father was in a good mood because he had already bagged a pair of woodcock. He looked around to see if there was anyone nearby and let his son reload the weapon. Milan opened the barrel by himself, took a cartridge from his father's hand and slipped it into the chamber like a veteran. They were a good twenty metres from the edge of the forest. When the familar whistle sounded, Milan aimed and hit the bird at the first attempt. His father patted his head in appreciation and from that time took his son with him during the spring break while he was home. Milan would often also come for the weekend. Hunting woodcock was one of the attractions of home.

"You've got a talent for shooting," his father nodded as they returned from the mountain with a rich haul, part of which Milan had shot.

"And when his friends visit him, what do they talk about?" Lajos pumped the widow of the Duke's servant.

"Hungarian, German and Latin, but they talk in their tinker slang."

"So in Slovak... hm... and do they sing any songs?"

"Yes, with their friends. Sometimes there are more of them here than in church. But they sing beautifully. Those songs of theirs."

"And where does he keep his books?"

The old woman, looking frightened, led the teacher to the closet from which Lajos took out Kollár's *Slávy dcera*, Ruppelt's Slovak National Songs, Sládkovič's poems, *Duma dvoch bratov* by Janko Kráľ, which the Štúr poet wrote on the occasion of the funeral of his great-uncle Vilko Šulek. He also found Štúr's writing, The Science of Slovak Speech. His vision fell on a sentence underlined in red pencil: "We have entered the service of the spirit, and therefore we must pass through a path of life of thorns."

"Well indeed, just wait and I'll show you. I'll borrow these books, dear lady. Goodbye," he chuckled at the door.

A few days later, at the suggestion of Professor Lajos, the Michaelis summoned Milan and threatened him with expulsion. Fortunately the boy was supported by Ferdinand Hirschmann, a professor of his favourite subject, mathematics, in which he was one of the best grammar school students, and his class professor, a convinced democrat, Samuel Markušovský, who taught Latin and Greek. He was a great favourite with poor students, encouraging them to learn, and telling them that lords did not need knowledge, but the poor did. Above all, however, he was saved by the fact that he was one of the best students of the school, for which he received a 10-crown scholarship from the Michal Institoris Foundation and was able to dine for free in the alumnea, the institutional dining room, saving twenty zlatky a year. His brother, Igor, was also threatened with expulsion, but Professor Ján Kvačala stood up for him. At that time, Milan had no idea where and in what situation he would meet his professor twenty-five years later.

CHAPTER 7
The Eighth Star

Despite tutoring and having a frugal way of life, Milan constantly struggled with financial hardship. If he saved something, he bought a book or necessary teaching aid. Through separation from his parents and friends from his native village, the 11-year-old boy suffered greatly, often afflicted with depression and self-pity. He'd weep alone in a corner in the attic, wondering how to make extra money for the journey home by train. The hardest moments came during his first Christmas without his beloved mamuška, papa, grandma Kubovička, the Christmas tree and traditional customs. Every year, on Christmas Eve, together with vergers and his brothers, they took care of and fed the livestock throwing them an apple for luck. Roast dumplings were covered with milk and sprinkled with poppy seed, his mother made cabbage soup with mushrooms and plums, poppy seed, ginger, cabbage, walnuts, dumplings covered in milk and plum balls of which he could never get enough; he missed it all very much. But most of all, he lamented not going on the traditional carolling walk after dinner with the other children. They would go from house to house, singing and wishing everyone a blessed Christmas.

He wandered with his brothers in the streets of Prešporok. The shop displays were already decorated for Christmas. A letter burned in his pocket, in which his father had written that they were sending cakes from the house and four zlatky – more they could not afford – and telling him not to come home for Christmas. However, the boys couldn't endure it, borrowed money and on Christmas Eve they took the train to Piešťany, from where they went to Košariská on foot. In Vrbové a well-known Brezová butcher, Poláček, nicknamed Tolar, who threw them some tasty sausages so they wouldn't come home empty-handed, took them by wagon. The boys appeared just as papa, mama, Ľudmila, Oľga, and Elena sat down at the table, with six-year-old Marína Želmíra in a wooden seat because her legs were paralyzed. Four-year-old Lacko and the youngest Mojmír, who wasn't even a year old, were asleep in the back room. At first there was a surprise with their father asking them to explain why they hadn't listened to him. But even he wasn't able to resist a smile when he looked at his overwhelmed wife and siblings. Milanko insisted to his father that the Košariská people should not call him the young gentleman, but as they had before, Milan. His father resisted for a moment, he was after all the son of a priest, but seeing that such a salutation did not really appeal to Milan, he acquiesced.

After returning from the winter holidays in Košariská, on 1st January 1891 with his brothers and friends he went over the newly opened Prešporok bridge, named after Emperor Franz Joseph. In the spring, when the rail connection with Sopron was opened, he made a trip to the historic city with his brothers. They liked it very much as it seemed the city breathed somewhat more freely due to the Austrian influence. Even in the Evangelical Lyceum that they visited most of the students were Austrians and Germans. They were surprised to find that Sopron Evangelical Lyceum was fifty years older than the one in Bratislava (Prešporok). There was a university more than a hundred and fifty years old in the city, which meant there were many students of which about half were of Hungarian and half of Austrian origin. When Austrian students found out that the three brothers were Slovaks, they invited them to their favourite restaurant, the White Rose, where Empress Maria Theresa had always stayed when visiting Sopron. Like the students in Prešporok, they also had a back room, where they often sang or boasted loudly. When the Slovak boys began to speak Magyar, the local boys indicated to them that they were in a society where Magyar wasn't very welcome and would prefer German, which they all understood.

"I've never had much to do with German, so at least I can practise it a little," smiled Milan.

"Lads, we want to tell you that we, who are sitting behind this table, are Slovaks and Austrians. We've had similar bad experiences with our Hungarian classmates and professors as you've had in Pressburg," said a student, who'd introduced himself as Karol, a Slovak.

"But they aren't as harsh with us as with you Slovaks, because we are mostly members of the Habsburg nation, that is to say, gentry, whom they all acknowledge, though through clenched teeth. The settlement was the work of the devil benefitting no-one except the Hungarian nobility," Karol added.

"Aren't you afraid to say such a thing?"

"No. There's a freer atmosphere here than you have. Moreover, our grammar school is the cheapest in the whole of Hungary and almost all students are from poor families. Those who studied here include Juraj Palkovič and Andrej Kralovanský, who was eventually rector here. Janko and Jozef Boor from Vrbové edited the magazine *Veniec*, later Dušan Makovický, Matej Bencúr and others. They are still mentioned here. And here is the patron and protector of the Slovaks, Mr. Bothár. They actually like Slovaks here," he said in fluent German to his Austrian colleagues who were smiling. "We know how Lajos and others like him bully you in Prešporok. Come here and breathe more easily."

Despite the scholarship that for Milan had been raised to sixteen crowns, he could not afford expensive accommodation, so with his classmate, Bálent, they moved to the house of the poor

Blanovarič family on Panenská Street 21. And his brothers, Igor and Paul, too, had fallen not only on financial but also national hard times. On 15th March, 1893, as every year, they celebrated the beginning of the Kossuth Revolution of the Estates. Since Kossuth had been an undergraduate of the Prešporok Lyceum, on that day it was compulsory to wear a red-white-green cockade on their coats. The Štefánik brothers, together with several other students, however, refused to pin them on, which immediately marked them out as pan-Slavs. They awaited *consilia abeundi*, conditional expulsion from school. If similar actions were repeated before the end of the year, they would have to leave the school. The Štefániks didn't lose sleep over this decision because they'd been thinking about continuing their studies in Šopron for some time anyway. Just days after the announcement of the conditional decision, Milan on Maundy Thursday, 30th March, wrote a letter to his parents on the occasion of his first Communion:

By the grace of God, I have lived to see the joyful and sacramental moment in which, for the first time, when I come to the Lord's Supper, I can join the adult members of the Evangelical Church. To God, my dearest parents, I have to give thanks for what I am and what I can do. Accept your child's gratitude for all your gifts. I beg You, forgive us everything, for our deeds and actions. I promise to correct myself and will strive to make You happy. Again I beg You, grant us Your family blessing to come to the Lord's table with a calmer heart.

The letter doesn't mention the *consiliu abeundi*.

Despite having As and Bs during the three years of his studies in Bratislava with only one C in German from his second year Milan agreed with his brothers that they would leave Prešporok. He sensed from his letters that even his father wouldn't object to their decision. Igor Branislav went to Kežmarok in1891, a student of the seventh year of the local lyceum, already a grammar school. His classmate was Janko Jesenský from Martin, chairman of the secret Slovak association, *Kytka*.

After arriving home for summer, Milan was praised by his father for his very good report. Compared to the previous year, he'd improved his mark in German to a B. For Hungarian and Latin he had As and even in the new subject, Physics he gained an A. He was particularly pleased that the boys did not unnecessarily arouse the anger of the professors in tense times, but had kept their Slovak character. For the first time in three years, Milan also had an A in Physical Education, despite his parents noticing a kind of malaise in him. He coughed, found it hard to breathe and from the least strain felt a sharp pain in his chest. From the resulting heart problems, his lips often turned blue. A doctor from Brezová diagnosed pleurisy. He ordered him to rest and gave him anti-inflammatory drugs. Granny Kubovička brewed him agrimony and the boy stayed in bed for a few days.

After a long time, he went to his almost forgotten children's observatory under Úboč. Even though it had almost disappeared into the undergrowth, in the evenings he'd go there to watch the stars. He looked at them every spare moment he could. Talking about the stars livened up the life of Želmíra in a wheelchair. He liked to take her for summer evening observations in the manse courtyard where he lent her his binoculars and fervently explained the secrets of the universe.

"Look through the cardboard tube. If you fix it so it can't move, you can see the movement of the stars. I watch what time this or that star goes from one edge of the tube to the other. Which planet would you like to know about?" he asked, pleased with his sister's interest.

"I'd like to know about Mars."

"Why Mars?"

"Because it just came into my mind," she giggled.

"It's a good choice because it is now very visible in the night sky. Mars is the fourth solar system planet in terms of distance from the Sun and the second smallest after Mercury. Of all the planets it most resembles our Earth. While we go around the Sun in 365 days, Mars orbits in 687 days. Our day lasts twenty-four hours, but a day on Mars lasts only half an hour longer. Their year lasts twenty-four months and if people live there, they look at the same stars as we do."

"Milanko, what are you talking about?" His father, who'd suddenly appeared, interrupted his conversation. "Except on Earth, there's no life elsewhere."

"That isn't known. People can't yet prove it," he objected.

"But our Creator has made it so that life is only on Earth. Thus it is said in the Scriptures and Scripture is holy, nothing of which can be questioned. Our faith preaches to us!"

"No one can know whether there is no life elsewhere other than Earth," he resolutely contradicted his astonished father.

"God knows it and he says so clearly. And you believe in God!" He looked at him sternly staring at the son who had fallen into a tense silence. Želmíra was ready to burst into tears, frightened as her father had raised his voice. "Yes or no? Have they made you an infidel in those schools?"

"I do believe in God, of course, I have only As in religious studies, but you teach us that the most important thing in life is the search for truth."

"Yes, that I've taught you. The most important truth is the word of God. And now to bed, it's late!" his father left the unpleasant debate.

For a long time, Milan's words whirled in his head and especially the strength that radiated from the delicate little boy as he defended himself firmly. He was also upset by the bad results of Milan's three-years-older brother, Paľko, who'd had to repeat a year at the lyceum. As he had the feeling that the teachers were biased against them, he didn't protest at all when Milan and Paľko informed him that they wanted to go to Šopron in the autumn. He was also encouraged by the strong position of Professor Daniel Bothár, who taught ancient culture and was the founder of the Lyceum Science Collection. He was known to be supportive of Slovak students because he came from Banská Bystrica.

Milan liked Bothár in particular for his interest in Czecho-Slovak literary relations. Although he wasn't taught by the professor, he was impressed by his interest in the Czech culture that he and his boys used to discuss. He taught Paľko Greek, but he had poor grades in that as well as other subjects, so failed again in Šopron. Milan finished his fourth year with worse results than in Bratislava, but he was one of the few to always get As in mathematics.

Šopron was at that time an important Hungarian student city with thirty-five thousand inhabitants. In addition to the Lyceum, there were two grammar schools, a vocational school, a business school, a higher girls' school, a military school and an evangelical institute of teaching and theology. Slovak students were frequent guests for tea at the lawyer, Ľudovít Bazovský. As the youngest, Milan was in charge of preparing and serving tea. He attracted the attention of older classmates with interesting stories about the stars. Bazovský once told him jokingly that he would be our Flammarion. The Hungarians would, due to him, have to change their folk song "Hét cillagból áll and Göncöl szekere" (Seven Stars Make Up the Big Dipper) to "Nyolc csillagból" (Eight Stars). The young Milan blushed, then confidently declared: "And I will be the eighth star."

Magyarization also grew stronger in Šopron, and the school authorities sought to disperse sibling students to different places. The pressure on the Slovaks escalated mainly in Protestant grammar schools, because the awakened Slovak youth came mostly from evangelical priestly and teaching families. Perhaps also because of Paľo's weak results, their father finally decided that Milanko and Paľko would be sent to the grammar school in Szarvás in the lowland country of the great plain of Hungary. Igor was about to finish his studies in Kežmarok. The decisive role was played by the fact that the Szarvás Grammar School had not only a good reputation, but also that their father spoke to Samuel Šaško, one of the school's teachers, who came to visit Brezová that summer. He persuaded his father of the selfless and tolerant spirit of the Szarvás establishment, where the director, Július Benka, the son of a Slovak mother, was at that time one of the most respected teachers in Hungary, and one of several professors of Slovak origin trying to mitigate the pressure for Magyarization. Štefánik was also persuaded by the fact that sons of Matúš Dul, the priest, Ján Trokan from Kostolné, Štefan Fajnor, and Milan's peer Vladimír Čobrda with whom he later became friends and matriculated with, all studied at Szarvás. So it was decided; from the autumn of 1894, that the highland boys would go to the lowlands in which they placed their hopes.

CHAPTER 8
Faith is Action

As far as the eye could see, vast fields of corn, wheat, barley, poppy and other crops stretched out providing nourishment for the inhabitants of not only Alföld, the Lower Land, but also a large part of Budapest and other Hungarian cities. The granary of the country. And especially the endless grassy steppe, over which herdsmen followed horses and cattle. The Hungarian *puszta*, where Paľko and Milan, boys from the Myjava Kopanice, felt their hearts grieving. Paľko couldn't concentrate on his studies, so after a while he left the grammar school. The fourteen-year old Milan remained alone in a far lowland without a single hill. In the spring and autumn it was bearable; when he could, he went from the town into the fields. He would close his eyes in the haystacks and draw deeply into himself the scent of hay reminding him of home. And the stars, too. He watched them at every possible opportunity. He imagined how the same Venus was shining over Košariská.

The Szarvás gymnázium didn't have a dormitory, so Milan and Paľo with two friends, as in Bratislava, lived in private accommodation. Samuel Kršniak, a furrier, took them into his family. The Kršniaks became almost second parents for both brothers, Milan's younger brother, Kazimír, also staying with this family during his Szarvás studies. By the time Milan was in his eighth year, Lacko, who stayed with Milan in the first year of his stay, came to study in Szarvás. Lacko knew almost nothing in Hungarian, so Milan often translated for him into the Slovak language. In addition to his own studies, he tutored his weaker classmates, rarely going to student entertainments but spending most of his time in his books. He often didn't have enough for himself, but he used to take home dinner from the alumnea so Lacko could eat a little. In the room where the boys lived, Milan wrote down the Latin motto of the industrious Benedictines: "Ora et labora!" (Pray and work!) He kept to the dictum throughout his studies.

In the room he'd hidden a letter in his desk drawer that his father had put in his hand as he left the house. This moment was deeply impressed into his memory. "In the lowlands you'll enter the age of maturity and it is good to enter into it in honesty, wisdom and dignity. Already you're a young man with a heart and a sense of openness, a truth-seeker. Try to stay that way. Like I have done, try to model yourself on Ján Hus, a man who always pursued truth at whatever cost. Look to him and draw moral strength from him in the moments of difficulty in which you will surely find yourself."

"Do you promise to behave as our Master Ján preaches?"

"I promise, father."

He realized that for the first time in his life he had not addressed his father as papa, but as father. His father hugged him and held him tight against his chest for a long time.

Slovaks began to move to the lowlands at the beginning of the eighteenth century after the Turkish wars. At the time of the arrival of the Štefánik brothers, they made up two-thirds of the population of twenty-five thousand inhabitants in Szarvás. The atmosphere in the town was filled with the coming millennium celebrations, the thousandth anniversary of the arrival of Hungarians in the Carpathian Basin. Although their arrival had been officially set as 895, the celebrations were shifted for a year for organizational reasons. The greater the problems which emerged in relations between Hungarians and Austrians, as well as Hungarians and other nationalities living in Hungary, the more the Hungarian state administration pushed to glorify the past and vice versa, to trivialize the real problems which existed. Parliament had passed a celebration law, and had earmarked the state budget for the construction of millennium memorials in all major Hungarian cities, especially for monumental buildings in Budapest. They built a new Parliament building in the capital, the largest in the world at that time. The majestic Országáz building with its unique architecture on the banks of the Danube 268 meters long, 123 meters wide and 96 meters high. They launched the operations of the modern Szabadság híd, the Bridge of Freedom, opened the prestigious Grand Boulevard, Nagykörút and started the first underground railway in Europe.

They reconstructed the Matthias cathedral in Buda and built the famous Fishermen's Bastion, the Royal Opera House, the Eastern Railway Station, *Keleti pályaudvar*, Margita's Island Spa and many other buildings that were largely built by Slovak carpenters and masons. The young Szarvás grammar school student read professional journals about construction and architecture with great interest. He was captivated by everything new and modern brought in by the rapid development of science and technical disciplines. At that time, Budapest was "Slovakia's" largest city, with over fifty thousand Slovaks living there, half of whom didn't even know Magyar. During the millennium celebrations Slovaks also built a complex of school, church and other buildings in Budapest, which under the name Luther House became the centre for the national, cultural and religious life of Slovak Evangelicals in the capital of Hungary. The jubilee exhibition, which at the time was seen by an incredible five million visitors, was supposed to demonstrate to the world the power and global achievement of the Magyars.

Milan experienced the febrile atmosphere of the millennium celebrations at the Szarvás Grammar School in the autumn of 1895 and especially in the spring of 1896, when on the occasion of the second anniversary of the death of Kossuth, a Slovak born to the Haviar family, who on 25th March, drunk from celebrating the millennium, caught the delicate boy by his legs and suspended him head down through the balcony railings, forcing him to pin the Hungarian tricolor and proclaim glory to Kossuth. Haviar, who in between had changed his name to Halmos, shook him furiously and harangued him in Felvidék Hungarian.

"To te nemfogs... call glory to our leader Lajos Kossuth... So! Will you or won't you?"

Štefánik, with his face red from accumulated blood, trembled with fear, but was silent. "As you like. You won't change your mind? I'll count to three, if you don't call, we'll let you go... aha... down there..." Students ran to the shouting and noise and waited tensely for what Halmos and his band would do.

"One two..."

" Nebolondúj... Are you crazy ?!" He's our Milan, my best friend," an enormous boy leapt at Halmos, trying to push the lout away.

"How is he your friend? He's a yokel from the Felvidék!" Vilmos pushed Halmos back. Seeing that other angry classmates were approaching, he pulled Štefánik up and placed him on the ground. The enormous Vilmos approached the frightened boy and straightened his shirt and loose tie.

"Listen, Haviar, because that's what you're called, you're not Halmos in any way. You're a disgrace! I'm as Magyar as a turnip born in Kispest of Magyar parents, but I wouldn't be so foolish as to behave like this even to my greatest enemy!" Then he turned to his classmates who'd gathered into a large group watching the situation.

"If you, idiots, think that we Hungarians will gain the respect and hearts of our highland brothers this way, you're hellishly mistaken. My dear Milan," he said to Štefánik, "I want to apologize to you on behalf of all your decent Hungarian classmates!"

Several of Vilmos's group nodded in agreement, but most just roared and moaned at him. Vilmos with Milan and two other boys returned to class, but Halmos and his cronies headed straight to the director. They protested vigorously to Benko, the director, about Štefánik's behavior and described him as a pan-Slav. However, Július Benko refuted them with a categorical statement, "Bear in mind that as long as I'm grammar school administrator in Szarvás I don't want to hear anything about pan-Slavs. The basic principle of our learning institution is tolerance and mutual respect, regardless of nationality, religion or family origin. And now go!"

That evening, Milan wrote a poem that began with the lines: "Arise, Slovak, weapon in hand, if you do not want to suffer torment any more!"

Thanks to the attitude of an understanding and correct director, as well as Professor Alfred Neumann, who taught him mathematics, he gained the respect and admiration of his classmates. Neumann publicly declared that Štefánik was a credit to the grammar school, that they'd never had such a mathematician until that time. It was widely known that not only Neumann, but also some other professors invited Milan for Sunday lunch so he could eat properly at least once a week. He was often invited by Professors Mocskonyi and Chovan; Milan's platonic love for Emília Chovanová resulted in several love poems. For the first time, he felt his romantic soul tremble from the touch of a woman's hand. His soul probably became the magnet that in future would attract women to this outwardly unattractive man.

He was given a scholarship for his diligence. While in the fifth and sixth years he received only a few zlatky, in the seventh year he received thirty-two and in the eighth, seventy for his Teleki scholarship, which put him among the best grammar school students, and enabled him to buy the Kralická Bible. But when he proudly showed it to Professor Rónay who taught religion, the latter was merely annoyed that Štefánik read the Bible in Czech.

"It's a sensation for Slavs," Štefánik said. "It's the first translation of the Bible into Czech from the original Biblical languages, Aramaic, Greek and Hebrew, and not from the Latin Vulgate."

"For us, however, the Bible, in the language prescribed for our schools, Hungarian, is a natural, even obligatory text," Rónay, the professor of religion, was becoming agitated.

"I don't think it is the language, but the content of the Holy Scripture which is essential," argued the diligent student. "And if you allow, I've read the text of both the Magyar and Czech New Testament and found some confusion."

"So read only Magyar and everything will be clear to you," the Halmos class leader broke in. His classmates responded with noisy laughter.

"But I didn't find the confusion in the language versions but in the content. In both there is the same lack of clarity."

"Lack of clarity in Holy Scripture?" Rónay shook his head. "Sohár, what is the Holy Scripture?" he called upon the nearest student.

"It's the Word of God."

"You heard, Scripture is the written word of God," the professor turned to Štefánik. "And you, a nobody from the Felvidék, want to convince us that there is lack of clarity in the Word of God? Are you telling us that the Father of our Lord Jesus Christ is lying? That we Christians have been reared largely on lies? Have you such a fine opinion of yourself?"

"Professor, I fully respect that the Bible is the word of God..."

"Well, I am relieved that Štefánik respects the Lord," the professor laughed, and the whole class with him. "How nice that you don't question the basis of our faith, the Divine Essence of Jesus."

"Of course, I acknowledge Jesus' Divine Essence, but it is just unclear to me..."

"What's not clear to you again? Everything is clear to everyone, nothing is ever clear to Štefánik!" Halmos jumped down his throat without being invited.

"Colleague Halmos, only enter the discussion with the permission of the teacher," said Rónay. Then he turned to Štefánik: "So what's not clear?"

"Professor, you may not like it, but for me, Jesus is a great being, perhaps the greatest motivator in my life. He is the Christian prophet we love. However, I think that Jesus would be more beneficial to us if we knew he was one of us, a man like you or me, who, through his wonderful life, worked his way up to such a level that God noticed him, figuratively speaking. Nevertheless, Jesus has both a Divine and human nature. Being the Son of God does not exclude that He is also the son of man."

"So what you say is correct. What don't you understand? That He's the Son of God?"

"Fundamentally do we know that He's the Son of God?"

"Are you really putting such questions to me, one of my best students of religion? Štefánik, I'm starting to doubt you."

"You've often praised me for doubting and seeking."

"Oh, how smart he is!" one of Halmos's supporters shouted out. However, the reaction of the class was no longer so enthusiastic; the students were growing interested in Štefánik's manner of argumentation and putting questions.

"The divinity of Jesus is simply given, it's the basic pillar of Christianity and I must warn you that everyone who challenges that is approaching a dangerous position of heresy," said the professor without conviction.

At that moment there was a knock on the door. A student came in to tell Rónay that he was to go to the headmaster immediately.

"I have to interrupt my teaching because the Rector has called me on an urgent matter." There was relief on his face that he would no longer have to debate with the restless and curious spirit of the Košariská boy. With the words Dicsértessék Jézus Krisztus (Praise be to Jesus Christ) he abandoned the class abruptly. Murmurings in the classroom followed his departure, but no-one attacked the slim blonde youth any more.

Halmos was also brooding over his questions, because after a while he waited for him and addressed him in Slovak.

"My apologies, I'm sorry about what happened..."

"That's okay," Milan smiled.

"Do you think we can ever be like him?"

"Who?"

"Christ."

"We can, we just have to believe it."

"How must I believe?"

"Just as Christ says. Act. Faith is action. I've underlined the following sentence in Saint Mark's Gospel, Whosoever wants to be great among you, let him be a servant."

His classmate looked at him questioningly for a long time.

In the afternoon, Milan and a few friends had decided to go out of town. The school janitor's son, János, was bringing the latest Borchardt pistol with a magazine in a rifle stock. At the grammar school Milan was known to have an unusually steady hand. He was a well-known shot. Even his greatest enemies acknowledged him, and when it was necessary to represent the school in competitive shoots, they always nominated him. And the Košariská marksman filled the school case with winners' cups.

CHAPTER 9
Isten áldja meg – May God Bless You

In the years that he attended Szarvás gymnasium, he had As in all subjects, except German in the fifth year. In the lyceum library he absorbed the Latin writings of Isaac Newton; *Philosophiae Naturalis Principia Mathematica* (The Mathematical Principles of Natural Philosophy), from which he learned to understand the laws of gravity and the laws of the motion of matter. He studied Kepler's laws describing the movement of planets around the sun, the effect of gravity on the movement of the moon and followed the paths of comets, passing long hours in the library, while most of his classmates spent time in every possible distraction. He devoured information about inventions that raised humanity to unprecedented spiritual heights. Traditional and new magazines about architecture, astronomy, philosophy, literature, learning of Tolstoy were increasingly seen in the hands of the diligent Szarvás student. Darwin's theory that all forms of creation, from the long extinct to the present, form a continuous chain in which the stronger destroys the weaker was of great interest to him. However, as a young man with a sensitive heart and unshakable belief in human morality, he was less enthusiastic about Darwin's thesis that life is an endless battlefield for living creatures in which the most moral doesn't trimph but the most physically powerful.

After finishing his fifth year in the summer of 1895 he decided to go to Liptov after a short visit to Košariská. Not only was it in the interests of the Szarvás Gymnasium, but it was also for the beauty of the Liptov countryside, which he wished to get to know better. During his stay in Liptov, he spent several days in Pribylina, where his future friend in Paris, Ján Lajčiak, was enjoying his post-secondary holidays. They stayed with the Ruman family, wandered through the mountains, picking mushrooms, fishing, hunting, and climbing up to Kriváň, where they slaked their youthful zeal by reciting patriotic poems. Janko confided in Milan his decision to become an evangelical priest, which he later succeeded in.

His gymnasium school studies had come to an end. Finally the 25th June, 1898 arrived when Július Chovan, the director of the gymnasium, handed him his *Testimonium Maturitas*, the matriculation certificate with "eminentes" – excellent in Hungarian, German, Latin, Greek, history, mathematics and physics, that is all the compulsory graduation subjects. In the subjects he didn't graduate in, he received excellent marks for religious doctrine and natural history and Bs in geography and geometry. Director Benko invited him to his office after the official act, which was an honour that only the most outstanding students received. When, after a careful knock, instead of the usual "tovább" he heard "come in" in Slovak, his face lit up with a smile. He knew Benko had full confidence in him. The director motioned him to sit down.

"Štefánik, I am proud of you and I sincerely congratulate you," he told him. "You are one of the best students in the history of our institution. A great future awaits you..." he paused briefly, but then continued. "I hope... I wrote to your father, who believes you should continue your university studies in Budapest. I agree with his opinion..." But when he saw that his words did not impress Milan, he explained further. "There are great conditions for Slovak Lutherans there. Indeed excellent... I believe that from the opportunities that Slovak students are receiving, studies in St. Petersburg, Warsaw, Belgrade, Zagreb or Vienna, Budapest is the most attractive. Our church has a strong background in Luther's court. Newspapers and magazines in the Slovak language come out there and last year they opened the Slovak Association in Lipová Street. You won't even be that far away home. I know how passionate are feelings for Slovakia are..."

"Rector, I appreciate your and my father's opinion. I was not told by my father that I was going to Pest, but I have already decided. You have forgotten to mention the city closest to the hearts of Slovak students, Prague," Milan responded with a decisive tone after a moment of hesitation.

"Prague? That nest of liberalism and ungodliness?"

Milan was silent.

"Do you insist on your decision?"

Milan nodded. "Štefánik, but... you have... so... disappointed me... And I believe that your father, as I know his piety and deep faith in God, will certainly not agree to this. Do you want to quarrel with him?"

Milan hesitated for a long time, then shrugged.

"If there is no other choice..."

"You know your father. He told me clearly it had been decided."

"I'm decided, too. For the Slovak cause, for which I want to fight, there is no better place than Prague. The best for the matter of a career is Budapest. But I have decided for Slovakia. I believe my father will understand."

The director pursed his lips and tried to persuade him.

"I've also talked to your favourite professor, Mr. Mocskonyi. He also sincerely likes you and desires only the best for you. He, too, believes that talented students, such as you undoubtedly are, should study in a domestic environment and apply their knowledge for the welfare of Hungary."

At that moment there was a knock on the door.

"Tovább," exclaimed the director.

Professor Mocskonyi entered the office. "Elnézést, szükségem lenne..." (I'm sorry, but I need...)

"Ah, Mocskonyi kolléga, nagyszerü, teszég tovább és foglaljon helyet..." (Ah Mocskony, my colleague, excellent, delighted, enter and sit down...) the director offered his colleague a seat in the hope that their combined forces would persuade Štefánik. "We were just talking, colleague Štefánik and I, about his future studies."

"I firmly believe you will decide properly. I believe that teaching, law, medicine or, if you pursue the family tradition of the Štefániks and become a priest, all professions are open to you," Mocskonyi said in a passionate voice.

"I understand you, gentlemen, but I have my dreams I wish to pursue in the hope that at least some of them will be fulfilled. I know it's not going to be easy because of the financial situation of our family, but I'm determined to pursue them."

"That's just why you should study in Pešťbudín. Our government supports outstanding students with excellent scholarships. Based on your study results and our recommendations, it's certain that you can count on generous financial support," Benko added.

"But at what cost? What would I have to renounce? What would I have to deny? And although I thank you for your support, surely you understand that I don't want to live and study on a foreign account, for a foreign conscience. I want to live a purposeful life, on my own terms, I want to be a man, not a cipher. I want to march energetically and conscientiously to achieve my goal, because only thus will I fully control my destiny. In one month I will reach the age of maturity and don't want to be constantly dependent on someone," Štefánik said firmly.

"My dear colleague, before the professor came, you opened your soul and told me that one of your dreams was to achieve a state in which Hungarians and Slovaks would live in mutual understanding in a common Hungarian homeland."

"Yes, that's truly my dream," nodded Štefánik.

"Professor Mocskonyi and I know your views and your dissatisfaction with the balance of power in Upper Hungary. But who can change this balance if not people like you? You young Slovaks have to join with young Hungarians and build a new, modern Hungary. And where else would you achieve this, if not in the capital?" said the director returning to the subject.

"Rector sir, you know that both you and Professor Mocskonyi, along with Professors Neuman and Chovan, are men I hold in the greatest respect and don't wish to oppose. But this is not about my career, I don't want to purchase a life at the cost of inactivity. I'd like to contribute my life to the construction of a temple of humanity and progress. And also, if you allow me, to the promotion of my nation. I would prefer not to talk about Upper Hungary, but about Slovakia. Therefore, I've decided to study in Slavic Prague. I'm not backing away and I'm no longer afraid of the future. I won't rely on any preferential treatment, luck or happenstance. I trust only in myself."

He was silent, he still had something on the tip of his tongue. His eyes had acquired a kind of reddish tinge. Both professors were silent.

"I understand you..." Benko sighed. "But I see that I can't persuade you. Well, I wish you good fortune in life. And I'll keep my fingers crossed for you. If I can help you somehow, I'll be happy to do so," the director said. Then he got up and embraced the surprised blond student. With the words "Isten áldja meg" (May God bless you), the Slovak lad and Hungarian professor hugged each other and the professor made a paternal cross on the lad's forehead.

CHAPTER 10
Not Humble in the Least!

The splendid summer of the penultimate year of the nineteenth century drew the new graduates of Szarvás gymnasium to their homes as quickly as possible. For Milan, this summer meant the end of being addressed as Milán and returning to Milan; the end of the words Felvidék, Kosarasa, Tót! It meant a return to Slovakia, Košariská, Slovaks, the end of stress, stomach cramps and the constant anxiety of a slip of the tongue or of expressing his own opinion. It meant the end of diplomatic self-control, the end of his first platonic loves, high school friendships, the unconquerable futile desire for home and Kopanice, the end of plains parched by the sun. Unfortunately, too, also the end of excellent Chabian sausage, paprika, *bableveš, perkelt, töltöt kápozste, székelykáposzte* and other delicacies. A return to *pirohy*, bean soup, dumplings, stuffed cabbage and *lokše*. He looked forward to returning to mamenka and papa, though he was afraid of this meeting. He was relying on his decision to study in Prague, despite parental opposition, being more acceptable to his father once he showed him his matriculation certificate with all As. He was encouraged that he would be an adult and reach his eighteenth year in less than a month. Yet his father's uncompromising and hard hand aroused anxiety. The closer he was to home, the more severe were his stomach pains.

As the last business day, 30th June, 1898, fell on a Monday, Director Benko decided that the certificates would be handed over on the Friday, so that students would have enough time to pack and get ready to go home. On Saturday and Sunday Milan said goodbye to Samuel Kršniak's family, to the families of Professors Chovan, Mocskonyi, Neuman, Achimus, Fertig, Liška and several others who had materially supported him during his studies. Early on Monday morning, he and several of his highland friends set off on the Mezötúr – Szolnok – Cegléd – Monor line to Budapest, where he was delighted with the novelty of *Keleti pályaudvar* (Eastern Railway Station), one of the largest and most modern railway stations in Europe at that time. He admired its eclectic style and could not take his eyes off the sculptures of the inventors James Watt and George Stephenson on the main facade. Looking at these giants, he closed his eyes and imagined what it would be like to have a statue built for him one day in some European city for important scientific inventions and discoveries.

He dreamed of glory and recognition; he wanted, as his father had commanded him, to spread the good name of the Štefánik family. From Budapest the oldest Hungarian railway ran through Vác, Párkáň and Nové Zámky to Prešporok. He had almost three hours before the arrival of the train to Trnava, with a transfer to the recently opened track to Jablonica, and so ran along the boulevard of Princess Štefánia to the building of the Evangelical Lyceum, where he remembered his student days in Prešporok. From there he ran under Michalská gate to the Danube where a monumental new equestrian statue of Maria Theresa dominated Coronation Square in front of the regional granary. The work of a native of Bratislava, Ján Fadrusz, it had been unveiled in May of the previous year, and at the time, in the cafés of Prešporok the visit of the Viennese court, headed by Emperor Franz Joseph I, even after a year, was discussed with pride and boastfulness. More than the statue, Milan was intrigued by the architecturally interesting incorporation of the entire square into the newly created Danube embankment. The river had been heavily brought under control through generous projects from the Italian patron and architect Grazioso Lafranconi. This project had fundamentally changed the face of the city over a stretch of fifteen kilometres. On the way back to the station, they passed the hotel *U zeleného stromu* beneath Michalská Gate and stopped in the newly opened *Mezey* Café on the corner of Palisady and the Uhelný market. At that time, no one knew that this popular café would soon be named Štefánik and that the beautiful boulevard would bear the name of the national hero shortly after the founding of the Czechoslovak Republic...

He ordered coffee with Prešporok nut cake. He tried to speak Slovak and to his astonishment, the waiter with a smile responded.

"Are you a Slovak?" Štefánik asked.

"I'm a native of Prešporok and every correct Prešpurák knows German, Hungarian and Slovak. And since I have a little Jewish blood, I know something of Hebrew," the waiter smiled, continuing the conversation in an unusually agreeable manner. "Shalom, Yom tow – good day, lehitraot – goodbye, tuda – thank you, slicha – sorry, achat, shtajm, shalosh – one, two, three... but I know up to a hundred. That's enough for me. Und wenn es notwendig ist kann their auch ungarisch, slowakisch und sogar russisch rechnen," he added in German.

"So you are native to Prešporok?" the young man had interested Štefánik.

"No, if you please I'm a humble native of Turčianska Stolica," he said cautiously.

"Are you afraid to speak Slovak?"

"Not all guests like it, and unfortunately, state detectives come here, I know them all, but now fortunately none of them are here now, so we can also speak Slovak. Our owner, Mr. Mezey, is also from Prešporok, but he is very tolerant. It doesn't matter to him whether a Hungarian, Slovak, Jew or Japanese pays for his coffee. And he gives it to the detectives for... so... they shut their eye... Well, one day I'll surely speak Slovak without fear. There is no need to make a fuss; silent water washes away the banks, as we say, he smiled winking at Štefánik, who returned his smile. "Please excuse me, I have to go, customers are waiting..."

He bowed and left.

Milan chose a few titles from the magazine rack and flipped through them with interest. *Pozsonyi Felvidék, Pressburger Zeitung, Die Wahrheit* and various German and Hungarian magazines were available to customers. The waiter brought his cup of coffee with cake and, as Štefánik was flipping through the magazines, he added: "We have one Slovak magazine. It started up this year. People like to read it..." and handed Milan a pink-gray magazine called *Hlas* (The Voice).

"Your owner must be areally brave man."

"Indeed he is," the waiter confirmed, bowing.

Štefánik leafed through the unusual magazine in its even more unusual language: a monthly for literature, politics and social issues. Issue number six, first year – 1898. The editor, owner, printer and publisher responsible – Dr. Pavol Blaho. Published in Uhorská Skalica. He went through the contents and was astonished. Every article had an interesting topic. Our Efforts, Magyarization, Hungary, all by Vavro Šrobár; On Popular Education and Education of the Intelligentsia, On National Success and Its Conditions, On Modern Popular Education,

Anton Štefánek. Instructive reading by Dušan Makovický, Slovak Socialists in Budapest, On Slovak Miners in Šálgotarján, An Image of Slavism, Minuted Report on the Activities of the Slovak *Detvan* Association in Prague and a number of other articles. Štefánik's hands shook with excitement; he hadn't anticipated finding a magazine in Prešporok that would address not only his mind but also his heart. He called the waiter and pulled out his purse.

"Could I pay, please?"

The waiter looked at him with a smile.

"Why are you asking if you can pay? German customers only call out Zahlen, bitte!"

"Also dann zahlen, bitte," Štefánik laughed as he handed a ten-crown note to the waiter. The young man took it and wanted to give him his change.

"It's okay, I just have a request for you. Could I buy this magazine?"

The waiter smiled, nodded and gave him a handful of coins.

"The magazine is a gift from me to you, sir. From today I'm expelling the word humble from my repertoire. Yes please is enough..."

"Absolutely! Not humble in the least! You are an educated person, obviously more educated than many of your customers, speaking multiple languages. How humble is that?"

The waiter smiled, looking into Štefánik's eyes.

"Yes, sir... And thank you. Excuse me, sir, what's your honoured name?" he asked.

"Do you think it might be important to you?"

"I have a nose for people," he smiled.

"Štefánik. Milan Rastislav. And yours?"

I'll become somebody. I'm called Chyľo Miloslav."

"Chyľo Miloslav," Štefánik repeated to himself. "So take care."

As they approached home, the boys' nervousness grew. But Milan hardly seemed to notice the scent of home and was too busy reading; by Trnava he'd read the whole magazine, some articles twice and would have missed the stop at Trnava station had not the familiar guide hurried him off the train. The others continued to Žilina and beyond to Orava and Liptov. At the new Jablonica station, which had been opened before Christmas in 1897, he was greeted by uncle Žídek. When they watered the horses, some of the passers-by asked the coachman who he was carrying. With a smile he replied: "A Slovak visitor from the Lowlands." The wagon passed through Hradište, beneath Kyseľová, Úboč and continued on the road beside the newly-built railway track to Brezová to be opened the following year. Soon they were at Brezová, where they continued through the town. Behind the hillside beside the evangelical church, the Bradlo rock rose up and the path flowed into meadows. It was already dark, with candles or kerosene gleaming in the windows. When he saw the silhouette of the Košariská church and the manse, his heart pounded with emotion. But then he realized that he had a serious interview with his father ahead of him. The smile vanished from his face, his stomach clenched. He was home.

CHAPTER 11
I'll Follow the Voice of My Heart

There was a strong pastoral tradition within the Štefániks and Milan's grandfather had also been a pastor. His father's authority was sacred and he and his father had minor differences of opinion, Milan felt self-reproach. Soon, however, he began to realize that he was now an adult and obeying his father's orders was more a matter of respect or dutiful expression of his love than a legal duty. He was delighted, though, when not only his mother and siblings, but also papa welcomed him with open arms. His mother was also relieved when his father behaved graciously because she had been worried all the time that Milan's decision to study in Prague would cause a fatal rupture in her family; she knew her husband was capable of casting aside anyone who went against his will. Milan's telegram from Szarvás, with information about his excellent report, had alleviated the bitterness that had affected her husband since Milan had written to them about his studies in Prague. After his son's arrival, his father controlled himself and didn't raise the matter, but tension at the Košariská manse simmered. The next day Milan went to Fedorko's grave, to which the grave of Jaroslav Sergej, who died in 1891 less than a year old and Mojmír Alexander, a three-year-old, had both been added.

The tension-filled truce lasted until early August, when the head of the house fell into a particularly bad mood. The manse had suffered a catastrophe as a marten or weasel or other predator from the forest had crept though the netting of the hencoop behind the house and slaughtered eight of the fifteen hens. When the priest saw the destruction, tears burst from his eyes. Milan and Paľko repaired the fence, but the damage had been done. From that day on, the pastor walked around peevishly growling at everything that didn't meet with his approval, regarding the event as an act of improvidence. Albertína knew him well and guessed that he would get rid of his anger by venting it on someone. And Milan wasn't in luck. His father looked for him all day but he did not appear in theyard until just before noon. As soon as his father saw him, he motioned him into his study. Milan knew that if his father called someone into his study, he would not emerge without a good dressing down.

The priest lit his pipe, sucked smoke into his mouth and blew it out.

"Where did you wander off to? You were needed to help bring timber down from the mountain."

Milan hated the tobacco smoke whose stale smell pervaded his father's study. When he wasn't wearing his vestments, he wore a short military-style jacket with lace, imbued with tobacco; if he wasn't smoking, he was taking snuff. Milan realized that he was hypersensitive to his father's smell.

"But... I had to arrange something..."

"To arrange something? Don't I even deserve an explanation from you?"

Behind his father's reproach, Milan sensed that he was angry not only because he didn't know where his son had been that day. Mama had whispered to him that his father wasn't satisfied with his decision to study in Prague and had been waiting for this moment.

"Well... I went to Brezová... For this... I have to send an application to Prague and this with it..." He handed his father an envelope from which he took a letter with the stamp of the Mayor. "From the town committee of Brezová... For reasons of hardship, no stamp is required... Certificate of poverty! It is confirmed by the directors of the municipality that Milan Štefánik, aged 18, of the Evangelical Augsburg Confession, a matriculated student, is in our community under the law of 1886 paragraph XXII. Section six confirms that he possesses no movables or real estate. His father Pavel Štefánik... hm..." his father cleared his throat and after a while continued quietly: "... the Lutheran minister in Košariská, for the community of Brezová belonging to Kopanice, lives in such material conditions that it is not possible for him to cover expenses related to his son's study, all the more so because his parochial position gives him such a small pension that he can hardly barely keep his nine-member family and possesses no private property. Brezová on the fifth of August 1898, signed by Szolnoky Ödön, notary and Cserny György, mayor."

His father read and remained silent. Remarkably he didn't shout. It was as if the mayor's testimony confirmed that the Štefániks were poor and that although the parish priest could act as he wished in the village, everyone knew that he was just a pauper.

"You see, here's more reason to go to Budapest. Our students have excellent conditions, scholarships and other support."

"Papa, you know I have always respected you and always will. I could go to Budapest, but it would be at a great price, at the cost of my complete loss of national identity. Didn't you tell me, papa, not to return home if I forgot that I was Slovak?"

"So you have already sent an application to Prague?"

"No, but I'm planning to."

"Without my consent?"

Milan was silent for a while, but eventually gathered his courage and said firmly: "Papa, I'm no longer a baby, even though I like being called that. And according to the law, I'm already an adult and can decide freely for myself."

"You could do that if you paid for studying by yourself. But while I'm paying for you..." he suddenly paused, realizing that he was still holding the certificate of poverty in his hand and that he would no longer be providing for his son. After a while, he continued in a milder manner.

"I know, Milan, that you have the right to decide for yourself, but above all I care about your well-being. You see in what kind of hardship we live and must understand my standpoint. Of course, you are my son, but we don't just have you. Your sisters and brothers study or want to study, too... And Pešť is the best for our people in all respects."

"At the cost of total Magyarization and loss of moral principles."

"Think of the Slovak schools, clubs, choirs, theatres in Pest. The newspapers – *Pešťbudínske vedomosti, Slovenské noviny, Cirkevné listy, Priateľ ľudu* and many others," his father added as an objection.

"Papa, I guess you didn't know that publishing those newspapers was outlawed a long time ago..."

His father began to lack conviction, his voice weakening and his son feeling almost sorry for him. At that moment granny Kubovička banged on the door of the pastor's room and hardly had she announced his brother-in-law than a sweaty bald man appeared in the doorway from under which the lawyer and Milan's godfather, Štefan Fajnor, grinned at the priest and his son.

"Good day, greetings to you all! I'm coming from Piešťany after a concert. I said to myself I can't not stop to see my dear brother-in-law and my precious godson."

"Well, it's good, in truth, that you've gone out of your way although the road runs only a few metres from the manse. And where is your carriage?"

"I was driven by a coachman from the spa, I've sent him to take care of the horse and in half an hour he'll come to collect me."

"Half an hour – absolutely not! You'll have dinner with us," the master of the house insisted.

"Why put yourself out? I got a reward for my efforts, aha, they gave me sausages, eggs, cheese. It will all go down nicely. There's more than enough for us, so I've brought this for you," and he put on the table a leather bag full of delicacies.

"What are we going to do with this?" Štefánik said unconvincingly.

"What? So many hungry gullets as the Štefániks have are hardly to be found in Kopanice! And we do really have enough as there are twice as many sausages in the coach. Just take it," and pushed the bag at his brother-in-law.

"Well, I don't mind, it's a welcome addition, a weasel has deprived us of ten hens... So, as you say, we truly don't raise children on cake in the Košariská manse... Here, Milan, take this to your mother in the kitchen. And let mama send in that five-year-old of ours..."

Milan took the bag and on the way couldn't resist taking out one of the smaller sausages and eating it. But when he returned, he felt an ache spread in his stomach. The pain grew stronger, but he clenched his fists so that he wouldn't give anything away. He brought two dram glasses and poured for his father and his guest.

"And nothing for you?" Fajnor looked at him in surprise. "You've been eighteen for a good month, if I remember correctly," he laughed heartily, pulling a tiny cup out of his pocket. "I carry this with me. One never knows..."

Without waiting for consent, he poured one out for Milan.

"Gentlemen, to your health. In addition, to Milan on your excellent matriculation. You're a credit not only to the Štefánik family, but to our church and the whole region. And as I know you, lad, the day will come when you will be the adornment and hope of this whole devastated nation. Pursue your dreams and don't be tempted by material benefit – life is about much more than money Follow first the impulses of your heart and only then your mind. If your heart calls you to Prague, listen to it. Try to succeed in life according to your and God's design. Papa says you want to go to Prague to study, and I totally approve. And I believe papa approves, too," he said encouragingly winking at Štefánik. He raised his glass with Milan and his father and drank it down. Milan looked at his father, and seeing that he didn't prevent him, drank it down, too. Surprisingly, his stomach ache subsided in a few moments.

"I'm for Pešť," Štefánik said coldly. "At Pešť University, a thousand Slovaks study law, philosophy a hundred and fifty, medicine four hundred, surgery two hundred... Milan, just imagine you could be a doctor or a lawyer. You would be helping the whole family, you're very talented. Director Benko wrote to tell me that you are one of the best students in the history of the Szarvás Lyceum. I remember Martinko Bzdúch from Brezová – he was a much weaker student than you, but he became an eminent doctor in Budapest. We've arranged accommodation for you with the Podhradský family. They're Slovaks from Senica like your godfather here..."

"Brother-in-law, don't cut the ground from under the boy's feet. Do I have to remind you of the words of Vajanský, who studied in Budapest? How many thousands of our poor brothers and sisters from all over Slovakia are working their fingers to the bone on the streets of Pest and starving? And how many souls will be lost there to our nation, to their families, to their communities, to their own salvation? Slovaks in Budapest don't expect anything other than moral destruction! This is what your Svetozár Hurban Vajanský, who drives you to distraction, says!" Fajnor's voice rose.

"Leave Svetozár out of this. After Štúr he's the most intelligent Slovak; let's be glad that we have such a man!"

"I don't like Vajanský's Russophilia, but we can certainly agree with him that the Budapest lords want to decimate us both morally and materially. You're right, Pavel, in Pešť, great scholarships and other support await our lads, but at the cost of their national identity. If you want Milan to lose his, send him to Pešť!"

"How many studied there and didn't lose their identity! On the contrary, they were strengthened. Kollár, Martin Hamuliak, Ján Palárik, Zechenter-Laskomerský, Paulíny-Tóth, Seberíni, Pavol Országh Hviezdoslav, Hroboň, Radlinský, Viktorin, Francisci, Červeň, Dula, Medvecký, Pietor and dozens of others graduated there, none of them lost their identity and they've all done very well in life."

"The ones you named studied there before the settlement! I know what I'm talking about as I studied law and theology there myself."

"Hope smoulders in Martin, in Vajanský, in Russia! Only the Russians are capable of saving Christianity. Czech freethinking is devastating for the Christian and he wants to go there!" Štefánik gestured violently.

"What are you talking about, Pavel? Don't you have a great image of Master Hus in your room? Wasn't he the most courageous Christian? Do you want to say that Hus and his followers, some of whom are also Štefániks, are ungodly?"

"My dear brother-in-law, you don't see this objectively, you are infatuated with all things Czech. You see yourself in Smetana."

"I would like to see myself in a Slovak composer, but unfortunately we have none. And don't talk, I beg you, about all things Czech, the Czechs are the closest brothers to us. I don't deny my justifiable respect for Czech culture. yes, I am in a friendly relationship with Adolf Heyduk, a great poet whose poems I've set to music, I am friends with Jarda Vlček, who has a Slovak mother so he understands us all the more. He founded and was the first chairman of the Slovak association, *Detvan*, which could also help Milan in obtaining financial support for study. What's wrong with that?"

"Of *Detvan* I've heard this. It's full of riff-raff, boozers and their offspring, wasting time singing in Prague cafés and beer cellars."

Milan watched his father and frowned a little at his words, but he didn't dare to enter the debate. In his mind, he thanked God for sending his godfather, who, as an authority recognized by his father had greater powers of persuasion.

"Don't run it down. It's an association supporting Slovak students and Czecho-Slovak reciprocity. And in Prague there's also a supporting association, *Radhošť* and for two years Czechoslovak unity has been active. They have collections in affluent Czech families for poor Slovak students.

"Milan doesn't need alms," he wanted to look at his son, but he lowered his eyes. Then he raised his voice again, "The Czechs will devour him. Just as they swallowed Šrobár, Blaho and others. To hell with what they get and with their new magazine, *Hlas*, they call it. They dare to be the voice of Slovakia... Bah!"

"And the Hungarians wouldn't devour him? You're all disappointed with the attitude of Vienna during the time of the revolution. They gave us the cold shoulder and therefore with the end of the Štúr and Vajanský era, you all uncritically turn to Russia. Aren't you all confirming by this the words about malice waiting for a saviour from outside, even if he is a Slav? Just as you are preaching Slavic unity, the imperial deputy, Masaryk, encourages every Slavic nation to follow a path of small, patient but, above all, its own steps. I am a Slavophile like you, but we must not confuse our fraternal relationship with the Slavs with uncritical Russophilia."

"You go on glorifying Tolstoy. And I know you've also awakened interest in him in Milan."

Milan could no longer hold back and entered the debate.

"Papa, my godfather isn't manipulating me. I've read War and Peace and Anna Karenina, and they are great works."

"Well, Tolstoy is a God-fearing man and a man devoted to Christ, even though his church is fed up to the back teeth with him, but don't mention the ungodly Masaryk."

"And weren't you yourself impressed when he went from the Catholics to the Evangelicals?"

"He's still an atheist."

"My dear brother-in-law, I admit that I don't understand your antipathy to the Czechs well. Yet your sermons in the temple are also Czech. Please, I urge you, dear brother-in-law, to give the boy your paternal consent."

This time Fajnor poured, Štefánik drank and stood up. When he had to think hard about something, he would go to the window and look at Úboč.

"And what would you like to study there?" he asked, gazing into the window.

Milan and his godfather looked at each other encouragingly.

"I hope it will be something worthwhile, from which you will be able to live a decent, godly life and help your siblings," his father suddenly turned to his son and brother-in-law.

"So, papa, you agree?" Milan exclaimed.

"On condition that you don't make things up with your stars or with an empty philosophy. It must be something proper! You excel in mathematics, physics..."

"Well yes... everywhere there's enormous development in science and technology. As I've already told you, I've decided to apply for the Technical college."

"Oh, yes, you already said that... I forgot... I guess I've drunk a little bit too much..."

"Because... because I... I firmly believe in the development of science and of everything that is noble and beneficial to mankind. I want to contribute to this endeavour, too. I'll give it all my devotion and love for my nation and for those who are and will be always dear to me. Above all, you my dear papa, my mamuška, my sisters, my brothers, my dear godfather and my Slovaks. I listen to the voice of my heart."

His father, nodding his head, walked over to his son, put a hand on his shoulder, breathed in, and said, "Write your application for the Technical college."

"I... I've already dared to do so..." he pulled out a neatly written letter and read slowly, "Request for admission to C. K. Czech Technical University in Prague for specialist engineering in architecture." He handed the paper to his father, but he didn't take it. But Fajnor, his godfather, enthusiastically reached for the paper, read it and smiled at Milan.

"You haven't signed it..."

Milan rushed to his father's table, pulled out a quill, dipped it in an inkwell, and signed the application. Then he went to his father, knelt down and kissed his hand.

"Papa, thank you."

Without a word, Štefánik went to the window. For the first time in his life, somebody had gone against his will and not lost, but triumphed over him. Although Milan was his dearest son, it was hard to bear. The lawyer, Fajnor, approached the silent boy and embraced him.

"You'll see, everything will be fine. You know your papa, he's a good man, he cares for you."

His father stepped back from the window and with a tender look stroked his boy's hair.

"So give it your best, Milan! It is a truly brotherly city that in the time of revolution sheltered our dear Jozef Miloslav Hurban with his whole family, shielding him from Hungarian revenge."

CHAPTER 12
Likewise in Times of Loss and Victory

Renowned Committee of the Association of Czech Engineers!

Despite the various repressions and persecutions that every native Slovak experiences at Hungarian schools, I finished the current year at the Szarvás Gymnasium, as written under A) in the attached matriculation certificate testifies to my excellent academic results and following the voice of the inner desires of my heart, I have devoted myself to pursuing my studies at the Prague Technical University. To enable me to fulfil this aim Československá jednota has given me 100 zlatky in generous support, which in my unfavorable material circumstances is a great help, but not enough to cover my different annual expenses and needs.

My dear father, a poor evangelical parish priest who, with his 500–650 annual zlatky pension, must keep a nine-member family is, unfortunately, not in a position to enable me to continue my studies in Prague. I have no other choice than to appeal to this high-ranking committee to grant me generous support, promising both diligence in my studies and in my private life in order to become worthy of devoting all my abilities to the benefit of the Slovak nation.

In the hope of a favourable hearing to my petition, I sign myself on September 5, 1898 in Košariská with deepest respect,
Milan R. Štefánik.

He signed, dried the letter with a blotter and put it in an envelope in which he placed the poverty certificate in Magyar from the mayor of Brezová with his own Slovak translation. He thought for a moment, knowing that it was the first official document he had written in Slovak. He smiled now realizing that if the Committee of the Association accepted his request, there would be a fundamental change in his life. When in July 1898 he'd read in the newspaper an invitation by *Československá jednota* to Slovak students going to study in Prague to apply for scholarships, he did so without hesitation. The next morning he went to Brezová to the post office, from where he sent it off. And then he prayed that Lord God would hear his request and enlighten the famous committee.

On his way home he didn't return directly to the main road, but turned left to the mountain, heading to it through the forest path to Bradlo. Something irresistibly attracted him to this enchanting hill that he'd look at from the foothills of Košariská's Úboč opposite. He went up to the highest point of the hill, which on its eastern side was partly overgrown with wild hops and bushes, but was bare on the western, northern and southern sides. He sat down on a rock warmed by the September sun, unbuttoned his tunic, sweaty from the steep ascent. His gaze glided over the ridges of the mountains; first he bade farewell to Klenová and Vrátna, behind which is Hurban's Dobrá voda. He recalled the visits of his uncle Miloslav to the Košariská manse, his talk about the proud Slovaks who, under his leadership, rose up against the oppressors. His forehead cleared; it was late afternoon and the sun was setting behind the Carpathian ridge. From his pocket he took a small notebook with notes, thoughts and poems. He leafed through it for the one that appealed to him most. He had written it last May in Szarvás after one of his many disputes with the proud and self-importnat Professor Rónay. Whenever sadness came upon him from their subservient situation, he was strengthened by the thoughts of the Myjava fighters who, under Hurban's leadership, took their guns and rose up against the Kossuth guard. He also wrote about that on that memorable May evening, when he vowed in Szarvás to do all he could to liberate the Slovaks. A warm south wind whirled though his shock of hair. He stood up, looked to see if anyone would disturb him, and when he'd made sure he was alone on the majestic Bradlo, began to read out aloud. "Rise up, Slovak, gun in hand, if you don't want to suffer more torment. You've suffered enough, now arise, don't submit, defend yourself like a man. You have friends, a strong body, so be bold!" He looked for a long time at the ridges of the mountains behind which the Czechs and Moravians lived, their closest Slavic brothers. His eyes lingered on Veľká Javorina, passed on to a view of Durila, Čupec, Vrch Slobodných, Kobyla and Žalostiná, a stone's throw from Senica where his beloved godfather, Fajnor lived, who'd convinced his father to let him go to Prague. Beyond Senica, was Hodonín, from where the fifty-year-old Tomáš Masaryk originated, an interesting man who the year before, as he'd just read in *Hlas*, had become a professor at Charles University in Prague.

On the first post holiday meeting of *Československá jednota*, the committee heard Štefánik's request and approved fourteen Slovak students with scholarships totaling 1,050 zlatky. Of this, a hundred were Milan's. He sent other requests, less fruitful but also approved. Prague, his long-held dream, had come true. He was going to study at a Slavic university where Czech was the language of instruction. Unbelievable! The Czechs had fought for the opportunity to teach in their own language during the Taaff government in 1882, when Charles University was divided into Czech and German. Due to the establishment of a Czech university, there had been an unprecedented development of Czech science and culture. The Czechs had a literacy rate of 97 percent, the highest in Europe. Their industry was strong; they were developing textile production, mining brown coal and hard coal, were suppliers to the monarchy of 100% nickel, antimony and tungsten and were developing large industrial enterprises that needed educated technicians and engineers. Names such as Tomáš Baťa, Emil Škoda, Emil Kolben, Václav Klement, Daniel Swarowski, Ferdinand Porsche, František Křižík and others had become synonymous with Czech technical self-confidence. A growing Czech patriotism was sensed at every step. Even though there were discrepancies between the more conservative old Czechs and the more liberal young ones, Prague demanded from Vienna the same status as the Hungarians in the monarchy. The National Museum had become a place gathering documents affirming the great history of the Czech nation.

The majestic architectural stylenamed the Czech neo-renaissance was abundant. Instead of wood and stone, new building materials such as concrete, glass and iron were used increasingly. The magnificent public and private palaces and spaces needed decoration and fine art flourished. Josef Myslbek created the statue of St. Wenceslas and Jan Šaloun the Hus statue in the Old Town Square. Cabarets, concert halls and exhibition halls were opened in which the works of painters at the very pinnacle of European art, Josef Mánes, Mikoláš Aleš, František Úprka, could be admired by a wide range of citizens. They still felt reverberations from the unique Jubilee Exhibition, which displayed the outstanding results of Czech education and culture. The symbol of Czech and Slavic solidarity was the collection for the Czech National Theatre, which was supported not only by Czechs, but also by many Slovaks, Serbs, Croats, and even the Russian Tsar. Ordinary people contributed as did important Czech noble families; Lobkovicz, Schwarzenberg, Kinski, Chotko, Kolowrat, Czernin and one of the greatest contributions was made by Emperor Franz Joseph I. When Crown Prince Ferdinand opened the theatre in June 1881, nobody knew the building would burn down in two months and the collection would have to be repeated. In an incredible 47 days, they collected the necessary million in gold. Healthy living was encouraged with the founding of the physical education association, *Sokol*, together with the periodicals *Hlas národa*, *Národní politika* and the increasingly influential weekly *Čas*, founded by Tomáš Masaryk.

Into this atmosphere came a proud, but poor student from Košariská, educated in Hungarian schools. He stayed at František Horn's in Vašková 6 in Královské Vinohrady. In those days it was a separate place with fifty thousand inhabitants, the fourth largest Czech city. Štefánik liked it not only for its modern architecture, but mainly because the vast majority of the inhabitants were Czechs, while Prague itself was almost half German. It was just as Milan arrived in Prague that the tram line between Múzeum and Flora was put into operation. Although later he moved to Chocholouškova

Street, then immediately aterwards to Klicperova Street and then later to Korunní třída, he remained faithful to Královské Vinohrady. It was a great place because the famous Hlava's Café Royal, known for its Slovak students, was at the corner of Francouzská třída and Vinohradské náměstí. Due to his experience of life in Budapest, he had no problem quickly adapting to the city's life. He rarely went out in company as he had no decent clothes and had to count every penny. Beer or coffee were beyond his means. From his home he'd brought Kollár's *Slávy dcera*, the poems of Botto, Hurban Vajanský and Sládkovič, whose poem, *Marína*, he'd concealed from his father. In the Štefánik household, erotic literature was forbidden.

He was a frequent visitor to libraries, museums and picture galleries. He would go to services at the Church of the Czech Brethren on Klimentska street in Prague's Nové mesto. After worship he'd wander through old Prague and absorb its long history. His favourite place was the Betlémské náměstí, where he'd sit on a stone wall and imagine the atmosphere of the place in the times when the famous Betlémská Chapel with the preacher Ján Hus was still there. In his honour he even grew a beard as he wanted to resemble him as much as possible.

From 18th October, he would go to the Zemská banka every month, where he was paid 10 zlatky monthly as support *by Československá jednota*, to which the Müller Geodesic Fund added fifteen crowns. These modest scholarships, barely sufficient to cover the rent and provide enough to eat, enabled him to start his studies. He enrolled in lectures on positional geometry, descriptive geometry, mathematics, physics, astrophysics, drawing and Russian. His roommate, Eduard Hron, advised him to save money by not buying a newspaper as he could only have tea in the coffee shop and read there. The best print selection was at the Royal café. He quickly became a regular. The waiters did not initially love him because of his frugality, but his cordial nature gradually won him the generosity of some of the other regular guests. He used to play chess with Stanislav Klíma, and sometimes the no-vice sculptor Franta Úprka, the brother of a famous Moravian painter Josef Úprka, also went there. From the beginning of the winter semester, Slovak students of the *Detvan* association, founded in March 1882, regularly gathered in the café. Initially, only Slovaks attended, but they gradually accepted every scholar who was at the heart of Czecho-Slovak rapprochement. Tomáš Masaryk became its most valuable member in 1887.

Štefánik couldn't wait for the first general meeting, which was held on 15th October. His desire to personally meet the editor-in-chief of *Hlas*, Vavro Šrobár, was so great that he came to the café two hours before the meeting began. Older and younger students came and walked past the unknown blonde youth into the back room, which Mr. Hlava had reserved for the Detvans, as he good-naturedly called the members of the association. Milan asked Hlava to warn him when Šrobár arrived. As soon as the chairman of *Detvan*, Šrobár, an undergraduate in the last year of medical studies entered, Hlava gave Milan a friendly wink. Štefánik stood up, greeted him, but he only responded with a quick handshake and hurried into the association's room. Twenty students gradually gathered of whom a quarter were newcomers. Šrobár greeted them and invited everyone to introduce himself, say where he came from and what he was studying in Prague. Milan was visibly nervous and remembered only the names Jozef Gregor Tajovský, who introduced himself as a student of the business academy and Žigmund Zigmundík, of those who had already spoken. When it came to him he stood up with a shy voice and said, "My name is Milan Štefánik, my father also gave me the second name Rastislav. I come from a family of an Evangelical priest in Košariská near Brezová. I'm a Kopaničiar and have registered for construction engineering."

"Won't you tell us more about yourself?" smiled Šrobár.

"Well... I could, but I don't want hold you up."

"You aren't holding us up, don't worry. We'd like to discover something about your hobbies, family, where you graduated, why you decided to come to Prague and so on. Like those who've just spoken. And if I may suggest – a little bolder... " he said encouragingly.

"Well, if you allow, Mr. Chairman..."

"What's this Mr. Chairman..." Šrobár laughed. "We're all equal and on first-name terms here."

"Well... if you, sir, won't give... sorry, if you won't."

"I'm Vavro and from now on I'm Vavro to you as well as to all the newcomers. As you are Milan for me," he said to Štefánik, shaking his hand.

Milan smiled and was encouraged to continue.

"I'm not used to talking freely in Slovak. You know, with the exception of three years of folk school, I went to Hungarian schools all my life, so now have to get used to it. You, my dear Vavro, had bad luck, but also good fortune that you were dismissed from the Levoča Lyceum and could graduate in Přerov."

"Not could, had to," Šrobár corrected with a smile, touched by the 'my dear Vavro'.

"But you're right, my dear Milan, that the time spent in Moravia helped me to learn Czech. But there's nothing to be afraid of. Slovak is enough for you to be understood. Here we are among our own."

"I came here to study against the will of my father. I was supposed to go to Budapest, but my heart drew me here. I want to learn as much as possible, study diligently and conscientiously to convince myself that I'm a good son to him. I know I'll have to turn myself around; we haven't been eating cakes where I come from. I know that my life will be a stormy river, but I know, too, that a rolling stone gathers no moss. I want to contribute to the betterment of humanity and to progress. I have great faults, but I feel there is also good in my soul. I'm grateful to you for accepting me among you and ask you to treat me with honesty and rigour. Papa taught me that there is only a lie between yes and no and therefore I apologise if I'm sometimes rude and direct. It's what I've been taught; to praise good and discourage evil. I'm not afraid of the great world, I'm not afraid of evil or good. I'll try to be the same Milan Rastislav Štefánik in moments of triumph and defeat. This is my promise. I hope I won't disappoint you. Thank you."

His sincere and simple words left an unexpectedly good impression among the people present. Someone cautiously started to clap and then the others joined in. The slim student sat awkwardly, bashful and quietly, more for himself than for others, just whispered: "Thank you, thank you." It was the first time he was publicly appreciated. To everyone's surprise, he stood up once more and repeated with some force: "You'll see that I won't disappoint you!"

He entered the work of the association with verve, preparing performances responsibly and reciting so fervently that at some points his face would pale and he'd have to take a deep breath, and briefly pause in his recitation. He'd clutch his belly and remain on his knees for a moment. Those present didn't not know what to do. Šrobár, as a nearly qualified doctor, jumped towards at him and measured his pulse. It was high. "Are you all right? Do you have cramps in your stomach?" he would ask worriedly, putting his hand to Milan's forehead who nodded.

"A little bit..."

"When did you last eat?"

He wouldn't answer.

"It's all right, it's okay... I'm sorry..." he'd apologize and continue his recitation.

Šrobár publicly stated that if he went on like that, he could be a great speaker. "Above all, pay attention to your health," he'd say paternally.

Vavro and Milan gradually grew closer, attending concerts and exhibitions. For Slovak students, members of *Detvan*, there were four free tickets to performances at the National Theatre. Milan was thrilled when he saw the famous Eduard Vojan in Mrštík's *Maryša* from the highest balcony.

Milan and Vavro would address each other as my dear friend, my dear Milan and my dear Vavro. Milan became not only a supporter but also a distributor of *Hlas* published by Šrobár. Therefore, it was difficult to bear when Vavro left Prague after thirteen years of study in Prague and returned to Liptov in March 1899, where he began his medical practice in the autumn. However, they soon met on the 6th and 7th of August during a holiday break of the young association around *Hlas*. An unpleasant situation arose, however, when the youth of Martin, opposed to the young members of *Hlas*, didn't come to Liptovsky Mikuláš despite an invitation. Šrobár was very discouraged. On their way home, he and Štefánik went by train together.

"I understand that we are in conflict with the conservative fathers from Martin, but you see, dear Milanko, neither do their sons understand us in hardly any issue. Almost the whole of the Slovak intelligentsia is opposed to us, fuelled with anger as they are by *Národnie noviny* and its offshoots, *Pohľady, Černokňažník, Hlásnik* and all the church magazines, both Catholic and Evangelical," he sighed, looking out of the window at the passing Liptov countryside. "They feel that the orthodoxy inherited from their fathers is under threat. Therefore, they consider us the enemies of the Slovak people, they fear that we want to go from the people and not to the people. They are dreamers and romantic philosophers in their musty Martin boozers but we must bring science, reason, practical solutions, activity. As Masaryk has said. When I met him with Dušek Makovický, Gusto Ráth and Fedor Houdek in Bystrička two years ago, his design for solving the Slovak problem captivated us. He was crystal clear: it lay in an incredible thing – activity. The difference from Vajanský and his companions, who just weep and fatalistically await help from Russia, is that Masaryk is calling us to act. So we decided to publish *Hlas*. We are in a conflict of peasant idealism with the modern. Vajanský has idealized Russia because he is influenced by his contacts in St. Petersburg and Moscow and has strong support in the uncritical Slavophilism of Kollár and Štúr.

Russia's help to the South Slavs, our Bulgarian brothers, is praised as a selfless manifestation of Russian solidarity with an oppressed Slavic nation. He does not want to admit that it springs from Russian imperial ambition."

"For my father, Vajanský is a pure and steadfast exemplar. But I understand them - they are both influenced by aggressive Magyar nationalism to which they react all the harder. We must get as many young Slovaks as possible on our side, especially those who study in Hungary. If we fail to unite and ignite the young for the national cause, Slovakia will be lost. There are only about sixty Slovak students at universities all over Hungary, which is almost as many as our *Detvan* has put together. There is such a lot of work in the club. But I will deal with it all somehow..."

"Why just you? I guess everyonewill be happy to help you, but I honestly do not know how as you're no longer in Prague," Štefánik shrugged.

"Hey, brother, don't worry, there are enough willing and dedicated people in Prague and Slovakia. But I have the feeling that you would like to get more involved and that keeping minutes is not enough for you," said Šrobár teasing him.

"I admit that working in the club and debating with friends is more fun than studying. There's only one big problem; that you have left Prague. There is no such authority, the older members can't direct the younger. Your successor, Ursínyi, won't show up more than he has to, the rabble, which he warned against, are now commonplace and morals are loose. Thank God Jožko Gregor and Žigo Zigmundík still go, otherwise I wouldn't have anyone to talk to properly. Gregor is more or less keeping things alive."

"We mustn't be discouraged, we must walk resolutely to our goal," he clapped Milan encouragingly on the shoulders.

"If it weren't for Professor Zenger, maybe I would move to another field. It was he who greatly encouraged me to be interested in astronomy. He talked very engagingly about his dispute with

Purkyně. And even though I'm an evangelist and he's a Catholic, I feel he likes me," Štefánik ruminated.

"Zenger likes the Slovaks, he taught in Banská Bystrica himself... Oh, there's a lot of work ahead of us. In *Detvan*, in *Hlas*... Listen, Milanko. In a moment I'll have to get off at Ružomberok. What are your plans when you arrive home?"

"I'll help with scything, working around the house, we'll certainly haul wood from the forest, visit relatives, friends and so on..."

"So if you were to stay a day or two with us, you wouldn't be missed, well..."

"Vavro, well, this kind of invitation can't be turned down. You're an excellent friend."

"Milanko, you should know that the doors of the Šrobár house are always open to you."

CHAPTER 13
Always According to the Truth

As time went on, he found that he was less and less interested in studying at technical school. Perhaps because of this, he plunged into work with *Detvan*, where he became the recorder on 14th October, 1899. He neglected his lectures, didn't do examinations and was only kept in good mental and physical health by the lectures of Professor Zenger on astrophysics.. The professor liked the enthusiastic student and they did experiments and research in his beloved field of astronomy. At length, Zenger persuaded him to move from Civil Engineering to the Philosophical Faculty. Štefánik claimed that his dream was to be an astronomer and he'd continue to follow a starry destiny. While his classmates partied, usually at the expense of more affluent Czech friends in the front rooms of Prague's pubs, he quietly drank his cheap lemonade or tea and devoured the Prague newspapers. To his acquaintances he became a sort of reproach and began to feel that he wasn't welcome at the Hlava's café, at the *U Čížků, U Trunečku, U Kuřího oka* or other wine taverns in Vinohrady. He had no time for entertainment and made extra money teaching private lessons. Professor Vávra asked him to tutor his son Bohuslav, who was attending secondary school. Vavra paid him royally and it was clear to Milan that it was a discreet form of support.

A breakthrough and great encouragement in Štefánik's bleak life as a second-year student at the technical university was the visit of his godfather, Štefan Fajnor, who came to Prague on 20th January, 1900 to the graduation of his son, Ivan, who'd qualified at the Medical Faculty. He came to a *Detvan* meeting and it was an honour for Milan that his godfather witnessed him keeping the minutes. He promised to tell his father, who constantly reproached him for passivity in his letters and suspected him of leading a feckless life. Fajnor was a well-known Hlasist advocate and critic of the centre at Martin and therefore was warmly welcomed in *Detvan*. It was clear that his words, in which he didn't name anybody, but said that he was ashamed of Slovaks who wanted to beat others with sticks because they didn't share their opinion, referred to Vajanský.

"Thank you for making such great progress in the free Prague atmosphere in which you live. Freedom of spirit, words, actions are the things that we must bring to life in our home. I would like to greet you from your many supporters in Slovakia and say that we are proud of you. You are future leaders and perhaps reformers of our nation. When we progress according to the principle of 'ours to our own and always according to the truth', we shall not perish!"

Even after Fajnor's appearance, some colleagues' attacks on him continued; in addition to his grammatical mistakes, they criticized his hard pronunciation of soft vowels. In vain, did he explain that he'd attended Hungarian schools, where Slovak grammar wasn't taught and that he grew up in the Kopanice environment where they spoke with such an accent. A disgusted Štefánik withdrew and devoted himself more to his own advancement. He visited interesting Prague families more often and above all he began to focus more intensively on the study of philosophy and opinions of Tomáš Masaryk. With his arrival from the University of Vienna, this man immediately widened the intellectual and political circles in Prague. When in 1882 the Charles-Ferdinand University was divided into the Czech Charles University and the German Deutsche Universität zu Prag, he became Extraordinary Professor of Philosophy at Charles University and then a full professor fifteen years later. It was he who convinced Šrobár and Blaho of the necessity of establishing *Hlas*. The ideas and actions of this man from a simple Slovak-Moravian family began to influence the path of Milan's life. Štefánik's decision to move to the Faculty of Philosophy was unconsciously supported by Masaryk's ideas. Above all, through his heroic defence of an unknown and poor Jew, Hilsner, accused of ritual murder, he gave courage to the young Štefánik. In great suspense he followed Masaryk's fight for the truth, which caused storms of nationalist and anti-Semitic protests. Mobs of furious students went into the streets and even threatened to kill Masaryk. However, in April 1900 he was satisfied when the appeal court in Vienna, referred the case to a new hearing after Masaryk's protests.

Masaryk's compelling struggle for truth fascinated Milan and he decided to enter a life similar to that of this amazing man. He wanted to get closer to Masaryk, so his decision to move to the Philosophical Faculty, where the professor lectured, was a natural one. After some hesitation, he wrote to tell his father. His father first responded calmly, persuading him to understand that he didn't come from a wealthy family, so he must also help his siblings. Moreover, he would one day be a father of a family himself, and therefore the engineering construction faculty was much more promising and practical than any philosophy or astronomy. When Milan again wrote to him that he had already made a firm decision, he got a letter that upset him so much that he had to visit hospital with stomach problems before leaving for home. Professor Eiselt warned him against nervous stress. Štefánik promised the professor that he would be careful, even though he knew in advance that it was a false promise. In the summer semester of 1900 he was determined to leave the Technical University. He stopped attending lectures for good; Professor Zenger was the only one there with whom he had a bond, but he had yet to mention his decision to him. He knew that the summer in Košariská would be difficult for him.

CHAPTER 14
Thoughts, Words and Deeds in Harmony with Conscience

Milan appeared at Košariská on 3rd July, 1900 shortly after being discharged from hospital in Prague with stomach problems. Fortunately, no surgery was needed. He was still weak, pale and visibly nervous and was greeted by his parents and siblings coldly. Waiting for the storm to break, he rummaged through the newspapers that his father always had at the manse. He had been moping around the house for two days, his father tiptoeing around him as if on eggshells. An explosion was expected at the manse, though no-one knew when.

When mama, with a serious and terrified face, came to her son in the garden to go to his father, he knew time had come for the first serious clash with his father's authority. His mother, according to his father's command, sat behind the table on his side. The head of the family didn't involve his wife in his affairs, but as this matter concerned the whole family, he insisted on Albertína's presence.

"How did you do in your exams?" His father demanded that Milan show him his index book where his marks were recorded. Although this question was expected by Milan, nevertheless his blood ran cold. In the second year of his studies at the Prague Technical University he hadn't passed any exams. In his index was only a note about his attendance of lectures and seminars on the subject of drawing.

"It seems that the great lord was hanging around in the hundred-spired mother and enjoying life. Fine..." said his father.

"Not quite," Milan said. "I attended some lectures and asked the ministry to credit at least two semesters. Professor Zenger, with respect, also recommended that I leave the school that I don't enjoy and go where I can find true fulfillment."

"So you didn't have time for school. And yet you had time for songs like this?"

His father pulled out one of the issues of *Hlas*, where there were a few poems.

"It's written here here how young people mock their fathers, and so does your poem: *"Smoking and beer over everything dear, newspapers perhaps from times not so near..."*

"How do you know that I wrote it?" asked Milan, surprised. "In *Hlas*, the authors aren't identified..."

"Did you write it or not?"

"Yes... I wrote it. Is it bad when I'm honest and open? Well, yes, it happened that the Technical University wasn't satisfying, but I'm not the first. Just out of respect for you, I told myself that I could manage it somehow, but it was just suffering. I couldn't expect a life there just a wretched existence."

"So smoking and newspapers... hmph ... And both the family and the church community, the life your father lives, your uncle, your godfather and all the courageous people who care for their family and lead an organized life are just good for ridicule?"

"I have nothing against organized family life, later on, once someone has achieved something and turns his gaze backwards rather than forwards. But I don't want to live for twenty-thirty years hence. Now, now I want to live. I want to fully and consciously control my destiny. However, I can only achieve this if I have a clear goal before me, towards which I will go resolutely. In that issue of *Hlas* that you hold in your hand there is another of my poems; you don't have to look for it as I have it by heart. *Alea iactas est*, before you a thousand roads. Choose one of them, choose, go on..."

"Yes – the die is cast, I know Caesar's words, I just don't know how they relate to the fact that you've decided to ignore your parents' sincere advice," he looked at Albertína, who regarded her husband as a source of truth.

"Isn't the goal to be a courageous and exemplary father or mother for a family?"

"The die is cast for everyone when they leave the family nest. I left it in childhood. Many of my friends were still wet behind the ears at the time. You sent me to Šamorín, then to Prešporok and then into the world forcing me to work on myself, for which I will be grateful to you until I die. You, papa, awakened in me an interest in knowledge, in discovering the secrets of life, in seeking the truth. Have I ever overestimated my powers? Have I ever retreated from any obstacle that got in my way? Haven't I always triumphed with the help of God? You say I don't have it, but where is the evidence that I lack talent, if not genius?"

"Don't you think you're a little conceited?"

"No, because it seems to me that I only have a duty to myself. Don't blame me for wanting to pursue the science to which my whole heart draws me. Papa, please understand me... Don't be angry, but anyone can be a father. Only a person who has dreams, though, can be an astronomer."

"Having dreams is all very well, I'm just asking you what you want to live from? What about your siblings? You know we're going to finance you from loans for which we will be liable and one day repay! Do you want to risk your ill-considered study of astronomy causing harm to your siblings?"

Milan was silent, he understood his father's fears, but he was firmly resolved to yield nothing of his conviction.

"Milanko, have you really changed your mind? You know you won't be able to go very far with astronomy in Hungary," his mother took his father's side. She thought for a moment and then spoke with great emotion. "Don't you see how we live here? We live in poverty because your father keeps faith with his origins. Magyar officials have offered him various advantages if he identified as Hungarian, but your father has bravely refused. Not even the superiors of our own church will help us, not even Igor…"

"Leave it, Bertinka, don't mention that!" his father grew heated.

"Mama, I know what I'm doing, and why I need to study philosophy and astronomy," he said passionately.

"So we should understand that you don't want to come home after your studies?"

"Mama, I'm twenty years old and grateful to you and to papa with all my soul for all that you have given to me in my life, but haven't I been in Prešporok, Szarvás even now in Prague, and survived and provided my own living? I have been standing on my own feet since I was ten years old…" he said in a tone in which there was a soft reproach.

"So you're not coming back…" his mother mumbled and wiped away a tear. Milan was silent.

"It would be proper to discuss such a thing as leaving the university with your parents," his father said shaking his head.

"And what would you tell me, papa? Only what you're telling me now. So it's better that I didn't consult you so that you wouldn't blame me for not listening."

"Milanko, can't you see that papa and I just want you to do well?" his mother broke in again. "If after all, you studied properly and then earned for your family honestly, bringing up your children in love, your father would gladly give you his blessing."

"Yes, mama. But I want to be an astronomer! I've been dreaming about it since I made my first telescope with poor dead Fedorko, may the earth rest lightly on him."

"I would immediately approve if there was a real chance you could feed yourself and your family as an astronomer. But they don't have observatories in the Czech lands and won't let you go to the German ones in Prague. You say that you don't want to go to Hungary and those few places in Vienna or Pula are taken. I know that you aren't very much drawn to Russia, so where do you want to apply your knowledge once you finish school?"

"When I embark on a journey, it will be one which'll lead to the highest accomplishment. In astronomy, in meteorology, but especially in cosmology, Camille Flammarion is the world's greatest authority. Scientifically examining the origins, evolution, and structure of the universe, he has demonstrated that the universe is governed by physical laws. He is also one of the greatest contemporary thinkers," Milan explained firmly, encouraged by his father's knowledge of observatories.

"Rubbish. What physical laws are there? The whole of creation is in the hands of God. God controls not only all things in the universe, but also the fate of our people. And as far as I know, your Flammarion is a godless blasphemer and agitator. He examines the afterlife and deceives gullible women. You want to go to such a person?" he said heatedly to his son, who went on enthusiastically.

"If I don't go to Flammarion, I can go to another authority, to a man who has demonstrated that the Moon has no atmosphere and the atmosphere of Mars contains water vapour and has discovered the new element of helium. He is a man who, as a sixty-nine-year old, built the observatory on Mont Blanc, Europe's highest mountain, the famous Frenchman, Jules Janssen. He has a large observatory in Meudon near Paris. I'd like to work for him!" said Milan with such enthusiasm that a smile appeared on his mother's face. But seeing his father's angry expression, she became serious.

"You're foolish, son. You have to realize that it's amazing for a boy from Košariská to get to Prague. But to Paris and to such scientific show-offs? It's unrealistic."

"Professor Zenger promised to write me a recommendation to Flammarion. And if not, I'll still get there. I'll break through!"

"Why do you think so?"

"Because I want to break through!"

"These are determined words," his father said through gritted teeth. It was evident that he had to be very restrained. "You're talking about a meaningful fulfillment in life. You overestimate yourself! And what fulfillment is there in observing a solar eclipse? What have your astronomers, one or the other, brought to humanity? What does humanity have from Janssen's finding that there is no water on the moon and no atmosphere on Mars?"

"Not water, but water vapour, and it's not on the Moon, but on Mars. And Janssen found that there was no atmosphere on the Moon. Papa, please understand me. You say I overestimate myself, but I ask you again: have I ever stepped back from an obstacle that came my way?"

"Man needs the word of God, and your science won't give him that! You're drunk on science, but its only result is to divert you away from God! And you, the son of an evangelical priest, do you still want to promote the spread of ungodliness?!"

He lit the pipe in his emotion and coughed slightly as it came alive.

"Flammarion is a world-wide authority," said Milan.

"Give me peace from your astrolabe. When I told Auntie Hanulech that you wanted to be an astronomer, she crossed herself and ran to pray for you. She's got more common sense than you!" his mother was furious, too.

"Well, if you follow Aunt Hanulech's advice, then..."

"You see, woman, now you have what I feared," Štefánik said reproachfully to his wife. "I knew that if he went to godless Prague, he would return to us as a freethinker. This is what we've been waiting for," he exhaled smoke furiously.

"Milan, the Word of God is the only one and this is in the Holy Scriptures that your father and our ordained priests explain to men. As did his father Paul, his godfather Miloslav Hurban, your grandfather and all their noble predecessors, the proclaimers of God's word," his mother tried to calm a tense situation.

"The word of God is spoken in ten commandments that no one actually keeps..."

"Not even your parents?" his mother asked in dismay. Milan was silent.

"Give me one example where I or your mother don't follow the Ten Commandments?" said his father.

"For instance the fifth, you must not kill. How can a priest be a hunter? How can you enjoy killing?"

"Sorry, I don't understand what you're reproaching me for? That I occasionally bring home something to eat from the forest?"

"I reproach you for killing innocent animals. Aren't they our fellow creatures?"

"God means not to kill a man..."

"It does not say you must not kill a man, in the Scripture it says you must not kill!"

Old Štefánik and his wife were silent because they couldn't find words to say to their son.

"All right, let's stay with man. So I'll tell you... I haven't... but maybe it is time... Killing a man doesn't just mean taking a rifle or a knife and taking his life literally. Killing also means when someone has long been humiliated and mentally tormented... It is a slow, gradual killing."

"No, I can't and I won't listen..." his father flared up in anger.

"Milan, stop, there is no better father and husband than your father," his mother objected unconvincingly. "I'm happy to be a help to your father by being his devoted and faithful wife..."

"He is not fit to hear such words!" his father stood up preparing to leave.

"Milan, son, how can you talk to your father like this? All the parishioners respect him, only his own son rejects him... that is bad, it is awful... it is..." Albertína wept.

"Don't weep and wail here, go and get the church boy to feed the pig. Can't you hear it oinking?" he snapped at his wife who'd risen from her chair crying. "Wait a second. We'll finish this quickly. So listen, my son, my wise one... if I can still address you as my son after your ravings of today... I said I had no inclination to listen to your delusions. If you intend to spread them here among my parishioners, I strictly forbid you to. Not as your father, but as the priest of Košariská responsible for the purity of our community. I'm not asking you to revoke what you said here, we aren't in Constance... but I am asking you, no ordering you, to swear here to stop spreading these mischievous words. And on Sunday you will go to church and the whole time beg God for forgiveness..." he looked pleadingly at his son in anticipation of his response.

"I will beg God but not for forgiveness. I will ask for understanding and not in the church, but here under Úboč," Milan said firmly.

"Son, son... God be with us... You shouldn't contradict your father. Papa deserves that you fulfill his will..."

"I've fulfilled papa's will and I'll fulfill it constantly. Papa has always taught me to live in truth, and I'm doing just that."

"Go to the hired hand!" his father yelled at his wife who'd stayed still as she felt she had to stand by her husband.

"So you insist that you won't stop this talk..."

Milan was silent.

"Okay... as you wish, but do not spread your rubbish here in Košariská, in Brezová, Krajná, Myjava nor anywhere in Kopanice! I can see you're too stubborn to change your decision...

"It's no longer possible and I've already received a positive notification from the Philosophical Faculty of Charles University."

"I don't need," father continued through clenched teeth, "for my parishioners to begin to walk with my son, who talks to them differently from their father and their church. If you can't promise me... surely you can acknowledge that I can't risk that you put me in an evil light by doubting not only my authority, but the authority of all the Štefániks, Jurenkos and even the Hurbans or Fajnors. That must be clear to you..." He spoke slowly, oddly resigned, rather sad, as if he hoped that Milan would still say something that would allow them to find a reasonable compromise.

But Milan was silent.

"It's summer and you will surely find a place where you can put your head. I'll give you time until tomorrow. Consider what you're going to tell me in the morning." He stood up and walked to the door without a word. He glanced at his wife: "Go find the hired hand, the cows are already mooing!" Then he turned to his son. "Consider soundly what you will say. Otherwise I no longer have a son."

Štefánik looked sadly at his father. He thought he saw a tear in his eye.

"Father, I would only tell you what I've already said..."

Immensely agitated to the point of despair his father went out without a word as if he was shrunk, bent by age and humiliated. His mother took advantage of his father's absence and crept carefully to Milan. She hugged him, pulled him to her heart and made the sign of the cross on his forehead.

"I will pray for you, wherever you are, that your thoughts, words, and deeds are in accordance with your conscience."

CHAPTER 15
It's the Meaning of Life That Counts

The next day, Milan packed his bags. Since childhood he'd been accustomed to packing and travelling elsewhere. It was not the first time he'd left the house; almost every holiday he'd gone around Slovakia as a "suppliant" raising money for the grammar schools where he studied. It was as if travelling were his fate. He also took things for Prague in case his father didn't relent and he'd have to travel from Ružomberok straight to Prague at the end of September. He went to see his mother, who told him tearfully that his father had gone on urgent business to Myjava in the morning. He only left a message for Milan saying that he didn't want to see him. It was obvious that old Štefánik could be as stiff-necked as his son.

"Tell papa that I'm not angry with him because I know that he isn't angry with me either. We are both Štefániks and we both stand by our beliefs," he smiled forcefully, seeing that his mother was on the edge of tears. He'd left the house many times, but this was the first time he'd left after a quarrel with his parents.

"Where are you going to go?"

"I have friends from my studies in all corners of Hungary... I'll see... perhaps to some friends from school. Most probably to Vavro in Ružomberok."

"Write to me soon, Milan. And do come home for harvest."

"That's up to papa. If he wants to see me... If not, I'll go straight to Prague. And don't worry, philosophy, astronomy, mathematics, experimental physics, integral calculus, general surface theory, planetography, and others attract not only my mind, but also my heart."

"Oh, my love, I don't understand what you are saying. But may God keep you and lead you to know yourself. You know papa – sooner or later his anger will fade... Well, here you go, here's something for the train and a bit of food." She pushed money into his hand that he refused to take. However, he was glad to accept a basket with bread, bacon, onions, peppers, sheep cheese, cakes and other provisions.

From Vavro Šrobár he had an invitation to stay in Ružomberok for an unlimited time, so he decided to use it. Besides, he'd already planned to visit him during summer. He wanted to discuss the future of *Hlas* and *Detvan*, therefore, his trip to Liptov was not such a dramatic escape after all. It was moreover a welcome excuse to leave home. He was just sorry that the grain crops were ripe at Kopanice and he wouldn't help his parents with the harvest. But father had decided so; let him regret it. On his way he went through Priepasné to nearby Polianka to calm his soul with his older sister Olinka, whose husband Eugen Hajtš had become a teacher there in February.

He stopped by his brother, Igor, who was working as a priest at Myjava and then headed in the direction of Liptov.

Vavro had opened a medical practice in Ružomberok fin November 1899 and for a doctor beginning his career,was already successful and relatively well-situated. He lived in a house with a pharmacy where he rented an apartment with surgery. Its owner was his classmate, Julo Griell, whose father, a pharmacist, was a man of substance in Ružomberok. After Šrobár's arrival, the pharmacy began to thrive even more, as patients could collect the medicines prescribed by the doctor straight away in the house. Mr Griell valued Šrobár, wanted him to be satisfied, and therefore had no objection to his Košariská colleague staying with him. Šrobár was known to speak in Hungarian only in unavoidable cases, which goaded the eyes and ears of the local Hungarians. Since everybody needed a doctor, they also had to accept that Šrobár's prescriptions were exclusively in Slovak and also Griell, the pharmacist, converted the German and Hungarian labels to Slovak at his request. The big green sign, *Gyógyszértár,* had underneath it the Slovak word for pharmacy, *Lekáreň*. At the turn of the century, before the almost completely Slovak Ružomberok was Magyarized, renamed Rószahegy and dubbed the 'Felvidék Debrecen', anyone who spoke in Slovak was instantly described as a pan-Slav, and thus a near enemy of the homeland and a traitor. Unlike the kabatos (turncoats) as he called the local renegades, Šrobár addressed everyone formally, thus circumventing the established Hungarian third-case plural.

They went on trips to Likava Castle, to Choč, Salatín, Hrabov, to Čebrať, but also more demanding hikes to Kriváň, Ďumbier and to the Kvačianska and Prosiecka valleys. When wandering through the beautiful Liptov countryside, Milan relaxed, recovered and gained strength so at least his mother could consider his holiday stay useful. He informed her regularly on postcards where he was and how his health was improving. He never forgot to greet his father. But he didn't answer his son's salutations.

The most amazing moments of the stay in Ružomberok were meetings with a local compatriot, Šrobár's friend Dušan Makovický. Although he had a medical practice in nearby Žilina, he often came to Ružomberok to see his parents and brothers. His father was an important entrepreneur; he founded the Loan Participants' Association, which he later turned into the Loan Bank and in 1883 he founded the Paper Wood Milling Works, which over time became one of the largest pulp and paper mills in Hungary.

Makovický was pleased by Štefánik's interest in the great literature and philosophy of Leo Nikolaevich Tolstoy. He talked about him with undisguised joy and fascination.

"I visited Tolstoy in October 1894. Initially I reproached myself for going to disturb such a great man to satisfy my ego just to see him. But finally I stayed with the teacher for a week. Imagine it, at his request! My heart was beating from excitement on the road from Tula station to the entrance to the vast Tolstoy park. When we arrived at the writer's house and stepped out of my carriage, he was just going out for his regular morning walk. He looked at me curious about who I was. A Slovak from Hungary, I said. He said he was very pleased to meet me and gave me his hand and apologized. I watchedhim until he went into the trees. I admit that I was surprised at at his wretchedness. He was sixty-six years old, but hunched-up, an old man worn out by work, his face tired and sad. But his gaze was lively, deep, calm and welcoming. His beard was like milk, almost to his waist. When he returned from his walk, he asked me about my profession. After I told him I was a doctor and worked in Innsbruck and Budapest, he urged me to tell him more. We had a long discussion until finally he invited me to stay with them and immediately called a maid to prepare a guest room. Then I helped Tatiana Lvovna copy the master's letters and with Mária Lvovna I treated the sick at his request. His eldest son, Sergei Lvovich, always sat down when we talked with his father about the parties in the Pešť parliament, about politics in Hungary, the Hungarian nobility, but he was most interested in Masaryk. He spoke quietly, but very comprehensibly, so my Russian was enough to understand everything. He was restrained, tactful, did not impose himself and it almost felt as though he were listening more than he spoke. He didn't deny the gentle-bred nobleman in himself and every discourtesy was loathsome and repelled him."

"And what did you tell him about us, about the Slovaks in Hungary, about our suffering?" Šrobár asked Makovický impatiently.

"We talked a lot about it. I told him everything about the situation, but he was well-informed..." he smiled, adding: "And we disagreed when I criticized Jewish profiteers because as with the Russians, they get Slovaks in the villages drunk and part them from their money. He asked me why I was so taken against them as it is not the Jews' fault that Russians and Slovaks drink. And I said whose is it then, when every tavern in the village is in the hands of the Jews... he didn't agree with me..."

"I know an incident when a Slovak had a tavern in the Kopanice and you know what happened? He also drank it away... And when he had nothing, he sold it to a Jew for a pittance," Štefánik said.

"I don't deny it," replied Makovický.

"Tolstoy is a man of action. He establishes schools, teaches peasants himself – we should follow him. He even criticizes the church, the nobility; he's a man without fear, a pity that we don't have such a person," Štefánik sighed.

"I believe we are sitting on our asses and waiting for a saviour, just as the parish priests tell us. We're like orphans in our own country..."

"Tolstoy had many exemplars," said Makovický. "Above all, Christ, but also Rousseau, Amiel, Descartes, Seneca, Kant and others, but, as he told me, he likes Pascal extraordinarily. He highly values that as a famous mathematician and physicist, the discoverer of many physical laws, the famous Pascal theorem, Pascal's triangle and other mathematical and physical laws, Pascal achieved incredible things in his short life. However, according to Tolstoy, his philosophical rather than his mathematical views are more important. At a young age he gained fame as an outstanding mathematician; desire drove him towards other studies. He didn't let anything stand in his way and although he was very ill, he suppressed the pain with work. His health deteriorated sharply until he finally died of a malignant tumour. But in his short life he did more than others do in ten lives. It's not the length, but the meaning of life that counts."

"How many years did he live?" asked the excited Štefánik, who was devouring Makovický's every word.

"Thirty-nine..."

CHAPTER 16
Feet in the Mud, Head in the Stars

After his transfer to the university in the autumn of 1900, he threw himself into his studies with verve and determination. His friends hadn't known anything like that before. The Ministry of Culture and Teaching in Vienna counted his two years of engineering studies as one semester, thus saving him some time. He moved back to the Hron family, but soon left for Mária Pittnerová's place on Korunná Street. In the first semester, he enrolled for thirty-seven hours of lectures on subjects that had excited and attracted him from the beginning; the mechanics of the heavens, an encyclopedic review of astronomy, experimental physics, the use of differential calculus and others. Encouraged by his summer discussions with Šrobár and Makovický, two former chairmen of *Detvan*, he attempted to resuscitate the association's activities at the general meeting in November 1900. He severely criticized Chairman Ursiny's speech, especially his departure from Czecho-Slovak reciprocity. A few friends supported him, but most rejected him and didn't even select him for a committee already dominated by Martin-oriented students. Finally, he withdrew from *Detvan's* activities.

From his entry into the Philosophical Faculty at Charles University, he devoted himself not only to astronomy studies, but was also an extraordinary student of technology and in the summer semester he even enrolled on a practical physics course at the Philosophical Faculty of the German University. At that time he became close to Professor Gruss, who lectured on his favourite subjects: general surface theory, solar eclipses and planetography. The young man dedicated his life to a single goal; to become an astronomer. Long into the night he sat over his books, denying himself even minimal movement. The worst, however, was his disastrous diet. He didn't have the money for good-quality food. The only pleasure he had was shooting at a club on the nearby Strelecký Island on the Vltava River, where he used to go with his roommate Edo Hron. He was the backbone of the shooting club and sometimes he got food or a bottle of wine for winning a competition, which he and Edo immediately consumed.

Milan's interest in poetry, literature and fine arts continued and so he proposed to publish an arts supplement for *Hlas*. In June 1901 he asked Pavol Országh Hviezdoslav for a letter of cooperation and support. But the response of the great poet was negative, and even worse, extremely critical. In this difficult period of his studies in

Prague, the refusal only deepened Milan's depression. The disappointed Štefánik wrote to the great Slovak poet: "You complain about the whole generation of young people, although I approached you as a private person. We didn't expect such a harsh reproach. We wish to work on enhancing our dear nation and you put us down in the very moment we wish to demonstrate our sincere enthusiasm and love for the noble and the good."

He wrote several articles and poems, in which he revealed his sensitive soul and fervent relationship with his homeland. "Sadness settles in our mountains, sadness blowing over a wide field. Discord, anger builds balefire so that brother hurls brother on them. And wild with furious passion, he throws himself into a furious fight. He wants to serve the common good, but with so little love, our nation is perishing."

His depressed mood from the decline of *Detvan* and, in particular, the pressure of his relationship with his father didn't help his health. He sincerely loved his papa, though he often wondered if there was more fear in this relationship than natural respect. The uneasy life of struggle and assertion in an unforgiving, fierce world led him to study the writings and life of Professor Masaryk. His courage and uncompromising struggle for the truth impressed him. He was fascinated by Masaryk's openness and courage to criticize his own nation even at the cost of condemnation on the part of the public and rejection of him as an author. Virtually the entire Czech public turned against him when he questioned the authenticity of the so-called Zelenohorské and Královodvorské manuscripts; crowds of students marched through the streets of Prague chanting slogans of an anti-Masaryk nature. But the passions of the mob did not interest Štefánik. Fascinated, he watched the stoic calm and determination of this brave man and his absolute faith in truth. His words were engraved in the young idealist's memory: "The basic precondition for raising the spirit is to fight for the truth. Fighting for the truth means working for the truth, living for the truth, working the truth.

We have a duty to confess the truth and stand by it. Even if we have our feet in the mud, our head must be in the stars."

Masaryk and Hus became two of Štefánik's dominant role models. Just as Masaryk was trying to walk his life in Hus's footsteps, so Štefánik would try to follow Masaryk's path. His wisdom, largeness of spirit and strict morality were examples to the young Slovak student. He also began to understand Masaryk's profound piety, which lay in his quest for Christ's truth. He publicly opposed students who were involved in anti-Masaryk bullying. Enrolment in Practical Philosophy and Titanism, which was taught by Professor Masaryk in the third semester at the Faculty of Philosophy, was a natural act which much influenced Štefánik's perception of the world. He spoke of Masaryk as "the sun shining on us, even though we don't see it".

Encouraged by Masaryk's lectures, he tried to revive *Detvan's* activity. And as so often happens, he who criticizes the most is preferred. On 19th October, 1901, Milan was elected the new chairman of *Detvan* and with great enthusiasm, he plunged into work. However, his full commitment to both study and work in *Detvan*, his excessive mental and physical exertion, stressful situations and, in particular, poor diet, deprived him of strength. Neither Radhošť nor Jeroným support funds were able to cover his basic living needs, so he scrimped on food. The constant and undignified pursuit of finance worsened his stomach problems until, finally, less than a month after his election, he ended up on 15th November 1901 with inflammation of his appendix on Professor Kukal's desk at Professor Maydl's clinic. At his own request, he was operated on only with lumbar anesthesia as he wanted to follow the course of the operation with his own eyes. Only his lower body was knocked out. The operation went smoothly, but Štefánik long after was tormented, sitting crouched, in pain from the operation. He didn't eat after the operation, just drank warm milk. As a result of his ill health he was unable to participate in the work of *Detvan*, intrigues were led against him and he resigned as chairman. In *Detvan* once more the Pro-Martin contingent, oriented towards Vajanský, was given power. The disgusted Štefánik finally resigned from *Detvan* in February 1902. He explained this step by saying: "I have observed for some time that the wind has been against my person and have been subjected to personal attacks. In addition, I observe a retrogressive spirit in the association."

Such petty struggles had exhausted him. He was nervous and prone to losing self-control, labelling some members of *Detvan* a rabble because they went to cafés and enjoyed student life. His assault outraged many of them. Somewhere in the depth of his soul he began to become alienated from such people. He decided he wouldn't judge them anymore so that they wouldn't judge him. He needed to clear his head and leave everyday tension and stress. He decided to interrupt his studies in Prague and took the opportunity to complete two semesters in Zürich.

CHAPTER 17
I Will Break Through Because I Want to Break Through

In the middle of April, Štefánik went home to Košariská to settle travel formalities at his place of residence before leaving for Switzerland. He also went to Brezová, where he attended a military levy on 19th April. The recruiting commission classified him as "incompetent, weak and anaemic". Before that, however, he'd had to repeat with a heavy heart the process that he'd almost got used to. He applied for a loan of 300 zlatky from the *Ľudová banka* in Trnava, which he needed to travel to Switzerland. The deputy, Veselovský, the parish priest of Myjava, his brother, Igor, and a friend from his Prague studies, a distant relative, Ján Kraicz, were his guarantors. However, a generous Prague sponsor, Antonín Dvořák, helped him most. The dispute with his father hadn't settled over time, and there was a slightly disturbing, fragile peace between the obstinate Štefániks. His father was mollified at least by his excellent study results and he learned from his mama that papa had been bragging in Košariská and Brezová that his son would be an astronomer, which encouraged the Prague student. His mother urged him not to associate with Prague antichrists, but Milan assured her that she didn't have to worry about his spiritual direction.

He got off the train in Zürich on 26th April, 1902, with a letter of recommendation in his pocket from his favourite Professor Zenger to a professor at the Zürich University of Technology, Alfred Wolfer, opening the doors to the Zürich observatory. He stayed at the beginning of Claudiusstrasse in *Pension Baumann* near the University Campus. When for the first time he entered the newly built physics pavilion, he started trembling. The ailing lad from Košariská was walking into a Mecca of technological education. *Eidgenossische Technische Hochschule*, the Swiss Technical University was one of the world's most renowned. Thinking that beyond one of the windows he was looking through stood the laboratory of one of the most famous professors, the Slovak Aurel Stodola, the founder of the gas and steam turbine theory, he proudly turned to walk vigorously up a wide staircase, determined to find the professor as soon as possible. He had a recommendation from Dušan Makovický, with whom Stodola was a friend. Finding the office of this popular professor, head of the Department of Machine Construction, who completed his studies at the school in 1878 and had taught there since 1892, was no problem. Unfortunately, the professor was on a long stay abroad and would then be preparing a lecture tour in Germany. However, the secretary noted the name Štefánik and promised to inform the professor as soon as he returned from Germany. Indeed, at the end of June, the secretary announced to him that the professor would be happy to receive him the next day. The 43-year-old Stodola, designer of the first heat pump in the world, the man who laid the foundations for the construction of steam and combustion turbines, was very affable. When he learned from Milan that he was a friend of both Makovický and Šrobár, he had much to reminisce about.

"I'm sorry to keep you waiting for almost a week, but after returning from Germany, I had many matters of priority."

"I congratulate you wholeheartedly, I read in the paper that you excelled at the German Engineers' Congress in Düsseldorf," Štefánik told him joyfully.

"Well, I didn't expect to have such a response. 18th June, however, seems to have been one of my more successful days. There were more than a thousand scientists from all over the world, barely fitting into the Knight's Hall. At first, I was a little nervous, as I hadn't given a lecture at such a grand meeting, but when I saw how my thoughts went down, as I say, I expanded."

"You truly showed them. I also want to show the world that we Slovaks can do something. I am inspired by your success. I want to go to Paris to Camille Flammarion or to the observatory of Professor Janssen, the world's greatest astronomer," the young man said enthusiastically.

"Ah, Paris, a great city for personal development, but also very dangerous, unless you hold to firm moral principles. I studied there at the Sorbonne and worked at Hermann-Lachapelle. I will give you one piece of advice; if you want to be a great scientist, behave as if you were already one. I realized that in Düsseldorf. At first they looked at me as a revelation; you know, the Germans are not accustomed to acknowledging others, but when I showed them that I knew something by being self-confident and proud, they bowed down and, I guess, gave me the greatest applause of all. You know, we Slovaks are a small nation and will only make a difference in the world by demonstrating knowledge. We can never win a war with weapons, but we can win a battle of the spirit. I feel that after the congress, I've strengthened my position in the scientific world and at the university, though some people begrudge me my success. But no-one can know how much it has cost me in time and effort to become a professor at the world's most famous technical university. Here there are experts from Germany, America, France, Austria, Hungary, England, Russia and last year our compatriot Ľudko Tetmajer from Krompachy worked here. We broke through. And do you know why?"

"Because you wanted to break through," Štefánik, who'd listened to Stodola as if hypnotized and almost leaped to his feet.

"Exactly. You want to be a scientist and science is the ideal means to show your mental and spiritual capability. Only science can push humanity forward, only science can answer the basic questions of our lives."

"I've chosen science as my idol."

"I was just the same at at your age. Science has literally dominated me, seduced me, is my love, my mistress, everything. When I decided to leave home years ago and come to Zürich, everyone around me shook their heads. Subsequently, they said behind my back, what did a poor boy from a Vrbica tanning family think of himself. I simply repeated to myself, if you decide to follow love, go to the place where it is the greatest, the strongest, the most excellent, to this university. So I'm telling you if you believe in the depths of your soul that you'll get to the famous Flammarion or Janssen, then you will. You just have to be strong enough, very strong... You'll miss your home, your family... Consider that people who are passionate about things are often alone..."

"Professor, I've been away from my family since I was ten years old... and... well... well alone... very much..." Milan reflected.

Stodola patted his shoulder with understanding.

"Solitude is the fate of every true man devoted to his cause. Even my friend Makovický complains of loneliness. I have written to him to tell Tolstoy that science cannot and must not become entwined with religion and tradition. Science must face forwards, not backwards."

"Dušan wrote to me that Tolstoy had requested him to go to him as a doctor," Štefánik said revealing his close relationship with Makovický.

"Yes, I know, and in his place I would accept the invitation wholeheartedly. I know how much Dušan longs for it. Members of a small nation have one advantage over those of the great nations. Their commitment is usually greater. The Russians, the Americans, the English and the French have it easier in life because they are from great nations. However, they are more comfortable, less aggressive and less serious. We have to grit our teeth first, but then we really get going," he laughed.

The bells in the church tower opposite struck noon. Štefánik was nervous.

"Professor, sorry, I'm really sorry, but I have to attend a lecture, if I can... sometimes come..."

"Come anytime. And if you have trouble, be assured that you can turn to me."

He shook the hand firmly of the enthusiastic student and for a long time he thought about the unusual visit.

Despite his unstable health and continuing financial problems, Štefánik felt that his stay in Switzerland would bring him closer to his dream of a career in astronomy. He registered for Professor Wolfer's lectures in Geographical Site Determination, Exercises in Astronomical Observation and Introduction to the Physics of Bodily Objects. He also went to the Philosophical Faculty of Zürich's other university, where he applied to attend lectures on differential and integral calculus and the fundamentals of electrical engineering.

After his stormy departure from *Detvan*, the Swiss peace, splendour of nature and hospitality of the locals calmed his soul. He noticed little things that had escaped him in the hurly-burly of Prague and went on trips into the city's surroundings. If the weather allowed he bathed in Lake Zürich or went to the more distant Lake Greifensee. However, he preferred going to the nearby hill of Uitleberg from which there was a magnificent view of Zürich, Lake Zürich and the crests of the Alpine peaks.

Thanks to the generosity of the building engineer, Antonín Dvořák, he could travel a little. To his sponsor, he kept accounts of every zlatka he spent on travelling. Besides a trip to Lucerne to the Vierwaldstatt Lake, he took a trip that moved his life forward enormously. On 6th July, 1902, he took a train early in the morning, bringing him through Winterhur and Frauenfeld to Constance, a German city on the shores of Lake Constance. Storm clouds were moving over the lake and he suddenly came across a place that caused him a tremor just to think of what had happened there exactly 487 years ago. On 6th July Ján Hus was brought to the meadow called Brühl by the walls of Constance.

When Milan arrived at the Paradise suburbs, paradoxically named so, to the west of the old town, an unknown man showed him a place in the lawn by the Old Walls where a stone, accidentally found in Lake Constance, had been set.

"That's the place," said the local as if ashamed. "Are you Czech?"

"No, I'm a Slovak?"

"I've never heard that."

"We are the closest brothers to the Czechs. And Ján Hus is as much a hero to Slovaks as Czechs. Also Master Hieronymus of Prague."

"Yes, they were both burned at this point. It's called the Old Ditch by the Western Walls. Both are heroes for us Swiss. They say it is a spooky place and on the sixth of July, on the day Hus was burnt, a terrible wailing can be heard. We residents of Constance consider these murders to be an eternal shame on our city." Milan thought about it for a long time and put a little of the earth of Constance into a handkerchief and knotted it.

The next day he went to the nearby Schaffhausen, where he saw the world-famous waterfalls under the castle of Laufen, where the upper Rhine falls to a depth of twenty-five metres with a width of 150 metres. Enchanted by the splendour of the landscape and the deep impressions made by Constance, he returned to Zürich on the evening train. A month later he went to Milan, Italy, where he visited the observatory and the library. He also visited Messina, Naples and Pompeii. After returning to Zürich in solitude he celebrated his twenty-second birthday. Again he had to deal with the dilemma of financing the remainder of his Swiss stay. Finally, after long consideration, he decided to apply for a loan of forty-five zlatky from his loyal sponsor, the constructor Dvořák, who, as several times before, accommodated the request of the student. He knew that Milan would repay every borrowed zlatka, including the, six zlatky which the trip to Constance cost him. Štefánik recorded for him every last groat. Professor Emil Schaer, a 40-year-old astronomer and optician of the Geneva Observatory, employed him during the last month of his stay in Switzerland to improve his lens polishing in the optical workshop. The professor favoured the promising astronomer and seeing his enthusiasm, he sold him, or better, gave him for a tenth of the price a photographic refractor, several more refractors, scarce lenses and mirrors with an intent to help Štefánik fulfill his dream and have his own observatory. He understood that the young boy from Slovakia was short of money. Therefore, by way of farewell, the scientist promised him that if he didn't have the money, he would lend him the equipment for good. An enthusiastic Štefánik later wrote to his friend, Marie Neumannová: "It's a dream, a fantastic dream. This means that with the components I already have, I'll be able to build an observatory that is comparable with the best. Bohemia will be beautified. I will work, I want to be a real person, I want to play a role in my nation, which I have never ceased to love. I don't want to go under, I must not drown. I feel that my health is returning, that I will soon be stronger than my unfavorable fate."

He also visited a house in Geneva which had been rented by two lovely older ladies to his favourite Dostoevsky and his wife Sofia in August 1867. In this house, their three-month-old daughter, Sofia, died and Fyodor Mikhailovich, despite the pain in his heart, wrote the first hundred pages of The Idiot in an incredible twenty-three days. He transformed his pain into a masterpiece. He didn't despair, didn't blame fate, suffered, believed and worked.

CHAPTER 18

What You Give Comes Back to You

At the end of September, Milan returned to Prague. As he stepped out of the train and caught sight of his loyal friend, Žigo Zigmundík, at the station, he had no idea how quickly and unexpectedly things would start working out in his favour.

When, after a half-year break, he showed up at the *Detvan* general meeting in November, there was a hum in the room, with those present suspecting that something special was brewing. Milan listened carefully to the discussion and at the end indicated that he wished to speak. At first he apologized to those whom he'd called a rabble and then outlined his ideas about re-activating *Detvan*'s activity, which was enthusiastically received by those present. "If I have ever called a Slovak student youth in Prague riffraff, it happened at a time of great exasperation. It is not what I really think and therefore I'll try to focus on the Slovaks in Prague, on our mutual learning and high-minded enjoyment. Let *Detvan* again become the hearth of cultural and progressive efforts, let it become a school and preparation for our future life. Let us support Czecho-Slovak reciprocity, knowing that the Czechs are Slovaks living in Bohemia, Moravia and Silesia and that

Slovaks are Czechs living in Slovakia." He left the general assembly as the re-elected chairman, and shortly after attended the *Corda Fratres* student organization congress in Palermo in Sicily.

The regular social evenings of *Detvan* at the *Na Bojišti, U Růže* and especially *U Kupce* pubs became very popular throughout Prague. On Wednesdays, when they were held regularly, it was impossible to get a seat. The inn had a solid piano, usually to accompany the tenor, Bohuš Haluzický, with whom others always joined in. Štefánik rarely sang, but he liked to dance; sometimes he even dressed in Detva costume. The most memorable evening was at *U Kupce*, when the French librettist, Gustave Charpentier, visited the inn on the occasion of the premiere of his opera, *Louisa*; the Frenchman was so impressed with the Slovak and Moravian songs that the *Detvan* members sang that he invited Haluzický and František Úprka to the photographer Tomáš on Wenceslas Square. There they had to sing with piano accompaniment into a phonograph. The songs were also translated and sent to Paris. Shortly afterwards, during the Slovácky evening at Žofín, there was a presentation of traditional customs from Slovácko (an area straddling Western Slovakia and Moravia including Brno), which Štefánik took part in together with some Moravians. During the performance, a dispute between the giant Frantisek Úprka and some drunken guests broke out. Štefánik wanted to settle it. Úprka grew enraged and inadvertently struck Milan who fell to the ground. There was applause from the hall because the guests thought it was a rehearsed scene. Štefánik didn't want to spoil anyone's enjoyment, laughed and joined in the fun again. An even more famous visit to *Detvan* was by the sculptor, Auguste Rodin, with whom Štefánik chatted in broken French in *U Kupce*. The social life of Slovak and Moravian students was further strengthened when Štefánik and his friend, Kalvoda, discovered a man who played Slovak folk songs behind the piano in the artists' bar *Monaco*. They didn't hesitate to rope him into their association. From then on Mikuláš Schneider-Trnavský became an important member.

In agreement with Vavro Šrobár, who in January 1903 decided to reissue *Hlas*, Štefánik founded an artistic supplement, *Umelecký hlas*, which he edited with the Moravian painter, Alois Kalvoda and the poet, Ivan Krasko. When it came out for the first time, it caused a sensation. Štefánik unusually and poetically described the goals of the new periodical. He threw himself into working with Masaryk's daily, *Čas*, under the leadership of the editor-in-chief Ján Herben. His regular Monday editorials about Slovakia gained considerable public notice and became very popular. Štefánik became a central figure among Slovak students in Prague and with characteristic verve, plunged again and again into the work of the association. He was attending fewer lectures, no longer receiving scholarships and had to finance himself. Since he didn't plan on pedagogical activity, he didn't need a state examination. However, he needed a doctorate and a written dissertation for future scientific work. He chose as his theme a new star in the constellation of Cassiopea, which had been discovered in 1572 by Tycho Brahe in Prague.

He watched events in Slovakia closely and was pleased to see that there were nationalist ripples gradually emerging at home. However, he was saddened by the knowledge that, unlike those in the Czech Republic, the masses were nationally ignorant, decimated and hypnotized by a single ambition; to curry favour with the Hungarian Empire and gain some kind of material benefit. The Slovak intelligentsia drowned in continual quarrels, and the generational dispute between the rising generation and the old Martin wing intensified.

He described his disappointment in *Čas* on 25th October, 1903, but nevertheless believed in the law of cosmic equilibrium, knowing that if he sent out a positive signal, someone he cared about would notice and respond to it. He had no idea that the article would catch the attention of two men with whom he had a strong relationship. The first was his father, the other the professor whose lectures he had so appreciated. So he was thrilled when Vavro Šrobár told him that Professor Masaryk, who regularly read *Hlas*, asked him for information about the author of such interesting articles about Slovakia. He said they were among the best, and was particularly interested in the October issue. When Šrobár told him who the author was, he showed interest in meeting him. It was the most beautiful message Štefánik had ever received in his life. It showed the truth of the principle stating that what you give comes back to you.

CHAPTER 19
Lack of Freedom is a Lack of Courage

When he knocked on the door with its simple nameplate *Tomáš Garrigue Masaryk*, his palms were sweating a little. For the first time in his life, he was meeting a man who was for him the embodiment of virtue and truth, a man whom he regarded as the successor to his idol, Ján Hus. Instead of calling 'Come in', the door opened and there stood a broad-faced smiling fellow with a beard, a huge moustache, a sharp gaze and an eagle's nose, on which were perched his characteristic spectacles.

"Good day, I'm Štefánik. I came as you said..."

"Milan, welcome, come in," said the professor, surprisingly in Slovak and pointed to a chair. He took a place opposite his guest. Štefánik was hesitantly silent. The professor looked at him for a moment.

"You came without a coat, it's chilly outside. Aren't you cold?"

"I can put up with it," he said without conviction. Masaryk looked at the small student and didn't understand where in this slender young man was so much of the energy and determination that he could feel in his articles, gestures and zealous expression.

"Do you realize that I've known you for a long time?"

"How?"

"Since I started reading your articles. Your political views are very modern and, like few authors, you base them on democracy, morality, justice, historical and natural law. And you write so poetically. Your articles have heart, they are clear and honest. You write that Slovakia is a margin of ravaged hills and that this margin needs to be fertilized. A lovely metaphor. Look, here are all your articles, whether from *Hlas* or *Čas*, I have them cut them out. If you allow me, can I occasionally quote from them?"

Štefánik sat thunderstruck.

"But... sorr... how do you know these are my articles? They aren't signed..."

"Their diction, style, thought processes, and especially their unusually direct flame of passion are typical of you. Vavro Šrobár also helped me a little in revealing the author," Masaryk smiled.

"You, Professor Masaryk, want to quote Štefánik the student?"

"If I may. You can quote me without fear in return. After all, we are almost compatriots. I know our places of birth are very close to each other. Hodonín and Košariská are about sixty kilometres away as the crow flies."

"You know I come from Košariská?"

"I have the habit of always getting to know as much as possible about the people who interest me. It pleases me that you speak Slovak in Prague, because I'm also a Slovak and we understand each other. I asked my colleague Šrobár to arrange our meeting. I want to thank you for writing in the Slovak section of *Čas*. You're doing excellently. Your sensitive and heartfelt thoughts about your native region appeal to me very much, for I am almost a Kopaničiar..." He fell silent and poured himself a glass of water. "Like you, I was poor and my usual diet was bread and dried plums; as a student, I gave private lessons. Like you, I went to a foreign language school. But there was one difference... you are now in university but I'd only just matriculated at your age," he laughed.

"As a twenty-three-year old?"

"Twenty-two... Just like you, at school, I learned basically only the subjects that I considered of interest and for the rest I matriculated no matter with what marks. You determinedly go towards your goal and concentrate on its substance. And that pleases me."

"Does it please you that I left the Technical University and transferred to the Philosophical Faculty?"

"For me it's neither here nor there if you are satisfied with it."

"It was my dream... though... my father threw me out of the house because of it..."

"I didn't succeed in such a daring exploit," his host laughed heartily. "I was self-taught, I read a lot and became a loner..."

"We are similar in this..." Štefánik said quietly.

"Dear Milan... I can tell you this... people who go firmly towards their goal are always alone because they don't have time for jollities. Only the strongest can be alone, without friends and often without love. That's why they're strong."

"Friendship is a crutch for a weakling. A real man looks for a friend in himself," Štefánik responded vigorously. "Yes, I'm lonely in my way of life, but my great consolation is that one day I'll be of service to a higher ideal."

"I fended for myself from the age of fourteen, nor did my father agree with the path I chose." Masaryk patted him encouragingly with his hand. "But we don't have to overdo this solitude. My apologies in giving you some advice, as I'm a few years older and I have some right to do so... With growing age, I understand that if you want to do important things, you have to move where they are decided. Therefore don't underestimate social contacts, they are the key to every big matter. I was fortunate because, during my studies at the University of Vienna, I was tutor to the family of Schlesinger, the director of the Anglo-Austrian bank who met the elite of Vienna, the great world. If the great world offers you chances, you need to take them. Even today I feel regret for not going to France, to the great world."

"Why didn't you go?"

"I didn't have the money... but then I realized that it was more of an excuse to myself. I just didn't have the courage. I didn't know French well and was frightened... I have German from my home, even a little Hungarian, and Hungarian words came to us from Holíč and Kopčany. At home it was never 'listen', but, Ide halgash! Go and study," laughed Masaryk.

"We only spoke Slovak at home, but we had to speak Hungarian in the higher schools. I also learned German and recently I learned a little French in Switzerland. I have to improve my French because... I've decided to go to Paris after my studies."

"Great! Unlike me, you have courage. What does your father say?"

"He doesn't know yet, but I already know he won't be enthusiastic."

"You'll only be happy when you follow the voice of your heart and not your mind. Only those who follow their hearts are truly free. You know, Milan, the problem of both Czechs and Slovaks is lack of freedom. Lack of freedom is a lack of courage. That is why we must instil courage in people and we can only do it by example. Czechs and Slovaks must become examples of courage. The only way to free yourself is not to rely on anyone and take matters into your own hands."

"Like Hus."

"Exactly. Being courageous, like Hus, Chelčický, Žižka, Comenius... I remember that when I became a member of the Reichstag thirteen years ago, the Emperor came to the Vienna parliament traditionally to greet the deputies. He shook each hand and as he came to me, shook his head and said: "Are you this Masaryk?" I nodded, but he continued without offering me his hand. At that moment, regardless of his majesty, I turned and left."

"What happened next?"

"I don't know, I don't go there any more, but they told me everyone froze... ha, ha..."

"That took real courage."

"Not really, I had parliamentary immunity, but the truth is that I got a reprimand from my Austrian colleagues. But there were also those who secretly shook me by the hand, which no one was supposed to do in the Austrian parliament.

"It must be shown to the great nations that we can stand by ourselves, that we are at least as spiritually mature as they are, although we cannot equal them numerically, simply that we are not afraid. You know, the problem of small nations is that they are always trying to emulate large nations. We continually strive, thinking we are larger than we are, sometimes copying countries from the east, then from the west. We are so overwhelmed that we don't have time for our own thoughts. But without them we'll never catch up with the world. Let me read something to you." Masaryk smiled and pulled a newspaper from his briefcase. "Whoever rails at small matters and doesn't try to change them, lives an unworthy life. The content of my life must be an effort to change to a higher morality. With intellectual improvement, I want to bring myself into harmony with the laws of the universe."

"Yes, I wrote that in an article," Štefánik joyfully smiled with astonishment.

"You wrote it precisely. A source of living water can only be found by someone who didn't lose a sense of moral purity in his youth. In everything, big and small. If someone deceives in little things, he will also lie in great matters."

"Yes, as Jesus says: let your speech be yes, yes or no, no!" said Milan.

"Our university pays professors who teach astronomy, the laws of mathematics, physics, logic, but also professors, if they can be termed such, teach undergraduates that the Pope is a representative of God on earth," Masaryk smiled wryly. "For me, religion is Jesus, not the Pope. Jesus was a prophet. A genius is for science, art, or politics, a prophet is for religion. And this prophet reiterates to us that his free decision should be the basis of every man's action." Masaryk poured water for his guest and himself again. "You see how we talk – as if we'd known each other for years."

"We know each other. I go to your lectures and you read my articles."

"I just wanted to tell you that I watch your words and your actions closely. It impresses me how they match. You're on your way to becoming a great person. I'll keep my fingers crossed for you. Whenever you have the time and inclination, my door here or the apartment on Školská Street is open to you. They're always open for people like you. It is an honour for me to discuss things with you. And one little thing... please, accept this as a sign of my honour and respect, my sincere support for a man I value who follows in the same path I have trodden."

Masaryk slipped a banknote into his hand.

"It's cold, buy a good coat."

CHAPTER 20

To believe, to love, to work!

A note was hanging on the door of the rented flat at the Neuberts on Korunná Street: Absent. He then transferred the label to Mrs. Petříková's to whom he moved in July 1903. Once a week he went to *Detvan*, finally quitting as chairman at the general meeting on 31st October 1903, on the occasion of its twentieth anniversary. His friend, Mikuláš Schneider-Trnavský, didn't pass up the honour of playing "Nad Tatrou sa blýska" on the piano in Štefánik's honour. Until May of the following year, he was still a committee member of *Detvan* and from then on devoted himself exclusively to his studies. He was determined to finish school as soon as possible and travel to Paris. Only his closest friends were privy to his plans. In a letter dated 25th August, 1903, to Vavro Šrobár he writes what is almost a confession: *"You are the dearest and the closest to me of my regiment of "friends". For the most part I know and can give reasons for this.. You were the first to indicate the vortex of my ancient-national and primitive ideals and so cast me into eternal restlessness, contradiction, anxiety, but at the same time you became an indirect cause and a stimulus for my progress. You've been my model in every respect, I have eagerly listened to your words, uncritically approved your actions, I have bound myself to you with all my youthful soul... I won't now describe how my development has gone, I can only assure you, dear Vavro, that my primary devotion and respect haven't disappeared; on the contrary, the flower is in full bloom drawing sap from the soil of conscious friendship. Never forget it, as I will not forget. I would like to help you in the desperate struggle with which your life is filled, but – as you know – my path is different."*

Occasionally but less frequently he would visit the family of the poet, Jaroslav Vrchlický. However, he was careful not to meet his daughter Eva, with whom he had an unpleasant incident. At one of *Detvan's* social evenings, she had refused to accept a bouquet from Štefánik in a very inappropriate way, tearing it out of his hand and throwing it away. The young man kept an admirable calm, as noted by Mrs. Bílá, the wife of the director of the Žižkov school, František Bílý, who was at the party with her sixteen-year-old daughter, Lidunka. She invited Milan and his friend, Bohdan Pavel to visit them the very next day. While Lidunka cast secret glances at Bohdan, Milan made a great impression on her mother. The invitations were then repeated regularly and often, but only for Milan. The lady listened attentively to Milan's stories about the stars and even acquired an atlas of the heavens and stars. Her eloquent guest spoke engagingly about his dissertation, which he was slowly finishing. Meanwhile, Lidunka had grown into wisdom and beauty and the two young people began to feel more than just friendly affection. Milan's conversation so intrigued the lady that her daughter laughed at her: "Mama, he's not coming to see me, but you; receive him yourself." He tried to pass on his enthusiasm for stars to Lidunka, too, but she wanted to talk to him more about love, the beauties of earthly and not heavenly life.

"Milanko, and what if you shaved your beard? It only makes you look older," she suggested after her mother had discreetly withdrawn and left them alone.

"Lidunka, ask me what you want, but don't wish me to remove my beard."

"Why? If you love me, you'll do it for me."

He shuddered at the idea that she should look at his unlovely, pock-marked face.

"You know, it may seem naive to you, but I had at a certain time, an almost mystical experience before. In Switzerland, in Constance..."

"I guess your experience is not related to your beard."

"To a certain extent, yes. You know, my hero is Ján Hus and I try to walk in his path in all aspects of life. He wore the same beard as me. I know, maybe it is ridiculous, but whenever I get into difficulties when I'm troubled in spirit, this beard reminds me of his suffering and I stand on my feet again."

"And do you often have to get back on your feet?"

"More often than you think... Well, I have to confess that since I've known you, I feel as if my life is lit by the rays of the sun. I see groves, flowering meadows, inhale their smell, listen to the squirrels and feel a certain Harmony of which you have become an important part..." Lidunka didn't even notice that he had taken her hands and was longingly gazing at her. She only noticed when his lips came close to hers and turned her face away quickly. In her embarrassment she felt a similar desire, trembled slightly and shyly lowered her gaze.

"Sorry, I didn't want to touch your beautiful soul..."

"No, everything is fine; as I look at you, I see that even your beard becomes you ... But as far as I know, Hus preached maximum restraint to young men in relation to young ladies. You don't follow him very much..."

"Well, man is just a weak creature, and not everyone has the will of Master Ján."

"Shall we go for a walk?" She smiled gracefully at him. It was a late June afternoon, the pleasant warmth and a light breeze enticed them to walk in the nearby park. He nodded.

"Mama, I'm going to accompany Mr. Milan," she called toward her mother's room. Without waiting, she took his hand and led him to the front door. Milan, though, went to her mother's room, bowed dutifully, thanked her for an excellent lunch, kissed her hand and said goodbye. The mother looked for a moment at the departing youngsters with an approving smile. Lidunka took his arm in the city park. He didn't resist.

After a while, they sat down on a bench, and Milan sensed the moment when he could tell her in the smallest details the words he'd been thinking over. He looked her tenderly, lovingly in the eye.

"What do you think, Lidunka, how would a girl I love reply if I asked her if she liked me enough to become my wife?"

He noticed that the delicate girl was blushing and felt the blood suffusing his face.

"I would like to care for her as a flower which no one should touch and whose fragrance would be only for me. Living and working for her would be the thought and purpose of my life. But I don't know if she wants to become my wife..."

Her cheeks glowed with a sincere smile and she lowered her gaze timidly. He returned her smile. They got up and walked slowly to Lidunka's apartment.

"My wife will be my queen. If it were in my astronomical power, I would carry her to the stars," he murmured.

"You obviously like to poeticize and dream," she teased.

"Only in dreaming is life worth living, because only then do we approach the absolute," he replied mysteriously and saw that Lidunka didn't understand him very much. Later, when her mother accidentally discovered a piece of paper signed Lída Štefániková on Lidunka's desk, she smiled with satisfaction.

In addition to being a regular at the Bílýs, Štefánik was a frequent guest of the family of the professor of technology, Antonín Vávra, where he tutored his son Bohuslav. He was also admired by the successful and attractive writer, Růžena Svobodová, twelve years older than he was and a relative of the construction engineer, Antonín Dvořák. He also regularly met with doctor, professor of histology at Charles University and confirmed bachelor, the Slovak, Jozef Rohoň. He also kept up relationships with the hotelier, Hauner's family, and visited other influential Prague families.

A further military conscription examination was undergone by Štefánik in Myjava on 13th April, 1904, with the result, "Incapable of bearing arms, general physical weakness. Decision: Not selected." He then went to Báčsky Petrovec for the wedding of brother Igor, who'd moved there from Myjava a year before. After a long time he also met his brother Pavol. In the large house of his new sister-in-law, Zuzka Šusterová, where they were staying, there were three unusually cheerful days. The lowland Slovaks, but also the Serbs, Germans and Hungarians, who lived in the village together with the wedding guests, sang Kopanice wedding songs together. When the lads intoned the Myjavská "I am a slender girl, a black-eyed girl. Who wants to know my name, I am called Anička", they danced through the whole village.

And then he returned to intense study again. He defended his dissertation satisfactorily and gained excellent results in his secondary rigorous examination in philosophy with professors Hostinský and Drtina on 19th June. Shortly afterwards, on 7th July, 1904, he also passed his PhD exam with unanimous excellence in philosophy and a satisfactory grade in astronomy and physics. Three months later, on 10th October, he passed rigorous examinations with professors Gruss and Strouhal and two days later, the Dean of the Faculty of Arts, his precious patron, the poet, Jaroslav Vrchlický, awarded him his Doctorate of Philosophy. The Vávras, Bílýs, Dvořáks, friends from *Detvan* and other guests attended the graduation ceremony, as did the man whose presence excited him above all, for he considered it an act of reconciliation: his father. He came without his mother who had to stay in Košariská with his ailing sister, Mária Želmíra. After receiving his diploma, Milan gave a moving speech of thanksgiving, bowing in front of his beloved parent, who allowed him to achieve this success. He also named all his precious supporters who'd helped him financially and morally through difficult moments. After the graduation ceremony, he and his father went to the Vávra family, where they had a celebratory lunch. For dinner they were both invited to the Bílýs. Shortly after the welcome speech and congratulations by the master of the house, Milan took the floor and thanked the Bílý family for all the good days spent with them. He'd barely finished when, to the great surprise of a number of guests, his father spoke. Unequivocally, he hinted that it wouldn't be against his will if Milan married the daughter of his hosts: "As in the heavens there are double stars, here, on earth, in human life similar phenomena occur, similar pairs appear, destined for a common journey through life as the stars travel through the universe." Milan glanced at Lidunka, who was blushing inordinately. She apologized in embarrassment and left the room.

"Honoured Mr. Pavel Štefánik," the master of the house hurried out an answer, surprised by his father's challenge. "We know that our Lidunka harbours warm feelings for your son, and knowing your son, nothing prevents us from saying yes to your request. However, I believe that we agree that our esteemed Milan, whose passionate desire is to become an astronomer, should first secure a stable place and then, when Lidunka is more sophisticated and older, a marriage can be celebrated."

"A good speech, I totally agree with you," his father smiled happily. "I think my son is happy, too," he said to Milan, who nodded in silence. It was clear to him that his father had achieved what he wanted: a public commitment that Milan would marry and start a family. The next day after his graduation, his father returned to Košariská. Milan still had the formalities of moving out of his temporary residence, calling on all his friends, all the kind and related families who'd supported him during his studies, settling up at the pawnshop, going to say farewell at the dean's offices, packing up and leaving for home.

As he expected, he was greeted by an enthusiastic mother and siblings, neighbours and well-wishers, known and unknown, also congratulating him. It wasn't so often that the Košariská gained a doctorate in Prague. But his father kept a cool distance.

"I'm not excited about your decision," he broke his strict silence in the kitchen in front of his mother. "From godless Prague to even more godless Paris. The French have forgotten God since their revolution."

"Papa, we need to focus on modern countries like France, the United States or England, where science is most advanced and where the best conditions for free human development have emerged."

"Without God, man is not free. Your Masaryk strongly condemned the evangelical and Catholic clergy and there is no difference between them for him, nor can there be. Here he writes how the doctrine of the Christian faith runs counter to science and how we should put truth before faith. But it is against God, it is blasphemy! Against his views are our *Cirkevné listy, Zochova Stráž na Sione, Osvaldove Literárne listy*, not to mention the *Národné noviny*. This Masaryk has completely dominated you."

"It's just redress for when the independent *Národné noviny* boasts having the support of the Upper Highland Clergy. Even the Hungarian, Jehlicska, is given space there, but let God pay for such *Národné noviny*. It'll be throwing out decent Slovaks from the nation for so long as it remains on its own," Milan said in annoyance.

The atmosphere in the house was stifling, so Milan preferred to visit near and more distant friends and relatives. Despite his cussedness, his father arranged a passport in Myjava, though the issuing office dragged its feet forever over the rebellious Štefánik. Finally, on 4th November, Nitra's deputy governor signed it and sent it to a notary office in Brezová, where it was collected by Štefánik's father two days later. They'd given it to him in the hope that he might not return to Hungary and stir things up. When his father handed him his passport, Milan felt that his father loved him, despite his continuing opposition. He could see his sorrow over his departure.

"My son, you know that we have several other sons and daughters, so we can't help you materially. I don't want to return to this unpleasant debate, but I have to ask you seriously whether you have financial support in Paris..."

"Papa," he replied emphatically, "you don't have to worry, I'm going to fund my two-year research stay at the Flammarion Observatory from the scholarship I get as soon as they publish my dissertation. Then I'll return home and lecture at the Department of Astrophysics at Prague University..."

"You don't say that with great conviction. How certain are you they'll make the work public and pay you?"

"I'll make some money and my friends will lend me some money," Milan immediately mumbled unconvincingly. "Professor Flammarion will take me and I'll make... uh... decent money."

His father looked at him sadly, knowing that his son was merely speculating, but he remained silent. "Well, dig deep. And maintain the honour and pride of the Štefánik family there." To Milan's surprise, he embraced him and held him for a while. When he released him, Milan saw ta tear trickling from his father's eye.

He packed the necessary things and went to Prague. Saying goodbye to his mother was not easy, but when he promised his parents he would be home again at Christmas, she calmed down. Milan gave a promise, but he had no idea how to pay for the train ticket. Fortunately, though, he had promissory notes in his pocket which he'd been issued with the help of Vavro Šrobár. In Prague, he dropped in on families and friends with whom he was in contact during his studies, saying goodbye to all of them. Professor Zenger wrote a letter of recommendation to Flammarion. Milan knew it by heart. But

if he was ever to get to Paris, it depended on one thing: money. So far, he'd managed to collect a few meagre resources. He therefore decided to make a last, desperate attempt shortly before his departure and after long deliberation wrote a letter to his devoted supporter, the building engineer, Antonín Dvořák, in which he asked for 165 zlatky. He finished the letter with the moving words: "Please don't consider me a man who uses your good offices excessively, but a man who uses all honest means to overcome misfortune. I'm sorry to express myself so plainly. I'm extremely tired and depressed."
The benevolent sponsor, as he'd done before, gave Štefánik money. Now he just needed to say goodbye to the woman he'd promised to take to Paris as his wife. He chose to visit Lidunka last of all. But her mother told him sadly that her daughter was at her grandfather's in Předmostie near Přerov and gave Milan Lidunka's farewell letter. He immediately took action; instead of writing an answer he travelled to her the next day. Nobody will ever know what the two lovers said.

With his friend, the sculptor, Bohumil Kafka, he set out on the express to Nuremberg and Strasbourg on 18th November 1904. They broke their journey in Nuremberg and also took a three-day break in Strasbourg, the capital of Alsace-Lorraine. They arrived at the political, artistic and scientific center of the world on 28th November. Without money, but with unshakeable faith. Paris welcomed the slight, timid-looking young man from the unknown Upper Hungary with cautiously open arms, which meant more an opportunity than a promise. He saw the city as his life challenge and decided to grasp it with all the strength and energy of his hard, Kopanice nature. His life thus began in a large foreign world. He knew he would only succeed in it if he fully believed, loved and worked.

CHAPTER 21
I Have Suffered for You

The city of boulevards, chansons, cabarets, bohemians, universities and theatres welcomed Štefánik with gloomy autumn weather. He was tired from travelling by night, but had barely put his things down in his small room in the *des Nations* Hotel on the Rue des Écoles, a street of schools hidden behind the Saint Éphrem Church, when he bought ten postcards to send to those closest to him. The first went to his parents. He reassured them that the trip had gone smoothly and he was well. He left the postcard with the hotel's receptionist and eagerly went out to the street, whose name seemed to predestine his mission in Paris: to absorb knowledge in a city where there was more than anywhere else in the world.

He took a deep breath of the damp November air and although there was a burning sensation in his stomach, he smiled resolutely at the home of his new life. He saw no obstacles and problems he couldn't overcome in his dreams. He was committed to everything, knowing that chances were waiting to be grasped. The busy Latin Quarter was full of students circling like bees round the hive of the renowned Sorbonne, which enchanted him at first sight. One of the unknown youngsters at the school was the Czech from Kožlany, Eduard Beneš, who studied Political Science there. Maybe in one of the cafés or corridors of the famous university, they would smile at each other, but fate did not bring them together in the city on the Seine for another ten years. He headed to the nearby *Soufflot* Hotel on Rue Toullier leading from the Pantheon to Jardin du Luxembourg with the Palais du Luxembourg, the seat of the French Senate. He wanted to find an old friend from secondary school, a boy from the Tatra mountains, Janko Lajčiak, who'd come to Paris a month before him to complete a two-semester course and gain a doctorate in theology. But at the hotel he was told that "Monsieur Lajsiak" came late in the evening. The talkative concierge added that the young foreigner was ruining his health because instead of enjoying Parisian life he was sitting in a university library or lectures for days. So he went on a first exploration of the neighborhood before returning to the hotel to ask whether the "m'sieur" had appeared yet. Around the corner was the complex of the Sorbonne, near the Pantheon with the remains of Voltaire, Hugo, Dumas, Zola, buried there two years before, Rousseau and many other important Frenchmen. He couldn't resist the impulse to go into the Pantheon, the temple of French glory. When he entered the monumental building, his heart pounded. The next day, he and Janko went to see a technical miracle, the sky-touching tower of the engineer, Gustav Eiffel, which was given to the public on the eve of the world exhibition in 1900. Built by three thousand metalworkers in twenty-six months, it was the most suitable place to become acquainted with Paris. Looking from the top of the tower down at the city that lay beneath their feet, they marvelled at what they saw. Milan realized how great the city was where he believed he would spend the best part of his life.

"Paris lies at our feet," laughed Štefánik. "This is where we've reached, the world's tallest tower. This Eiffel must be an incredible man; they gave him a hard time and discouraged him wherever they could, but he did it. We aren't on a tower but on a monument to human will, determination and skill. We stand on the symbol of a new era of science and technology. Isn't it amazing? We've come to the heart of the modern age from wooden houses with straw roofs. What a symbol!" he enthused. "And we'll break through here!"

"Truly, we will," his five-year older friend put a hand on his shoulder. "We have no alternative…"

"Like your prophet Ezekiel," Štefánik told him.

Lajčiak looked at him, raised his head and stared sadly ahead in the direction of the east.

"Kriváň, from where we looked at our Tatras, is over there somewhere. We'll go back some time. But first we'll do what we have to do."

"I feel that a wonderful future is waiting for us. Now we've got here, we can't let fate slip out of our hands. Our will can overcome all mental and physical weaknesses," Milan broke off his dreaming. The boys looked at each other and inadvertently clasped each other's hands. They looked down at the crowd scurrying like ants led by an infallible instinct, without a conscious goal, fulfilling only the primordial nature of life.

"Oh, look at those cabs, hackneys, vehicles, coaches, omnibuses on huge wheels, I guess for twenty people. Look at the trams and cars, at those crowds of men in expensive suits in the English fashion, at those glittering embossed lorgnettes, silk top hats and straw boaters on their heads, satin gloves and snow-white shirt fronts. Look at the snobbish parasols although the sun is almost absent and the November wind is chilling us. A regiment of top hats, working jackets, beautiful toilettes, thousands of biped creatures with made-up faces, boasting the name of human. Look how the bourgeois forces its way through as if the fate of the world depended on its full wallet. Look at the head of that mademoiselle over there, aware of her charm, a flock of wasters around her. How many useless lives of futile existence! They don't understand that the difference between animals and humanity is free will and yet the vast majority of people don't follow it," Štefánik shook his head.

"I bet those lorgnettes and crinolines are largely borrowed. Look at that cricket and listen to his sad song. Nobody throws money into his hat, people don't want to listen to plaintive songs, they want to be happy and cheerful even at the cost of borrowing it. But they all pretend to have it..." Lajčiak meditated.

"Don't worry, I'll return all the money I've borrowed as soon as I earn something," Milan said conclusively.

"Milanko, I wasn't thinking about you. I mean that unconscious mass. We're at least going for something, we've got a clear goal before us; I want to be a shepherd of souls, a good shepherd, and therefore I want to learn as much as possible about my prophet Ezekiel at the Sorbonne. You came here because you want to be a counter of stars. We'll break through; there's no need to fear."

"You say exactly what Professor Stodola says. He, too, broke through. As did Eiffel, who built this miraculous tower. It's said they only gave him permission for twenty years and then he must dismantle it. I'm telling you here that nothing will be dismantled because this will be Paris's most famous building. I'll introduce myself to him, he must be an incredibly daring man. Thanks to him, we're now almost in heaven. Don't you have an excellent feeling as a future priest?"

"And you as a future astronomer?"

The young men glanced at each other understandingly.

"We have to go down slowly. Stop dreaming and speechifying! Let's march to the entrance to hard reality," Lajčiak laughed.

Reality was worse than Milan had imagined. And the gloomy weather only added to his mood. The first snow flakes fell on the city and it was cold in the cheap hotel. If he wanted to have more wood for heating, he had to pay extra.

His friend Bohuš Kafka, with whom he'd arrived, had moved to a rented studio in Montmartre, to which he often invited him, only it was two hours on foot as cabs or omnibuses were expensive. When depression came over him, he'd make his way across the old town to the heights of Montmartre, where he could at least get warm in Kafka's studio. There he met other Czech artists who were in Paris on study visits: the sculptor Otakar Španiel, the painters Ludvík Strimpl, Tavík František Šimon and Hugo Boettinger. The young men invited him with them to the artists' cafés, but Milan usually declared he had duties, though he would have liked to have gone with them. He didn't go because he had no money. For lunch he went to a cheap restaurant, *Amiot*, but two and a half francs for lunch was more than he could afford. There were days when he only had a baguette and a cup of warm milk, and when he didn't even have that he made do with the warm tea that the caretaker occasionally brought to him out of compassion. He didn't get the promised money from Dr. Rohon; Professor Zenger's recommendation letter lay idle in his pocket. The hours and days of waiting for Camille Flammarion to receive him were endless. Twice he went to his observatory and although his assistant politely assured him that the famous scientist would be sure to receive him at the earliest possible date, he hadn't yet kept his word. He was beginning to get a bad impression of Flammarion's behavior. His second hope, Professor Janssen, had been stuck in Italy for several months and it was unknown when and if he would ever return, because he was caught up, in his old age, by mysticism and pursued astronomy less. He'd saved as much money from Šrobár's loan as he could; he couldn't count on help from home. His father was broke and only later did he learn that his brother Igor didn't write to him because he didn't have money for a postage stamp. He was helped by his sister Ľudmila and her husband, Imrich Zmertych, his sister Oľga with her husband Eugen Hajtš and his sister, Elena, with her husband Emil Izák as far as their modest means allowed. But it was him from whom they expected to receive money soon...

The moments of cold solitude were relieved unexpectedly at the feast of Saint Nicholas, at least for a few hours, when Janko Lajčiak took him to visit the family of a wealthy Slovak businessman, Daniel Benko in the luxurious neighbourhood near the Palais Royal. A successful furrier from Blatnica, he'd come to Paris eight years before, when Hungarian officials withdrew his licence for participating in the National Congress to protest against the millennial madness in 1896. He stopped trusting the authorities. He was afraid that a similar punishment would be imposed within the territory of the Austrian Empire and as he had been considering a move from Budapest to Vienna, he decided on Paris instead. He opened a fashionable fur salon, which prospered from the first moment, because a master of the fur trade, Benko, inheritedfrom his ancestors not only a skill in craftsmanship, but also in creativity, due to which his fur coat designs quickly became a Parisian hit.

The dinner that the maid brought to the splendidly laid table was, after a long time, the first proper meal he really had an appetite for. But immediately his aching stomach returned. Madame Benková noticed it and Milan had to explain that the food was excellent, but he had some digestive problems following unsuccessful stomach surgery.

He was sincerely delighted that their charming daughter, Mimi thought it was funny that he wrote poems.

"So you, Mr. Milan, are a poet?" she shook her head in disbelief.

"My dear Miss Mimi, whoever often casts his mind into space to discover not only its great hidden secrets, but also the coordinates of his soul, must be a poet. And I often gaze into the stars."

"It must be wonderful to see stars through a telescope as if they were in the palm of your hand."

"It is. I promise you and your honoured parents that as soon as I become an associate of Mr. Flammarion, I will invite you to the observatory. I feel it won't be long. He sent me a letter to say that I should visit him in four days."

"The famous astronomer and philosopher, after whom a crater on the moon is named?"

"Exactly," said Milan proudly.

"That's wonderful! We'll keep your fingers crossed for you."

On 11th December he took Professor Zenger's letter of recommendation on the suburban train from Paris via Chevilly and Orly to Juvisa clutched tightly in his hand. A few times he checked if he had the professor's gift for Flammarion in his bag: a glass tube containing precious radioactive dust from Jáchymov. Somewhere he'd read that the power of the imagination is enormous, so he closed his eyes and imagined how he'd work at the Juvisy-sur-Orge observatory, alongside the famous astronomer he'd already met in Prague. Flammarion received him along with Janko, who was to be the interpreter. Milan tried to speak French, but he thought it better to leave it to his friend. The famous astronomer talked to him jovially, read Zenger's letter, took the tube, looked at it and then gave it back to Milan.

"The tube can be dangerous, but there is a certain Mrs. Sklodowska Curie, maybe you've heard of her that works with radioactive materials, maybe it should go to her... And as far as you are concerned, my young friend, French astronomy adorns not only our science, but the science of the world. You surely understand that the prerequisite to succeed with us is a perfect knowledge of French..." Flammarion circled around Štefánik with his hands behind his back. He didn't even look at him to give him a clear indication of his position. The young man became nauseous and shaky, his heart pounding at the thought that Flammarion wouldn't take him. He asked for permission to sit down and drank water without asking. Flammarion looked at him gloomily.

"But so that you won't say that Camille Flammarion is a cruel person, I'll make a suggestion; write the scientific work you would like to certify with me. It won't be a hindrance if you rework your dissertation. Then come back. Naturally, it must be in French..."

Štefánik, with ample help from Janko, again despairingly tried to explain his scientific dreams to him, but Flammarion added coldly as a true pragmatist.

"I still think," Flammarion interrupted him, "that your place is in the Meuden observatory with Janssen. However, he and his daughter have been observing the sun in Italy for several months and the date of his return is uncertain. It should be sometime in the spring." He returned Zenger's letter and jovially offered his hand to both young men.

A bruised Milan walked out of the massive observatory building. He didn't understand or rather didn't want to understand that he had lost. When he thought he'd have to last into spring with his modest finances, his head dropped. That his plans had been thwarted was hard to bear. In the first moments he cursed Flammarion and could have smashed the table in anger. The idea that he'd have to return home to Upper Hungary, or just to Prague, was beginning to make him sick to his stomach. On arriving at the hotel room, he was so upset that he vomited the little milk he had drunk. However, he gradually calmed down and got a grip of himself in the Štefánik manner. He decided not to eat, but to learn French so that Flammarion couldn't tell him from a Frenchman. He enrolled on a course for foreigners, attended lectures at the nearby Sorbonne and sat down amongst French native speakers and absorbed their language. Janko bought him a French conversation and grammar textbook. He fought and strengthened himself as usual by reading the Bible. He bought a French version and put it beside the Czech. He learned not only French faster, but also remembered Christ's words better. He always opened the Bible at the page he needed most. Even now he read: "If you suffer, know that I have suffered before you."

CHAPTER 22

A Miracle is the Consequence of Faith

The city on the Seine was dressed in Christmas decorations and the streets were marvellous. However, he spent little time in them; it was cold and he had only an old, tattered coat. Moreover, with the arrival of the first frosts, he got worse, often had a headache, heartburn, and ate little. There were weeks when he put food in his mouth only once a day; and then, when he ate, he suffered cruel stomach cramps. He envied the generous Hlávek scholarships of his friends, but they sensed that Milan was too proud to apply for one. In the end, only Janko remained for his hard moments; as a priest in Budapest, he had earned a little but had to be thrifty. He was troubled by his father's urgent letters, where he occasionally went from being conciliatory to being harsh, even threatening. As mama added a few fearful words at the end of each letter, Milan understood very well under what kind of pressure from his father she must be. He acknowledged that his mother's desire for him to return and wait for Janssen at home was logical; he would be stronger on good Košariská air and on his mother's home cooking. But he was determined to achieve his goal,the basic prerequisite for which was French. He couldn't learn it in Košariská. However, his father wouldn't recognize such an argument and so communication between the two stubborn Štefániks went from bad to worse. Unfortunately, even Lajčiak had no time to waste as the date of his doctorate had been set and so he spent almost all his time studying in the Paris libraries. Most of the time, Milan was alone and not accustomed to having his door knocked on apart from an occasional visit of the old hotel owner or caretaker;he assumed that the caretaker was bringing him wood. But to his astonishment Mimi Benková was standing behind the door.

"You, Miss Milka?" he couldn't help but stare at her.

"Aren't you going to invite me in?"

In his embarrassment, he merely mumbled and motioned her to enter.

"I was going around the neighbourhood and giving our customers Christmas gifts from my father, so I stopped by."

"How do you know my address?"

"Mr. Janko kindly gave it to me... It's really cold here, Mr. Milan. In such cold you probably won't sing about violets to me... Can I sit down?"

Shaking from excitement and the cold, he pushed the shabby armchair towards her and sat down on a rickety chair. He drew the curtain to silence the noise from the busy street. You had to pay extra for a quieter room on to the courtyard. He handed her a book by Mikuláš Schneider-Trnavský.

"There it is."

"Let me find it myself," she leafed through it eagerly and after a while she found the poem. She started to read it aloud: "My dear little girl, would like to be married... uh, I wonder who or what kind of situation inspired you..."

"I just wrote it..."

"I don't want to be wed, nor has anyone asked me," she laughed.

"But there is a bloom in your cheek," Milan replied, humming his line. "I feel somebody is about to ask you... I noticed Janko's gaze when we were together..."

"Mr. Milan...? I thought you knew that Mr. Janko had a girl at home in Liptov, a Miss Hroboňová. Please, don't repeat what he has confided in me..." Inadvertently she reached for his hands pleadingly and held them for a while. "You've got very cold hands... I'll have to go... what if you were to accompany me a little bit so that they don't think at the reception desk that I'm one of those three-franc girls..."

Walking down the stairs he offered her his arm and smelt the scent of her body and fur and felt the velvet of her gloves. Something like a cold chill ran down his back. The fragrance of the woman confused him. He couldn't breathe walking with Mimi down the Boulevard Saint-Michel almost to the Seine. Earnestly he told her about his experiences from Switzerland and Slovakia, but he felt that she wasn't listening, just smiling secretly all the time. When they came to the cab stand, they changed the subject:

"I wanted to ask if I could come to pay you and your family the compliments of the season. I'll be alone here."

"Oh, I'm sorry, we're going to Vienna for Christmas. My father's already gone to open a salon there. But we'll be back for Epiphany. Please come then. And if you would like to send home some Christmas gift, we'll take it for you and send it on from Vienna..."

"Um, you're very kind, but..."

"I understand. So a peaceful Christmas and a happy new year to you," she leaned over and pressed a kiss on to his cheek. She ran to the cab, stepped in, and the coachman cracked his whip. She waved from the window as he stared sadly at the rattling vehicle until it was completely lost in the noisy crowd. On his way to the hotel, he stumbled on some fallen leaves mixed with streaks of snow. He didn't notice the decorations in the streets. Christmas only filled him with hopelessness.

His Czech friends tried to distract him from time to time, so he was taken almost against his will to various bohemian establishments of a better or worse reputation. Once they took him to the famous cabaret, *Le Lapin Agile*, in an inconspicuous house in the middle of Monmartre, where Apollinaire, Utrillo, Modigliani and his peer Pablo Picasso used to go. At the time, none of these famous artists were there. It was a small space with a small podium, jammed with scuffed stools, full of smoking and drinking men, strikingly reminiscent of the Hungarian gentry. They shouted at the scantily clad girls who boldly revealed their powdered and scented breasts. Milan averted his eyes and tried in vain to introduce more serious topics. However, the guests hadn't gone there for serious debate, but for distraction. He'd dined on rabbit in wine and for almost the same price, three francs, he could choose one of the drunken ladies, ready to give him her body. Provencal wine had played its part and a tough inner struggle was unleashed in the young Košariská man. "The only way to resist temptation is to yield to it," said the painter, Španiel. One of the prostitutes introduced herself as Edit and she was especially drawn to Milan. He went with her behind the curtain where they caressed each other. With a heavy heart, he paid for an expensive cognac, but he gave himself water. When she ordered another without his consent, anxiety appeared on his face. But Edit drank the cognac and indicated to him that she wanted a third. Then he got up from his chair, went to the bar, paid the account and told his friends that he was leaving. Španiel later made him a plaque with his portrait as a reward for his heroic resistance to temptation. However he couldn't help thinking that with the ten francs he paid for the cognac, he would have had food for three days.

After the unsavoury event in *Le Lapin Agile*, he was ashamed of himself. He'd spent almost half of his weekly outgoings on a drunken prostitute and was asking money from people who loved him. If only they knew... After the New Year, he'd have to pay his bill not only for December, but also for January, as the owner had stopped trusting him after his November payment was delayed. He was now requesting payment in advance, Šrobár's money was slowly dwindling and Milan had no other income. He was already asking money from almost everyone and felt embarrassed. He didn't dare ask his siblings and was worried about his sister, Oľga, who'd stopped answering him. He knew that she'd moved to Szepes Olaszi, now Spišské Vlachy, but he didn't know that, after four-year-old Olinka and three-year-old Elena, her third daughter Klárka had been born, so she and her husband had enough worries to sustain a growing family.

At length he sat down at his table, opened the inkwell, dipped the pen into it and began to write. "My esteemed Professor Vávra..." He wondered where he'd found the courage to ask the professor for such a high sum; he was becoming desperate. The next day he went to the main post office and in low spirits dropped the letter into the mailbox.

He was supposed to spend Christmas Eve with Janko, but he'd been invited to one of the suburban evangelical branches, so he stayed alone. He bought a small spruce and hung candy, apples and cheap candles on it. The sounds of music, singing, noisy shouting, the jingle of omnibuses, and whinnying horses came from the streets. Unlike Christmas Eve in Hungary, where people spent the evening together by the Christmas tree, Parisians visited Parisians, drank, enjoyed themselves, happiness radiating from the poorest eyes. When the bell from the nearby church of Saint-Sulpice rang for the sixth hour of Christmas, he lit candles and prayed. Despite the tension between him and his father, he felt sorry for his family, who also remained alone with his lame sister Marína. He opened a bottle of wine that he'd kept as a special treat. But he didn't even finish a small glass because his stomach was heaving so much. At midnight he couldn't stand it, he put on his old winter coat and went to the church of Saint-

Sulpice. But before that he wrote to his father a New Year's greeting in which he humbly asked him why he wasn't answering his postcards. On his way to the church he dropped the postcard into the mailbox. Although the church was Catholic, the welcoming holy atmosphere embraced him. People's eyes shone with joy and generosity and when *Douce nuit, sainte nuit, dans les cieux l'astre luit* began before the end of Mass he didn't hold back and sang with his whole heart. In a French Catholic sea he sang the Slovak-Lutheran version of 'Silent Night'. All at once he felt good, feeling the warmth of home inside. People smiled at the foreigner and after Mass they exchanged the blessings of the season. Returning their blessings, he found himself unwilling to leave the church. However, after the last believer had left, the church clerk closed the massive wooden doors and he returned to his cold hotel room, sat on the side of his bed and wept. Sorrow as large as the sea entered his soul, as freezing as the solitude of a Christmas Eve in Paris. An incredible depression overcame him. Despite the pain in his stomach, he poured another glass, which only made it worse. He bit into a cold baguette but had no appetite for it. A strange hitherto unknown feeling of futility and unreason descended on him. Janssen didn't have to come back at all and, if he did, he might deal with him as Flammarion had. His dreams of the stars were becoming increasingly unreal. He couldn't return home. Lidunka was waiting for him, but only on condition that he found a solidly paid job, of which he had no prospects. From the shelf he chose Masaryk's book 'Suicide as a Mass Social Phenomenon of the Present'. He flipped through it slowly. Suicide, according to his beloved teacher, had become a common phenomenon due to the loss of piety and the fall in moral standards. People are more susceptible to evil under the influence of growing affluence. Man has the advantage over the gods in that he can take his life... It occurred to Milan that he could play God. He'd take a life that had no value... Death in Paris, a beautiful death... He smiled in resignation, forgetting that a miracle was the result of faith. His glance fell on to the chest of drawers at the bottom of which he'd placed a glass tube of uranium powder. It was a violent poison used in colouring glass and glazes, containing carbide that quickly wrought destruction. He pulled the tube out of the drawer, but feeling cramps in his stomach, he lost consciousness for a moment. Somehow in a semi-conscious dream it seemed that someone was knocking at the door. Frightened he returned the tube to the drawer and went to answer. The concierge was there.

"I'm sorry to interrupt, but I see your light is on. I've been looking for you. You've got a telegram. From Prague... I wish you a merry Christmas."

He opened the telegram and read: "Today money has been sent to your account in the Banque Lyonnaise. Vavra."

CHAPTER 23
Serve Beauty, Spread Happiness!

Professor Vávra's financial help came at the last moment. He had needed to share his loneliness with someone, but only wrote cheerful letters home. So he wrote the truth to his second mother, Mrs. Ľudmila Vrchlická, whom he trusted without reservation:

Much loved mother! I'd flown into the arms of despair and only your "Religion of limitless goodness" saved me. Only your goodness, your sincerity, your tenderness has restored me to life. My life is a tough struggle and I never share my misery with my parents. You who are next to them in my heart, must feel this.

The situation had now changed miraculously and money also came from his faithful companion, Vavro Šrobár, the doctor Ján Slabej, a friend from *Detvan* Fedor Houdek. The editor of *Cirkevné listy*, Jur Janoška and the priest, Michal Bodický from Krajné, also helped. This abundant help allowed him to rent a sunny rooftop room at the hotel, Cluny Square on the crossroads of the boulevards, Saint-Michèle and Saint-Germaine. He stayed in the Latin Quarter, but closer to the Seine and the city centre; and now the sun shone into his room and could keep his aching stomach warm. The sunny hotel room improved his mood and a new friend brought a smile to his face, Ludvík Strimpl, to whom Bohuš Kafka, a sculptor from the so-called "Czech colony" group of artists, had introduced him. He gradually became acquainted with Jan Dědina, Václav Hradecký, František Kupka and also met on several occasions the famous Alfons Mucha, who had lived in Paris for seven years. There were more omnibus routes to the hotel and so his friends whom he met at the tavern opposite Cluny came to see him more often.

In a more optimistic mood he wrote to Lidunka: *"I've walked over rocks and thorns, scrambled to the very top, difficulties did not intimidate me, and... finally I've found myself under the tree of knowledge. At least my life is no longer the sad valley of the damned... with pious respect, I embrace Harmony. Peace and Beauty float around us and penetrate to Your heart; I welcome them with sincere love. Because in love is purpose, happiness and virtue. But only in limitless love. Let us defend ourselves against misfortune, let us do good. My life is stormy and will be full of struggle. I would like to share happiness, but if I fall, I want to fall alone. I say to myself, I command myself: look at the stars when something troubles you and measure the matter well. The stars guide my life, the stars call to me, serve beauty, spread happiness. An astronomer devoted to his work inevitably becomes a poet."*

In the spring, Ludvík traveled to Prague, where he was preparing his own exhibition and asked Milan to pay a little attention to his friend, Hanuš Kolowrat, who'd arrived in Paris to improve his French before starting his diplomatic career. Kolowrat's arrival was a pleasant respite from the gloomy winter. They became friends quickly and since Kolowrat was a good marksman, they would go to different shooting galleries with Španiel and Kafka. Friends made bets with onlookers as to which of the two would hit the most bullseyes. Milan almost always won and would return home with a nice heap of money.

Above all, he was reading all possible material about Janssen and his family, learning French, having resolved that on Janssen's return he would be so proficient he wouldn't need Janko to interpret. His friend took his decison with a smile. Fifty zlatky from the Myjava Savings Bank came, so they went to a café from time to time, an escape from the hotel or park benches.

"Vavro wrote to tell me that Makovický has definitely left Slovakia and gone to Jasná Poľana to work as Tolstoy's doctor," Štefánik informed him and ordered both of them tea in the Cluny tavern. It was an amazing feeling that after such a long time he could invite a friend if only for tea.

"I think Dušan couldn't do anything better. At home, only a monotonous medical life awaited him with a surgery full of patients and endless night duties Now he's with the world's greatest sage."

"I envy him. Talking to Tolstoy, that is."

"If you really want to, you could have the opportunity."

"I don't know if my health would let me travel that far..."

"Do you have problems again?"

"Not again – I continually have them. It seems to me that pain and suffering are my lasting condition. I think I have a stomach ulcer. Since that failed Prague operation, the pain has been constant. I've had almost no relief from it..."

"My dear friend, look at yourself. Look how your hair is starting to fall out? It's not normal at your age. Your forehead is slowly becoming the crown of your head. And do you know why? Because you are always pining for something. Money one day, platonic love the next. Then again for news about Janssen, then because you aren't reconciled with your father. And then... I'm sorry, but we're friends and, that's why I'm telling you openly... Maybe I'm wrong, but please, listen to me... I think your pride is also a big problem..."

Milan looked at his friend uncomprehendingly.

"I know, it's not good to hear, but I know you... are stubborn and tenacious. If you set your sights on something and don't achieve it, you rage, you're irritable and often hurt those around you..."

"So you want to say that I have to go home? Has my father been manipulating you as well?" he exclaimed.

"You see, you're getting upset now. I don't want you to return. On the contrary, I want you to go towards your goal, but to humbly accept the obstacles that appear on your way. The Lord has his purpose with you and obstacles are part of it."

"I don't deny," said Milan, surprisingly quietly, "that since childhood I have constantly had to fret over something... Maybe my greatest pain comes from losing my home. Can you imagine leaving home and never returning? As a ten-year-old boy, I went to Šamorín and then on to Prešporok, Sopron, Szarvás, Prague and now here... and God knows how much of the world is still waiting..."

"Why are you whining? You decided for yourself, so put up with all the obstacles. And if I may say so – even the suffering. Don't think that only you have health problems..." he said carefully, but he immediately changed the subject: "What about your Count?"

"Kolowrat?"

Janko nodded.

"Well, we meet, he's a fine lad and with some of our artistic rascals, we go to the rifle range. Shooting is his hobby, and when he saw me doing well, he invited me as his paid coach... you won't believe where... Imagine a pigeon shooting meet at Monte Carlo. However, he set a condition, that I mustn't miss the target once with 150 shots..."

"And did you?"

"Not once."

"So you're going to Monte Carlo... God, that is incredible, congratulations to you," said Janko, shaking his hand.

"We're going on 15th March... An incredibly interesting and pleasant person. You know what he told me? I was likeable because of the pock marks on my face; apparently in his family all the men are ugly..." Štefánik laughed loudly. As soon as he'd laughed, he noticed how Janko suddenly paled, staggered a little and babbled something incomprehensible. Milan understood that he was looking for water and poured him some quickly from the decanter on the table. Janko swallowed it. Those sitting around saw two strangers curiously chatting in broken French, followed by an unknown language.

"Are you all right?"

Janko nodded unconvincingly and coughed a few times. Milan noticed that a few drops of blood had run from his nose. He wiped them off with his own handkerchief.

"Do you have anyone to take care of you?"

His friend was silent.

"I'd better not go to Monte Carlo..."

"My blood pressure is a little high, otherwise everything is fine. Sometimes it comes over me... You have to go to Monte Carlo, it's your chance to get to know some interesting people and make a little money. You just have to promise me one thing..."

"And that is?"

"That you show them there and win!"

"Very well, if you insist!"

CHAPTER 24

To Experience Eternity in Seconds

On the afternoon of 16th March Štefánik and Count Hanuš Kolowrat, of ancient Czech aristocratic stock, stayed at the Hotel Hermitage, one of the most luxurious hotels in the most luxurious city in the world, overlooking the infinite horizon of the glittering Mediterranean. Hardly had a hansom cab drawn up in front of the hotel than two porters rushed to it and loaded their entire luggage, including two double-barreled shotgun rifles in leather cases on a strange cart. Kolowrat was worried that he might have problems with the Vienna Ministry of Foreign Affairs if his participation in the clay pigeon competition was revealed. Therefore, he decided to go to Monte Carlo incognito and Milan would play his colleague, another count. He bought him a long black frock coat, a white shirt with a starched collar, a tall black top hat and black leather gloves. When Milan tried on this outfit in Paris, he couldn't help laughing, but somewhere deep down inside he enjoyed looking at himself in the mirror. Hanuš, as he amiably addressed the temporary count, took him to a photographer and gave him a magnificent picture of this "shooting outfit". Not so long ago he'd been thinking of suicide, now he was a mysterious count in paradise. The next day in his outfit at breakfast with Hanuš, sitting in the dining room with its valuable historical frescoes and heavy crystal chandeliers hanging from the ceiling, every guest with their own waiter, he felt as if he were in heaven. He was experiencing luxury living for the first time and couldn't believe that it was his destiny to be a guest in this ethereally beautiful hotel. As Count he was in one of the best apartments. When Hanuš told him that the competition would last for up to five days and he would be in this miraculous city for almost a week, his happiness made him forget to write home the postcard he always did while travelling. In Paris, they had prepared diligently for the competition for almost a month, so were in excellent form. There were two hundred shots in the competition with each marksman having two shots at each pigeon for the first 125 and only one for their last twenty-five shots. There were five shooting posts and the clay pigeons were filled with coloured powder to prevent arguments about whether the target had been hit or not. Both friends had amazing success, hitting each pigeon with their first shot. With the same total number of points they were winners and the acclaim was unending. Spectators were plying them with flowers, when a shout came from the stands: "Bravo, Monsieur Štefánik!"

The name Štefánik sounded very Slovak, without a hint of a French accent. He almost fell off his feet when in the auditorium he saw the lady who'd entered his lonely heart in Paris, Mimi Benková. He apologized to Kolowrat and with his arms full of flowers rushed over to her.

"My God, Milka, what are you doing here?"

"I'll explain everything to you, go and enjoy the celebration, the spectators are asking who you are."

She wrapped her arms around him. He was holding a huge bouquet, which he immediately put into her arms. After the enthusiastic celebrations, she waited in the stand with the bouquet. Hanuš, adding to what she had from Milan, also put his bouquet into her arms.

"Gentlemen, I will not even be able to carry them both," she smiled embarrassed. The two gentlemen took her bouquets and headed for the hansom.

"Milord, let me introduce Mimi Benková to you, daughter of the famous Parisian furrier," said Milan.

"I'm Hanuš," Kolowrat smiled jovially. "We'd be honoured if you accepted an invitation to dinner."

"I'd love to," she replied immediately, and now Milan noticed the graceful dimples in her cheeks. She was truly beautiful and enchanting. At first glance, it was clear to Hanuš that the Law of Attraction was operating between Mimi and Milan.

"First of all, we have to drink to today's triumph."

She was accustomed to luxury, but when they walked out onto the terrace with its magnificent view of the evening harbour, illuminated by smaller and larger steamboats and yachts, the magical atmosphere enhanced by a romantic nocturne of Chopin played by a white-haired virtuoso, she was at once captivated. When a waiter brought on a silver tray a special edition of 1889 Champagne, produced for the hundredth anniversary of the French Revolution, a strange wave which she had never felt before in the presence of men flowed through her.

"Gentlemen, you were amazing," she drank to the two of them.

"Well, it turns out that the astronomer can survive stellar moments for quite prosaic reasons. In fact, dear friend, I don't understand how you could learn to shoot so perfectly in just a month," wondered Kolowrat.

"It's easier than you think. Since my youth I've shot at flying targets. Not at clay pigeons, though."

"Did you shoot live targets?" Mimi said.

"Yes, woodcock. Every spring, my father and I went into the woods and in the early evening, when they started to break cover, I'd train for my future success at Monte Carlo," Milan said, smiling. "This shotgun has the greatest credit for our success. I confess that I had never such a weapon before," he admired, looking at the weapon. "Beautiful," he gently stroked the rifle along its barrel.

"A classic beretta," Kolowrat said, smiling. "It's not the quality of the gun that counts though, but that of the marksman. Your performance was incredible!"

At that moment the waiter came and told the young trio that their table had been set. On their last evening in Monte Carlo the Count had ordered a table in the conservatory overlooking the sea. The sun was setting behind the ruins of the ancient castle in nearby Eze. They spent a few hours together enchanted by the atmosphere of the medieval city. There on the heights, intoxicated by the wakes of steamers on the sea from Genoa to Gibraltar, with a suspicion of Corsica opposite and the distant shores of Africa beyond, Milan inadvertently touched Mimi's hand and she surprised him by taking hold of his. He looked her in the eyes, but was unable to read anything in them as she lowered them quickly. Hanuš noticed the blush on her face and winked at Milan, handing him a plate of five snails. There was nothing else for Milan to do, except join the other two gourmets.

"My dear Mimi, I guess we should find out what has brought you to Monte Carlo," Hanuš broke into the delicate situation.

"Well... not a very pleasant affair. In the New Year the noble Russian Prince, Volkonski, whose family are related to Tolstoy and are very close to the Tsar came to father's salon. He promised my father to speak to the Tsar on how Russia could help liberate Slovaks from the Hungarian yoke. My father didn't want to offend such an important person in the Imperial Court, so he made him a tailor-made fur coat without asking him for a deposit. But to our surprise when father and I brought his coat to the Ritz Hotel, they told us that the prince had suddenly left for to Monte Carlo. I found the hotel where he was staying but unfortunately, they told me there that he'd lost almost all of his property in the casino and had barely been able to pay his hotel bill. He'd packed up and said he was travelling to his Siberian governorate. You can imagine my father's disappointment. He's a great admirer of the Russians. He relies so much on their character and honour, and suddenly something like this happens to him…"

"I understand you; such a betrayal is hard to bear. But if you have that fur in Paris, I might find a solution to save your honoured father at least from a commercial loss. I'd like to buy it from you. Slavs have brothers everywhere, don't they, Štefánik?" he paraphrased Kollár's statement, giving Milan an ungrudging smile. "Tomorrow, before we leave, we'll settle the whole thing." Milka glowed at the notion that her father was in no danger of losing money. After dinner, they conversed in the smoking room for a while, where the gourmets tried out the latest Cuban tobacco hit *Bolivar*. Milan also tried to puff on the expensive cigar, but his head span, so he apologized. Mimi laughed and asked if she could try. Hanuš offered her a new humidor, but she smiled, taking the cigar from Milan's hand and slipping it into her mouth. She coughed and the company chuckled. The count finished the cigar and went to his room with a remark that everything they had consumed would be, of course, at his expense. They ordered champagne. The wine began to exercise its power over the young people who weren't used to alcohol. The end of March evening was unusually warm and cloudless. Milan took Mimi's hand and walked out on to the terrace, where he described the stars to her.

"For the first time, I feel that life is no longer a sad valley of the damned... just see how much harmony there is in those stars. Everywhere around is peace and beauty. I'd like to live a beautiful life, to experience eternity in a second. It's these moments that carry me to eternity. I wish they'd never end... I don't know if you have the same feelings, but for me, this stay in Monte Carlo is a miracle, and you're its most exhilarating part." He felt how Mimi clasped his hand more strongly as she turned away from the sea and looked directly into his eyes. He took her other hand and approached her lips. There were nothing besides them and the stars on the terrace.

"Hanuš's advice that everyone should eat garlic snails was very sensible," she laughed repeating his irony. It was long after midnight, and an unpleasant chill had crept from the sea to the terrace.

"It's very late, I have to go..." she said cautiously in the hope he wouldn't let her go.

"It's cold and your hotel is far away... the count ordered me a huge apartment. So I'd be sorry if it were to remain unused... unless you refuse, I'd be happy to give you one room..."

"I think it would be a shameful pity if the apartment remained unused," she laughed, with a smile more sparkling than the champagne of that captivating evening.

CHAPTER 25
Knock and the Door Will Open

In his hotel room he'd stuck a picture of the Meudon observatory on his wardrobe to keep it in front of him. He already knew the front view by heart. He imagined how he'd work or even live there and was determined to turn his desire into a reality, the power of imagination dragging him out of bed every morning. He went on learning French, studied Janssen's works, secretly went to the Meudon Observatory Park, felt the energy of the place of his dreams and met friends to drive away his loneliness. He'd play chess with Tavík Šimon regularly on Friday at the popular Café Cluny. That evening, however, it was a little different than usual. They'd been looking forward to an evening meeting Tavík's new friends, who'd come from Prague and were staying on the other side of the Jardin du Luxembourg on Rue Madame. Milan enthusiastically described his experiences with Hanuš, who had to come to say goodbye before returning to Vienna. In a weak moment, Milan admitted to Tavík that two months before he'd been so depressed that he'd seriously thought of suicide. Perhaps if he hadn't received a telegram from Engineer Vávra at the last moment, literally a call from heaven, he wouldn't have been there that day. Tavík listened gravely, feeling that his younger friend needed to talk, to vent all his distress and joy.

Count Kolowrat arrived just as they were about to start a new game. It was already the third and Milan had lost both of the games before. He was out of sorts as he took losing badly, so the arrival of friends at least gave him something to smile about. Hanuš had spent the whole day saying goodbye to acquaintances, leaving the artistic "riffraff" till last. Milan knew he'd be travelling the next day, but was a little disappointed by the perfunctory nature of his leavetaking. He had intended to invite him for at least two glasses of wine and thank him for the wonderful moments he had enabled him to enjoy in France. This young man was as excellent as his father, who was known to have funded the visit of Božena Němcová in Slovakia years before, an event which helped raise the Czechs' awareness of Milan's nation. The two men gripped each other's hands firmly, embraced each other, both with red eyes, and promised that their friendship wouldn't be broken even at a distance. Likewise, Hanuš said goodbye to Tavík and disappeared with an embarrassed smile. When the chess players wanted to pay after a while, the waiter told them that the gentleman who'd left shortly before had paid the bill.

They walked out into a dreary street and headed down the boulevard Saint-Germaine. At the omnibus stop they boarded the fastest, pulled by three horses, and headed for the centre of the Île-de-la-Cité.

"Wait, wait, where are we going? You said they were waiting for us at the Jardin du Luxembourg, but we're going in the opposite direction," Milan exclaimed.

The omnibus stopped on the island by Notre-Dame Cathedral, where they went on foot behind the cathedral, to places in Paris where there were no official attractions. They entered a strange, gloomy building, moving among dense crowds of silent pedestrians who entered grimly and even more grimly left the building. Milan walked from room to room like a sleepwalker among the morbidly curious. Children wept from the horror and wandered to their parents, themselves numb with horror, yet unable to tear themselves away from the dead, often mutilated bodies laid in the vitrines behind glass.

"My God, Tavík, where have you brought me?"

"This is the sadly named La Morgue de Paris. A public morgue where the murdered but especially the bodies of suicides are exposed to help their relatives and acquaintances identify them for the police. There are many foreigners among them... those who have no-one here and have lost hope... you know, there's paradise in Paris, but also hell, and taking a life here is nothing unusual. I come here often to study anatomy. But I'd rather paint you alive..." Milan couldn't fit all of it into his head. "Well, let's go so that Bohuško, Hugo and Otík haven't claimed all the pretty girls."

The same fast omnibus brought them to *Pension de la Famille* on Rue Madame, where an agreeable surprise awaited him. The hotel room was pleasantly warm with bottles of wine, fruit, baguettes with ham and cheese and other things good to eat stacked on the tables, cabinets and free shelves. Otík Španiel, Hugo Bottinger, Josef Mario Korbel, Bohuš Kafka and Milan's best friend, Ludvík Strimpl, joked merrily with three young ladies.

"These are our compatriots who've come to Paris for a few months on study stays and like all decent fellows, we're helping them start out. If the ladies permit, I'd like to invite them to join our "rabble", as Milanko over here has nicknamed us," said Tavík to the girls. Milan shook hands hand with everyone, but remembered only one of them, Neumannová, next to whom was a free space on an old couch.

Kafka poured out wine for his chilly friend, but Milan took a glass of water instead.

"What's happened Milanko, you're so thoughtful?"

"We were in the morgue," Simon explained laconically.

"The morgue? For God's sake, why?" Marie couldn't contain herself.

"Artists often go there to study anatomy, but Milan hadn't seen it until today. The building of the dead, the famous Paris Morgue, a place where bodies are displayed behind glass, dead bodies of the drowned pulled out of the Seine, suicides and murder victims, for identification... Of course, it's visited more than Notre Dame, it's a booming business!"

"It is incredibly unethical to earn from the dead..." said a scandalized Milan who'd yet to recover from the shock.

"But highly profitable... well, I see you can't get it out of your mind," Ludvík handed him a glass of wine, but Milan refused again. He got up and made tea from the steaming kettle. "Stomach again?" enquired Hugo.

"It's nothing serious..." he replied unconvincingly.

"Yet again..." Strimpl said irritably, looking at the troubled Štefánik with some disdain.

"Without pain nothing great can be born..." Marie encouraged him.

Milan gratefully nodded in agreement.

"I never complain, but if there's too much pain, I can't hide it, whatever I do. However, when a person firmly chooses to go after his goal, he must count not only on physical but also mental pain. I know that today's pain is my strength tomorrow."

"Can I ask what is bothering you in this beautiful, playful and cheerful city?" asked Marie.

"Is your problem only physical? I feel like you have some other troubles..."

"No, I don't. Or perhaps only my nature that doesn't know how to compromise. It despises dishonest or half-hearted behaviour and hates empty phrases. And perhaps even my impatience, which butts at things more than it should. You know, a few days ago I spent a few days in heaven. Yes, literally in heaven, in unimaginable luxury and plenty. Nothing like that will ever happen again in my life..." And he fervently told her of his experiences of Monte Carlo. But she was unimpressed.

"And should the purpose of life be luxury and wealth?"

"Certainly, I have other ambitions than to be rich, but unfortunately we need oxygen to breathe. And if I want to work scientifically, I need a material basis, because focusing on real science in an unheated room, hungry and ailing, is almost impossible."

"I've heard you came here to fulfill your dream to be an astronomer. I know that you're waiting for Professor Janssen's invitation and waiting is an ordeal for you, but I think patience is a quality of great people."

"You're right, maybe I lack all greatness. Impatience is one of my worst qualities, and inactivity is a pain to me. But now I feel that after all I have suffered, my goal isn't far away..."

"Listen to the two of you – you might want to give us a little of yourselves. Milan, show the ladies something of your magic art," Kafka implored his friend.

He was sorry to interrupt a conversation with such an interesting lady, but when Marie also urged him to perform his magic tricks, he pulled some cards out of his pocket and shuffled them. His hands flickered; it was obvious he was really dexterous. He picked four aces from the cards and spread them on the table. Then he asked Marie to put the cards back into the rest of the pack and shuffle them. He took the shuffled stack of cards and called on the ladies present to guess where the aces were. They tried but failed. Thanks to Milan's tricks, the party livened up. The young ladies talked about what was new in Prague and the young men told them the secrets of Parisian life. They even sang some Slovak, Czech and Moravian songs. It was almost midnight when the neighbours banged on the wall begging them to stop.

In a slightly better mood, with the good feeling that he had new friends in Paris and under the influence of the coming spring, he went to Janko Lajčiak's room on Rue Touillier near the Sorbonne more often. However, Janko was fully involved in his dissertation on the prophet Ezekiel and didn't have much time for his friend. When they had a little money, they'd go to the Café Chartier on Boulevard Saint-Germaine. He didn't dare to go to the Benkos; Mimi hadn't shown any wish for a deeper relationship with him after his beautiful experiences in Monte Carlo. What if she was to wake up one morning and the dream had disappeared? French was the oney activity he devoted himself to continuously. He had plenty of time, so he went to Juvisy to see Flammarion, whom this time he found in a better mood than when they first met. He stayed with him a whole afternoon and was praised for his progress in French when they said their goodbyes. Through willpower he suppressed his abdominal pains and attributed the occasional bleeding to changes in the weather. His mood was not improved by still sharper letters from his brother, Igor, who, most certainly under his father's influence, evermore strongly recommended him to return and live an honest life. He didn't even respond to the letters. Abandonment tore his soul, his unhealthy heart fell into an abyss of regret which was soothed in the rare moments he received modest financial help from his sisters Oľga or Ľudmila. Several times he went to Meudon in the hope of learning the joyful news that Janssen had returned. He'd already memorized the long linden alley rising to the observatory dome. He also went to the observatory on days that weren't for the public. He sat in the silence of the vast observatory park, closed his eyes and imagined he was working, perhaps even living there, that Professor Janssen was his beloved chief and he was the happiest man in the world. He prayed, pleaded, promised, until things began to happen that convinced him that there must be a righteous force controlling his destiny in the sense of what was written in the Gospels: "Knock and doors will open for you."

On the way home one day he was caught in heavy rain. He ran into the hotel thoroughly soaked. There, however, a more pleasant surprise awaited him: a package from the Benkos with a jar of Slovak honey, a bottle of preserves, dried fruit and a note from Mimi cordially inviting him to visit her and her father.

The receptionist handed him a telegram tamped "Urgent", the sender of which was Camille Flammarion. He read it eagerly, sat down in his chair, his pulse racing. He read it again. The receptionist saw his enthusiasm and smiled with the happy hotel guest. Milan looked at the message with elation. He'd believed in a miracle that would fundamentally change his life. Outside, it was steadily pouring down, but for him it was the most beautiful day so far in Paris.

CHAPTER 26
Growing to the Stars

"The day after tomorrow at 9:30 am we'll pick you up at the hotel and go to Meudon. As I promised, I'll introduce you to Janssen. He returned two days ago and is curious about you. Bring the tube with the radioactive dust. Flammarion." There it was in black and white in the telegram.

Milan had been eagerly looking at his watch since nine. He'd wondered if he should wear the frock coat and the top hat Kolowrat had bought him in Monte Carlo, but finally decided to wear his standard student clothes and only the cravat from the Hanuš clothes. He carefully folded Professor Zenger's cover letter into his pocket. Flammarion was very friendly and optimistic on his way to Meudon. Milan had the feeling that he'd already put in a word for him to Janssen. Indeed, his reception at Meudon was unusually cordial. Upon his arrival, Janssen's assistant quickly took him across the whole observatory. When Milan found himself in front of Jules Janssen, the most important astrophysicist in the world, he could hardly utter a word. The eighty-year-old scientist leaned forward from his ancient chair and patted his arm in a friendly manner.

"I understand you, young friend, I understand... You've been waiting for me for six months... six whole months. The fact that you haven't given up and gone home is a testament to your true interest..."

Then, for three-quarters of an hour, they talked in the presence of Flammarion. Milan's French was already sufficient for such a conversation. Yet it seemed to him that Janssen was excessively reserved or perhaps just tired. He struggled hard to attract the astronomer's attention.

"Sir, I noticed your spectroscope... I believe that after minor adjustments to the collimator, its resolving ability could be substantially increased."

"What do you mean?" said Janssen.

"I worked with a similar spectroscope in Zürich with Professor Wolfer and I improved it. It's too early to say for sure, but if I could get to know the device, I could suggest a solution."

Janssen paused for a moment, seemingly not paying attention to Štefánik's remark, more interested in his dissertation and the situation at the Prague faculty, until he finally stood up and gave Milan his hand.

"It was a pleasure to meet you. And thank you for the radioactive powder..." He took himself to the door and a terrified Milan wanted to shout out if that was all there was, that he'd let him leave after so much waiting. But Janssen stopped and before he left the room he said: "Come and look at the spectroscope tomorrow morning. I'll be waiting for you at eight. You know, old people get up early..."

It was Saturday, 22nd April, 1905, and the weather was beautiful from dawn. Rubbish collectors were sweeping the streets, stall holders were unloading goods for the market, bouquets were being tied at the station. From one he bought eleven Bordeaux tulips for Mrs. Janssen and seven whites for their daughter Antoinette Marie. At seven-thirty he got on the train at Montparnasse, heading towards Versailles. For the first time, he was travelling by early morning train, crammed with workers hurrying to work. Rural women travelling with fresh vegetables, eggs, milk, and cheeses were travelling on trains in the opposite direction. The station scenes reminded him of train journeys from Trnava to Jablonica and home to Brezová. In free Paris, even the women with bundles on their shoulders looked at him more joyfully, while at home they travelled gloomily looking down. At seven o'clock he arrived at the station in Meudon, where he was about one and half kilometres from the observatory. He set out with a brisk stride, full of enthusiasm and expectation. At half past seven he was sitting in the observatory's large park. Mrs. Janssen noticed him, so the caretaker let him in. He served him tea and Milan waited for a while. Shortly after, an affable middle-aged man with a beard just like his came into the guest parlour.

"Hello sir, I'm Gaston Millochau, Mr. Janssen's assistant."

"It is an honour to meet you, I've heard a lot about you," Štefánik bowed.

"I'm instructed to take you to the laboratory to see the spectroscope. Mr Janssen asks you to come to his office afterwards."

"Would it be possible to pass on these bouquets to Madame and Mademoiselle?"

"I think you'll be able to hand them over to the ladies in person," Millochau smiled, putting the bouquets in a vase.

In the laboratory, Milan stayed longer than he'd expected, but in less than two hours he put a spectroscopic sketch into Janssen's hand with a design for improving it. The old man looked at the scheme for a long time, then summoned Millochau. Together they bent their heads over Štefánik's suggestion.

"Interesting, interesting... a good solution. Well, Mr. Štefánik, you can stay here and finish your repair. Let's see how the first spectra turn out. And thank you for the ampoule of radioactive pitchblende."

Milan would have liked to jump up and embrace the old man.

"Sir, you can't imagine what I'm experiencing now. Yesterday you said I'd been waiting for you for six months. No, I haven't been waiting for you for half a year, I've been waiting for this meeting all my life. I have the grandest of dreams and can assure you that the spectra results on the modified spectrograph will be excellent. Can I remain right here and proceed?"

"Well... uh... naturally... Gaston will take care of you."

He plunged into work with unprecedented energy. He felt that his stomach was starting to flare up again from excitement and he had to sit down from time to time to keep his head from spinning, but he worked until late at night. The next morning, his eager footsteps on the stairs woke up the household. Alone in the laboratory, he sat down, folded his hands and prayed that the Lord would bless him with the fortune that was beginning to smile on him. A day later, Janssen's daughter Antoinette came to see him, astonished to see a picturesque rainbow of colours formed by the splitting of white light after it had passed through the glass prism in the spectrophotometer he'd improved. Immediately she informed her father, who hurried in to the laboratory to see the excellent results of the observations of the self-confident foreigner. On 24th April, he called Milan to him. He looked at him searchingly and then spoke with surprising emphasis.

"When I came to Meudon in 1876, the observatory was almost in ruins and you see its splendour today. I'm proud of this observatory. So you can understand that I won't take just anyone here..."

Milan's face flushed red with fear that he'd done something wrong and the old man had reconsidered accepting him.

"But I'm taking you. So I've decided," he declared his judgment.

Štefánik's face lit up, his brown beard trembling slightly as he breathed deeply for a moment, searching for words.

"Dear sir, I don't even know how to express my gratitude to you."

"You have great dreams and that's the biggest proof of your value. If one can dream, one knows how to live... I dreamed from my youth that I would observe the stars and the eclipses of the sun from the highest mountains... But I had a serious accident and many wrote me off. So I invented a special lightweight stretcher and persuaded my friends to carry me up to the peaks. It's not important how you reach the peak, but that you do it, even if you have to crawl. From tomorrow you are officially in our observatory, for the moment on an unsalaried basis but with *honoraria*. I'll do my best to get you a regular salary as soon as possible... Where are you now?"

"In the Latin Quarter at the Hotel Cluny Square on Boulevard Saint-Michel..."

"Well, you can tell the hotel owner that you are moving to the observatory from 15th May. My wife will prepare the small apartment in the attic. To be closer to the stars," he smiled with satisfaction, and a similarly joyful feeling seemed to enter his soul as burned in the little Slovak at that moment. Milan found it difficult to contain himself while listening to these words. In imagining what a reputable scientist had to go through until his dream became a reality and the sacred Meudon Observatory his new home; how many mishaps, hardships, suffering, humiliations, enmity and envy he'd had to overcome, thinking of the sacrifices of his parents, sisters and brothers, of Fedorko, who was the first to watch him at the little Košariská observatory, he trembled and tears welled up in his eyes.

"My dear sir, I don't know how to thank you and your honoured wife. I promise you, I'll never disappoint you but will do everything to bring joy and light into your life. I promise you…"

"If your enthusiasm is anything to go by, I judge that you will indeed be an astronomer. Just keep in mind that one doesn't fly to the stars, but one grows to them," Jansen smiled, patting him encouragingly on his shoulder.

To make his day's happiness complete, when he came back to the hotel there was notification from his bank, where he was informed that he'd received money from a Ružomberok financial institution. At last, he could repay his debt of 320 francs to Professor Vrchlický. Full of joy, he went to the post office and wrote a card to his father:

"Monsieur le Pasteur Pavel Štefánik, Košariská, Brezová, Horná Nitra, Hungary: My dear papa, my dear parents, this is to inform you that I have fulfilled what I promised. I've become a member of the famous Janssen observatory and will move there on 15th May. Write to me at my new address, Paris, Observatoire du Meudon, 898."

CHAPTER 27
You Can Do it!

He watched the birds in the crowns of the trees from the skylight in his observatory apartment, not knowing whether it was a dream or reality. He had had similar feelings ever since he moved to Meudon. He didn't want to believe that after so many troubles he'd got his own, though modest, clean, sunlit apartment in the house, where his amazing patron with his excellent wife and daughter lived. Despite not having a permanent contract, he also received a small fee as a private assistant to the professor, a great source of satisfaction compared to the previous erratic income he'd had until then. A stable income... unimaginable. He felt that he was beginning a new phase of life, beginning it with unbreakable will and energy, with the hope that his dreams of the stars would come true, and in particular that he wouldn't disappoint the generous people who trusted and supported him. Sometimes he was remorseful about his outstanding debts. He had always managed to put them at the back of his mind by believing that his creditors were doing well, and that the money they'd invested was for something meaningful. He was only sorry that he couldn't number his father among these people. He believed, he hoped, he pleaded with God that he'd show at least a little joy in the fundamental change in his son's life in the letter he expected from him. He'd also gained the trust of Janssen's family. Since he was in the building of the observatory, he liked to help them with the housework, occasionally grazing a favorite goat of Mrs. Janssen. Most of all, though, he worked from early morning until late at night. After a short period of time, however, it turned out that some things in the Observatory weren't as they had first seemed. After Pierre Jules Janssen and Camille Flammarion, Henry Deslandres, Janssen's colleague, was the third greatest astronomer in France. He'd already reached fifty and knew that without a leading position in the observatory he would never really stand out. But old Janssen was hindering him in his career and, of course, the foreigner Štefánik, who had wormed his way into the favour of the director, was a thorn in his side. Since Janssen had showed his colleague the spectroheliograph that Štefánik and Millochau had improved, he was visibly jealous of the new colleague. Milan, of course, reacted emotionally and it didn't help his peace of mind or the tension in his stomach.

On Saturday, 27th May, after a night of rain, the sun was emerging and Meudon park glittered in the morning dew; the birds in expectation of a glorious day were twittering from dawn. Milan was lying in bed, though he should have been in the laboratory for some time. It was as if he had gunpowder in his head; his pulse had risen to almost a hundred and he had severe stomach cramps. At night he'd hardly closed his eyes; he'd been to the toilet several times and his stools were almost black. There was a tingling in his elbows and he felt on the verge of exhaustion. He'd decided to write an apology to his colleague, Millochau, and ask for a day off when Janssen's maid knocked and told him from behind the door that the professor was asking him to come immediately. She turned around and left, so Milan couldn't tell her that he was almost unable to stand on his feet. But he couldn't fail to fulfill his professor's wish. With pain in his head, bent with stomach cramps, he knocked on Janssen's office door. The old man was waiting for him smiling and in a good mood. Milan collected all his strength to keep his condition from showing.

"My dear young friend... you've been in our observatory for three weeks now and surely it hasn't escaped your attention that there are some tensions between me, my co-workers and the group of my colleague Deslandres. I understand him. He's impatient because my position will most likely come to him. And rightly so. He's a great astronomer, just a little jealous. So I'm not convinced that there will remain, when one day I stop being the director, such a position as is now opening to you under my directorate. I'm eighty-one years old and there is more behind me than in front of me.

Therefore, you must proceed quickly. You know that for a long time we've been carefully planning a trip to Mont Blanc to view the Sun and Mars. The expedition will depart from Paris on the tenth of June and will be led by our colleague, Millochau. The number of participants is already closed, but I've proposed a little change to Gaston. You. Do you want to take part in the expedition?"

There was a roaring in Milan's head, the chirping of birds and the noise of the wind in the crowns of the trees were stifling Janssen's words and at first he didn't even hear what the professor was talking about.

"You're probably in shock from my news, so I will repeat it to you again – I have suggested you as deputy head of the Mont Blanc expedition. Do you agree?"

Now, Milan fully realized what had happened. The first thing that occurred to him was to excuse himself because of the state of his health, but he immediately dispelled that desperate idea. An offer like this came only once in a lifetime and even if he were to die on the expedition, he'd go. "Professor, I'm sorry to be so silent, but it is such great news to me that I can hardly catch my breath... Of course I will and assure you that I won't disappoint your trust... Professor, how can I repay you for your kindness..."

"I'll support you while I live," he gave him a paternal pat on the shoulders. "Now go, I'm somehow tired today."

As though in a swoon he walked downstairs to his room, collapsed into bed and fell asleep from fatigue. After an hour, the pain, surely from a torrent of positive emotion, stopped. He went straight to the laboratory, where he stayed until dark. He went out to the balcony to breathe the fresh air and enchanting smell of blooming lindens. The alley had been blooming for days and he only realized it then. In the dimness between the trees he saw a figure walking on the path. It stopped, calling out his name. The balcony was lit by the setting sun, but there was already darkness between the trees.

"Who's there?"

"Don't you recognize me? It's Janko."

"God, what are you doing here?"

"Well, you haven't called me, so I've come uninvited."

He ran down the stairs and excitedly embraced his friend. He took him to his room and made tea. He didn't have anything else. As soon as they'd sat down, he told Janko his great news, but his friend didn't display any great enthusiasm.

"What is it? What's wrong? Isn't it great news? I'm going up the highest mountain in Europe! I, a young man from Košariská, will prove all those wrong who didn't believe me, who care only for petty money, who don't know about science and its profound meaning! Now I'm no longer a supplicant, but a member of the observatory, a pupil of the famous Janssen..."

Janko sat down and sipped a little bit of tea. Suddenly, Milan grimaced in pain, but did everything he could not to show it. His stomach was acting up again, though it had seemed better in the morning.

"Fair enough – I wish you this success from my soul. But there are rumours that you will have to pay for the expedition yourself, even the instruments you have in the laboratory you have to pay for... And then there is your health..."

"Where do you know this from?"

"Milan, if you are asking for loan guarantees not only from friends but also from strangers, it means that your family, especially Igor, refuses to be liable any longer for you. So I wonder how you will pay for the expedition... Sorry, I didn't come to dissuade you from going, but you should show more responsibility to those who love you."

"I have other influential supporters besides my narrow-minded family. Hanuš Kolowrat promised to be a guarantor for me. I already have a steady income and am repaying at least the interest. Things are improving..." he said, more to persuade himself than his friend.

"I wish, I wish... But look at you, you can barely walk up the stairs. How are you going to get up Mont Blanc?"

"I assure you that I'll manage it!"

The young men stayed for a while longer more in silence than discussion. Milan was irritated by his pain and by Janko, whom in all likelihood had been sent by a well-meaning person to talk to him about going home. He quickly showed his friend round the observatory, the laboratories and said goodbye to him on the stairs. He was so weak he was afraid that Janko would notice. When he later returned to his room, he found an envelope with a fifty-franc banknote and a message on the table: "Contribution to the Mont Blanc Expedition. I'm keeping my fingers crossed, I know you can do it! Janko."

CHAPTER 28
For a Person of Strong Resolve, Nothing is Impossible

On Wednesday, 7th June the sun briefly rose for the young Slovak from a sea of clouds; following a speech by Camille Flammarion he'd been admitted to the French Astronomical Society despite being a foreigner. Five days later on Monday, 12th June, he embarked on the evening express to Geneva. In the night, his condition became so bad that he had to lie down and a benevolent fellow traveller lent him his pillow. In Geneva as soon as he arrived at the hotel he lay down. The next day, he took a short walk to remind himself of the places that had been in his memory since four years before when he'd been grinding lenses for Professor Schaer. At noon he took the train to Chamonix, where in a hotel room he gave himself two days to get well.

The expedition was financed by the state, but everyone had to get personal belongings by themselves. He recalled the Benkos with gratitude; they'd given him leather gloves, a special jacket, a leather hood, a warm scarf and other useful things. He had bought mattocks, dark glasses, rucksacks and most of the other equipment he needed with a loan from the bank in Ružomberok though preferred not to think about how much remained in his account and what he would live on after returning. At a height where air pressure is only half as high as in Paris, a level which may result in death in people with heart problems, he realized with astonishment his own sense of indifference. Before leaving he'd taken out a life insurance policy knowing that if the leader of the expedition, Millochau, had known what his condition was, he wouldn't have taken him. Gaston Millochau, the seasoned mountain guides Eduard Ravenel, Claret Tournier and Carrier, along with eighteen bearers, all went to Chamonix on 17th June to attempt the ascent to Janssen's observatory on the summit of Mont Blanc. The storm clouds looked ominous but the tight-lipped men still set out, despite the warnings of experienced climbers. As far as they could, they trudged up on the backs of mules. Other members of the expedition joined them at the *Cascade du Dard* mountain restaurant though there was doubt whether they had chosen the right time for the demanding ascent during which hundreds of kilos of material had to be carried. Millochau's wife said good-bye to them with tears in her eyes, her resilient husband looking at the black clouds with mixed feelings.

At ten o'clock they arrived at the *Pierre Pointue* Mountain Lodge at a height of two thousand metres, where the owner prepared a simple lunch for them. The mules stayed at the lodge and the men continued on their own with only their backpacks and their thoughts. After passing the Bosson Glacier, they heard a huge rumble behind them, two avalanches collapsing into the depths just after their passage. At 6 pm they arrived at the *Grands Mulets* hostel. The next day the weather was extremely unfavourable and so they continued more slowly and cautiously. Three times they slept in improvised bivouacs or rather lean-tos of rough boards nailed together. The hardest night was at the hostel on Grande Boss, where they arrived on 19th June at 5 pm. The wind had broken through the door damaged by inconsiderate tourists and the chalet and the stove were covered in snow. It took two hours to make a temporary bivouac with mattocks and an old bucket dug out of the snow. Twenty men, crammed on the floorboards, slept close together in a small space. The next day they set out before ten on the last section of their ascent. The summit of Mont Blanc, the White Mountain, seemed to have been reached, but in fact there were still about five hundred metres to climb. The snow pitilessly reflected the sun's rays and some men had weeping ulcers on their faces. At noon they were caught by a windstorm that created an electric field and sparks on climbing poles, caps and gloves. Štefánik was tired to death and needed to take frequent breaks. But the others couldn't wait for him as it was late afternoon. Finally, on 20th June, 1905, at half past five, they reached the summit where they were welcomed by Janssen's Observatory, a wooden two-storey building, reminiscent of an overturned ship, which had been designed by the famous Jean Eiffel. The first floor was covered with snow, which had blown in through the cracks. They quickly assembled the stoves they had brought. Gulps of hot tea tasted like the best champagne. Wherever they found a place they lay down. The stove soon died out and in the morning they could barely recognize each other. Their eyelashes, beards and moustaches were white with ice and their tired, frozen bodies were barely able to move. During the night there had been a gale and the building had been completely buried in snow. Two guides scrambled over the roof and managed to release the doors and the skylights. When they unpacked their equipment, they found that they had left the main crates with biscuits, dried milk, and other food behind in Chamonix, so they could only depend on what they had brought in their rucksacks. The porters said goodbye to them and promised to bring the food crates in a day or two at the latest. The next day, the storm turned into a hurricane. One day passed, then three, then a whole week, but no one came. Observations couldn't be made and, despite drastic economies, food was low. On the tenth day, they began to search for food, hunting for frozen remains of bread or cheese from behind the pots, cans and bowls. An old steak discovered had to be cut with a wood saw. During the gale no-one set foot outside the observatory for three days.

Although it was June, it was minus ten degrees Celsius on Mont Blanc. Fortunately the reserves of coking coal were sufficient but it was difficult for Milan to breathe in the thin air. He searched for the cracks in the planks through which it blew; it made his breathing a little easier. At first he took his pulse, but when it remained at 140–150 beats after a week, he stopped measuring it to avoid unnecessary anxiety. The men didn't know that three rescue expeditions had been sent to them, but all had turned back due to the extraordinary weather. The snow accumulated; several times they tried to carry telescopes and measuring instruments through the windows, but there was no point because they could barely see each other. Milan didn't eat at all and just sipped warm tea. However he noticed a strange thing; his stomach didn't ache at the top of the mountain. When he realized that, despite the terrible conditions, his stomach was fine, he exuded hope and stayed in good spirits, which Gaston Millochau, who he was now on first-name terms with, was at a loss to understand. The worst was at night when the light of the kerosene lamps cast ghostly shadows. In his thoughts he returned home to Košariská, recalled student times in Prešporok, Šopron and Szarvás, flew to his loved ones in Prague and to friends in Paris. Wrapped in heavy blankets, he watched the shimmering shadows on the wainscot walls and suddenly realized that he was grateful and happy despite all the cruelties of fate which he had suffered. Half a year ago he was thinking of suicide and now he was at the top of Mont Blanc. Outside, the gale which would accompany him throughout his life, howled. But it gave him strength, like a Viking strengthened by the harsh northern wind.

The observatory shivered in the wind, the frozen boards cracked. One of the two guides who'd remained stirred restlessly, Gaston was snoring loudly. *"Lord, I promise that if I survive this, I will always remain faithful to what you have granted us, to freedom of will and understanding. I will use it to better myself and humankind, always remaining faithful to the cult of truth, beauty, energy and strength. I do not want my life to resemble the dead heavenly bodies that merely flow through the Cosmos, shining with lustre gleaming for observers and then disappearing forever, without leaving a trace."* At the top of his notebook he wrote: *"I truly want to be a citizen of the world, so even on Mont Blanc I am a faithful son of the poor Tatras, the Slovak nation."*

The storm didn't stop. Nobody said it out loud, but it was clear to each of the five starving and frost-bitten men that if the weather didn't improve, Janssen's White Mountain Observatory would slowly turn into a white grave. A point came when food remained for only one day: a box of frozen sardines, a third of a frozen loaf, half a pound of sugar, and tea. Getting back on to the path was risky, but it was death to remain. So on the third of July they started down in the storm. The wind knocked the men to their knees like ninepins, a glacier cracked near Vallot and created a deep though narrow rift that couldn't be circumvented but had to be crossed with a ladder. Millochau slipped and only the alert Milan, who'd already crossed with the two guides to the other side, lay down and pulled him up with the help of a rope. That evening before six, they reached the cozy room at *Grand Mullets*, where they found powdered milk, canned food and cheese. They finally ate. The next day, at 7:00, the descent to *Pierre Point* began, from where they continued to Chamonix, where they arrived on 4th July in the afternoon. Milan stayed in Chamonix for several days to recuperate. He was heartened by an article in the local newspaper, *Revue du Mont Blanc*, which said that "the expedition of Gaston Millochau set a world record length of stay on Mont Blanc, 18 days and was attended by Mr. Milan Štefánik, whose performance was proof of his remarkable stamina." Janko Lajčiak in Paris conscientiously collected all the newspaper articles written about the world record. In each one Milan was mentioned.

On 20th July, he returned to Meudon, where Janssen's family congratulated him, despite the expedition's lack of scientific success, and even invited him to dinner. He was surprised by a bouquet of flowers; he'd almost forgotten that he'd be twenty-five the next day. He wrote a short postcard home in which he told his parents that, after returning from his forced sojourn on Europe's highest mountain, he felt completely cured. In every cell of his being he now felt like an astronomer. On the day of his twenty-fifth birthday, he took a trip to the seaside spa town of Ault-Onival on the English Channel, where he celebrated his holiday in the cozy penzion of Madame Petit in the agreeable company of Bohuš Kafka, Karel Špillar and Tavík Šimon. Czech artists would stay there regularly with this lovely lady as she rented rooms for an incredible five francs a day with full board and Milan was extremely sorry that the day went so fast. The recollections of this pleasant trip to the sea, however, were quickly rained upon when he realized that the expedition to Mont Blanc had cost him 350 francs and he was almost broke again. When Janssen invited him on a trip to Alcosébre, Spain, which this time he'd lead personally, to observe the solar eclipse, at first he enthusiastically agreed, but then realized that he had no money for it, even though it was officially funded by the French Academy of Sciences. But the idea of being with his beloved teacher in the summer seaside climate outweighed his diffidence. After some hesitation over whether his request would disturb his relationship with Lidunka, he again turned to his proven sponsor, director Bílý, who lent him 300 zlatky. But he urged his potential father-in-law to keep quiet about his request to his wife and Lidunka. Jaroslav Vrchlický helped him with almost the same amount. Thanks to this support, Štefánik finally reached Janssen in Barcelona and joined the expedition.

Several Paris daily newspapers published interviews with Professor Janssen before the Spanish expedition and mentioned a doctor of natural sciences from Prague University, Milan Štefánik, who would also be a member of the expedition. Milan kept the articles religiously. There was wonderful weather in the Spanish coastal town on 30th August, 1905, and the three-minute observation of the total solar eclipse yielded excellent results, which was lucky because although such a phenomenon occurs seventy-four or seventy-five times in a hundred years, over half of the observations had been unsuccessful because of cloudy weather. Štefánik designed a special telescope for the purposes of this observation, consisting of a Prazmovský telescope with a focal length of 0.8 meters and a Duboscq spectroscope with a carbon-disulphide prism, making the device very accurate. Janssen immediately telegraphed to the Academy of Sciences, highlighting Štefánik's great work with the spectroscope. Then followed the most enjoyable part of his professional and social career so far. With the famous professor, he visited Valencia, Toledo, Escorial, Burgos, San Sebastian, Barcelona; a reception at the royal court, during which he was received by King Alphonse XIII, was the highlight of the triumphant journey. Everywhere he presented himself as a Slovak from Hungary and used every opportunity to explain the inauspicious situation of his nation.

Janssen, with whom he became very close during the Spanish trip, then sent him to the first International Union for Cooperation in Sun Research to Oxford, where he met many major scientists for the first time. He took his first vigorous step into the world of astronomers in place of his benefactor and second, "French" father, Janssen, who, during Milan's visit home, presented the report "Spectroscopic Investigations of the Solar Eclipse on 30th August, 1905 in Alcosébre" at a meeting of the French Academy of Sciences on 9th October. It was received with great acclaim.

Returning from England, Štefánik's relationship with his colleague, Deslandres, deteriorated sharply. Deslandres was the observatory administrator, while Pierre Jules Janssen was the honorary director at that time. The young, passionate foreigner had become an unpleasant competitor to Deslandres. Milan felt the tension in their relationship and strove to strengthen his position through relentless work. He refused to comply with Deslandres' instructions during an infrared observation experiment, saying that the director was still Professor Janssen, and that he would only follow his instructions. Deslandres turned sharply to leave, inadvertently knocking over a pile of Milan's notes and scattering them on the floor. After his colleague had slammed the door, Milan bent over to pick them up, but his head span and he lost consciousness falling to the floor, where a servant soon found him. He wanted to take him to a pharmacy where, at that time, first aid was provided, but Milan refused. At his insistence, they called Otík Španiel, who'd promised to take him to the studio of his teacher, Charpentier, where he would be under constant supervision. On his way to the cab, Milan fainted again. Fortunately Španiel kept his head and ordered the coachman to go at a gallop to the nearest pharmacy. After a few drops of ether, he came round, but he passed out again on the next journey. So they had to hurry back to Španiel's studio, where a physician confirmed a cardiac weakness and prescribed medication to stimulate his heart. Štefánik slept surprisingly well that night, so his friends took him back to his Meudon apartment the next day. The sight of his home gave him strength and he quickly recovered under the careful supervision of Mrs. Janssen. At last, he was able to travel albeit not in the best mental and physical condition to Prague and then Slovakia.

CHAPTER 29

Don't You Want to Triumph as Well?

He stayed in Prague for three days in early October. He visited the Vávro and Dvořák families, met his old colleagues from *Detvan*, looked at the plans of the municipal house that they'd just started to build and admired the unusual construction of Čechův Bridge, which was growing at a fascinating pace. He could barely take in all the beautiful new Art Nouveau buildings sprouting up around the breathtaking city. He had a ride in the latest Laurin & Klement car model and admired the great expansion and confidence of the Czechs. But his arrival in Slovakia after his experiences in the world metropolis on the Seine and the no-less-lively and vibrant Prague always brought back to him the tragic situation in which Upper Hungary was situated, eternally slumbering in the harsh Hungarian grasp. The view of peasants with hoes constantly bending forward seemed to symbolize the nation's position in its own country, arousing sorrow in him, but also defiance and desire for change. However, the worldwide development of industrial production had not bypassed Upper Hungary, where the families of rich landowners had begun to switch to manufacturing. The Andrássy, Coburg, Csáky and Pálffy families had all invested money earned through agriculture into industry. In addition, Slovak nationally-conscious entrepreneurial families, such as the Makovickýs, Houdeks, Jančeks in Ružomberok, the Stodolas and Pálkas in Liptovský Mikuláš, were also investing in industry building new factories and modernizing old ones, becoming key regional employers: there was production of seed drills in Lučenec, Northrop's weaving mill in Ružomberok, a shrapnel factory in Lučenec, *Cvernovka* in Bratislava, the Siemens-Schuckert electrical engineering plant in Bratislava, an enamel plant in Fiľakovo, Dynamit Nobel and Apollo in Bratislava, gun cartridge factories in Bratislava and Komárno, *Sandrik* in Dolné Hámre, a textile factory in Ružomberok, a cement factory in Ladce, ironworks in Krompachy and Podbrezová, a textile mill in Žilina, railway workshops in Vrútky, a sugar factory in Šurany, the metalworking company of C.A. Scholtz in Matejovce, a drapery in Banská Bystrica, a furniture factory in Turčiansky Svätý Martin, a paper mill in Harmanec, a mint in Kremnica and more. Opportunities for work were concentrated in the districts of Bratislava, Komárno, Turiec, Liptov, Spiš, Gemer, Zvolen, Nitra, Hont and Tekov. Only Northern and Eastern Slovakia remained traditional small-scale farming regions, without much hope of better living standards and so natives of Kysuce, Orava, Zamagurie, Zemplín, Šariš and Abov moved to industrial areas, but more often overseas to the United States. A quarter of the Slovak population left their homeland while those who had no money for ship or train tickets, suffered the misery and hopelessness of the majority in Upper Hungary...

For Košariská every homecoming of Štefánik was a holiday. Close and distant relatives from children to old men sat in the manse. Each of the villages was curious about information from the world, coming directly from their French "astrolabist," as they lovingly nicknamed him. The locally dignified Mr. Štefánik, after his son's successes on Mont Blanc and in Oxford, had become reconciled to Milan's stubbornness, the coldness in his behaviour gradually softening. He even encouraged Milan to write about his achievements in *Národné noviny*. Mother couldn't hide her pleasure in the arrival of her boy and joyfully plied him with his favourite plum balls and poppy rolls. His siblings Ľudka, Oľga, Igor, Pavel, Norika, Laco had flown off into the world; Lacko, a notary in Spišská Nová Ves, and Igor, a pastor in the lowlands, were furthest away. Only Marinka, bedridden, and Kazimír, 12, remained at home.

He went to see Igor in Palanka, from where he returned straight to Paris. He wondered if he should go to Košariská once more, but the heart of a woman whose call he couldn't resist drew him back to Paris. He sent a letter from Slovakia to Marie Neumannová, full of surprisingly, warm words. "I want to live for you, I want to walk always by your side... Yours is a beautiful soul..." He had barely settled back before he was hurrying after Marie in the Rue Madame. It was a raw November, a sad, tearful time, as if destined for melancholic farewells. They walked the paths of the Jardin du Luxembourg, the soaked, tiny gravel crunching beneath their feet.

"It has gone incredibly fast," sighed Marie. "We've barely met, I have to go home."

"It was on 26th March, I saw you in the guesthouse for the first time. It was surely for me the most beautiful evening in this empty city full of people..."

He stood up and took her hand. She didn't resist.

"Do you really have to leave?"

She nodded. He wanted to say something, but his lips refused to comply, only trembled.

"So I wish you well... And write as soon as you arrive. I will also write to you... I'll be home again at Christmas, I'll stop for a few days..."

He sent apologies that he was unable to attend Janko Lajčiak's defence of his dissertation on the prophet Ezekiel and his Doctor of Theology graduation at the Sorbonne in early November due to important retinal sensitivity tests. If Janko had been more insistent, he might have gone, but he didn't want to provoke Deslandres unnecessarily. However, he went to a performance of Ibsen's A Doll's House, to which Benko, the furrier, had invited both of them. From the theatre they went to the Benkos for the evening, where Štefánik proposed a toast to Janko's success and compared it to the *Magnum Decus Hungariae*, the great decoration of the Hungarian homeland, of the Slovak Matej Bel of Očová.

After dinner, he and Janko went into Paris. From the Palais Royal, they walked alongside the Louvre to the Place de la Concorde and continued scrupulously kicking up damp leaves on *la plus belle avenue du monde* – the world's most beautiful avenue, the Champs-Elysées, where the nightlife was vibrant. Occasionally, a fashionable convertible went past followed by night-time riders on their new Harley Davidsons.

"Just look, dear friend. The hum of omnibuses, carriages, cars, the laughter of cheerful throngs, the buzz of people on the move, the yells of street sellers. Everything stirs the air and creates a mighty, nervous-sounding chord, the music of the crowd. My God, what a kaleidoscope, what a comedy! Everyone thinks they are an important wheel in that big machine and yet we are all just ephemeral sparks struck from flint with which immense natural powers play their game. We sparkle and then disappear forever into limitlessless darkness. If I perish now at twenty-five only those closest to me will remember me and in two and half thousand years not even a trace of the endless glory of Paris will be left."

"You're being sentimental," objected Janko.

"I'm not sentimental or hysterical. I'm just thinking of how best to determine my destiny with a firm hand. I don't want to be blind and surrender to the winds of chance. I don't want to live on a foreign account, a foreign conscience, to be an extinct star. Look up at the sky. Many of the stars we see are long gone."

"Are they?, Even though we can see them..."

"They remind me of human life. Only someone who leaves something behind them has lived a meaningful life. Only a star that has shone has lived. This disturbs me in my research and, I confess, depresses me. I search in the stars for coordinates of my soul so I can have faith to look to the future on the basis of knowledge. However, I realised that we, astronomers are only digging the distant past. If I consider that the light from the Andromeda Nebula, one of our neighbouring galaxies, has travelled to us for over two million years, while humanity, according to science, appeared forty thousand years ago, it is clear that we aren't examining what is happening now, but what was happening before there was even a hint of humanity..."

"Everything is born and dies, and our earth is going to die some time. As humans are born and die, so do planets die. That is the law," said Lajčiak calmly.

"There is only one way I can achieve my goal," Milan said philosophically.

"And what is your goal?"

"To be a famous astronomer."

"That is all? Sorry, I thought you had more ambitions. I thought you wanted, at the very least, to better yourself and your nation. Slovakia is experiencing hard times. If something doesn't happen in the foreseeable future, Magyarization will kill us off. And you merely dream of the stars... Sorry... That is why I'm returning home so I can in a small everyday ministry encourage the people of the parish in the matter of the nation."

"So you're not returning home just for the pleasure of Mademoiselle Hroboňová?" he teased his friend, adding slyly: "Miss Benková would not be overjoyed to know it... I feel she has set her sights on you."

"Milanko, we are probably different in this. I like to gather knowledge abroad, but to leave home forever? I don't have the strength for it nor would I want it for any price. Ezekiel, my hero, my prophet, lived in the most critical times of the Israeli nation, an age that demanded a man with the fortitude to help men overcome the difficulties that historical circumstances had put before them. Armed with a firm will, rare viewpoint and deep feeling, he triumphed over the obstacles he faced with unheard of courage. Don't you also wish to triumph?"

CHAPTER 30
If You Want It, You Already Have It

In mid-November 1905 Štefánik travelled to Slovakia again. He briefly stopped at Košariská and then went to Vavro Šrobár to arrange and sign new loans. He couldn't hide his indignation when Vavro told him of electoral fraud.

"The brother of your friend Aurel, Emil Stodola, who stood in the neighbouring Liptov constituency told me that Interior Minister Kristóffy warned him during his election battle with Lányi, the government candidate, that he shouldn't agitate too much, otherwise "Jön egy kis magyar királyi eröszak," there would be "a little royal Hungarian violence". Although Stodola didn't succumb to threats and fought bravely, he lost. They eliminated his voters."

"And how?"

"Simple. Some they refused just because if someone was called Hrnčiar and Hrnczár was on the list, they didn't allow him to vote. The electoral lists were deliberately written in Hungarian to give the chairs of the election commissions a reason to reject Slovak voters. One man wasn't allowed because he'd registered as Juraj Koreň, but the Commissioner didn't find any Juraj in the lists, only Koreň. The

Commissioner argued that he had registered himself incorrectly because, according to the Hungarian method, the surname should go first. They deleted virtually all the voters who registered with a Slovak name. And there was no secret ballot. Anyone who the Commissioner graciously allowed to vote had to call out the name of the candidate he wanted to vote for. So you can imagine how many had the courage."

"What an incredibly dirty business," said Milan angrily.

"Your precious sponsor and our great nationalist, the deputy from Senica, Frank Veselovský has just spent a year in Vacovský gaol just because he demanded the use of the Slovak language in primary and secondary schools in Upper Hungary in his election campaign..."

Milan was breathing hard and found it hard to control himself.

"This is how it looks in our place, Milanko. Disorganised, drunken, dejected Slovakian gangs, against whom fight determined Hungarians armed with fanaticism, violence and mammon. And whoever joins them will also gain mammon. Who wouldn't be enticed or intimidated by threats?"

"The Slovak intelligentsia! We must be the first advocates for the people. That's our task. Yours here, mine there, dear Vavro! Without our presence in the countries where decisions are made, we won't see freedom. It's futile for educated Slovaks to be active in Zagreb, Budapest, Prague and St. Petersburg. The future is in London, Paris and America. Paris is full of educated foreigners who work in the name of their peoples. Czechs are there like poppies, Hungarians, Russians, Romanians, Bulgarians, not to mention Poles. And Slovaks? I'm there alone, completely alone. Before climbing Mont Blanc, I was stopped by a man in Chamonix asking whether I was a Pole. When I said I was Slovak, he shook his head; he'd never heard of us. If the world doesn't know about us, we don't have a chance. And our chance is only with the Czechs. Czambel and the Budapest linguists should be sent word that their efforts to break the rapprochement with the Czechs are foolhardy. Attempts to squeeze out Czech from the ecclesiastical language of the Slovak Evangelicals are blind!"

"Well, it's starting to boil over everywhere. I don't think this government administration will last very long. People are already starting to rebel. Imagine that in mostly German and Hungarian Prešporok Slovak workers from *Dynamitka, Apolka, Káblovka, Patrónka, Cvernovka, Stollwerck* and other factories have been demonstrating. Hurban, Vajanský, Hodža and Juriga, were there, amongst an unprecedented five thousand people. I'm telling you there will be new elections in a year."

"I agree. And you should run for election," said Štefánik.

"I confess that I'm starting to think about it, I've gained a strong position in Ružomberok. And Father Hlinka also promised that if I decided, he would campaign for me. You can't always live on your knees!" he exclaimed pugnaciously and pausing for a moment, added: "I just hope there will be elections…"

"There will be!"

And there were elections, but when the two friends made their farewells before Christmas 1905, they had no idea that the coming year would test the strength of their courage and will to the limits.

CHAPTER 31

My Soul Weeps, My Fist Is Clenched

The escalation of the Hungarian demands for a de facto detachment of Hungary from the Austrian Empire caused a crisis in the monarchy. Emperor Franz Joseph I dissolved parliament and its building was occupied by the army. New elections, which lasted from 29th April to 9th May, 1906, were held. Despite blatant fraud and coercion, Slovak deputies achieved their greatest electoral success so far with seven Slovaks elected, although they should have had around fifty deputies, according to population. Štefánik's father fervently organized elections in Košariská. On the election day under his supervision, young men prepared and decorated carts with Slovak flags and slogans, 'For our language', 'For Universal Suffrage' and 'For our Shirts'. They were willing to fight for a Slovak candidate. But Štefánik's disillusionment was intense when he was told that the Slovak candidate had withdrawn under duress. The pastor, with a pale face and a rambling voice, told the disappointed voters what had happened. The candidate for the city of Ružomberok, Vavro Šrobár, was also unsuccessful despite the fact that he was supported by the extremely popular Catholic priest, Andrej Hlinka. For this support, the bishop of Spiš Alexander Párvy punished Hlinka immediately after the election by banning him from the office of parish priest and in June imposed an even stricter sentence: he was banned from serving Holy Mass. Šrobár and Hlinka were finally arrested in June.

In Paris, influenced by bad news from home and constant financial pressure, Milan fell back into depression. In addition, his eyes were inflamed. But instead of resting, he went to the laboratory where his rival, Deslandres, had decided to do the same experiments with coloured shutters as Štefánik had done. Two days in the laboratory instead of in bed damaged his health for three weeks. Although his eyes had not yet completely healed, he wrote scientific articles for the Academy which were published in *Comptes rendus*; he was becoming a name in scientific circles. Even the prestigious Chicago magazine, the Astrophysical Journal, published his scientific analysis, which gave him justified pride and new confidence. He even wrote articles for old Janssen, who published them as his own with Milan's consent. He enjoyed a joyful moment on 7th March when, at the meeting of the Astronomical Society, Ján Alojz Wagner, a Slovak popularizer of astronomy and meteorology, became a member.

There was a tense atmosphere at Meudon, though, so he was glad when Janssen requested him to repeat the observations of the sun from the Mont Blanc Observatory with his colleague, Millochau, and the Russian astronomer, Ganski.

Before Milan went to the Alps, Mimi Benková came to Meudon with a kind request from her father to check on a new fur shop he was planning to open in Chamonix. When Mimi added that her father wanted to entrust her with running a business in a town fast becoming a fashionable winter resort for the rich, Milan couldn't hide his elation. The idea of being in Chamonix with a young lady with whom he had spent unforgettable moments in Monte Carlo, excited him enormously. And for Mimi it was evident that this adventure appealed to her.

"My greetings to your father. I wish him good health and... I will, of course, be happy to meet in Chamonix. There are comfortable trains with berths going there."

"Excellent. I'll tell father that with your help, he will have good prospects in Chamonix."

He travelled to Chamonix in early July and stayed in the Alps for more than two months, during which he climbed Mont Blanc three times. This time, the weather favoured the expeditions. From Chamonix he went to Geneva twice to Professor Schaer, who lent him some instruments. Back in Paris, a pleasant surprise awaited him. The Academy of Sciences gave him an award for his research on telluric lines in the infrared spectrum. It was his seventh work to attract the attention of this prestigious French institution, a member of which was the famous Jules Henry Poincaré, mathematician, astronomer and philosopher, who was interested in helping the scientific advancement of the young foreigner. After a joint proposal by Poincaré, Janssen and another influential member of the Academy, Guillaume Bigourdan, Štefánik received an official commission on 19th November from the Academy of Sciences and the *Bureau des Longitudes*, a research institute for research in all astronomy sectors, to lead a French expedition to Turkmenistan to observe the solar eclipse. Henry Poincaré, who personally presented Štefánik's works in the Academy, played a key role in this. Through the Academy, Štefánik also met Raymond Poincaré, Jules's cousin, who was later five times French Prime Minister and President during the First World War. Milan was delighted to have been chosen as the expedition leader. He also received an offer from the main observatory of the Russian Academy of Sciences in Pulkovo near St. Petersburg to establish heliographic studios there. But though they offered him a permanent place and a decent salary, he felt that, despite his disputes with Deslandres, his position in the French scientific world was stable and so politely declined the Russian offer. In addition, the prospect of new findings in the observation of the solar eclipse to occur on 14th January, 1907 was indeed very attractive. They started the preparations for the expedition immediately and his joy would have been complete if he'd had enough money for his activities. The Academy of Sciences and the Bureau des Longitudes couldn't help him as a foreigner, so Marie Neumannová had to help again with the considerable sum of 6,000 zlatky.

He left Paris on 19th November, going through Prague to Košariská for a new passport. He arrived home on 29th November. The first news he heard, however, drained him of his elan and enthusiasm. The trial of Vavro Šrobár and Andrej Hlinka had just begun in Ružomberok. They'd held Hlinka in custody for investigation since his arrest. The imprisonment of the popular priest caused such an outrage in Liptov that the Budapest government had to occupy Ružomberok with military police. Hlinka, Šrobár and another thirteen defendants were tried for alleged insurrection against the Hungarian nation, for alleged calls for criminal actions during Šrobár's election campaign and for their participation in public protests. Foreign journalists also attended the scandalous trial so people abroad learned about the situation in Slovakia. Andrej Hlinka said in his emotional defence:

"You won't turn me! You won't break me! I was born a Slovak, I am a Slovak and I will be a Slovak! And when I get out of gaol, I'll just continue where I left off. To my last breath I'll fight for the divinerights of the Slovak people and the Slovak nation!"

He arrived in Berlin on 6th December and went on to Pulkov. Due to an unfortunate fall he broke his arm and stayed here for a week. With his armed unhealed, he continued with the rest of the Russian expedition through Moscow, Samara, and Orenburg to the capital of Uzbekistan, Tashkent. From there, they went to the last railway station in Chernyaev and continued for forty kilometres by caravan through unknown and dangerous desert, camels transporting his 13-metre folding telescope. They were accompanied by their security guards, a number of Cossacks but they wouldn't have helped very much in the event of a raid. They reached the almost two-thousand-five-hundred-year-old Tajik town of Istaravshan, the Russian Ura Tyube, on 29th December. But his injured arm not only prevented him from writing, but also made it difficult for him to handle the instruments. Doctors advised him not to proceed on the journey, but not fulfilling the task was unthinkable for him. In Tashkent, Štefánik received the news that Hlinka had been sentenced to two years' imprisonment and a fine of 1,500 crowns. Šrobár received half the punishment: a year in prison and a fine of 900 crowns. The indignant young man wrote to his friend Vavro: *"My dear Vavro! How much narrow-mindedness, fanaticism, and bestiality! The world doesn't want to believe me when I tell it the sad rumours that have come from home. My soul weeps and my fist is clenched. In four to five weeks I'll come to Slovakia and look for you. Be valiant and convinced that many thousands feel with you. Greetings to your friends and accept this sincere embrace from your faithful brother Milan."*

Vavro read the letter in his cell on the ground floor of Szeged prison, where both of them had been escorted. After a few days, they pushed in another convicted man, a man with a bull's head and hardly any neck, with thick black hair and a moustache. He was vigorous and radical in his uncompromising left-wing views, admiring Endre Ady and Petőfi, hating the rich and happy to declare it. He introduced himself as Béla Kohn, the son of a notary from Szilágycseh in Transylvania. At that time Šrobár had no idea in what incredible situation he would meet this man a few years later.

CHAPTER 32
Improve Yourself, You'll Improve the World

On the day of the solar eclipse, 14th January, 1907, snow fell, so the whole expedition failed. With his Russian colleague and friend, Ganski, with whom he'd taken measurements on Mont Blanc a number of times, Milan packed up their instruments and left Ura Tube four days later. The hospitable Tajik, Sarti, regarded the astronomer as a prophet because he could predict when the solar eclipse would be. He gave him expensive furs, carpets, and even three gold buttons, inlaid with emeralds and diamonds. He later gave the gifts to the people to whom he was indebted. Before leaving Central Asia, he took a detour to Bukhara and Samarkand, saw the Kalyan minaret, the Mausoleum, walked round the palace of Tamerlane and then headed back through Tashkent, Orenburg and Moscow. Although there were thirty-degree frosts, he couldn't forgo a meeting he'd dreamed of, an encounter with the greatest thinker of those times, the man of whom, after his death, it was asserted that the First World War would never have broken out had he lived. Štefánik's friend, Dušan Makovický, arranged for Lev Nikolaevich Tolstoy to receive him at his estate on the first of February.

Makovický was Tolstoy's personal doctor for a third year, although initially he'd been invited by his wife Sofia as a temporary replacement for Nikita, a doctor who was sent to the Far East for the Russian-Japanese War. In addition to Tolstoy and his family, Makovický also took care of the sick from the surrounding villages. Milan and Ganski spent the last day of January in Tula, from where they went to Kozlovka-Zásek station the next morning. There, Dušan met them with a sledge pulled by a pair of gray geldings. Within the hour they'd passed through the gateway to the Count's estate. The driver kept the horses at a steady pace beside a frozen pond up a birch alley, at the end of which Milan heard a piano.

"Lev Nikolayevich likes to play the piano," explained Dušan.

The sledge stood near the porch steps. Milan was surprised by the modesty of the house. The average Parisian bon vivant had a grander place than the world's most famous writer. A servant bowed to Dušan and his guest, took Milan's overcoat and led them through the library up the stairs to the main hall. The piano chords resounded and when Milan saw the genius from behind, playing beside his daughter, Alexandra, a thrill ran up his spine. So it is him, the man who created a whole movement, a man followed by young and old, with same opinion on many issues as he had. He felt nervous in the personal presence of this moral authority that millions of admirers treasured as almost a saint. Makovický put his finger to his lips so that the players weren't disturbed and they listened to Chopin's Nocturne for a while. Milan wandered through the spacious, bright hall, dominated by a large dining table, set for ten people. There was a round table with a stylish table lamp and eight armchairs. Tolstoy's bust stood beside a large glass display cabinet. On the walls was a portrait of this master of words along with pictures of what were probably family members. In the opposite corner was a comfortable chaise longue with a chess table on which pieces were set up for a game. When the music was over, Tolstoy wiped his forehead with a white scarf, breathed for a moment, then stood up. As soon as he saw his doctor with his guests, his thick eyebrows rose and his mouth with its white beard formed a warm smile.

"Alors, mes chers amis, soyez les bienvenus!" He gently stroked the piano and remarked, "Music is a stenography of the emotions. I love music."

Alexandra curtsied and disappeared quietly.

"Dear Milan Pavlovich, welcome," Tolstoy went to his guest, extended his hand and spoke fluent French. He also welcomed Ganski with a warm handshake and signalled to the guests a place on the sofa beneath his bust. When he noticed Ganski and Makovický didn't understand, he asked for permission to speak Russian. Štefánik, pleasantly surprised that Tolstoy had known his and his father's name, waited politely for the head of the house to sit down and then took his seat on the sofa.

"Dušan Petrovič, our Slovak and Slavic angel, has told me a lot about you, your country and her problems. He loves Slovakia so much I've really begun to consider moving there. But you know, I'd have to be a little younger, because at this age... Though, truth to tell, I'd rather quit this place immediately..." he resignedly waved a hand and paused. "I hear that you've come from Turkmenistan."

"We went to observe the solar eclipse, but it snowed all the time, so unfortunately we have no results."

"Don't be disappointed, science is as creative as art. It depends on many external and internal circumstances, and those who blame you for failure don't know what it is to create. I've heard that you're a good chess player."

Surprised Štefánik looked at Makovický, who shrugged.

"If you've got no objection, I'd like to invite you for a game, but first, of course, you must taste our excellent tea. And then, if you allow, honoured guests, we'll have lunch together." Tolstoy announced the following programme in such a tone that Milan couldn't have refused even if he had wanted to. Fascinated, he realized that he was playing chess with one of the greatest geniuses of the day. They sat down at the table. Tolstoy turned on the clock, lit a cigarette and opened the game, but it was more of an accompanying activity to their interesting conversation.

"You're one of twelve children?"

"Yes, my father is a Protestant priest and having many children is a tradition with us."

"Well, you see how close your father is to me. My Sofia Andreevna gave me thirteen children, and I'm not a priest," Tolstoy laughed. A white-gloved servant poured tea for them. "You Evangelicals are followers of Hus and Chelčický and are congenial to me in this. I have fundamental problems with our church and so was expelled from it. But the church isn't important to me, Christ is. If we want to change the world for the better, the only way is Christ's way of non-violence and personal example."

"Excuse me, your Excellency..." Štefánik began.

"Be quiet, Milan Pavlovich, with this Excellency, I'm a simple man, the writer Lev Nikolayevich," said his host.

"Excuse me, it may not be fitting to argue with a great person like you, but if we follow the path of non-violence, how do we change the world? Do you think evil will give up its positions voluntarily?"

"You speak like this Prague professor..." Tolstoy laughed, "what's his name... he was here twenty years ago, sometimes he writes to me..." he turned to Makovický.

"Masaryk," Štefánik added.

"Yes, yes, Masaryk. He, too, argued with me. Well, a struggle is nothing but a twist in the spiral of violence. Nobody has solved anything in the long run by fighting. Look at Europe. The Turk beat the Hungarian and what does the Hungarian do? Nothing but dream of revenge. The Hungarian oppresses the Slavs and what do the Slavs do; they don't think about anything else, just how to break the heads of the Hungarians."

"But we aren't attacking anyone, we're just defending ourselves from oppression. I think it's our sacred right," objected Štefánik.

Tolstoy pondered for a moment, moved a piece on the chessboard, and continued quietly with a slightly lisping voice.

"Two years ago, a revolution broke out and the Tsar suppressed it with force. And what did he achieve? Only more and more rebellions and no prospect of an end to violence if an end ever comes at all. Violence can only be fought by the power of the spirit. If we answer evil with evil, we merely strengthen it. However, if we respond to evil with good, if we turn the other cheek to a blow, we'll destroy the evil in man. Evil is weakened by good. The ideal of revolutionaries is equality, fraternity, freedom, and the task of the Tsar is to create an ideal that overcomes these ideals. All that can be achieved by force is new violence. One day, if the revolutionaries remove the Tsar's dictatorship, there'll be a dictatorship of workers and peasants. What can we achieve with this?"

"But that would mean a general retreat from evil. Do you think that if the Slavic peoples didn't rebel, our oppressors would voluntarily grant what we have the right to, fair participation in elections, use of our language, equality with the Hungarians? It is also a question of national honour. In Anna Karenina, you describe your feelings exactly when the Turk humiliated Russian pride and you went into battle against him..."

"If we ceased to constantly privilege national thought and as an ideal built human love based on the Ten Commandments, there would be eternal peace in the world."

They finished the game, which naturally ended with the victory of the great writer. Then they sat down together at the table where they were joined by Sofia Andreevna and Alexandra Lvovna. After lunch, they said farewell. Dušan took them back to the train to Kozlovka, where he embraced his friend. Full of emotions from the meeting with Tolstoy, they continued through Moscow to Pulkov, where he and Ganski wrote a joint report. He also said farewell to his precious colleague and hurried through Berlin and straight to Prague, where Marie was waiting for him.

CHAPTER 33
The More I Learn, the Freer I Am

The encounter with his platonic love, Marie, was disappointing for Štefánik. He thanked her for her financial support so far, and hoped it would continue. Marie's mother didn't refuse, but she made it clear that if he had serious intentions towards her daughter, he should be more interested in how to support his future family. She indicated that it might be time to return at least part of the money he'd borrowed; it would be best to move to Prague and become an Associate Professor at Charles University. Her suggestion was such that he couldn't react to it. He was fond of Marie but was in no way willing to give up his promising career as an astronomer. She was sorrowful to realize that she couldn't hope for a deeper relationship with the eternally restless stargazer. When he took his leave, he hoped that the woman to whom he'd uncovered his feeling in letters would remain a good and ungrudging friend he would always be able to depend on. But his heart wouldn't belong to her.

On his way from Košariská to his brother Ladislav, who worked in Prešporok as a lawyer, he stopped in Pezinok to see Žigo Zigmundík, with whom he had been friends since his studies in Prague. Žigo's father was an astronomer, albeit an amateur and whenever he went home through Prešporok he also stopped to see Žigo's sister, Alžbeta, with whom he felt very comfortable. In Pezinok, some drunken Hungarian deputies, Smrecsányi, Kovács, Bresztyánszky and Csizmazdia, entered Štefánik's compartment and warned him and two other passengers not to speak Slovak, becoming very rude about Slovak politicians, among others Vávro Šrobár. Štefánik warned them to stop it because they were insulting his friends and courageous people and nobody had the right to forbid conversation in Slovak. The Hungarian deputies started yelling at them, scolding them and waving their fists. The three men, however, continued to speak in

Slovak calmly, which inflamed the inebriated deputies to the point of madness. They pulled out clubs and Smrecsányi even pointed a revolver at Štefánik. Who knows what the end of the matter would have been if a group of Slovak workers from Vajnory, travelling in an adjoining compartment, hadn't responded to the shouting, and decided to stand up for Štefánik and his fellow passengers. Later, an indignant Štefánik, wrote an open letter to the opposition Social Democratic magazine, *Népszava*. "In Turkestan between Kyrgyzstan and Tajik, I was safe, in Hungary, I was attacked on the railway near Prešporok with a revolver and stick by members of the Hungarian legislature." Cynically they replied: "Poor Frenchman, bear in mind that you are not in a cultured country but in Asia." When he visited the United States three years later, his countrymen also knew about this incident.

After returning to Paris, a pleasant surprise awaited him: Janssen's Gold Medal, which he was awarded on 10th April at the General Assembly of the French Astronomical Society. Encouraged by this success, he embarked on preparation for the Third Congress of the International Union for Cooperation on Sun Research to be held in Meudon. However, in his home observatory, he was coming under increasing pressure from Deslandres. The older Janssen could no longer fight for him openly, so Milan, feeling he would have to leave his flat in the observatory sooner or later, rented an apartment in the popular Latin Quarter at Leclerc 6. Deslandres officially announced to him on 22nd May that he was dismissed from the astronomical institute of the observatory. It was a foretaste of Štefánik's definitive forced departure which he attributed to the director's resentment about him receiving the Janssen Prize. However, he didn't move into his new apartment. At the beginning of July, his health became so bad that he needed daily care, eye inflammation together with severe stomach pain leaving him bedridden. The Janssens had kindly given him a room in their Bellevue Villa in Meudon. At his bed, the Millochaus and Mrs. Janssen and her daughter alternated, as well as thirteen-year old Štefan Repta from Košariská, the son of a classmate of Milan's from primary school. As he had promised Juraj, he taught Štefan French, introduced him to the great world and instilled in him social etiquette. Štefan, who he addressed as Monsieur Étienne, was very helpful to Milan. He took care of his post, helped the gardener, grazed the goat and helped out at home. After six months, Monsieur Étienne returned home and, when his horrified mother caught him cleaning his teeth with a toothbrush, she ordered him not to show the strange thing to Košariská people as they would be ashamed. An educated and attractive man, he later moved to Vienna to advance his career.

Štefánik's condition didn't improve, he fell unconscious and there were moments when the doctor feared the worst. Finally, there was no other solution than to take him to the mountain air of Chamonix. Devouassoud, a factory owner, provided a place for him and Štefan in his villa.

In Chamonix, from a letter from Vavro, he learned of yet another blatant offence of the Hungarian government against non-Hungarian nations, one intended to be the last nail in the coffin of a dying Slovakia. In June, the Emperor signed laws on Hungarian school policy which had been submitted by the Minister of Education, Count Albert Apponyi. Only one lesson a week of Slovak was to be taught, and that as an optional subject. The executioner of the Hungarian peoples had raised his axe and struck. Teachers had to swear to work to fulfill the idea of the Hungarian state. At the front of each school there had to be a Hungarian state emblem with the initial words of the Hungarian anthem, "Isten álld meg and Magyart!" (God bless the Hungarian!). The name "Slovak school" was banned with a fine of 500 crowns imposed on anyone who didn't obey. Milan envisioned his Košariská teacher, Kostelný, having to teach Košariská children in Magyar, though not only they, but the teacher himself had no command of the language. His indignation made him worse and yet he had no idea that the cruellest event was still to come that year, not only for him, but for all Slovaks. His stomach problems had worsened to such an extent that he was bedridden for two months but the beautiful surroundings of the town and the fresh mountain air helped him and he returned to Meudon at the beginning of October. Soon after, however, his condition worsened when his sensitive heart was disturbed by a tragedy which newspapers everywhere wrote about.

Consecration of a new church, build from the small contributions from people in Černová near Ružomberok was planned for the 27th October 1907. People demanded that the church be consecrated by their beloved native, Andrej Hlinka, who was at that time suspended. Bishop Párvy therefore decided that another priest would ordain the church. On the day of ordination, around a thousand villagers gathered at the church and refused access to the coach carrying the officials Pereszlény and Veveric and the dean, Pazúrik, who was to consecrate the church. When Veveric whipped the horses and drove them straight into the crowd, a villager, Jozef Demko, grabbed their reins and tried to stop them. Then the commander of the gendarmes, a Slovak, Ján Ladiczky, issued an order to shoot. Vavro Šrobár arrived at the scene of the tragedy immediately and tried desperately to rescue who he could. In vain. Fifteen people lay dead on the ground, with ten seriously and sixty lightly wounded. In March of the following year, fifty-five people were sentenced to prison for periods ranging from six months to three years, with fines and loss of property. The Černová massacre sparked outrage in the office of the French Minister of Foreign Affairs, Pichon. Nobel Prize laureate Bjørnstjerne Martinius Bjørnson, Robert William Seton-Watson alias Scotus Viator, French writer, Viliam Ritter, Czech parliamentary deputies and even the president of the Austrian parliament sent protests to the Hungarian government.

Štefánik decided to go to Slovakia as soon as possible, moving from Meudon to his new apartment on Rue Leclerc beforehand. On Christmas Eve, he arrived in Košariská from Vienna and had barely greeted his parents and siblings, when the postman came to the manse with a telegram, one of the saddest he ever received. Mrs. Janssen informed him that on 23rd December, 1907 Pierre Jules César Janssen had died. Milan could not control himself and wept. He'd lost a second father, a benefactor, who'd helped him in his most difficult times. From now on he would have to wander through the thorny paths of his solitary journey among the stars by himself.

CHAPTER 34
Departing from Time

In the summer of 1908, millionaire Joseph Vallot, owner of the observatory at Grande Boss under Mont Blanc, after Janssen's death, appointed Milan as a properly paid director of his and Janssen's Observatory. He had a solid income for the year, for which he was supposed to dismantle the now dilapidated and weather-beaten Janssen observatory. Vallot, an entrepreneur, often invited him to his salon, where he endeared himself to higher society with his flawless conduct, illusionist tricks and fascinating observations and tales of travels. He met the prominent politician, senator of Upper Savoy, chief councillor of the Chamonix canton, chairman of the Paris city council, Minister for Overseas Territories, radical of noble birth and influential French Freemason, Émil Chautemps, who later became a pivotal supporter. Milan had no idea that he and Chautemps' seventeen-year-old daughter, Yvonne would become close friends.

He used the relative peace of mind in Chamonix to prepare an expedition to North Africa where he intended to fulfill one of his dreams: to open his own observatory. He was greatly helped by Senator Chautemps, who provided discounts on travel expenses and at the same time entrusted Štefánik with tasks related to the French colonial administration. These weren't public and had nothing to do with astronomy. His cooperation with Chautemps marked the entry of the young astronomer into the world of politics.

Marie Neumannová also provided him with financial support for the expedition; he would be happy to relax in the solitude of the Sahara Desert after the strenuous work of dismantling Janssen's observatory. He sailed on 7th April 1909 on board the General Chanzy from Marseille to Algiers, from where he continued by train through Blidu, Berruaghia, Boukhari, Ain Ousser and Djelf to the Saharan oasis of Laghouat, where he made a number of meteorological observations and measurements. Here he was invited to visit the living Arab saint Manabut. He had no idea that he would have a similar mysterious encounter with another sage a few years later in faraway Polynesia.

"You're an artist, aren't you?" Manabut asked, gazing at him with dark eyes.

"I'm an astronomer, a scientist."

"A scientist is an artist and art consists of studying and imitating nature. Everything invented and to be invented by science has long been achieved by nature. However, nature reveals its secrets reluctantly and only to noble souls. Therefore while examing nature, time is the most important. Time is patience and it takes time to learn patience. The ancient Greeks knew two times, one called *chronos*, which is time that controls man and doesn't fulfill him, and the second, *kairós* , which is time that man controls and which fulfills him. Whoever is able to live in *kairós* is happy. You're on your way to living *kairós*, but there are still too many instances of *chronos* in your life."

Štefánik listened with interest and the saint wasn't taciturn.

"You scientists explore external phenomena. Yet the only thing that makes sense is what is inside a human being, because only through your interior will you understand the meaning of your life. You examine what the world consists of, how it works, but you don't examine the essential, the human. If you know the human, you'll also know the universe perfectly. Science teaches a person to prefer matter to ideas, the consequence of which is a fear of losing matter, but also one day of becoming matter. Yet where we all return to is without time. Those seeking truth and doing good move away from time-controlled space and towards eternity. The most noble of people, after understanding and fulfilling their tasks, depart forever to places without time and won't return to the material world. All their life in this world is for one thing: departing from time."

CHAPTER 35
Weaknesses are Stairs up to the Heights

From Laghouat, he continued southward into Ghardai, where he ate mostly couscous, drank muddy magnesia water and covered himself with a blanket infested with bugs on cold nights. On his way back he stopped off in Berouaghia and Medea and returned to Algiers via Blid. This physically demanding journey, where the average temperature was 33 °C lasted from 8th April to 20th May. He hadn't recovered completely when he made a four-day trip to the ruins of Carthage in Tunis, from where he wanted to return to Europe. However, he had to prolong his stay in Tunisia due to a sailors' strike, so went to a holy place of Sunni Islam, Kairouan. He meditated there in Uqba, one of the largest mosques in the world and took part in the ceremonial dances of the fanatical sect of Si-Mahmed-ben-Aiss, who fed on live scorpions in one of their rituals. With his open and friendly nature, he made friends everywhere. Hunting in the desert he demonstrated his marksman's art, which opened the doors and hearts of the locals, as desert nations have great respect for a good marksman.

After the strike he returned to Paris via Malta, Syracuse in Sicily, Catania, Taormina, Naples, Rome, Pisa, Genoa and Marseille on 9th June, 1909. In Rome, he received the sad news of the death of his godfather, Štefan Fajnor. On 13th July, he travelled to Geneva to meet the American industrialist, millionaire and philanthropist, Andrew Carnegie. This was mediated by Hill, the American Ambassador to Berlin; Štefánik was hoping to win over the American to the idea of building an observatory in Africa. Unfortunately, though, Carnegie offered no support. Disappointed, Štefánik went through Munich to Slovakia. As usual he visited his sisters and friends, but he was mostly drawn to see his friend Vavro in Ružomberok. But the meeting with Šrobár added little to his optimism.

"We're going through a bad time," Vavro said in his surgery. "They lie, cheat, beat us and get us drunk as only they know how. And the worst part is that we give in to them and aren't ashamed of it. The nation is in complete moral decay. Whoever has any sort of ambition, packs up and leaves. Only the old, impotent and, I'm afraid to say, incapable, stay. At times I reflect on whether our efforts make any sense, on whether those almost continually drunken masses want to change their position at all. Consider this: recently I was called to a patient in night, we went on a dung cart for about twenty kilometres. I entered a filthy cottage, a room full of people and animals stinking to high heaven. A young woman lay groaning in a corner. A drunken neighbour had broken two of her ribs with a stake. The young woman's husband was in America, otherwise the neighbour would have been killed in revenge. I treated her and when I sat down at the table, the father of the bride came and asked: "Will she live?"

"If she stays in bed, she'll improve."

"Thank you, Doctor, I know you're a good man, I know your father, I also wanted to vote for you when you ran… but…"

"Why didn't you vote?"

"Well, I'll tell you the truth… uh… the priest said you wouldn't give us a drink… well, and what do we get for our vote, if we don't drink at least once and for free?" I tried to condemn this despicable practice and convince him of the importance of parliamentary elections for the Slovak people. He listened to me calmly, even with a smile, but when I finished, he replied almost in anger, "I've been a voter for forty years, I've always heard promises that if we choose one or the other, it'll be easier for us. But it just gets worse and we pay more and more taxes. Gentlemen's promises, sir, are gypsy words. So we may as well choose the drink. That's the surest vote every time."

"I am convinced that the cause of this chaos and ignorance is that we lack a national consciousness, a moral tribunal, a clear genius of science. We live too one-sidedly for politics. But if only it were politics! We're not increasing awareness but just stupid petty national delirium!"

"Milanko, Milanko... you live in your own world, in your imagination. The delirium is not national, but real, from drinking."

"Well, I'm not contradicting you, only saying that you identify just the first part of the problem. They drink because their lives have no meaning, no goal. If you want to take the drink from them, you have to replace it with something, you have to give them something to think about, an idea. Something they can also offer to their children. But we're just agitated, envious, grudging, acquiescent. We speak Slovak in the kitchen, but Hungarian in the tavern so as not to anger the nobleman or tavern keeper. We make the language of Slovak a graven image, turn a healthy democracy into a celebration of torn breeches and foster opportunism instead of honest religious and philosophical education."

"Go tell the nation in the pub..." Šrobár laughed.

"The role of a nation can't be different from that of an individual. Even a peasant must understand that only someone who uses every moment to deepen his intellect is living purposefully. It is logical that the smarter a peasant's mind is, the clearer and fresher his relation to the world will be, the deeper his judgment, the greater his understanding, and not as now where every maid servant can deceive him."

"You put it beautifully, but what is the practical solution?"

" It's simple – science!"

"Science?"

"I don't mean puffed-up academics, for me science means organizing, genuinely trying to decipher the riddle of existence. To give maximum content to our lives and also to the life of the last peasant."

"Everything you say is beautiful, but how do you want to educate people when little by little they aren't even allowed to speak in their own language? I'm sorry! Your thoughts are a beautiful dream, but we have to act! Especially at home."

Štefánik fell silent; he understood Šrobár's words as a gentle reproach.

"I... won't come to Slovakia again for a long time... well, I'll tell you... My ultimate goal is and will remain astronomy and above all the establishment of an independent, modern equipped observatory. I'm approaching this goal quite quickly. There are two or three observatories in the distant regions of the southern hemisphere, but not one in an equatorial region. I have a place in mind, a certain island of Polynesia, to where I'll lead a scientific mission in the near future... "

"I admire your courage, May your bold resolutions bring success!"

"Thank you... but for that... I need money... I want to ask you very nicely if you might not renew your signatures on the exchange bills... on my long journey, I'll insure my life in case something happens to me, so my debts will be paid..."

"Well, I assume you aren't going that distance on your own initiative, but on the authority of a state institution."

"Of course, I'll get an official commission from the Bureau de Longitudes to observe the passage of Halley's comet on 18th May in Tahiti, then I will go to the Tonga Islands, where there'll be a total solar eclipse. They'll give me some equipment, I'll borrow other equipment, but such a journey requires a great deal of money, and, to be honest, again I encounter an old problem: even if they wanted to, they can't fully fund me because I'm a foreigner..."

"Somewhere I read that the comet contains gases that can damage our planet when it approaches."

"So it's claimed, but the comet has passed by the Earth at least thirty times with no ill effect Every seventy-five years it goes past, and as you can see, everything is fine."

"When it comes close to Earth, it always brings with it regret and tribulation. It's a comet of misfortune which has always caused fear and horror in people and brought disasters, earthquakes, wars. I just hope nothing bad happens to you, brother," said Šrobár. "Milanko, Milanko, Miňo you're such a positive fool... to go so far for some comet..."

"Observing the passage of Halley's comet is a privilege, and every astronomer would give half his life for that. Actually, I'm sailing round the globe. I'll go to America first, all the way to San Francisco, from there down to French Polynesia. I'm going to make observations in Fiji, Vavau, New Zealand, Australia and Tasmania. You know, I think there'll be enough time to show weakness when we're old. Weaknesses are not stairs to the heights, but from them."

"Sure, sure, that's nice, but have you thought seriously about your health problems?"

"Doctors recommend me a stay in the Pacific. I think a year away from the stresses of Paris and from Europe will do me good."

"My precious friend of mine, you know I like you and I'll always stand by you. Naturally, I'll sign the bills."

Štefánik was moved by the kindness and with reddened eyes stood up and embraced his friend.

"My dear Vavro, I want to tell you that if there is a heart on this earth that truly and sincerely loves you, look for it in a distant foreigner in Paris. As God is my witness, I have met many people, well-disposed, precious, but you, my friend and teacher will always remain first in my heart. May time and distance never divide us."

CHAPTER 36
Paradise in the Heart

From Slovakia, he hurried through Munich and Geneva to Chamonix, where he stayed in the hospitable villa of the Devouassoud family, gathering strength before a journey that no astronomer had ever made before. He communicated with the scientific institutes *Bureau de Longitudes* and *Bureau Central Météorologique*, but also with Professor Schaer, from whom he asked to borrow a 21-centimeter short-focal mirror with a large prism and a lens telescope, which the ungrudging Schaer then gave him. Štefánik was also given a telescope tube, eyepieces, photographic equipment and other technical equipment. However, he also had to think about more prosaic things, kitchen utensils, tools, tropical clothing and medicines, which greatly increased his shipping costs. He also took French and German dictionaries, Masaryk's sociological work on suicide, Physics by Zenger, Poincaré's Reflections on Electron Dynamics, and more.

At the beginning of December, he noted in the newspaper an interesting report on the celebrations of the 74th birthday of the American writer, Mark Twain, who, perhaps under the influence of his poor health, said with characteristic irony: "I came in with Halley's Comet in 1835. It is coming again next year, and I expect to go out with it. It will be the greatest disappointment of my life if I don't go out with Halley's Comet. The Almighty has said, no doubt: Now here are these two unaccountable freaks; they came in together, they must go out together."

Štefánik spent the turn of the year preparing intensively for the greatest event of his life. For seven weeks he didn't sleep more than four hours a day, almost forgetting to send a Christmas greeting home as he had to answer over five hundred Christmas and New Year's greetings he had received from all over the world. He never failed to thank everyone and wish them happiness in a year which was to bring new hope into his life. At the same time he was busy seeking funds he hadn't received from official sources on the grounds that he was a foreigner. In addition, he also sketched the designs of his inventions, one of the most interesting a design for a colour photography and cinematograph apparatus which he presented to the Chassevent firm. The patent was published when Štefánik was in Tahiti, but by then he was too absorbed in the construction of an astronomical observatory to care. In order to facilitate the handling of formalities and improve his financial situation, he applied for French nationality.

He hoped that a longer stay in a subtropical climate, by the sea, in the embrace of the green of the island's mountains and clean air far from civilization, would also help his health. In February he went home for a few days to say goodbye to his loved ones and on 12th March sailed from Cherbourg to New York aboard the German ship, George Washington. But hardly had he gone aboard when he came down with a fever in his cabin. He spent five of the seven days of the voyage in bed, ate almost nothing and just drank warm milk. While he was on the Atlantic Ocean he was granted a residence permit in France on 18th March, 1910, which made his situation a little better, but he could only file for his nationality permit after three years. In New York, he met his brother, Paľo, who was working on First Avenue at a Hungarian restaurant and at first glance it was obvious that Paľo had succumbed to the lure of alcohol. He pleaded with his brother and warned him; he knew that Paľo's problems with alcohol were greater than he admitted.

"Oh, my dear brother, if you were a street sweeper, I wouldn't be ashamed to embrace you, just don't drink."

With these words, the abstemious Štefánik bade his brother farewell.

He visited the Yerkes Observatory of the University of Chicago from where he continued to San Francisco. Here serious boarding problems occurred. He had to pay an unexpected three thousand dollars because the transport company had falsified his documents and not even the intervention of the consul in San Francisco helped. He was cynically advised to file a lawsuit but this would have delayed him, and he didn't even have the money to pay the costs. He had to decide whether to go back to France or pay the transport company the money from what little he had, leaving him only eighty francs for the whole trip to Tahiti. There was no other course than to pay and hope for a miracle. Disappointed, he stated: *"If there are several noble people in America, there are even more corporations and people without conscience or shame. I feel that the people of the United States have lost a sense of anything that doesn't concern trade and that their god is the dollar. A father doesn't know his child, brother brother, friend friend, if he is to make a few miserable pieces of gold. How disgusting! Money doesn't have a name but an owner. They bow down to wealth and devote hardly any attention to the treasures of the heart and soul. In this country you seem to be surrounded by thieves. I'm the victim of such American 'dexterity'."*

Finally, he sailed from San Francisco and on the steamboat *Mariposa* wrote in his diary words expressing the innermost turbulence of his soul, fears and hopes, but above all his enormous inner strength. "A day passed, then two. Now we've had a week of sailing and a sweet lethargy has taken over my body, my soul falling into an abyss of desire to know the mysteries that have filled us and the world. I think of protoplasm and feel like a giant that has ascended to the heights of ideas. I look at the dust that floats to the heavens, and feel wretched, strapped to the ground and to harshness. My eyes flash with light but also I shed tears. More often, however, they shed tears that your neighbour can't see and run down your chest instead of cheek to make your heart tremble."

He learned from the ship's captain that the strange prophecy of the writer, Mark Twain, had come true. He died on 21st April, when Štefánik saw the comet from the ship. For the first time a presentiment of evil silenced him... On 27th April, 1910, the *Mariposa* arrived in Papeete, the capital of Tahiti, the largest island of the French colony of the Society Islands, forming part of French Polynesia. From his very first moments on shore, he understood why the famous Paul Gauguin had decided to spend the end of his life in Tahiti and the Marquesas. The fairy-tale landscape, lush greenery of the mountains, reaching up to two thousand metres, palms, ferns as tall as small trees, red anthurias, violet-gold heliconia, red hibiscus, oleander, the yellow-green fruit of the breadfruit, figs and many plants he'd never seen before, were all bathed in beautiful sunbeams over an azure sea. He realized that this was the paradise that Gauguin had been looking for. Thanks to the support of Senator Chautemps, doors were initially opened to Štefánik by local representatives of the colonial administration, generous in their help in building the observatory – at least until the moment the local governor was accused of fraud. Through his reports, Štefánik had been told in Paris that he would find a weather station here, but the entire meteorological equipment on the island consisted of the local pharmacy barometer with financial resources sent from headquarters apparently ending up in the pockets of local chiefs. Štefánik criticized the governor for his lies, which caused a sharp cooling in his relations with the the island's officials. The governor dismissed the workers from the construction of the observatory, a certain officer called him "an arriviste Austrian" and the quarrel ended with a challenge to a duel, one which the officer backed down from at the last moment. Despite this, Štefánik was keen to build the observatory on Mont Faiere Hill above Papeete. A local entrepreneur, Joseph Amédet, with whom he quickly became close, organized a state agreement for the lease of land for its construction.

Time was inexorable. The day of the transition of Halley's comet in front of the sun, 18th May was approaching and he could only rely on the locals who started to like the eternally smiling incomer. To him, he was a mysterious white man called "Taata hio fetia", the man who talks to the stars, or "Eripene hapate", the man with eyes the colour of the sea current. Finally, a wooden observatory with a tin dome was built with the help of Amédet. Unfortunately, the key day of the comet's transition was cloudy, so six months' preparation came to nothing. However, he managed to establish a network of meteorological stations not only in Tahiti, but also in the islands of Rapa, Tuamotu and the Marquesas; more importantly, his health greatly improved.

Štefánik travelled by horse-drawn carriage across the island and came to the settlement of Papeari. Fifty kilometres from Papeete in a pigpen he discovered Gauguin's glorious woodcarvings and rescued them from the manure.

He became friends not only with Catholic missionaries but also with the sailors of the French gunboat, *Zélée* (Zealous), in which he visited many islands of Polynesia. Among other things, *Zélée* was supposed to guard the coal warehouses in the Papeete harbour, along with the depots for the new fuel, diesel, which was increasingly being used by ships of the world fleet. The gunboat's commander, Lieutenant Henry and his wife, the Baroness de Rougemont, became his inseparable companions.

Despite the fact that missionaries had forced beautiful Tahitian girls to lengthen their short skirts and cover their bodies with shell necklaces, nudity was still the most natural state for their bodies. Fascinated, Štefánik watched the beautiful, slim Tahitians bathing like naked nymphs in the Tahitian bays. He couldn't paint like Gauguin, so he photographed them.

He celebrated his thirtieth birthday with Joseph Amédet, who'd lived in Tahiti for twenty years. When the police director, on the governor's orders, removed him from his house, Amédet accommodated him. He suggested his new friend buy the largest of the islands in the Austral archipelago, Tubuai, 670 kilometers south of Tahiti, and then colonize it with Slovaks with agricultural experience. And with the help of Chautemps, they actually bought the island.

In Pittsburgh, USA, which was the second largest Slovak city in those times after Budapest, an advertisement looking for colonists was published in the National News. However, because only forty families responded and the island was far from trade routes, the ambitious plan failed.

He was reminded that there was a real world around him by the arrival of the Austrian admiral ship at Papeete, sailing on its usual route around the world. The Austrians left a heap of newspapers and magazines on the island that he read after they'd left. From Prague there was the magazine, *Čas*, from which he learned that on 20th November, 1910, in the presence of a single person, his friend, Dušan Makovický, Lev Nikolayevich Tolstoy died alone at Astapovo railway station.

But the time for his departure from the earthly paradise was nearing. He set off on 24th February, 1911 to the west, toward the island of Vavau, the largest island of the Tonga archipelago, two thousand kilometres away from Tahiti. On the island, he planned to observe a total solar eclipse. *Parahi,* Tahiti, farewell, Tahiti. However, he didn't sail directly to Vavau, but made a detour to a mysterious island in the middle of the endless Pacific Ocean.

CHAPTER 37
Pain is Suffering for the Weak, a Gift for the Strong

On 26th February, Štefánik's ship sailed to the port of Uturoa in the north of Raiatea, the second largest of the Society Islands, dedicated to the first god of Polynesian mythology, Taaroo. The holy island of Raiatea, a prehistoric spiritual center of Polynesia, once called Hawaiki, is located right in the middle of the Polynesian Triangle, bordered by New Zealand in the southwest, the Hawaiian Islands in the north and Rapanui (Easter Island) in the east. On Raiatea Štefánik was attracted to the place where the Tahitians had told him was the sacred stone building of the Taputapuatea in the Opoa Valley on the south-eastern limb of the island. The place called Marae was for the secret rituals that the local shamans celebrated. The irregular rectangular surface surrounded by a metre long stone wall was dominated by a rock placed in the centre, rising to a height of three metres. After the arrival of Christian missionaries, the mysterious buildings of Marae were gradually destroyed, one last actively ritualistic but forbidden building remained. On other islands, too, the sacred places of Marae had been built, but the cornerstone had always to be from Taputapuatea. Polynesia has the shape of an octopus and Raiatea is exactly in its centre, a place where they welcomed the new-born, and with the ritual of tangihanga, bade farewell to those who departed to eternity. Mara priests, shamans, after sunset were able to communicate with the dead preparing to return and at sunrise with the living who had already reached paradise. They brought human sacrifices to the Polynesian war god, Oro. The priests communicated with the god of war and were able to determine precisely the time of an impending conflict anywhere in the world. Members of the priesthood were worshipped as gods, so it was almost impossible to gain contact with one of them. Štefánik succeeded, however, thanks to his frequent trips around the Society Islands where he'd made a name for himself and gained the trust of the locals.

At night he had to undergo a ritual of which he was afraid, but which overwhelmed him with curiosity and hope. At exactly midnight, eight locals embarked with him from a wooden hut near Uturoa on an outrigger vessel and after about an hour approached the south-eastern limb of the island. In front of and behind him, two pairs with torches walked silently, the remaining four staying on the boat. As the outrigger approached he'd noticed an unusual square stone structure that looked like a metre-high wall. The longer side was about thirty metres long, the shorter about five metres less. They came to a metre-wide hole in the centre of the narrower side and entered. In the flickering light of the torches and in the glow of the stars of the southern sky, a slim stone about three metres high, before which a fire burned, stood in the centre of the space. They brought him in front of the stone and in broken French called on him to wait. He was startled when the blast of the conch shell sounded. He looked back. Two locals were approaching through the western wall opening he had entered by, followed by a white-haired, majestic old man in a flowery shirt, lit with flickering torches. His neck was adorned with a garland of flowers woven with strips of palm leaves. Someone alternately sang then muttered. Another two men followed the old man carrying two bamboo seats. The old man came to Štefánik, took his hands in his and shook them a few times with extraordinary power.

"You're in Taputapuate," he said in excellent French, "in a place where gods, priests, and men are born and buried."

He gestured to one of the two men by the fire to bring a large stone container with a pale brown liquid. The man handed the shaman the vessel and two hollowed out halves of a coconut. The priest held the container, muttered something, shouted and then poured the beverage into both coconuts. He handed one to Štefánik, clapped three times and drank the drink of cinnamon slowly. He gestured to the stranger to do likewise. When they'd drunk, the nuts were exchanged, this time with Štefánik clapping . He knew he'd drunk a ritual drink of kava and that it was a mild drug which would induce euphoria. Polynesians sipped it on festive occasions.

"After three sips, your path to spiritual levels will be easier. I've heard you can talk to the stars. Is it true?"

"I'm an astronomer and I try to understand them."

"Only the elect can understand the stars and the priests are those. If you understand the stars, not from your own will, the Great Spirit has chosen you. The star in our culture has always been a symbol of the victory of the spiritual principle over the material. However, this principle only prevails for those who have prevailed over themselves. A person can defeat thousands of enemies with the sword, but such victory doesn't have the value of a single victory over one's own weaknesses. I am Turai, descendant of a priestly family. If you knew that the great comet would be at its brightest on 18th May last year, then you are chosen."

"I'm a scientist and we can calculate it."

"We can calculate it and we don't need any instruments. There'll be a total solar eclipse on Vavau on 28th April."

"Yes exactly. I will observe the eclipse," Štefánik stared at the shaman.

"And what will you find when you observe it?"

"Well... how can I... I'm going to analyze the colour spectrum, photograph the sun's corona, measure the length of the rays, analyze the coronary mass distribution around the sun's disk, examine the reasons for the curvature of the polar rays..."

"And why? Will your examining help to improve a person? To make the world more loving and understanding? We've known navigation for two thousand years, we've travelled according to the stars. This island is the centre of an area of thirty thousand islands," the shaman said, slightly irritably, with narrowed eyes looking at the foreigner. He turned his head, then gestured at the men standing by the fire. One took the jar of kava and the other brought a coconut. At a nod of the priest's head, this man cut it with a single slash of his machete. The priest took one half, the man handed the second to Štefánik. At the command of the shaman, they both poured water from their halves of the coconut into a natural vase, from which it slowly trickled back into the empty halves. When the vessels were filled, the shaman indicated he should drink. Štefánik didn't recognize this ritual. In a moment he felt well and his stomach pains subsided.

"You suffer a lot. You're in pain now. From the colour of your face, I can see that your stomach and kidneys are bothering you. Is that so?"

"It's not that bad," Štefánik forced a smile. Since the morning before, when he'd boarded the ship, his bowels had been knotted and he'd had occasional kidney cramps. He begged God not to suddenly afflict him with a colic; he would struggle to conceal the pain from the shaman.

But after ingesting an unknown liquid and powder, he felt the pain disappear, and the old man looked at him more kindly.

"You are destined for great pain, be grateful to the Great Ruler for that. Pain is suffering for the weak, a gift for the strong. The great ruler gives it only to those whom he wishes to make strong. In order to tolerate suffering, according to our rituals, you will be dedicated to the god, Or. His symbol is a falcon. You French call him "faucon pélerin". Legends say that the first falcon took off from the nest exactly at this place called Taputapuatea. This brave warrior symbolizes the forces of light, spiritual brilliance, nobility, dignity, courage and especially freedom. If a falcon appears over a person's grave and flies up to the sky, the person's soul goes straight to paradise. According to our shamans, falcons are the only creatures of the animal kingdom that do not die. They leave the empire ruled by time to the realm where there is no time."

The priest paused.

"It's dawn. From now on you'll be accompanied by the strength and wisdom of the falcon. I'd like to tell you joyful news, but I can't. The comet flies to the earth once every seventy-five years and brings evil. It can't be avoided, nor will you avoid it, but you will endure evil more easily due to this initiation. The Christians will experience a great evil in the coming years, much innocent blood will be spilt, kings will fall into the dust and new rulers will rule with the same sword and fire like their predecessors. Your journey with the stars is true, but you won't walk long on it."

He gestured to his countryman, who handed him a tiny shell. The shaman took it in his hands, put it to his mouth, breathed on it and chanted something incomprehensible. "Open it."

Štefánik opened a shell in which was a beautiful gleaming pearl with a diameter of about a centimetre.

"The pearl is the symbol of the soul, the shell is the symbol of the body. The body's role is to be strong to protect the soul. A white pearl is a symbol of spiritual purity, wisdom and generosity. Every time you depart from these virtues, the pearl darkens."

In a moment the boat was already sailing north. The sun's rays reflected off the endless surface of the water. The new day replaced a night that had been lost in eternity.

CHAPTER 38

The Shaman's Prophecy

Water has the same status for Polynesians as the earth has for landlocked nations. Štefánik scooped up salt water in his hands and rubbed it on his forehead. A golden color appeared on his fingers, the rest of the mysterious substance that must have passed from the shaman's forehead to his own during the farewell ritual. Despite having not slept all night, he didn't feel tired. Before midday the gunboat, *Zélée*, sailed to Raratonga Island in the Cook archipelago and from there continued west and arrived in Auckland on 8th March. He spent three weeks there. Before leaving, he loaded bags of cement on to the ship to erect concrete columns on Vavau as a base for his instruments. From New Zealand, he continued on the *Atua*, to Nukualofa, the capital of Tonga, English and Australian expeditions also sailing on the same ship. After a short stay, he then arrived on April 4th at the port of Neiafu on the island of Vavau and stayed in a Christian mission. Despite his poor knowledge of English, he immediately began to organize preparations for the observation of the solar eclipse, due in three weeks. He was aware that any repetition of the failure of his previous observations in Turkmenistan and Tahiti would damage his hard-won authority in professional circles. With the help of the gunboat's seamen and local French Marist brother missionaries, he installed simple instruments, a telescope, a grid spectrograph and a Schaer photographic lens on Paris hill, about seventy metres high, north-east of Neiaf. He'd left the other instruments at the Tahiti Observatory. Compared to the much better-equipped fifteen-member English expedition led by the astronomer, Lockyer, who arrived on a warship and brought state-of-the-art instruments, Štefánik's observatory was very basic. He quickly won over the locals with his spontaneity and charm, however. Where he could, he helped them and the locals gratefully helped him in preparing and constructing his apparatus. He helped the local nuns to nurse the sick and often the kindness and goodness of the nurses brought him to tears. When a poor boy died in a local hospital, he himself made his coffin and took part in the funeral rites. During heartfelt conversations with Father Macé, he confided in him about his own trauma, the misunderstanding between father and son, and discussed the issue of free will, telling the astonished priest that his views were close to those of Thomas Aquinas.

The rainy season had ended and the heat had eased off, which not only facilitated installation but also the observation itself. A crowd of locals on 28th April, at the 9th hour 36th minute and 46th second, closely following the foreign white man, cried out in astonishment. It had been a sunny day a moment earlier but it suddenly went dark; the sun, hidden behind the moon, had died. The rumbling of the waves breaking against the cliffs was echoed in the faint murmur of the coconut tropical forest, the mimosa closing its flowers as if night had come. The birds fell silent, the butterflies settled to sleep among the flowers that closed their petals and crickets began to cheep in the dark. Frightened to death, natives jumped into the sea, calling out that evil spirits had carried off the beneficial rays of the sun and they had to cleanse themselves ritually before death struck. Štefánik reassured them that the whole phenomenon would not last long and the sun would soon return. When he proved to be right, they kissed his hands and worshipped him as their shaman. Thanks to Štefánik changing his observation plan due to the arrival of light clouds, he achieved the best results of all of the expeditions that observed the eclipse on the island of Vavau that day. About a kilometre north of Neiaf was the Australian camp and near them the British base. In fact Štefánik gained better quality pictures than all the observation groups from Melbourne through Norfolk, the Tonga archipelago, the Danger Islands, Samoa and Mexico observed the eclipse that day. As a result, his name in the scientific world was spoken of again with greater respect.

After the observation, the instruments were packed and Štefánik took his leave of his new friend, Father Macé, who later wrote to him: *"According to the admission of individual Australian astronomers themselves, you yourself achieved the best results. This news quickly spread to Vavau, our locals celebrate a victory and are proud of you and France. They like to attribute a share of your success to the help they have given you. This joy confirms that you have won their hearts, for which I congratulate you and thank you. Australian newspapers have also written about your success – I quote: Mr. Štefánik has achieved the best results. The success you have achieved is all the better because you did it alone without a single helper, working with enthusiasm, without rest."*

Finally, he set out on a nearly three-month journey west through the Fiji archipelago, Sydney, Australia, Sri Lanka and the Suez Canal. From there he went on to Marseille and Paris, where he returned on 20th July, 1911. He handed over a report on both observations to the Academy of Sciences. The Vavau results caused a stir in scientific circles, but political leaders were particularly attracted to his activities on the strategic islands of Tahiti.

The man for whom his knowledge of Polynesia was of the greatest interest, was Senator Chautemps. Štefánik became a frequent guest of this remarkable family, meeting with them not only out of courtesy and gratitude for the senator's generous support, but also because of his two beautiful daughters, Marguerite and Yvonne. He felt that the younger, Yvonne, liked him and was flattered by her interest.

On his way home, he could not bypass Mělník, where from 1907 his love, Marie, had lived with her mother. When he saw the Neumann villa, his heart beat with desire, but in no time at all a fear came upon him that Marie and her mother wouldn't accept him, a man with a restless nature. In his thoughts he ran through the letters that he had sent her on every possible occasion: *"I live in the sign of your love, everything must be completed honestly and for our good. Don't forget, I want to live to resolve great moral and scientific problems, but above all I want to live in harmony with you. Write to me a lot and often. I kiss the hands of your good mother, of whom I often think with sacred love and admiration. My dove, be healthy, trust in the future and in your loving Milan."* Marie harboured similarly warm feelings for the charming scientist. Yet the idea of living with a man so much in love with science brought doubts to her mind. At the moment when it seemed clear and transparent for her, something strange came from him. "It was as if he lived two lives, one purely spiritual, rarefied, the other the life of a man entangled in business activities he didn't understand and in which he couldn't succeed. Sometimes he was irritable, but he was never bad. He often talked about his native region, and then tenderness and love entered his blue eyes. The suffering of the Slovaks touched him very much. Despite having many friends, he felt lonely during the years that I knew him. He didn't judge anyone and he himself refused to be judged."

He continued to Košariská, where he stayed for about a month. He believed that after his next visit to Prague, he would bring good news to Marie about the possibility of obtaining the post of associate professor at Prague University, as well as building an observatory there. "It's a dream, a fantastic dream. This means that with those elements I already have, I'll be able to build an observatory that will equal the very best. Bohemia will be adorned. Because I am definitely going back to you, to my true homeland. I will work, I want to be a real man, I want to work in my nation, which I have never ceased to love."

Unfortunately, his dreams didn't come true. His deteriorating state of health forced him to return to Paris, where he spent almost all of November. An unexpected antidote to his bad situation was the prestigious Wild prize, awarded to him by the French Academy of Sciences at a meeting on 18th December 1911. "The reward of two thousand francs is given to Mr Štefánik for his invaluable observations at the Mont Blanc Observatory, for having set up a Tahiti Observatory at his own expense, observing the passage of Halley's comet around the Sun and the Solar Eclipse on the Tonga Islands." As he received the prize he ran over his recent Pacific journey in his mind and the prophecy from the shaman from Raiatea came to him. "Your journey with the stars is true, but you won't walk long on it." He quickly drove away this grim thought and became intoxicated with the sense of his first major recognition. His star had begun to rise.

He spent the end of 1911 in Mělník. It emerged that Marie didn't see her future life in union with a man whose thoughts pursued travel and stars more than her. They still exchanged some letters, but with the definitive end to Štefánik's hopes of returning to Prague, their relationship ended.

CHAPTER 39
The Titanic Didn't Happen

Returning to Paris, he recovered somewhat and devoted himself to sorting out the artifacts he'd accumulated from his travels. His apartment near the Paris Observatory on the sixth floor of the neo-classical house on Leclerc 6 was transformed into an exhibition of trophies. The hallway was dominated by drums, spears, arrows, boomerangs and other weapons of primitive peoples as well as bowls, vases, stone statues, ceramic and wooden ritual items from Turkmenistan, Sahara and Tahiti. Oriental rugs and cushions were exhibited in both rooms, as well as Gauguin woodcuts, musical instruments, binoculars, astronomical aids, icons with exotic motifs, Jewish menorah, gems, pearls, embroidery and infinite numbers of books. In every room there was a library with not only specialist literature in Czech, German, French and Russian, but also with biographies of his heroes, Shakespeare, Napoleon, Dürer, Copernicus, Watt, Stephenson, Fulton, Ressel, and the work of the philosophers Pascal, Nietzsche and Spinoza. His bedroom was decorated with pictures of Czech friends and his bust by Mario Korbel dominated the living room.

The star of the Košariská "astrolabist" had truly risen after his return from Tahiti. His report on the observation of the Solar Eclipse at Vavau had been personally read by President Henri Poincaré at the Academy of Sciences, an honour bestowed on very few. In March, he learned that the *Bureau de Longitudes* had decided to resume the mission in Tahiti in order to complete and expand the astronomical site there. The idea of returning to his dream, the island of paradise was overpowering and he immediately began to prepare for the journey. He decided to go the same route as before, through America and across the Pacific to Papeete. He intended to travel by the most modern and luxurious ship then in the world, a fifty-thousand-ton, almost three-hundred-metre long giant called the Titanic. However, even better news came on 13th April from the Academy of Sciences: they'd approved forty thousand francs for a combined Brazil – Tahiti expedition, to start in August. Therefore, he immediately cancelled his reservation of a ticket on the Titanic. A few days later, the world learned the terrible news: the White Star Line's unsinkable pride had hit an iceberg on 14th April, 1912 at 23:40. and sunk to the bottom in three hours. Štefánik did not know whether to mourn or rejoice. He had little time to think about the intentions of Providence. By 17th April, he'd become a member of the expedition of Professor Bigourdain, director of the National Observatory, which had explored the partial solar eclipse. The observation was in the fortress of Corneilles-en-Parissis near Paris.

In May, at Issy Les Moulineaux near Paris, he'd first tried flight by plane. Three years had passed since the first miraculous flight of the heavier-than-air machine over Paris and later over the Channel by the French constructor, Louis Bleriot, but Štefánik was one of the first people ever to fly by plane. The first Slovak who not only flew but also constructed a flying machine was a younger fellow student of Štefánik's from Szarvás the Békéscaba native, Andrej Kvas, who in 1911 flew 72 kilometres without a break. At that time, Štefánik didn't sit in the pilot's seat, but on the second seat of the open monoplane for two people. After a safe landing, he couldn't hide his euphoria. He had no idea that the aeroplane would become his destiny, but it was clear to him that a machine that could take people to the heights would become an interest of his alongside astronomy. From then on, he went to the airport whenever he was free, gradually learning the secrets of flying. He was troubled by the problem of the machine's over-dependence on weather conditions, and so proposed to place a hollow circle with mercury in the fuselage which would bring the aircraft into a horizontal position according to its inclination. His ideas were professionally redrawn by his artist friends which may have been a key factor in his stabilizer eventually taking hold.

He was granted French citizenship on 27th July, 1912. The first to congratulate him on this was Senator Chautemps. As usual, they settled in his beautiful parlour. The family was on vacation in Chamonix, so the two men had enough time for a memorable discussion. Chautemps was familiar with Štefánik's health problems and offered him herbal tea, pouring cognac for himself.

"Being a Frenchman, although naturalized, is a great thing, opening doors to important institutions and personalities. It's great news and I'm happy for you. You'll no longer have to rely on the good will of sponsors for your research – the state will officially support you."

"I want to thank you – I know that without you, my application may have failed. and aware of the chances that my new homeland gives me. France, after all, is one of the world's strongest powers."

"All because of your excellent work. What you accomplished on Mont Blanc, in Spain, Algeria and Vavau, despite the bad weather, is amazing. Your name already has a solid reputation in scientific circles, therefore allow me to make a request... Hm... I'd like to ask you to give a lecture on your travels, especially on your Polynesian journey..."

"Tell me more."

"My dear friend, you're a man in whom I have complete confidence, and therefore, with the sincere approval of our community, I want to say that it would be on the grounds of our lodge. More specifically, it would be attended by members of a number of lodges. There is such an interest in you."

"Lodge? Do you mean Masons?"

"Yes."

"Um... That's strange... I knew you were a Freemason, more precisely, I suspected..."

"Really? Names of members are strictly confidential."

"Your name was revealed to me by a female antique shop owner in Chamonix," Štefánik smiled secretively.

"I don't understand... We don't have women in the lodge..."

"But you go to her to buy Masonic symbols... Circles, Angles, Hammers, Swords you use for initiation rituals, medals, needles, triangles, stars..."

"I don't buy them only in Chamonix," Chautemps smiled. "I see you're interested in our fraternity..."

"I'm interested in noble people. When I arrived in Paris, I bowed to Voltaire and I'd already read the work of the mathematician Diderot in Prague."

"I know that you are a mathematician, an astronomer, philosopher, traveller, scientist and humanist, but above all, I know you as a man who works relentlessly to raise himself. In terms of your values, behaviour and enduring work, you're already a Freemason. Gothic cathedrals are so beautiful because the stones from which they were built were worked to a perfect smoothness. We masons, cut the stones to our own measure and endeavour to do it as well as we can. Cathedrals are perfect because they are built in a complete harmony of spirit and matter. Balance is the fundamental principle of our existence. Death has to be in balance with life, with extinction, a breath taken with a breath exhaled, a woman with a man, also love with hate."

"What if hatred prevails?"

"It cannot be prevented but our task is to help love. It's up to each person to stand on the side of love or hatred. Our authorities are spiritual personalities, regardless of their religion. There are Christians, Buddhists, Muslims and Jews among us. We follow God's commandments, not church dogmas. That's why the Catholic Church hates us. A Freemason can't be a man who hates; we regard xenophobia and racism as mental illnesses. Only wise people may join. Wisdom is the symbiosis of reason and heart, thought and feeling. We follow the ethics of Christ's Sermon on the Mount. Our motto is the motto of revolution: Equality, Fraternity, Freedom."

"As far as I know," Štefánik smiled, "Dr. Guillotine was also a Freemason who, in revolutionary times, proposed execution without trial, and designed the execution tool himself."

"I see you already know something about us. Yes, there are hateful people among us, and we are not immune to evil. However, we do everything to have as many noble people as possible among us, men such as Benjamin Franklin. He was, by the way, when he was American ambassador to Paris, a member of the same lodge as Voltaire. Goethe, Pushkin, Mozart, Schiller, Diderot, Liszt, Washington, Stendhal, Oscar Wilde, the freedom fighter Giuseppe Garibaldi, Carlo Goldoni and the recently deceased Mark Twain were also Freemasons. You'd be surprised how many great contemporaries there are among us, but our regulations prohibit us from revealing the names of Masons unless they themselves publish them."

"The names you mentioned are known, but it is said that the Prime Minister, Briand, the builder Eiffel, the designer Citroën and my friend Alfons Mucha are also active in the Paris lodges…"

"I can't deny or confirm these names for you," Chautemps smiled. "However, you will be able to personally see who works in which lodges. Will you come and lecture to us?"

"I would be honoured."

"Excellent, thank you. However, you understand that you will be bound by silence, even if you are not a member of our brotherhood."

"Of course."

"So come on Tuesday in two weeks to Cadet 16. It is the site of the French Great Orient and a number of other lodges also convene there. You'll meet influential people who'll be happy to help you. Mutual assistance is the fundamental principle of our brotherhood."

Since acquiring French citizenship, it had become much easier for Štefánik to find financial resources. In gratitude for being granted French citizenship he announced his donation to the country of the buildings and astronomical instruments in Papeete. His new homeland appreciated this gesture and in no time the leading academic institution, *Le Bureau des longitudes*, commissioned him to observe another solar eclipse in Brazil. From there he planned to continue to Tahiti, but due to difficult shipping connections he had to abandon his intention.

In August he joined his friend Jaromir Kralicky in Bordeaux on the *Amazone* steamer Through Lisbon, the Canary Islands, Dakar and the Brazilian port of Recife, they continued to Rio de Janeiro, where they arrived on the morning of 10th September. When sailing across the equator, his stomach troubles returned, but fortunately soon stopped. Along with their expedition, another eight arrived on the Brazilian coast, settling in the Passa Quatro Nature Reserve, three hundred kilometers northwest of Rio. This time, Štefánik had excellent equipment with him, including a two-ton, ten-metre-long telescope, which was pulled by ox-drawn carts on to an observation platform at 1,500 metres. Unfortunately, on 10th October it rained during the eclipse, so none of the expeditions achieved the desired results. An unexpected compensation for his disappointment, however, was a meeting with the President of Brazil, Hermes da Fonsec. After this reception, they packed up their precious instruments and sailed on the *Atlantique* from Rio, back to Bordeaux, arriving in Paris on 8th November. The two-week voyage was a welcome opportunity to recover from his Brazilian stay. Listening to the sea and watching the stars, Štefánik pondered: "The voice of despair and the delight of millions of different beings merges into one wave, whose rhythmic surf lulls my soul out of resistance and coaxes from it peace and strength. So it was long ago and so it will long continue to happen, forever. We are cosmic only through dust and an arbitrary gift. Wretched is he who has realized the true value of life and things…"

CHAPTER 40
My Brother, You'll Be My Enemy

He could never wait to get home, had gone to Parisian shops in good time and bought gifts, carefully writing a list so as not to forget anyone. At Christmas 1912, he came home for the first time not as a Hungarian, but as a proud citizen of the French Republic. His brother, Lacko, had recently had a wedding, taking the excellent Ilonka as his wife, so Milan stopped off in Trnava to greet them. Then they came to Košariská. He was met at Brezová station as usual by Štefan, the coachman. From the whoops of fellow passengers and the brisk running of horses, which also seemed to demonstrate their joy at the arrival of the Parisian, they sped beneath Bradlo to arrive at the Christmas Eve table in time. They were warmly welcomed, and as they were late, sat down quickly. His father first welcomed the new family member, Ilonka, then said the customary Christmas Eve prayers. After dinner, the children took their gifts from under the tree and the biggest one went to his father, a new black suit from Paris. And they didn't even notice that some of the neighbours had joined them and that the parish priest and Kazimír had disappeared. When there was a mighty knock on the door, his mother exclaimed: "Who is it?"

A voice came from behind the door.

"Open up!"

"What do you bring?" the housewife asked.

"Health, happiness, abundant holy blessings!" his father repeated these words three times, then his mother went to the door and opened it. Behind it was his smiling father. It was the same every Christmas.

"We beseech you for one hundred chickens, one hundred ducklings, one hundred pigs!"

Kazimír appeared before his father and loudly recited: "We beseech you for a hundred heaps of wheat, a hundred heaps of rye, a heap pounds of barley!" His father then poured barley onto the table, on which his mother placed a small napkin and a candlestick with a candle in it. After this traditional ritual was enacted, Milan's tales stretched deep into the night.

The next morning, they went to church where his father preached. After the service, the verger took a bowl and passed among the faithful who threw small copper coins into it. He then tied up the bowl with a coloured cloth and went to the sacristy. At that moment Milan came up to him, took him to one side, untied the cloth, slipped into the bowl two hundred crowns in banknotes, bound the cloth up again and put a finger to his lips. The churchman nodded in understanding.

After the holidays, he returned to Paris through Vienna. The times were getting worse. The newspapers brought disturbing news as propaganda against the Serbs grew stronger. During Štefánik's stay in Košariská, the Hungarian Parliament unexpectedly approved extraordinary measures in the case of war.

On 1st April, after returning from enlistment, recruits from Košariská and Priepasné decorated their new hats with *sabatčáky*, bundles of coloured ribbons. In a good mood, their parish priest, Štefánik, interrupted them. He'd come to ask which of his parishioners had been conscripted. He stood in the doorway, greeted those present and began to talk to the boys: "My boys, what awaits you…" But he couldn't say any more, he was unable to move and fell. When her husband was late coming home, the priest's wife went out into the forecourt of her house every moment with terrible foreboding. Štefan Kopecký then appeared and in a loud, trembling voice blabbered something about apoplexy. It wasn't long before a haycart appeared in front of the manse, sombre men carrying the pale priest, barely breathing, on a pile of straw. The men carefully took him out of the cart and put him in the back room. Shortly afterwards, Doctor Roth came to examine him. But the pastor's health fast deteriorated and he never got out of bed again.

Despite his worsening condition, however, he still wrote to Milan about how he was looking forward to seeing him at home before he left for Tahiti. Then he lost consciousness and though Doctor Roth tried various medications, nothing helped. At the beginning of April, the whole family gathered, except Oľga and her husband, who'd fallen ill, and brother Paľo, who was wasting away somewhere in New York. Together with his parishioners, they prayed by the bed for his recovery. When the old man's condition surprisingly improved, Milan, hoping that his father was recovering, went back to Paris. But as soon as he entered his apartment, a messenger brought a telegram from his mother: "Apank beteg, gyere haza azonnal. Mamad." (Father is sick, come home immediately. Mama.) He understood that it was bad with his father but didn't manage to see him alive again. Pavel Štefánik, sixty-eight, died on 15th April at ten o'clock in the morning. The funeral took place three days later, hundreds of parishioners, thirteen teachers and nine priests all coming to say farewell to the pastor on the afternoon of 18th April at 2 o'clock, in beautiful warm weather. Senior Pavel Sekera said with feeling the words of valediction; the teachers' choir and that of the Brezová church sang the funeral chorales. The funeral had to be postponed for two hours because Milan was delayed.

After the funeral he visited relatives and friends, including his sick sister Oľga in Spišské Vlachy. He was sorry that he couldn't stay with her for longer, so he wrote a letter promising to come in May and visit her again. But he wasn't to visit his sister, Oľga, nor any of his loved ones. Before he left, he managed to see his aunt and his godmother, Emília Fajnorová in Lučenec, to whom he gave a pearl. It was as if he knew the mysterious stars had told him it was the last time he'd see those closest to him. Before he left, he and his brother Ladislav went to the fresh grave of their father again, embraced and he said sadly: "This is how life is. The clouds are moving. Here we stand beside each other as brothers and soon we may stand against each other in opposing armies. I fear, my brother, that we'll be enemies, fighting each other. It'll be a hard fight, but good will prevail... Then it'll be good with us too... I'm convinced of it."

He travelled away and returned no more to his native country.

CHAPTER 41
A Prophecy Fulfilled

The year 1913 seemed to be the best Europe had ever seen. On 24th May the German Emperor, Wilhelm II, celebrated the wedding of his daughter, Victoria Luise, to Prince August von Braunschweig and invited both his cousins, the British King George V and the Russian Tsar Nicholas II. The mood was familial; the rulers addressed each other as Willy, Niki and George and to prove the inextricable nature of Anglo-German friendship, King George dressed in German uniform and Emperor Wilhelm in British. The reason for the celebration was not only the wedding, but also the twenty-fifth anniversary of the Emperor's reign.

The French President wasn't invited by the monarch to celebrate his jubilee. There had been tension between Berlin and Paris since the defeat of France in 1871. The French had an undisguised desire for revenge and the return of Alsace and Lorraine, which they'd had to relinquish to the German Empire. Outwardly peace ruled in Europe, a wonderful summer called people to swimming pools, where water slides appeared; fashion designers were becoming bolder, skirts shorter, dance floors sagged, funfairs bulged at the seams and the rich bet huge sums on their favourite horses. From London through Berlin, Paris, Budapest to St. Petersburg, there were premieres of operas, new museums opening, libraries, spas and telephones becoming accessible to the middle class. In European capitals, metro lines, roads, sewers, water mains, and hygiene levels multiplied. The consumption of meat, soap, wine and tobacco reached record levels, the Austrian writer, Stefan Zweig writing: "Europe had never been so strong, beautiful, rich. Deep in their hearts Europeans honestly believed in the wonderful future that had just begun." Germany was the most dynamic country alongside the US. In Berlin alone, in the splendid year of 1913 more than a hundred cinemas were said to be in operation, and a stadium for 33,000 spectators was established in which the opening ceremony of the 1916 Summer Olympics would be held. Germany grew as stronger and mightier voices called for an increase in German living space; in Berlin they also included Austria in this area. This unified Germanic force needed raw materials, especially oil, located in the Middle East. However, in the *Drang nach Osten* (Desire for the East), the Serbs and their loyal ally, Russia, stood in the way. In Berlin, a fundamental question began to be asked in political and media lobbies, *"Germanentum, oder Slawentum?"* (German or Slavic?). Few noticed that the number of German soldiers had increased by 130,000, military service in France had been extended to three years and the Russian Duma had decided to increase the standing army by 460,000 men before 1917. The United Kingdom, the only country with no compulsory conscription, had the largest military and commercial fleet.

Test cruises had already taken place in the newly built strategic Panama Canal. Whoever controlled the sea route from Europe through this canal to the Pacific Ocean would be master of much of the world's seas.

Štefánik's chance came in July 1912, when the French Parliament passed a law on building a wireless telegraphy network between French colonies. The central station was supposed to be in Tahiti with connections to the stations on Marquesas and New Caledonia. The project was all the more relevant because the British already had a similar station on the island of Raratonga, while the Germans had built a station on the German Samoa archipelago. Štefánik strengthened his argument by stating his aim to build a radio station in Tahiti.

He informed Senator Chautemps, who didn't seem enthusiastic at first. But when he told him that the German company, *Telefunken*, had a secret plan to build a wireless telegraph station on one of the Galapagos Islands, he sat up and took notice.

"How do you know? Not even our secret services have such information," the curious senator asked.

"Thanks to Hungarian."

"Hungarian?"

"In the port of Papeete, the Austro-Hungarian cruiser the Empress Elizabeth docked during my stay. The sailors liked the beautiful Tahitians so much so they prolonged their stay. And since they have great liquor in Tahiti, the drunken officers also talked about what they shouldn't have. Especially as the Hungarian nationals regarded me as theirs," Štefánik laughed.

It was decided. He drew up a project that Senator Chautemps endorsed and presented to the Chairman of the Assembly, Deschanel. He approved it. Štefánik's position unexpectedly improved when the French government instructed the State Secretary of the Department of Trade Fleet, Anatole de Monzie, to prepare a proposal to use the Panama Canal for the commercial, military and political aims of France. Paris had no coal storage base for commercial and military vessels near to the Panama Canal. For French experts the most ideal country for these goals seemed to be Ecuador, An even better place to build a base for the French Navy in the Pacific being the Galapagos archipelago, belonging to Ecuador, about a thousand kilometres from the mainland. The Galapagos Islands were the perfect place to build an amplification station for radiotelegraphy links between French Polynesia, French Guyana and Paris and when de Monzie and Chautemps were wondering who the most suitable candidate for implementing this bold plan would be, they came up with a single name: Štefánik. De Monzie remembered him well. His excellent and passionate lecture at the Masonic Lodge, of which de Monzie was a member, had made a deep impression on him and he asked Chautemps to be introduced to him. The four-years older under-secretary, known for his ambition when he was Minister of Justice as a twenty-eight-year old, sensed an opportunity. The ambitious Štefánik was for him the ideal implementer of bold plans. At their first meeting they understood each other De Monzie expressing his confidence in the Slovak He made no secret of the fact that he was present at his lecture at the French Grand Orient, although Štefánik hadn't noticed him among the many Freemasons dressed in the same black suits and white sashes. However, he felt honoured when de Monzie confirmed to him that the legendary Prime Minister, Aristide Briand, himself sat among the top dignitaries.

"There should be a French wireless station on the island of Floreana in the Galapagos Islands," de Monzie said vigorously as they agreed on a common goal after a long talk.

"I'll do it!" Štefánik said, looking at him daringly. In a corner of his soul, he believed that he would move to his dream of Tahiti after the task. For De Monzie, the whole event was so spectacular that he agreed. In those pre-war times, it was no problem for de Monzie to raise money for political and military tasks, especially when the project was backed by Prime Minister Barthou. Moreover, French intelligence services had reported American interest in buying or renting the Galapagos Islands. Since the declaration of the Monroe Doctrine, the Americas for Americans, Europe for the Europeans, the action which Štefánik undertook in the French interest required extraordinary diplomatic skill. In any communication between the domestic French authorities and the authorities in Peru, the letter X would be used as code for Štefánik.

In August he travelled from Le Havre to New York, officially, as an astronomer, to build an observatory in Lima, unofficially to obtain a concession to build a broadcasting station in the Galapagos

Islands and to persuade the Ecuadorian government to let France rent out an island as a naval base for its merchant fleet – all, of course, very discreetly, so that his journey did not arouse the interest of other great powers.

In the USA, he behaved as a tourist, visiting the Niagara Falls, Chicago and Los Angeles, before finally, on 17th September, sailing from San Francisco to Tahiti. Sailing across the Pacific Ocean towards the shores of Ecuador, he wrote in his journal: *"I am approaching Tahiti again without reaching it. It seems to me to be a symbol of my existence. I imagine the most diverse and fantastic ways of getting there, but I can't reach the port. My health is broken, my finances exhausted, at times I feel mentally undermined and the years are running by. My life is complicated. Yet, I'm still alive so perhaps my effort is not wasted; perhaps I have contributed and go on contributing to humanity's progress. I have great defects, but I feel that there is some good in me."*

He stayed there for less than three weeks, greeted friends on board the gunboat, *Zélée*, told Captain Destremau the news from Paris, handed over some secret ciphers, and was back in San Francisco on 30th October. From there through New Orleans he sailed to Colón and continued by train to the capital of the country, Panama.

He noted in his diary: *"The character of the entire canal zone is North American and thus thieving. Americans have strongly fortified the canal, having obviously decided to hold it and use it for themselves. The zone will be protected by five thousand soldiers and no one will be able to live there. With one arm they hug it and in the other they reach into your pocket,"* he wrote of the US relationship with Ecuador. *"Their ultimate goal is the economic enslavement of Ecuador. But Ecuador must be strengthened and be a barrier to North American expansion."*

France as one of the superpowers, moreover the original builder and designer of the canal, was interested in strategic locations on the route from France via the canal to its Pacific territories where it could safely store coal for its ships. Floreana Island was the ideal place. Right after his arrival, Štefánik built up important contacts, establishing links with the director of the Quito observatory, Tufiño, who had studied in Paris and was a friend of Henri Poincaré. Tufiño promised to help him build a weather station in the Galapagos Islands. Štefánik heard about an opportunity to rent Floreana Island for 99 years for three million dollars, a million of which would be a bribe to President Plaz. But he strongly rejected the proposal. However, the United States also had an interest in the Galapagos Islands, and, as it turned out, so did the German *Telefunken* company. He feared that if the Americans didn't get the islands with money, they'd provoke a war between Peru and Ecuador or arrange a declaration of "independence" for the Galapagos, as they had done in Panama.

After learning that the Ecuadorian government had invited a German military mission to the country, he was received by General Leonidas Plaza, President of the country, at the request of the ambassador Francastela. Štefánik was informed that President Plaza was known for his corruption and German agents were wheeling round him. Consequently he thanked him for his promise of support.

"At this point I also convey the friendly feelings of the very influential French personalities who can and want to be useful," he added. "However, to avoid complications of any kind, the delicacy of the situation requires absolute discretion."

Finally, the President persuaded the responsible ministers of the Ecuadorian government, who accepted Štefánik's proposals for reorganization of the astronomical observatory, meteorology, and in particular the creation of a French TSF wireless telegraphy network, including the Galapagos, throughout Ecuador. He even managed to deceive the British Embassy, which had been closely following his activities. The mission ended in great success.

"Mission accomplished, the licence to build TSF gained," he telegraphed on 2nd December 1913, to de Monzie.

"I can't do anything other than testify to the dexterity of Mr. Štefánik, who has achieved results without attracting attention," wrote the enthusiastic French ambassador to Paris.

At the end of his stay in Ecuador he spent long days in bed, however; he couldn't eat and vomited what little he got into his stomach. At the beginning of January 1914 he left Guayaquil going via the Panama Canal back to France. The demanding and stressful stay in Ecuador had worsened his health and most of the voyage he spent in bed, stricken with pain. He wondered why he had to suffer so much, why God hadn't given him health that would allow him to fully enjoy life. Why had fate chosen this path for him?

Occasionally he went on deck at night and stared at the starry sky, reflecting on life: *"What a world of desolation without poetry. I don't have a homeland anymore. I drag myself through the world, work for my ideals, but for how long can I endure it? And I have to go on. I have a poor mother and must help my brothers and sisters. I can also be useful abroad for my Slovakia. But my soul is afflicted and my body is worn out. God grant me a better year."*

But God didn't grant his wish. The fourteenth year of the new century was worse for Štefánik and the world than he could have imagined. His stomach pains became unbearable and after a word in his favour from Anatole de Monzie, Professor Montprofit urgently operated on his stomach pylorus at Angers on 20th March. The operation was so harrowing he felt he was going out of his mind. His hair grew grey from suffering, but the professor assured him that his life was not in danger. The pain subsided a little, but as soon as he ate the smallest piece of food, it came back and sometimes left him unconscious. Štefánik was dismayed when a strong young man from the adjoining room was operated on for a similar diagnosis, but died soon after. After a month of convalescence, however, he thanked the professor, bought the nurse, Julie, a bouquet of flowers and returned to life to encounter other triumphs. And losses. His iron will lifted him again from suffering and steeled him against pain; he pulled himself together and in July he departed on the ship, *Montréal*, from

Bordeaux to Morocco. Mobilization caught him on 2nd August in Rabat. He had no idea that his brother, Ladislav, had in those days enlisted in the Hungarian army. As he feared, they found themselves in opposing armies. The prophecy from his father's funeral was fulfilled.

PART 2

war

CHAPTER 1
Honneur et Patrie

When Franz Ferdinand d'Este, the successor to the Austrian throne, decided to visit the manoeuvres in Bosnia and Herzegovina despite warnings from the civilian and military intelligence services, none of the imperial families tried to stop him. However, the Serbian Ambassador to Vienna immediately warned the Austrian authorities that the successor to the throne should remain in Vienna because of the acute possibility of assassination. Even so he went to Bosnia with his wife without any adequate protection. Incomprehensibly Vienna didn't ask for security nor did the Austrian commander-in-chief in Sarajevo, which was commonly done with less important visits. Moreover, the selection of the date of the visit, 28th June, was grossly provocative to the Serbs, as they commemorated the defeat at Kosovo on the day of St. Vitus. The authorities ordered the Serbs to create tribunes to line the route and insisted on a humiliating "spontaneous" jubilation from the watching crowds. After a tour of the barracks, a column of five cars set off for a tour of Sarajevo. Suddenly a young man jumped out from the people on the riverside, struck a telegraph pole with an object then tossed it towards the heir-to-the-throne's vehicle. The object bounced off and under the following car of the Duke Boos Waldeck and exploded. The grenade injured eight people in the escort as well as sixteen spectators. Despite the Grand Duchess Sofia urging him to stop the visit immediately and return to Vienna, the Archduke was not persuaded and ordered that they visit the military hospital. However, the chauffeur Loyka started in the direction of the original route and so he had to stop the car. As soon as the chauffeur reversed, a young man, Gavrilo Princip, jumped out of the scaffolding to the right of the car, leaned against a spare tyre and fired a shot into the archduke's neck. Princip's second shot hit his wife in the stomach. Both Ferdinand and Sofia died in a few minutes.

In Europe, it was thought that the assassination had been deliberately provoked by Vienna, succumbing to pressure from Berlin, and that they had simply sacrificed the successor to the throne, Franz Ferdinand. His uncle Emperor Franz Joseph I hated with all his soul the successor to the monarchy, so in the imperial court it was as if nothing much had happened. What followed, however, was what Vienna and especially Berlin needed: a pretext for war. On 23rd July, Vienna submitted an ultimatum to Belgrade, the conditions of which were achievable only at the expense of an unprecedented humiliation for the Serbs. The ultimatum was presented with devilish precision just as the French President, Raymond Poincaré, had left St. Petersburg, where he'd been negotiating with the Russian Tsar Nicholas II. The British Minister for Foreign Affairs, Edward Grey later described the Austrian ultimatum as the most insulting text he had ever read in international diplomacy. Nevertheless, the Serbs met the demands of the ultimatum, except on one point: deployment of Austrian observers in Serbian territory. The point, of course, could have been discussed if Vienna had been interested in peace. However, Austria-Hungary wanted war. Franz Joseph under the pressure of his government and furious generals connected to Berlin didn't even wait for an answer and announced the mobilization of half of his army. The only person who dared to object was Hungarian Prime Minister Count István Tisza, who warned the Emperor that the declaration of war on Serbia was a fatal mistake. The Austrian Emperor, under the pressure of the fanatical Foreign Minister Berchtold, signed a letter to the German Emperor, conceived by the Minister, in which he stated: "The assassination of my nephew is a direct result of Russian and Serbian pan-Slavism, whose sole purpose is to destroy my monarchy. Therefore, as a power factor, Serbia needs to be eliminated." Without any consultation, the German Emperor promised the Austrians the support that militaristic circles in Vienna were eagerly awaiting. On 28th July 1914, Austria declared war on a ten-times weaker Serbia and on that same day began to bombard Belgrade. On the day of the declaration of war, the Austrian ambassador came to inform the Pope and asked him to bless the Austro-Hungarian army. Pius X replied: "Tell the Emperor that I cannot bless either the war nor those who desire it. I only bless peace." The ambassador asked for at least a blessing for the Emperor. The Pope bowed, saying: "I can only pray for God's forgiveness for this. The Emperor will be glad if he does not receive a curse." He didn't receive one because Emperor Franz Joseph I died in the third autumn of the war fall after a sixty-eight-year reign. His successor, Charles I (Charles IV of Hungary), symbolically slashed a sword at the four corners of the world in honour of the tradition, promising to protect the realm from an enemy coming from any side. At the fourth slash the sword dropped out from the hands of the King, which those present interpreted as a bad sign for the empire. They weren't mistaken. The crumbling monarchy and the powerful Habsburg dynasty had only two years left. In the meantime, however, more than seventeen million innocent men and women were to die on both sides, mostly in the prime of life, among them forty-two young men from Košariská and Priepasné, almost all the young men from both villages. In Europe desolation remained, a crippled and lost generation that would have to cope with psychological trauma, the fall of empires, kingdoms, the Tsarist regime and the creation of new states in their place. Perhaps the most important of these in Europe would be the Republic of Czecho-Slovakia.

The sixty-year-old widow, Albertína, less than half a year after the death of her husband, vacated the Košariská manse to a new parish priest, Michal Valášek, who took over the parish in September

1913. With her daughter Mária, the widow moved briefly to live with her daughter, Elena Izaková in Myjava. In the spring of 1914, she decided to leave together with Mária, Ladislav's wife Elena and her daughter, Elena to the Lowlands to live in Báčska Palanka with her oldest son, Igor. The Hungarian authorities had labelled Igor a pan-Slav and after the outbreak of the war, he was under permanent police supervision, equivalent to house arrest. The Štefániks were in a difficult situation; sons Kazimír and Ladislav served in the Austro-Hungarian army, Pavel Svätopluk hadn't finished his veterinary studies and lived an improvident life in the USA, Milan was a citizen of the enemy country, and the sons-in-law were enlisted in the army.

Since the outbreak of the war, Štefánik had broken off contact with his home. As a French citizen and, moreover, an Air Force officer he'd become a traitor to Hungary. The authorities prevented any correspondence with his family. Two days after the outbreak of the war, he arrived in Casablanca with the official task of ascertaining the conditions for building an observatory in Morocco. The unofficial reason for his journey, however, was to map out the situation for the Department of Overseas Territories in response to reports of German efforts to obtain approval from the new Sultan of Morocco, Yusuf ben Hassan, to build a naval base in Agadir.

But Štefánik did not begin his planned activities. On Monday, 3rd August, General Louis Hubert Lyautey, resident minister of France in Morocco, which was in fact a protectorate, received him in Rabat at his headquarters. The white-haired General with an immense moustache welcomed Štefánik with a secretive smile in the presence of the top French colonial officials and army commanders. A protocol official asked Štefánik to take his place opposite the General under a portrait of Raymond Poincaré. The General resident was standing next to the French flag, welcomed the astronomer in an unusually friendly manner and instructed a subordinate to read the official letter from the Navy Department: "In 1913, Mr. Štefánik was entrusted with a mission to Tahiti and the Republic of Ecuador, gave evidence of his first-class capabilities and demonstrated remarkable service to the merchant navy and the French expansion." The General thanked the aide and took a telegram from an envelope. "My dear Mr. Štefánik, I would like to inform you that on 20th July, the President of the French Republic, his Excellency Mr. Raymond Poincaré, agreed to your appointment as a Knight of the Legion d'honneur at the Elysée Palace. You'll receive La Croix de la Légion d'Honneur upon your return." The General took two steps towards Štefánik and, seeing his sincere emotion, embraced him as if he were a son.

"I have reviewed the list of holders of the order of La Légion d'Honneur. You are the first Slovak to receive it. So my congratulations are all the more sincere." He squeezed his hand and all those present congratulated Štefánik. The General offered him a chair by the table on his right. After taking his place, Štefánik and other guests sat down. They drank to his success, but the atmosphere was oppressive.

"Your Excellency, gentlemen," said Štefánik, "my joy is immense. I am determined to do my best to be worthy to wear La Croix de la Légion d'Honneur, which I've been granted before I deserved it. Once again I thank the French President and my French homeland. And you, mon général, thank you for mentioning my Slovak nation."

Then he sat down. There was a long silence which the General interrupted.

"Unfortunately, our French homeland has no reason for the joy you have. We haven't met, gentlemen, in good times. The day before yesterday, Germany declared war on Russia and today, I'm very sorry to be the bearer of bad news. A dispatch informs me that the German ambassador to Paris ascertained from Prime Minister Viviani whether we would insist that Russia stop their mobilization and if France would remain neutral in the event of a war with Russia. Viviani replied that we would act according to our interests. Berlin has presented us with an ultimatum: to declare neutrality in the event of conflict and to give Germany our fortresses in Toul and Verdun as an expression of goodwill."

"It is a disgrace... an act of shameful insolence!" outraged voices called. There was a furious buzz in the room.

"As I said," the General continued, Germany declared war on Russia on 1st August and the next day gave a humiliating ultimatum to Belgium, which proudly rejected it. We replied to Berlin that we reject its demands and proclaim mobilization. Today, Berlin declared war on us and attacked Belgium. They are attacking a defenceless country whose neutrality they themselves have guaranteed. It is an unacceptable violation of international law. Gentlemen, it is clear that a German attack on Paris will occur within days."

The General's voice faltered, but then he resolutely added: "They'll get what they want. We'll give them hell on our land and return with interest Sedan and all the injustices that have been done to France and our allies. To our homeland! Vive la France! Vive la France!"

He stood up and everyone drank. Then they sang the *Marseillaise* in full voice. Their faces lit up, filled with determination, hearts burning with French pride. La Grande nation began to rise not only in Morocco, but everywhere in the world. And with him all the people of good will. "Our London ambassador has informed us," the General said quietly, "that Britain will declare war on the Germans in the coming hours."

"Long live Britain, long live Russia!"

"My dear sir," the General said to Štefánik, "I am really sorry that the day we officially informed you of your status as Chevalier of la Légion d'Honneur is the day of the de facto outbreak of a World War... I know you are from Hungary, for us an enemy country. On the decree signed by the President of the Republic, it is written that you are from Košariská in Hungary. I've found some information about you and your homeland. There are about two and a half million Slovaks living in Hungary. Don't take this badly, but as yet I have heard nothing about your nation. All the more we appreciate you joining us and becoming a French citizen!"

The General gazed at the tiny, disturbed man with his emotion-filled blue eyes in expectation of an explanation.

"Your Excellency, gentlemen," Štefánik sighed hard, "I believe you will understand my thrill. First of all, I want to thank France, my new homeland, from the depths of my soul, and you, the General Resident, for the manifest honour that I have received. You've asked me, honoured General, who are the Slovaks. We are an ancient Slavic nation who've always lived in Central Europe with our Czech brothers, with whom we form one nation living in two tribes. Slovaks are Czechs living in Slovakia and Czechs are Slovaks living in the Czech Republic. Prague is as Slovak as its Czech We are equally oppressed and deprived of civil and human rights, Czechs by the Austrians and Slovaks by the Hungarians. We can't use the language spoken by our mothers at any school. They beat us for wanting to speak our language, to have our own state, equal electoral rights and that we want to be Slovaks and Czechs. We don't want anything but to be a nation recognized and respected, like the French."

Štefánik's enthusiastic speech moved those present. Someone cried out: "Vive la Slovaquie!"

Štefánik turned to the Major who had called out, his face brightening.

"Did I hear right? Vive la Slovaquie? I've never heard anything like that before. Thank you, I thank you with all my heart. Gentlemen, let me drink to the health of my nation, which is outwardly your enemy, but in our hearts is with you. I believe that when this war is over, Slovaks and Czechs will be your closest allies. Vive la Tchécoslovaquie!"

Something incredible then happened. They all joined in and in distant Rabat there was a call for the glory of Czecho-Slovakia.

Tears came to Štefánik's eyes. The General went up to him and pulled an envelope from his pocket.

"Sir, you'll be able to fight for your two countries. You have to go back to Paris immediately. Here's your recall order. I wish you good luck. The first military transport from Rabat is leaving for Bordeaux tomorrow. You can join them if you wish."

At that moment his aide went to the General and handed him a pale blue encrypted message form. He read it carefully, then read it again. Those present watched his face gravely.

"Gentlemen, what we've been expecting has happened. The German Ambassador, Wilhelm von Schoen, left Paris at 22.20. An hour ago, a German aircraft crossed the French border in the department of Meurthe-et-Moselle and bombed the city of Lunéville. The dice have been cast; we will return this to the Germans with interest!" he added as if to himself.

There was a grave silence which Štefánik finally interrupted.

"Sir, I want to go to Paris with your transport tomorrow."

The general mobilization in the Austro-Hungarian Empire in the first phase involved reservists born between 1882 and 1889 and recruited newcomers born up to 1893. The Austro-Hungarian armed forces after mobilization increased from a peacetime number of 450,000 men to 1,421,250 men. Lads from Slavic nations made up 52 percent of these. Among them there were four hundred thousand Slovaks. One of them was Kazimír Konštantín Štefánik. Milan's second brother, Ladislav Dušan, was luckier with the draft; he was born in 1886 and so was called up a few months later. Brothers Fedor, Mojmir and Jaroslav weren't called up. They were lucky; they had died in childhood...

Milan presented himself for the draft on 11th August to the 102nd Infantry Regiment in Chartres. However, he wasn't taken because of bad health and an acute stomach complaint. Despite presenting a document that he'd been properly drafted in 1912, his medical condition deteriorated so much that he was afraid of being permanently removed from the records of conscripts due to physical disability. Not only did they not take him, but they had to hospitalize him in the Boucicaut public hospital in the 15th district of Paris, intended for indigent patients and employees of the department store, *Bon Marché*. Štefánik was welcomed here with disdain, because they believed that he was pretending to be sick to avoid military service. In addition, the hospital was Catholic and the staff knew that Štefánik was a Protestant, which didn't contribute to the quality of health care for him. He was threatened with another stomach operation. After treatment with powerful medication, however, his condition improved and he was transferred to the Fondation Chaptal sanatorium in the ninth district. Here, during almost three weeks of convalescence, he was visited by friends from both artistic and political circles. A frequent visitor was Senator Chautemps, his daughter, Yvonne, often accompanying him.

One week after the outbreak of the war, the Slovak National Party (SNS) suspended its activities. It justified its passivity by not giving the government cause to use repressive measures against the Slovak population. The SNS declaration of 5th August, 1914 declared: *"Our position is given to us by an inborn love and loyalty to the supreme ruling family. It matters to us that our homeland, our monarchy be maintained in its entirety, and emerge victorious from the coming war."*

Štefánik concentrated all his energy and contacts on one goal, getting into the army. He was afraid that the military authorities would place him among the unfit so he asked his friend Paul Raphael to get a recommendation for him from the famous pilot Henri Farman, in whose reconnaissance machines he had flown several times. The war inexorably began to impinge on the life of Štefánik and his relatives. By the time he'd left the hospital, he'd read that on 24th September, the flagships of the German Pacific fleet, the armoured cruisers *Scharnhorst* and *Gneisenau*, had docked in the Tahitian port of Papeete to replenish their coal reserves. In the Pacific, Germany had a number of important colonies and was determined to do more than defend them. These included the Bismarck Archipelago, German New Guinea, Emperor Wilhelm Land, Melanesia, Solomon Islands, Northern Mariana Islands, Carolina, Micronesia, Marshall Islands, Nauru, German Samoa, and a few smaller ones which they intended to expand at the expense of the British and French. The gunboat, *Zélée*, on the orders of Štefánik's friend Captain Maxim Destremau opened fire on them, but against a much stronger calibre and the solid armour of both cruisers had no chance. After the Germans returned fire, the *Zélée* sank, though the crew of 100 men fortunately survived. For the law of balance to be fulfilled, less than 3 months later a British flotilla sank both ships with almost 2,000 sailors on 8th December.

On 14th October, 1914, a member of the French Academy of Moral and Political Sciences, a commissioned officer of the Légion d'honneur, the philosopher Étienne Émile Boutroux, invited Štefánik to the magnificent Palace of the French Légion d'honneur on the Rue de Lille in Paris. After performing a ceremonial ritual in the great hall before the enlisted knights, officers, commanders, grand officers and holders of the Grand Cross, Boutroux informed the Grand Chancellor of the Legion that the astronomer Milan Štefánik, born in Košariská in Hungary, authorized for foreign missions, assigned to the observatories in Meudon, Paris and Mont Blanc, had met all the conditions for admission as a member. Then he gave way to the Grand Chancellor of the Council, Division General and Commander of Paris, George August Florentin. Štefánik knelt on his right knee.

"On behalf of the President of the Republic and the power entrusted to me, I elevate you as Chevalier de la Légion d'honneur," Florentin pronounced the mandatory formula. Štefánik stood up and approached the Grand Chancellor. From a tray held by an adjutant he took a white cross in a green garland and pinned the insignia to his chest. Then he kissed him and squeezed his hand firmly.

Štefánik became the first Slovak to hold the highest French honour, introduced by Napoleon Bonaparte. The password counsel of "Honneur et patrie" would from then on accompany him all his life.

"Mon cher Monsieur Štefánik," the Grand Chancellor said with a smile, "forgive us for delaying our council, but we were held back by circumstances known to us all when German troops threatened Paris a few days ago to the level that, for security reasons, the government had to move to Bordeaux. The old adage, *fluctuant, sed non mergitur*, they bend, but do not snap, applies to our capital. Thanks to the great abilities of Marshal Foch, together with French and British soldiers, we have achieved a crushing victory on the Marne River and the government has returned to Paris. Certainly, dear Mr. Štefánik, admitting you to the Council in the absence of the government would not be dignified," he joked.

"Sir, ladies and gentlemen," Štefánik began his speech of thanks with some emotion. "This day was supposed to be the most beautiful in my life. Unfortunately, it is not. A world war has been unleashed as a result of the moral turpitude and gross materialism of the Germans. My heart has split into two. One half belongs to my beloved homeland, Slovakia, which is part of the hated Austro-Hungarian state. The second belongs to my new homeland, my dear France. These halves are at war. Yet a person has just one heart that wants to beat for love, happiness and beauty. How to deal with this conflict?" He thought for a moment, then turned to the Great Chancellor. "I request that you use your position so that I can quickly enter the French air force as a pilot. I think my experience of flying, meteorology and astronomy will be of benefit to France. Je vous remercie cordialement, I give you my heartfelt thanks."

No sooner had he spoken than there was a sound of sirens. German Pfalz, armed with heavy machine guns and cluster bombs, were approaching the city again.

"Gentlemen, I end our celebratory assembly. Mr. Štefánik, I think you're right. Against those up there", he pointed at the sky. "We'll deploy every capable and courageous man. You'll be one of us. Thank you," the Grand Chancellor said.

He read in his newspaper that his respected professor, a deputy in the council of the Austrian empire, Tomáš Garrigue Masaryk had left Prague with his daughter Olga on 18th December and gone to Italy. From there, in January 1915 he moved to Switzerland, where he settled in Geneva. Before the end of 1914, Masaryk met representatives of the British secret service in the Netherlands to support him in his pro-Western resistance, as they feared Russian penetration into Central Europe and the strengthening of Russia's influence. By then, Alois Rašín, Přemysl Šámal and Edvard Beneš had established a secret resistance organization, *Maffia*, that organized domestic resistance to the monarchy. On Masaryk's orders, Catholics weren't allowed to become members of the secret organization.

On 28th September, 1914 in Kiev, a Czech fighting unit gathered under the military flag. About 7,000 Czechs and Slovaks living in Russia swore loyalty to their battalion. They had no idea that they would gradually become the foundation of the state's army, which at that time was only dreamed of by a few daring wishful thinkers.

CHAPTER 2
Father Against Son, Brother Against Brother

Štefánik closely followed the development of the French, Russian and Serbian fronts and read all available newspapers. He was pleased to read that Tomáš Masaryk and Lev Sychravý had founded the Central Office of Revolutionary Committees for the Independence of the Czech Lands and Slovakia in Geneva. Czech associations in

Switzerland, USA, France, Great Britain and Russia issued a statement informing them that the Czech nation didn't wish for war and desired the victory of the entente powers, which would deliver the Czechs from Austrian slavery. A similar statement was issued by representatives of all Slovak organizations in the United States, where some 700,000 Slovaks, a third of the nation, lived at the time of the outbreak of war. The Slovak League memorandum, drafted in Pittsburgh on 10th September 1914, demanded for the Slovak nation "complete self-government and self-determination on political, cultural and economic fronts" within Hungary. Apel followed up the memorandum to all Slovak organizations, in which Albert Mamatey formulated for the first time a call for the creation of a common state with the Czechs.

While generals and politicians wove their dreams of victory, soldiers in the trenches dreamed only of ending the senseless killing and returning home. Trench warfare on the Western and Eastern Front had turned into a struggle for survival not only with the enemy, but also with nature. In the trenches, only a few dozen metres from the enemy, the British, French, Germans, Russians, Austrians, Hungarians, Slovaks, Czechs, Serbs, Croats and others all froze. From 20th December, the snow-fed rainfall fell on Europe. The trenches were knee-deep in freezing mud in which hungry rats and lice ate the dead. The mud stank not only from the corpses, but also from the excrement of the soldiers who'd had to soil themselves where they stood. To leave a trench meant certain death.

The soldier, Graham Williams, from the London Rifle Brigade was freezing on guard in the morning of Christmas Eve in a forest near Ypres. Shivering from the cold, his feet freezing in the soaked puttees, with a frozen hand he tried to unstiffen his solid military cloak. He was thinking of one thing, home. A hundred metres away from Graham Williams, a German corporal, Peter Hartmann freezing in the same stench and frost also had his mind on one thing, home. Suddenly Graham became alert. He felt as if he were dreaming. From the German side came the tones of a famous song; Silent night, holy night All is calm, all is bright... A chorus of deep, sad, male voices. He couldn't resist and put his head out as did other British soldiers. Nobody shot at them. They looked toward the German trenches, over which there were Christmas trees, decorated with candles. "Stille Nacht, heilige Nacht, alles schläft, einsam wacht..." Graham stared uncomprehendingly at his friends and suddenly some of them began to sing: "Silent night, Holy night, all is calm, all is bright..." From the French trenches, "O, nuit de paix, Sainte nuit, dans le ciel..." From the frozen trenches near Ypres a song of witness floated to the heavens from German, British and French lads dying for the power ambitions of their politicians and generals whom they hated with their souls. A soldier named Amiens was imprisoned because in response to a General's question about the difference between a military exercise and a real battle, he replied that there were no generals in a real battle. Graham Williams pulled a candle from his pocket, tied it to his rifle, lit it and lifted it up. All his comrades emulated him. He stepped out of the trench and followed the others toward the Germans, who were coming closer to them. Then they smiled at each other, embraced and shook hands. They were joined by more and more men though they were not to know that on that Christmas Eve, they wished each other peace and tranquility on both sides of a forty-five-kilometer-long section of the front. German and British military bands played songs together, soldiers sipped tea, and in the Ploegsteer Wood, the Saxons shared their kegs of beer with British forces and were served traditional Christmas pudding I return. They shared their stories in broken German or English and found out they were much the same people as each other, freezing for their masters in the same shit and mud. When officers began to join their soldiers, the generals began to perceive the dangers being born in Ypres. The danger was called PEACE. When the British and the Germans helped each other carry away and bury their dead, the battlefields were dominated by a frozen silence. The earth was frozen, so they dug communal graves together. When they buried those who had been shot, the German and British chaplains served mass. At the conclusion, they prayed together: "Our Father, who art in heaven, hallowed be thy name... Vater unser im Himmel, Geheiligt werde Dein Name... Notre Père qui est aux cieux! Que ton nom soit sanctifié..." Soon there was a general order to terminate fraternization immediately. Those who refused to return to their positions were to be executed. The remainder said goodbye and went back to the trenches to kill each other...

Despite his health problems, Štefánik's dream came true thanks to the intervention of Emil Chautemps. On the 26th January, he received a despatch from the War Department, announcing that he should report to the 102nd Infantry Regiment in Chartres and collect military equipment. From there he would be transferred to a military flying school where naval officer and airman, Štefánik's peer, Pierre Cayle was charged with the rapid preparation of fighter pilots. Fourteen new Farman aircraft were available at Chartres Military Aviation School, which belonged to the Dijon Air Group. In January the course began and on 11th April the first twenty-five graduates left with a diploma in machine management for the MF – Maurice Farman, one of whom was Štefánik, who had been promoted on 3rd March to corporal. He received a class R diploma for reconnaissance flights and was transferred from Chartres for further training in the MF 54 fighter squadron in Le Bourget. At that time, Anatole de Monzie took Štefánik to the famous Parisian salon of Sarah Claire Boas de Jouvenel, who'd recently divorced his friend Henry de Jouvenel. There were many people in the salon and Sarah barely noticed the young officer.

Eleven days after being promoted to the rank of temporary air Lieutenant, he was transferred to the 10th Army on 14th May, which was part of the Northern Army Group under the command of Marshal Foch. Štefánik arrived there when this army was preparing for a decisive counteroffensive in northern France. Intense fighting began on 9th May in the area of Artois, the Czechoslovak company *Nazdar* in the French Foreign Legion's combat formation also taking part. Forty-three members of the company fell and a hundred were badly wounded. Štefánik also took part in the offensive, carrying out reconnaissance flights over German trenches, which he even photographed. His aircraft was hit several times by German anti-aircraft artillery and on 3rd July he was forced down in a wheat field. The plane broke up during the landing, but fortunately the pilot with his mechanic, Bourdon, escaped without injury. He waited for the arrival of nightfall and eventually rejoined his unit. Before every intelligence flight Štefánik would check to see if he had a loaded pistol. In the event of capture, he would have been punished by the death penalty as a traitor to the Austro-Hungarian Empire. On the front he spent forty hours in the air and carried out thirty combat reconnaissance flights. With Bourdon, he was instrumental in mounting a telescope and radio station on his aircraft, a novelty in the Air Force.

At the beginning of June, at the headquarters of the General Staff in the castle of Brias, he dared to contradict the Chief of the Northern Army, General Foch. He warned him of possible losses that threatened the Air Force the next day.

"Why do you think that?" Foch didn't understand.

"There will be a storm," said the prophetic Lieutenant. The General was convinced and there was a storm the following day. At Foch's command, General Weygand, Chief of Staff of the Northern Army Group, invited Štefánik to dinner. The passionate Lieutenant impressed him so much, he soon gave a lecture on meteorology for General Staff training. Immediately afterwards, General Foch appointed him Chief of Meteorological Service to the Northern Army Group. For this reason, he was often sent to Allied Army Headquarters in Chantilly, north of Paris.

On 1st May, the luxury liner, *Lusitania* with 1,959 passengers on board sailed from New York. They'd decided to travel despite the German Embassy's warning that the ship would be sailing in the war zone in British waters, so passengers would travel at their own risk. The unsuspecting passengers didn't connect the date of the voyage to the recent disastrous defeat of Britain and the allies by the Ottoman Empire in the Dardanelles, nor the battle of Gorlice, where the Germans and Austrians broke the Russian defences. The Allies were beginning to lose and in both London and Paris, there was a strong call for a US entry into the war. But President Wilson had refused so far. The ship headed east, strangely without its usual escort of destroyers. Shortly before it set sail Winston Churchill, First Lord of the Admiralty, wrote a letter to Walter Runciman, the President of the Board of Trade, stating that it is "most important to attract neutral shipping to our shores, in the hope especially of embroiling the United States with Germany. If something happens to some ships, all the better." It happened. The *Lusitania* astonishingly slowed down on 7th May instead of speeding up. It became an easy target for German torpedoes. After interception by a single German submarine torpedo U 22, the huge ship sank in eighteen minutes with the loss of 128 US citizens, including children. The sinking of the *Lusitania* fulfilled its purpose. It provoked indignation in the United States and people demanded an end to US neutrality. President Wilson decided to revoke the US embargo on loans to the fighting parties. The largest US bank, J. P. Morgan, lent $500 million to Britain and France in October 1915. To be sure, they also lent to Germany "just" $27 million.

After the promise of London to recognize Italian claims on Dalmatia, Italy declared war on Austria on 23rd May, 1915 but not yet on Germany. The Adriatic Sea was declared Italian by which they automatically embarked on a conflict of interest with the Serbs, who were also interested in Dalmatia, and, like the Italians, were on the anti-Austrian side.

In May, while Masaryk was writing a memorandum on the future Czecho-Slovak state for the British Foreign Ministry, Karel

Kramář was arrested in Prague. Alois Rašín was arrested the following month.

On Sunday, 6th July 1915, the five hundredth anniversary of Jan Hus's burning, Slovaks, Czechs, Russians, Serbs, French, Slovenes, Croats and, naturally, Swiss were gathered in the Reformation Hall in Geneva. In an emotional performance, which was essentially an open statement of foreign resistance to Austria, Masaryk said: "There is no reconciliation between the Czech and Austrian ideas established in our country by force with the help of the Counter-Reformation. We hope that this great world war will bring our nation to freedom and that we will live to see Czech independence in the spirit of all Czech parties. As Palacký said, we existed before Austria and will exist after it."

Two days later after leaving Geneva, a friend of Štefánik's from Sorbonne University, Professor of History, Arnošt Denis, called on the powers to "repay their debt to the Czechs and Slovaks and help them free themselves from the Austro-Hungarian carcass". Naturally, the treasonous activities of the Austrian citizen and deputy of the Imperial Assembly, Masaryk, didn't escape the attention of the Austrians, who sent warnings to the neutral Swiss government. In fear of vengeance from Vienna, the Swiss issued a statement by which every foreigner who committed anti-Austrian propaganda was warned to return to his country of origin. That would have meant a death sentence for Masaryk. On 4th August, Friedrich Habsburg signed an international arrest warrant and issued an order to seize his property. Masaryk left Geneva in August 1915 with his daughter Olga and went to France. It was not a moment too soon as Austrian secret police in neutral Switzerland were watching his every move. When Štefánik learned that his favorite professor had come to France, he tried to make contact with him. However, Masaryk didn't respond. Shortly after Masaryk, Beneš also emigrated and went to Geneva on 3rd September. From September Masaryk was active in London, where he arrived on a Serbian passport. His friend Seton-Watson linked him with British military intelligence to whom he gave information on the Austro-Hungarian army. His son Ján was honoured for bravery in combat and promoted to First Lieutenant in the Austro-Hungarian army, in which Štefánik's brothers fought as well. In a fratricidal war, father fought against son, brother against brother.

CHAPTER 3
The Weak Wait for an Opportunity, the Strong Create It

The madness of the war reached new levels, both sides feverishly developing more and more devastating and terrifying weapons. On 22nd April, 1915, green and yellow clouds appeared over British and French trenches near Ypres, gradually merging into a compact, green-yellow sky from which nothing escaped. German officers had released 150 tons of deadly gas from thousands of bottles, which the wind took over enemy positions. For the first time in history, poison was used against an enemy in war. 1,200 soldiers died immediately and three thousand were blinded for life. The deadly chlorine gas was invented by a German chemist, Fritz Haber, who may have personally directed the attack and whose wife Klara committed suicide after this chemical weapon was used. The personal tragedy of Haber was the fact that as a Jew he served German anti-Semitism.

In contrast to the largely static trench warfare in the west, massive combat movements took place on the eastern front, which soon stretched from the Baltic to the Black Sea. The key point of the fighting was the Austrian crown's territories within the boundaries of historical Galicia and also around Bardejov, Humenné, Medzilaborce, Snina, Stropkov and Svidník, where war was waged from November 1914 to May 1915. Three days after declaration of war the Russian government ordered a general mobilization in order to help Slavic Serbia. The next day Germany declared war on Russia. The delicate balance of power crumbled, a hellish machine in an atmosphere of whipped up nationalism spun out of control. In the west the Germans counted on a lightning defeat of France and the transfer of armies to the east to help Austria-Hungary fight Russia. Russia, on the other hand, had the goal of defeating the weaker Austro-Hungarian Empire and then Germany, thereby dominating Central Europe. The Germans scattered the Russians in East Prussia at Tannenberg, while the Russians scattered the Austrians at Galicia on the San River. The Germans didn't keep their promise to the Austrians and left substantial forces in the West in the hope of victory over the French and the British. The Austro-Hungarian armies thus became twice as weak as the Russians after mobilization. The Russians approached the border of German Silesia, the November offensive of General Brusilov bringing Russian troops and even its supreme commander to the village of Zborov near Bardejov, where Brusilov stayed on 20th November, 1914 in the house of the notary, Joseph Schultz.

Štefánik understood that it was necessary for France and his allies to have the sincerity of Czech and Slovak efforts demonstrated not only in speech but above all in fighting. He'd fly deep behind enemy lines. On 3rd June he and Captain d'Aragon miscalculated their flight distance, however, and ran out of gas when returning from a reconnaissance flight. During the emergency landing, the aircraft was damaged but the men escaped without injury. His exploratory flights were beneficial in the planning of French attacks, but it was little for an ambitious airman. He wanted to prove his skill and especially his courage in combat. At the same time, he was looking for an opportunity to influence Czechs and Slovaks fighting against the allies.

At the time, the Austro-Hungarian troops hadn't yet been deployed on the western front, so on 31st August, at the time of Masaryk's arrival in Paris, he left at his own request to support his Slavic brothers on the Serbian front. The Serbian army was fighting with incredible determination against a huge force. Out of 450,000 Serbian men, 180,000 had fallen. Since March 1915, a French squadron of MFS 99 had a strength of 9 officers and 85 men serving nine aircraft.

With his mechanic Bourdon and his orderly Garon, they headed for Févent Castle, where he'd been invited by the hero of the Battle of Marne, the Chief of the Northern Army, General Ferdinand Foch. Soldiers in blue coats and red trousers stood in front of the entrance but though they were impressive, in the field they presented an easy target for the enemy. Štefánik persuaded Foch of the necessity of agitation on the fronts where the Czechs and Slovaks were fighting, most of whom were on the Serbian and Italian fronts. He begged him to explain to the leaders of France that the morale of the Slavic soldiers in the Austro-Hungarian army was very low and that they didn't want to fight the Russians and the Serbs.

After a long conversation, the Chief of the Army personally accompanied Štefánik to his car, which was considered an unusually friendly gesture.

"Honoured Lieutenant, during your tenure in the 10th Army, you have, in addition to the valuable knowledge of a scientist, also shown the fine qualities of bravery, cool-headedness and considered courage. You have shown evidence of the most perfect military spirit. My dear sir, we are at war, so we can't say for sure whether we will ever meet again. In the short time that I've had the opportunity to communicate with you, I've understood that if we had more such determined soldiers as you, the victory of our forces would be certain. The Tenth Army feels your departure with great regret. Thank you."

"I'm part of a state that has an historic mission in this war, to defeat evil. Therefore, I don't for a minute think that evil will win. France will be the main winner of this war under your command!

During the time, my dear General, that I've had the opportunity to be close to you, I'm convinced that you are not only a great soldier, but also a man with a great heart, amazing inner strength and immense character. They rightfully say that you are a successor to Napoleon."

"I don't think so," the General smiled. "There was only one Napoleon. Do you know why he was so successful? Because one of his principles was that the weak wait for an opportunity, the strong create one."

After leaving the car, the General stared for a long time at the billows of dust that Štefánik's vehicle whirled up. That devilish Lieutenant had completely turned his head.

CHAPTER 4
I'll Give Up When I Die

After the Cer and Kolubara battles, the Serbian Air Force had only one aircraft. On 2nd March, 1915, a French "air fleet", with eight Maurice Farman aircraft, material and air personnel came to the rescue. The French air unit was located at Banjica airport near Belgrade, where it remained until the retreat of Serbian troops in the fall of 1915. Its task was to conduct reconnaissance flights over enemy positions.

From Marseille, Štefánik went to Piraeus and from there through Salonika to the headquarters of the Serbian troops in the town of Ralje, where the crew of the MFS 99 (Maurice Farman Serbe) squadron was accommodated in makeshift tents. He arrived when the Serbian army had been reduced to 40,000 men. On the evening of 26th September, the entrance tarpaulin to the largest tent, which was at the same time the place of the squadron commander, kitchen and dining room, was pulled aside. It was pouring, a cold wind was blowing and the men, who were just preparing for dinner, glanced coldly at the short, wet man who was shaking rain mixed with snow from his Lieutenant's cap.

"Bonsoir, I'm Lieutenant Štefánik," the new arrival said dryly.

"Welcome, we were waiting for you," said Major Roger Vitrat. "Dinner?"

The guest nodded. The major invited him to the table. Štefánik pulled a bottle of the best Courvoisier from his briefcase.

"A small entrance fee to the club," he smiled.

"Oh, Napoleon's cognac, bravo, Lieutenant, a good beginning," one of the pilots remarked. During the meal he answered many questions heartily and with respect for his colleagues. The atmosphere gradually relaxed and the airmen came to life. Before midnight, the Lieutenant pulled out his cards and cheered the airmen up with his tricks. From the very first moment, he won the sympathy of those present, even though they detected a foreign accent in his French.

"You come here in difficult times," said Vitrat. "On 7th October, the German Field Marshal Mackensen began a German-Austrian offensive against the ten times weaker Serbs. Germans, Hungarians, and Bulgarians have broken the front line on the Sava."

"The Bulgarians betrayed..." one of the officers spat out acidly.

"They betrayed as they betrayed... Berlin promised them a part of Macedonia, which the Serbs claim, so they joined them," Vitrat declared. "We won over the Italians from the Germans on the other hand. It's said that they've been promised much of Dalmatia. That's how it goes in politics."

"We've basically lost the Serbs. They're interested in Dalmatia, but as we've promised it to the Italians, they no longer trust us. I'm afraid that they see our presence here just as a kind of propaganda," said Štefánik. There was a note of remorse in his words. "But the

Italians did declare war on the Austrians. Their former ally... hm... The spoils promised by the deal are bigger."

"Excuse me, I don't want to be rude, but according to your accent I guess you aren't a Frenchman," one of the pilots suggested.

"I'm a naturalized Frenchman, but I'm a Slovak from Upper Hungary."

"So I understand why the negotiated movement with regard to your Slavic brothers Serbs is a matter of regret to you," Vitrat turned to Štefánik.

Štefánik was silent.

"Well, let's be fair, we were happy to join the English-Russian agreement to divide Turkey. We even refused to sell aircraft to the Serbs, although they were willing to pay in cash..." one of the officers said.

"I'm sad that the angry Serbs, disappointed by the inaction of the Allies, regard all prisoners as the same criminals and don't recognize whether they are Hungarians, Austrians or Slavs," said Štefánik shaking his head.

"And do you wonder? They should go back to their assurance that they'll get Dubrovnik and Dalmatia."

"In spite of all this, I believe that Serbian places will allow me to recruit among the Czech and Slovak prisoners who, as I have been informed, account for half of the total of 77,000," said Štefánik.

"I'll keep my fingers crossed, but I'm not sure. You haven't seen the shit that Austrians and Hungarians do to Serbian people. Those beasts hang old men, women and children, burn villages and destroy Orthodox churches. They aren't engaged in war, but a criminal expedition. In almost every village there is a gallows in the square on which the Honved troops hang people just as a warning. Some of them were said to be swinging too much on the gallows, so they nailed them on to make sure. Are these people human?"

The commander put a few photos on the table and Štefánik's stomach turned over.

"I'm afraid that in such a situation, the Serbs don't distinguish very much whether those who execute their relatives en masse are evil Hungarians or good Slovaks. They all have the same uniforms..."

"I always carry a vial of poison. I wouldn't like to end that way... If they catch me, it's clear that as a traitor they aren't going to cuddle me," Štefánik said dryly.

"Then don't take on the bad guys! Our task is to fly over enemy positions and give information to Serbian headquarters. If we can put down a Gerry or a Bulgar, it's only a bonus. Anyway let's go bed; tomorrow's first reconnaissance flight awaits you," Vitrat said pleasantly.

"They'll try to squeeze us, but we will not give up!" said the Lieutenant.

The next day, before breakfast, he sat bent over his maps and studied the terrain where he would be flying. As soon as he was ready for the aircraft, he flew some practice flights over Banat and Báč. Four days later, two German reconnaissance planes appeared over Kragujevac. Štefánik had been in his Farman for half an hour in the air and started to follow them. When two more machines joined him, they managed to drive off the German aircraft together with machine guns. On the first of October, after the mist disappeared from Palanka Airport with Bourdon in a Farman, he embarked on a reconnaissance flight. When returning to the airport over the top of Kovijon, his engine was hit at six hundred metres by a German Albatros which had suddenly appeared near them. The engine stopped but Štefánik masterfully glided down to an area covered with bushes near the airport. The plane was damaged, but fortunately nothing happened to the pilot and the mechanic. A moment later airmen and mechanics came running and after finding out that they were both saved, burst out laughing.

On 3rd October, however, German bombing began, and so the squadron moved to Niš. When the alarm went off on 11th October, Štefánik happened to be talking to Captain Labry during some light drizzle. A moment later a Hungarian plane appeared over the airport. Štefánik and Bourdon fueled and loaded up with ammunition and gasoline like lightning, jumped into their machine and took off for a two-hour dogfight. Štefánik's Farman returned with a few hits, the pilot stepped out of the plane, came up to Captain Labry and carried on talking to him as if nothing had happened.

During nearly four hours of flight on October 25th, he and his Serbian observer, Captain Božović, were shot at by Bulgarian artillery. Bulgarian pressure forced the Serbs to retreat towards the Albanian border. Štefánik got to Kruševac and after repairing the aircraft continued on to Raška, the new headquarters of the General Staff of the Serbian army and his squadron. Due to lack of gasoline they'd had to make an emergency landing in a field near the town of Alexandrovać. After refuelling, he took off with Bourdon, but found that the aircraft had a damaged propeller and again made an emergency landing. They tried to repair the machine, but enemy movements made it impossible and so they destroyed the machine. They loaded the usable parts on to a vehicle and went on to Raška.

An unusual event happened in Alexandrovac; on 4th November he met his old friend from his Prague studies, Ján Procházka, who hardly recognized him. He'd shaved off his abundant beard so the expression on his face couldn't help but register the hardships of war and his persistent stomach problems.

"Milanko, what are you doing here?" exclaimed the astonished Procházka.

"Janko, is it you? Well, what am I doing here?" Štefánik shrugged as they reached out to embrace. "I came to help the Serbs and recruit some of ours. If I should die, let me be buried in a part that is forever Slavic... And what about you?"

"They evacuated us from Čuprije, I'm the director of the sugar refinery there... It's said that Kragujevac, where the Serbian headquarters was, has fallen... Where are you headed?"

"To Raška."

"No longer possible. The road has been cut off and the only retreat is towards Priština. The 10-times weaker Serbian army has succumbed. The Entente welshed on the deal. 80,000 lads were sent against the Bulgarians, but they landed in Salonika and headed straight north along the Vardar. They've left us to our fate," Procházka stated bitterly.

"I've got to contact my commander," Štefánik wondered aloud.

"You can forget that completely!"

On Saturday, 6th November, Štefánik decided to destroy all parts of the aircraft. After lunch with Procházka and Bourdon, they set out with the most necessary things on a small cart on the 150-kilometre road, to the airfield at Mitrovica, not knowing if it would end at all. They spent the night by the Lesenovačský stream in the open air, went on slowly, sometimes pulling the cart themselves, but it got harder and harder. The dirt roads, especially on mountain passes, had become total mud pits. By Brus they were completely bogged down and could only carry on thanks to the help of retreating Belgrade bakers. They slept by another stream and stayed overnight in the open-air cemetery at Razbojna, exposed to the persistent rain and snow. Daytime temperatures were about eight degrees, at night they dropped to minus two. They couldn't fall asleep for the cold, so chose to go through the Janko Klisura pass at half past four in the morning to avoid frostbite. At the River Brvenica, Procházka said farewell to them and the two soaking, frozen airmen continued under threat of attack from Bulgarians in their calamitous journey to the Albanian hills. A retreating unit from Kragujevac gave them an ox, which could hardly move its legs by itself, so each time they climbed, both had to help the starved animal pull the cart. The roads were full of trudging soldiers trying to save their lives. Dead animals and frozen soldiers lying on the sides of the roads shocked them at first, but they gradually got used to them. In the mountains, on 10th November, a bunch of starved peasants fell upon them during the night, but with the retreating soldiers they fought them off.

Climbing the slippery terrain took 12 hours. During the ascent, a bag of grain was torn by the Serbs and spilled into the mud. The starving Austrian, Hungarian and Bulgarian prisoners began to brawl, stuffing into mouths chattering from cold and hunger handfuls of grain mixed with mud. By the third day Štefánik was shivering from chills and his stomach refused to take in any food. Bourdon tried to give him some warm tea and looked for a doctor in the crowd of retreating soldiers, civilians and prisoners, but everyone was too busy struggling to save at least their own life. A mother, carrying her baby wrapped in soaked rags, noticed after some time that the baby was no longer moving and was frozen. An exhausted old couple decided to finish with everything and sat resignedly on a soaked rock way from the road where snow and rain slowly, mercifully freed them from earthly hardships. Bourdon harnessed himself to the ox-drawn wagon and pulled the cart carrying the rest of the food and ailing sick Štefánik. He realized that if his friend did not keep moving, he would die. But he just rested his head on a ragged sheepskin and curled up in pain. He alternately fell in and out of consciousness and when he came round in the darkness he barely sensed the creeping shadows of mud and snow. In moments of consciousness, the words of a shaman from Raiatea Island came back to him. "God does not send suffering to the weak, but to those whom he has chosen to be strong. Be friends with pain and search for its meaning. To come to this hell was your own decision."

On 12th November they managed to reach Priština, from where Bourdan took him by train to Kosovská Mitrovica. His condition had deteriorated considerably. To be certain, he decided to hand over his personal papers and secret notes to his friend, Raoul Fabry, who, as a Russian scholar, had been assigned as an interpreter to the Serbian General Staff. Fabry found him in Mitrovac, in a Turkish hut lying twisted in pain with his head resting on a sack. When he approached him, Milan forced a smile.

"Mon cher ami... I'm done for. The propeller of my plane broke; landing after the engine went was very hard. When it crashed my wound reopened. I don't have any strength, I'm bleeding into my stomach, I don't even want warm milk – that was all I could get down. You've always been my confidant. Promise me that you'll pass all this to Masaryk on your return to Paris."

He pulled out papers and a sweat-stained, damp notebook from his breast pocket.

"Here is everything I have in my heart and everything we have to do to free my homeland. Here are my designs, a letter for Masaryk, plans, projects and lists of Czechs enlisted in the army. My last wish is to be buried in a grave without a name, so that the enemy won't find me. The Austrians would hang my corpse."

"My dear Lieutenant, Milan, no, no, you aren't dying. I know you well and I know you've already experienced worse than this. Was it easier to spend three weeks without food in a frozen shed on Mont Blanc?"

"Thank you for your comfort, but then I could see a way out. I don't see it here. Not with this enemy bombardment and all the people's despair."

"Dear friend, God is testing you and death is only a possibility. If you choose it like a coward, God won't condemn you for that, he won't judge anyone, but he certainly won't lift a finger for you. But if you choose life, God will commend you for your brave decision. Anybody can die, but to live, my friend, to live... We'll get you to the port at Vlorë, put you in Italian hands. Our Italian allies who'll take you by ship to an Italian hospital and from there to Paris."

"How do you propose to get me to Vlorë, 350 kilometres across snow-covered passes?" Štefánik smiled bitterly. "At two thousand metres, when I can barely make it to the toilet? The enemy will be here any minute, I don't want to fall into their hands, I don't want them to hang me."

"Major Vitrat has decided Captain Dangelzer would take you to Prizren by plane."

"Not in any event. You mustn't weaken the squadron even by a single combat machine. And there is no hope for me anyway."

"Lieutenant Štefánik, you are a soldier and you must obey orders. The Major has decided and it's settled!"

"That's good of him, but Prizren is not Vlorë."

"In Prizren you'll refuel and continue to Vlorë."

"From Prizren to Vlorë? It's at least three hours across the Čierny Drim mountain pass. No one has ever flown over it, especially in such weather."

"We can leave you in Prizren, Dr. Dominique Dumas will take care of you, but the Bulgarians are moving devilishly fast. Dumas can escape from Prizren, but you can't in such a state. Do you want to fall into their hands?"

"I don't have the strength…"

"So you're going to give up when you've already travelled the road of death? Several hundred Czechs and Slovaks who have joined the Serbs from the prison camp in Niš have overcome the same road of suffering and reached the ship to Valona, from where the Italians sail to Asinar Island. There the men are preparing to go west to the Czechoslovak army!"

At the mention of the Czechoslovak army, Štefánik's face came to life for a while, but the cruel hardships he'd withstood in the mountains had taken almost all his strength.

"And the booming you hear is the Bulgarian guns!" Fabry insisted.

Štefánik remained silent for a while, then quietly asked: "Does Dangelzer have experience of flying in the mountains?"

"Captain Paulhan volunteered. He's the most experienced airman we have here."

"Captain Louis Paulhan, the French aviator who won the London-Manchester race and became famous for defending Belgrade?"

"The very same."

Štefánik sat up, his eyes bright with the old optimistic gleam.

"Can I get some warm milk somewhere?"

"I've brought you some," Fabry handed him a thermos. Štefánik drank in gulps.

"Fine, I'll even go to death with Paulhan. I think you're right about those obstacles. I'm starting to feel that the bigger they are the more energy I have to overcome them."

"I'll contact your friend Senator Monza right away and inform him that you'll be in Brindisi tomorrow. They'll take you by submarine. As far as I know, it is the nearest Italian naval base," Fabry informed him enthusiastically.

"Thank you, my dear Raoul."

CHAPTER 5

Whoever Dies Without Desires Has Lived a True Life

The apocalypse of war took a new turn. The English and the French landed in Salonika, the Germans conquered Warsaw, Bulgarian Slavs began killing Serbian Slavs, the dead were counted in millions and the world got used to it. The war also entered popular language; in the Allied countries, hamburgers were renamed "Freedom Sandwiches", a German Shepherd was now called a "police dog," in Britain they ceased to use the name "Cologne" for perfume, forbade the playing of Beethoven, Wagner, Mozart, stopped teaching German and sauerkraut was renamed the cabbage of freedom. In Germany they stopped drinking French cognac and Russian vodka and instead of the usual greeting Guten Tag used *Gott Strafe England*

(God punishes England). In London, people looted German shops and threw German pianos out of the windows. Despite dancing ladies and noble sons exempted from the war, the Hungarian *czardas*, increasingly popular in Parisian dance halls, was strictly outlawed.

Fear of the progress of Russians in Galicia, where Austro-Hungarian soldiers were blessed by field chaplain, Jozef Tiso, as well as the possible arrival of the Russian army in Prague, aroused pathological reactions among Austrian and Hungarian state officials in the monarchy. If a police patrol heard someone begin a greeting *Držime sa* (We will keep going), they were put in prison as Vienna claimed this was a secret Slavic signal. In Upper Hungary, diligent officials devised ways to get more money from the population to finance military costs. In Nitra, on the Town Hall Square, they erected an iron Turul bird and sold nails that were hammered into the wooden base of the statue. The price of a gold nail with the name of the donor was 50 crowns, the price of the silver nail 10 crowns, an iron nail for workers cost one crown and for students and children 20 hallers.

On 22nd October, 1915, representatives of the Slovak League in America and the Czech National Association signed a five-point joint document in Cleveland, United States that entered history as the Cleveland Agreement. The first point of the agreement was the demand for the state independence of the Czech lands and Slovakia and the union of the Czech and Slovak nations in a federal system. The document spoke of "the joining of the Czech and Slovak nations into a federal union with full national self-government for Slovakia."

Štefánik was in agony in Kosovska Mitrovica when, on 14th November 1915, a declaration of the Czech Foreign Committee in Paris began the official anti-Austrian resistance. It effectively declared war on Austria-Hungary and was signed by the deputies of the Austrian Parliament, Tomáš Garrigue Masaryk and Josef Dürich, as well as representatives of Czecho-Slovak organizations in Russia, France, England and the USA. Despite the fact that there was no mention of Slovaks in the statement as agreed in Cleveland, the President of the Slovak League in the United States, Albert Mamatey and its secretary, Ivan Daxner the Elder, signed the declaration in the interests of demonstrating Czecho-Slovak unity. Unfortunately, the statement didn't meet with greater international reaction.

Despite heavy fog, the Farman aircraft with Captain Paulhan and Štefánik, wrapped in several layers of clothing, took off from Prizren towards Vlorë on 22nd November, 1915. It left just in time because the first Bulgarian patrols had already begun to penetrate the outskirts of the city. Sitting behind Paulhan, Štefánik had only a hand-drawn sketch of northern Albania on his knees, which was almost unreadable in the rain, fog, ten-degree frost and the eighty-kilometre speed. Out of caution, Paulhan didn't fly at the maximum speed of 120 kilometres because the mountains that they had to fly over were 1,500 metres high and the altimeter only went up to 1,200 metres. They seem to have been protected by an unseen hand; the mist momentarily dispersed just as they were flying over rocks barely thirty metres from the wings away. Paulhan had pushed the plane a few yards up at the last moment and they cleared the rocks. After half an hour, the clouds parted and when they saw the Adriatic Sea they gave a thumbs up. But this was premature as the Italian port guard fired on them as they approached to land after three and a half hours of flight. Thanks to Paulhan's brilliant airmanship, they landed on a wet meadow. The Italians came to capture them, but when they discovered who they were, they were taken to the port which had already been informed about Štefánik. Deputy de Monzie, through his contacts, had arranged for the transport of Štefánik by torpedo boat to Brindisi. The next day, 24th November, 1915, the French Lieutenant was hospitalized in the Regina Margherita hospital in Rome. On the same day, the Serbian Front finally fell. The heroic and betrayed Serbian army collapsed in the historic fields of Kosovo. As a result Germany had managed to connect directly with its ally, Turkey through the humiliation of Serbia and Bulgaria.

His friend Raoul not only contacted Monzie, but also described Štefánik's desperate state of health, exhorting him to intervene in Rome because the seriously ill and injured Lieutenant urgently needed surgery and the best care. Fortunately, Monzie's wife was a close friend of one of Paris's most influential ladies, Sarah Claire Boas de Jouvenel, who was happy to intervene with her Roman friends. They provided Štefánik with the best doctors, who gave him such care that an operation wasn't needed. Štefánik quickly recovered: the beneficial Mediterranean climate of the Eternal City soothed both his body and mind after his Serbian hardships. Sometimes he started out of sleep at night, dreaming of frozen corpses lining the distressed road of Kosovo. After the hardships in the icy mountains, the warm and clean Roman hospital seemed like a miracle to him. After a long time, he could consider life, the world, the future in peace. He was thirty-five years old and felt infinitely tired. He recorded his thoughts, insights, and desires in his diary. "I know that the life I have is short, so I have to make the best use of what remains. If I do, I will die peacefully. We sigh that life is short, but we waste it so recklessly. I wander in the world alone and sad, my only happiness is to become useful. I believe in a higher ideal, I want to serve. You look for a goal in life? Make preparations for death. Whoever dies without desires and regrets has lived a happy and true life."

One day he thought he was dreaming. A lady entered the room, accompanied by the director of the hospital, a senior doctor, several unknown ladies and senior Italian officers. Wracked with pain, he realized that it was Margherita of Savoy, the queen dowager. She spoke a few encouraging words to him and listened carefully to the war experiences of the young pilot. At that time, he had no idea that the Queen dowager's court mistress of ceremonies, a priestess of Venosa, would soon enter his life and help the young officer enter not only the Margherita's family circle, but open doors to important and influential Italian politicians. He had no idea that a fateful Roman lady would appear in his life.

CHAPTER 6
Help me Liberate My Country!

A week after his discharge from hospital, he travelled by train through Genoa and Nice to Paris, where he arrived the day before the feast of Saint Nicholas. He asked his friend, Anatole de Monzie, to take him with him to the palace on the Boulevard Saint-Germain, belonging to the writer, Madame de Jouvenel, the former wife of the journalist, Baron Henri de Jouvenel. Sarah de Jouvenel was the daughter of a wealthy Jewish entrepreneur, Alfred Boas, the owner of several hotels, but most of all a zinc factory, in the time of war a strategic raw material for the production of medicines. Although Henri de Jouvenel, the editor-in-chief of the influential newspaper *Le Matin*, had divorced Sarah, he had remained on good terms with her. The opportunity to thank her came the very next day, St. Nicholas's. He bought gifts and with a huge bouquet, he and Anatole went to the famous Paris salon. The beautiful woman, less than a year older than Štefánik, was surprised by the strange gallantry of the foreigner. He came in a military uniform, but Anatole introduced his friend as a famous astronomer and traveller. For a while, Štefánik's eyes wandered over the luxurious furnishings of the drawing room lit up by the latest fashion: electric lamps – they had still used candles the last time he was there. He looked at the solid furniture, the brocade curtains, the extravagant dresses of the ladies present and the black suits and anthracite jackets of quality wool, complemented by white shirts with the stiff collars of distinguished gentlemen. Some of them had black top hats on their knees.

"Madame, let me give you the real pearl of Tahiti Island as a thank you for saving my life."

Štefánik handed Sarah a small box with a shell in which a beautiful pearl was hidden. The Baroness gave a whoop of surprise, dropped her guard and enthusiastically planted kisses on both Štefánik's cheeks. She circulated the pearl around those present who responded with admiration.

"Amazing, beautiful, true Tahitian pearl…"

"In the east, they call pearls the Orient, the rising sun," smiled her satisfied guest. "According to them, it is the task of every person to take out the pearl from the shell and cultivate it. We have a precise amount of time for that. It's like when a pilot has a certain amount of gasoline and since he doesn't know what to expect on his journey, he tries to fly straight to his destination. However, when we extend our flight with spins and tricks in order to vainly attract spectators, we may waste our gasoline and not make it to our destination."

"I think it is a matter of experience. The pilot may take on gasoline and start again," objected Sauerwein.

"A pilot yes, but a person won't get a second chance."

Štefánik felt that several of them already knew about him and it turned out that the mistress of the house had spoken of him to her friends. It was obvious that they were eagerly awaiting the conversation of the mysterious man who spoke excellent French, but from his accent sounded like a foreigner. The energy of the vivacious fellow with sparkling blue eyes actually filled the whole salon after a while. His hostess patiently presented the guests, who asked him questions, and when the young Lieutenant seemed unable to remember a name, she repeated it discreetly. Under the influence of fresh experiences from the front he didn't restrain himself and began to describe the daring flights he'd made with Major Vitrat's squadron. There was a deathly silence in the salon at his recollections of the dreadful journey on the corpse-littered road through the mountains. Nobody dared interrupt the Lieutenant and one could sense from the silence of the ladies and gentlemen that they felt French complicity in the defeat of the heroic Serbs. His hostess sensed the unease and asked Štefánik to return to his more pleasing trip to Polynesia. He was piqued that Sarah had steered him away from the sensitive subject of French failure in the Balkans.

He realized that during his first visit it was not appropriate to embarrass the influential host or guests.

"When we built a telegraph station in Tahiti, the locals wanted to know what it would be like. I told them that thanks to this device, people would be able to send messages long distances. Imagine! They weren't at all interested in how technically feasible it was, but they wondered if it could send bad news. When I told them it was, they were disappointed. According to them, it would be a great telegraphic device that could only send good news."

"It would be an invention that would change history. You should work on that," laughed Madame de Jouvenel.

Then the hostess took Štefánik under her arm and took him to the other end of the salon.

"You brought me a gift, let me also give you my books on this beautiful day of St. Nicholas. What else can a writer give? This is my book of fairy tales, my precious friend, that gentleman, wrote the preface," she pointed to a smiling seventy-year-old with a gray hair and wide waxed moustachios drawn out into thin points.

"I am France, Anatole," the man approached Štefánik, bowed and shook his hand.

Štefánik flipped through the book for a moment, and said with astonishment: "But this is what Mr. Ariel has written..."

"That is my pseudonym; female writers, with few exceptions, aren't accepted among male writers very much... That's why I appreciate having precious friends among gentlemen of the pen." In this second book, I try to give the reader a few rules of the game called life. It's called: *Quelques règles du jeu de la vie*," she handed her book to her guest. "In this case, too, a dear man wrote for me, who... you won't believe it but he is also with us today, he's been very curious about you. Monsieur Paul Valéry," she pointed to a forty-year old man seated at the table.

"Oh, sir, it is a great honour for me. I had the honour to read your Introduction to the Method of Leonardo da Vinci. I congratulate you!" Štefánik smiled.

"Let me introduce you to my other dear and excellent friends," she took him intimately by his elbow and walked him through the drawing room decorated with beautiful frescoes, paintings, brocade curtains and crystal chandeliers. "Mademoiselle Louise Weiss, my dear cousin, a journalist, surely the future owner of *L'Europe Nouvelle*. Despite her youth, she has qualifications that enable her to teach and at the same time is the secretary of Senator Perchot," she smiled secretly. Louise smiled sweetly at the guest, her eyes dropped a little and she blushed. "Monsieur Jules Sauerwein, Head of Foreign Affairs of *Le Matin*, Monsieur Philippe Berthelot, Head of the French Ministry of Foreign Affairs, whom I personally call the architect of our foreign policy," she said to Štefánik and whispered intimately to him: "Do you know that his chief and close friend is our Prime Minister and Minister of Foreign Affairs, Monsieur Aristide Briand?" she smiled significantly and continued: "Monsieur Hubert Lagardelle, whom we call a bourgeois revolutionary, has already introduced himself..." Štefánik slowly approached the guests whom the Baroness introduced him to. "Ladies and gentlemen, friends, I have already told you about our dear guest, Monsieur Štefánik. He should have been here earlier, but his health problems delayed him in Rome, where he was treated for injuries and illnesses from the Serbian front, where he endured, as we have heard, incredible hardships. You have confirmed, sir, that modesty is the prerogative of great men. You've told us the beautiful experiences of your travels, but have barely mentioned the heroism of the war..." She smiled and offered him a place beside her. He politely refused to drink absinthe and asked for a cup of tea.

"You don't drink?" asked Valery with astonishment. Štefánik shrugged apologetically. "In a country of wine that is a very serious offence," he smiled mischievously.

"It doesn't sit well on my stomach..."

"That's why you're so serious. Many of us are members of the European Order of Wine Knights, and little suspected that there's a teetotaler in our environment. We wine knights say that those who drink together don't fight together," the poet smiled.

"Well... I've already experienced people who drink together and under the influence of alcohol beat each other up," said the guest. "And I sense that there are Germans and Austrians in the European Order of Wine Knights. It's strange that you now wage war against each other. It seems that wine doesn't always connect..." Štefánik smiled good-naturedly and drank his tea. There was silence, no one knew how to argue against it. "Well, I believe that once this war is over, you'll drink together again, but here I promise you that I'll drink in my new liberated country, too," he smiled.

On his pale face, the gloom of recent suffering could be seen and the occasional stomach rumble indicated that he had still not fully recovered. He put his cup on the table, spread out a map and asked unexpectedly: "What do you see on this map?"

"What do you see on this map?"

Those listening just smiled with embarrassment.

"It seems to be a map of Austria-Hungary. But only at first sight. I see Czecho-Slovakia, Croatia and other countries that will be formed after its defeat," he said with his dream glowing in his eyes. "This is Upper Hungary, we call it Slovakia. Here is where I was born. Slovakia is the sister of your Alsace-Lorraine, ruled there by foreign overlords against the will of the Slovaks. Look, my friends, this is how they treat civilians," he said, suddenly placing on the table a photo showing a gallows where Serbian peasants, men and women were hanging.

"Do you want to say that Austro-Hungary is a dysfunctional state that needs to be liquidated?" asked Sauerwein. Štefánik shook his head. "That is impossible. You can't blame the state for all excesses. It is necessary to rebuild this state from the ground up, preferably as a republic, but to liquidate it would mean total destabilization in Europe. In the eighth point of the war plan of the agreement, it is said that Austria-Hungary would be a threefold monarchy made up of Austria, Bohemia and Hungary. I think that would be best for you Czechs."

"You need to have more incisive arguments if you want to persuade Monsieur Jules Sauerwein," laughed Sarah.

"I'll convince not only Monsieur Sauerwein, but anyone who has a heart. Monsieur Jules," he turned to the head of the foreign section of *Le Matin*. "I'm not a Czech, but a Slovak, and I'll explain to you how Slovaks live. You grew up in a French environment, you went to French schools, you spoke French at home, you graduated in French, you sing your French songs, and you also professed French in love, didn't you?"

"I still do... I don't understand where you're going. How else but in my native language can I tell a beautiful woman, je t'aime?" he laughed.

"So it is logical that every nation should have the right to use its language in schools and offices?"

"That's a matter of course."

"It goes without saying in France, but not in Hungary. In my home country I wasn't allowed to speak Slovak at school, I wasn't allowed to read Slovak books, people are persecuted and imprisoned in our country for speaking in Slovak, they are taught only in Hungarian in schools."

There followed a silence that Madame de Jouvenel finally broke.

"I remember a story from Prague a few years ago. From an automobile, I asked a passer-by in German for directions. He didn't answer me. I turned to my mother, uncomprehending, and asked her how to say it in a foreign language. When that gentleman, he turned out to be a university professor, heard French, he smiled and politely said: "In French, Madame..."

"You don't have much love for the Germans and Hungarians, do you?" Louise Weiss turned to Štefánik.

"I can recommend Louise to your attention. As you can see, she is not only beautiful but also a very promising journalist. She's an assistant to Senator Perchot, director of the Radical Journal, who's a frequent guest in my salon," smiled Sarah.

"The pleasure is on my side," Štefánik said bowing and continued: "We Czechoslovaks like them like this. Let me read." He pulled out the Austrian newspaper, *Wiener Zeitung*, read from it, at the same time translating: "The military order of Emperor Franz Joseph I of 17th April 1915. With great pain I order imperial and royal infantry regiment number 28 to be erased from my army for betrayal and cowardice. The regimental flag may be stored in a military museum. On 3rd April, 1915, in the battle for the Dukla Pass, two battalions of the 28th Infantry Regiment surrendered with officers without the use of a single weapon to a Russian battalion, inflicting the greatest disgrace and shame on themselves. Let Regiment number 28 be eternally erased from the list of Austrian regiments and the Czech soldiers and officers survive to let their blood be shed for this serious offence." Štefánik read, poured his tea and continued. "The Viennese monarchy is rotten, three-quarters of its inhabitants are dissatisfied."

"What you have read out testifies, of course, to the nature of the relationship of the Czechs with the ruling family, but I don't feel, nor does anyone in our ministry of foreign affairs, nor in the government, that the monarchy is rotten and must be broken," Philippe Berthelot intervened. "If we have the right information from our allies in London and St. Petersburg, they haven't even taken the view that Austria-Hungary is inoperative. Certainly, some corrections need to be made, giving more space to nationalities, but we consider the demolition of a unit that is a guarantee of stability in Europe to be premature.

"I firmly believe, sir, it's just your... I beg your pardon... daring dream," Paul Louis added to Berthelot.

"Yes, but dreams are to be fulfilled. I would dare to contradict you. Obviously, Germany has a clear ambition to become a world power, taking over from France and Britain the rule of their colonies and the world oceans. To meet this goal, Germans especially need fuel, meaning the oil that is in the Middle East. The Berlin-Istanbul rail link will come into operation in a month's time, on 15th January next year. This is no coincidence."

"My dear colleague, be reasonable, the traditional Orient Express has been on the Paris-Constantinople line for twenty-five years. Are we therefore to claim that we also have ambitions in the Middle East?" Berthelot objected.

"And don't we?" Lagardelle laughed. "And doesn't Britain?"

"But this train won't be called the Orient Express, but simply a Balkan train. And it will only start to run because our painful loss at Gallipoli has allowed Mackensen to group the triple powers against the Serbs and defeat them. I experienced first-hand what happened afterwards: Austrians and Hungarians mass hanged and shot Serbs, including women and children. And thus the defeat of the Serbs has allowed the re-establishment of Berlin-Istanbul. Austro-Hungary is only a German vassal in which one third, the Austrians and Hungarians control Czechs, Slovaks, Croats, Serbs, Slovenes, Bosnians, Poles, Ruthenians, Italians, Romanians..."

"Slovaks are Hungarians, after all. That was what the Hungarian Prime Minister said..." Louise Weiss said hesitantly after a long pause.

"That's the problem. We are all citizens of Hungary and, in this sense, are Hungarian, but Magyars mark all Hungarians as Magyars..."

"Excuse me, sir, your passion is admirable, but your goal is more than a little utopian. The agreement among the treaty powers is that Austria-Hungary needs not only to be preserved but strengthened to create a strong counterbalance to German expansion in Central Europe," said Paul Louis, editor of *Petit Parisien*. "Your vision is impossible through and through, foolish even."

"My goodness, this cake is wonderful," Sauerwein tried to relieve the tension.

"If the English had such cakes, the Germans would undoubtedly attack them," laughed the journalist.

"True, English cuisine is not worth much," de Monzie added.

"Like the German. That is why they leave the English in peace," Sauerwein laughed.

"At least they have a sense of humour," added de Monzie.

"That and their cuisine is all they've got left," Štefánik added, and the company laughed. He pondered for a moment and looked at Louis piercingly. "Sir, sorry, but having a homeland is our real goal and I believe you can help us. The only thing I ask of you all is to help me free my homeland, our nation." Suddenly his face turned pale, his voice fell silent and he sat down heavily, breathing with difficulty. Sarah poured water for him, but a painful cramp made it impossible for him to put a cup to his mouth. Paul Louis, who was closest to him, grabbed his shoulders firmly and, along with Anatole, led him to the next room where he was put on a couch. After a short time, he calmed down and slept in the bedroom of his hostess.

The next day he was taken to an apartment on Rue Leclerc, but his pain and stomach cramps returned. He had black diarrhea and the right side of his abdomen ached terribly. His friends concluded that leaving him alone would be very risky. He was so weak that he couldn't even carry a bucket of coal from the cellar himself and so the Strimpl family decided to accommodate him at their place.

After a few days he'd recovered a little. It was at Ludvík Strimpl's that he met Edvard Beneš, younger by four years, shortly after Saint Nicholas' Day on 13th December. From the first moment they understood each other; their thoughts, opinions and, in particular, goals were in accord: they both wanted to do everything to break the Austro-Hungarian monarchy. They met almost daily, fervently discussing plans for further collaboration with Professor Masaryk, who was working in London. Štefánik took

Edo with him to Madame de Jouvenel's salon a few days later. It was a time of science and the salon celebrities were the scientists. They could only be surpassed by soldiers. Štefánik fulfilled both qualifications.

His condition had temporarily improved somewhat, and so, two days before Christmas Eve, Mrs de Jouvenel invited him to a friendly meeting where Aristide Briand, the re-elected Prime Minister, was present. This meeting was Štefánik's first entry into the world of top politics. But the intensity of explaining to Briand the goals of Czechoslovak resistance affected his health so much that he was taken to the auxiliary hospital in Neuilly-sur-Seine the next day. Despite severe pain, he wrote a letter to the Prime Minister:

Paris, 24th December, 1915
Sir Prime Minister,
the Manifesto attached here is the one to which I drew your attention during our audience on 22nd December. The Czecho-Slovaks passionately appeal to the powers that have declared their wish to fight for the rights of nations to a free life. They issue this challenge before the gigantic conflict decides definitively the fate of humanity and without fear of the terrible reprisals of the German-Hungarian horde. This Manifesto will be the most eloquent memorial if the four-power axis tragically succeeds in destroying this friendly nation. It can also be a starting point for a new, fruitful policy with immediate consequences for the Balkans and Austria-Hungary. Fate has put great power in your hands, Prime Minister. On your will now, the fate of nations depends. Ten million Slavs from Bohemia, Moravia, Slovakia and Silesia place trust in your political prescience and patriotic power.
Štefánik. Hospital, Victor Hugo Boulevard 26, Neuilly-sur-Seine.

This letter, which he asked Professor Hartmann to deliver to Briand, was the beginning of Štefánik's political struggle. Of course, the professor came to meet him and then instructed the patient to be taken to the operating room, where he loosened the cramped folds in his intestine. The surgery was difficult, the professor performed a resection of his stomach, duodenum and liver.

Štefánik noted in his notebook: *"If we want to be free in the future, we must act as though we are free now. We don't attack, we only defend our rights. We must defend them if we don't want to lose human dignity. We will win because our mottoes are love, work, honesty, the mottoes of future, hopefully happier ages."*

CHAPTER 7
Obstacles Strengthen Us

He followed news of developments on the fronts and was not enthused. He thus preferred to shorten his long convalescence by reading the biographies of Copernicus and Napoleon, and the philosophical works of Pascal and Nietzsche. He was visited by his Czech friends Tavik Simon, Hugo Boettinger, Amédet the entrepreneur, whom he'd met in Tahiti, Anatole de Monzie, Senator Chautemps, the poet Camille Mauclair and especially Louis Strimpl, whom he'd also entrusted with the key to his apartment. The Strimpls lavished flowers on him and supervised his flat not only during his absence, but also during his travels abroad. However, his most frequent and faithful visitor was Eda Beneš, who followed up Štefánik's contacts and developed them.

When Masaryk arrived in Paris on 28th January, his first steps led to Neuilly. Beneš took him there after he'd found out that Štefánik had important contacts in Paris; he'd persuaded Masaryk to come to Štefánik from London as soon as possible. With Julius Sauerwein and Professor Denis, he organised a series of lectures for Masaryk at the Sorbonne in Paris. It was necessary to act, because Madame de Jouvenel was informed that on 3rd February, Prime Minister Briand would receive Professor Masaryk and Štefánik.

Masaryk often visited Štefánik during his Paris stay. The young Slovak man felt almost a son's respect and love for this man. In conversations with the Moravian-Slovak professor, he realized that in many field he had a better understanding with him than with his father. The professor, enchanted by the spontaneity and sincerity of the young man, was equally impressed and confided in the convalescent problems of a personal nature.

"Do you know, Milan, that you and my Herbert are almost peers? You were born in July 1880 and he in May... Herbert, unfortunately, died last year of typhus in Galicia while helping soldiers attacked by the disease... He was thirty-five. He was an amazing artistic talent and painted great portraits. A year before him our Alicka was born, and in October 1886 our son Ján. I'm a little angry with the boy, he lives too irresponsibly. I wish he were more like you. He didn't even matriculate, so ten years ago I sent him to America to my friend, Crane, to learn a little bit of life. But he's hypersensitve and couldn't cope. Unfortunately, he started drinking, and so in 1912 he ended up in an institution with a suspected mental disorder, hebephrenia. Now he is somewhere among the Austrian war transports, I hear he's a Lieutenant and even got a decoration for gallantry. So you see, father is fighting son..."

"It's the same with us. I've heard that my brother Kazimir is in the Hungarian army. God knows how our home is managed..."

"Don't worry, everything will be fine. I believe deeply in the power of destiny, in the power of will and that a person will achieve everything he firmly believes in. And we will achieve it... My Ján will certainly be fine and maybe the experience from the front will open his eyes... I believe he will survive..."

"How is your dear wife?"

"Her mental world is fragile, she is being taken care of in a very good sanatorium..." Masaryk shrugged his shoulders.

"What would I give to know how my mother is managing..." Štefánik sighed.

Masaryk came to Milan on the second day after he'd been received by Aristide Briand. Although Štefánik could hardly stand on his feet, he came to the breakthrough meeting with Masaryk personally. His guardian angel, Madame de Jouvenel, persuaded a friend of her former husband, the single French deputy from Martinique, Henry Léméry, to do everything possible to have Štefánik and Masaryk received by the Prime Minister and Minister of Foreign Affairs, Aristide Briand. Léméry actually led both men to Briand.

Professor Hartmann welcomed Masaryk with Beneš to his office and then brought them to Štefánik's room. When they arrived, a tall, strong man came out of Štefánik's room, greeted the guests warmly and continued on his way.

Milan, seeing Masaryk, couldn't restrain himself and, despite the stomach bandages, stood up from the table and gripped both his hands.

"Milanko, Milanko... how many times do I have to tell you that you are in hospital and should be lying in bed and not sitting at a desk. But this time I forgive you. Yesterday we saw a great deal of success, thanks to you."

Štefánik squeezed his hands and his eyes gleamed with emotion.

"Hello, Edo," Štefánik greeted Beneš. He sat on his bed and his guests settled into their usual chairs.

Professor Hartmann objected in English that the young man should conserve his strength more.

"It won't be possible. I didn't spare myself on the front, and I certainly can't afford to stay in bed."

"How come? I'm your doctor and I've ordered you to."

"Monsieur le professeur, vous savez comment je vous aime, mais... but with all due respect to you, my mental state doesn't allow me to lie idly in bed, although my physical condition may make it seem that a bed would be my best friend at the moment..." Štefánik laughed.

"This man could convince the dead," said a resigned Hartmann.

"Sir, as we know Milan, he will never rest. Only after his death," laughed Masaryk.

"My father, truly I'm so tired that I feel as if I'm being ground into dust," he said in Slovak, so that Hartmann didn't understand him. The professor apologized, offered to fill the tea pot standing on the table and left the room. Beneš and Masaryk watched as the smiling Štefánik struggled with pain.

"Milanko, Milanko, where are the times when I read your articles in the Prague *Čas*," Masaryk recalled. "You captivated me."

"Professor, talk to me informally."

"You're no longer a student, and how we conduct ourselves requires some dignity, the expression of which is formal. But I promise both of you, my friends, that when we succeed, we'll meet as friends. My God, time has gone by unbelievably fast. When did we first meet?" Masaryk pondered.

"I remember it exactly. It was 23rd October, 1903. Vavro Šrobár sent me to you..."

"Yes, yes, I remember. I see that your ability to persuade people hasn't changed. I remember one of your phrases: "Slovakia is a land of ravaged hills, and the land has to be fertilized..." Today you're a French army officer – who would have thought it ...you've achieved great success that will be very useful for our cause. France is key for us at this point, and we don't have another like you in such a great position in Paris..." he clapped Milan's arm. "Tell me, how did you convince Prime Minister Briand to accept us?"

"I've been working in Paris for more than ten years, I'm a French citizen, I fought on the front in the French Air Force and I've got influential friends. In this case, Madame de Jouvenel and Monsieur Lémery helped us," he smiled secretively.

"The reception was excellent and I want to thank you again for everything. Also for your excellent interpretation; alas, my French is not that good... I just sometimes felt you were the only one at the audience. And this a few days after a serious operation. To fence with your arms in front of the French prime minister wearing a bandage on your stomach... you put the arguments to him in such a powerful way... And, if that wasn't enough, you got him to have his office issue an official report of our reception. It was an excellent suggestion. Thanks to it, all the French press took notice of the reception, and the important media in Britain, the USA and Russia also published information about this breakthrough diplomatic success of the Czechoslovak foreign resistance. The world's public has begun to learn in detail about the conditions in Austria-Hungary for the first time. Our dear friend, Auguste Gouvaine, even posted a fine commentary on the statement in the *Journal des Débats*. And this, Milan, is to your credit," Masaryk said, while Beneš watched them solemnly.

"Thank you," Štefánik smiled modestly. "I'm sorry that the Prime Minister had you wait, but he insisted on receiving me first. And I'm sorry you had to come twice from London to be received."

"The fact that they cancelled the audience the first time may have saved my life."

Štefánik looked at Masaryk uncomprehendingly.

"It's so. I'd already bought a ticket on the Sussex when Dr. Beneš called giving me your message from the hospital postponing the audience. So I returned the ticket. And the Sussex was sunk by a German submarine on the way... As you can see, a seeming inconvenience can sometimes be an advantage. I also want to thank you for ensuring my interview with Monsieur Sauerwein of *Le Matin*. Excellent, excellent... We must write for Monsieur Briand the promised analysis "Sur la situation militaire" with maps and our ideas of the post-war order. Although Dr. Beneš wasn't at the reception, he'll certainly be interested in being involved in the preparation of this material." Masaryk looked at Beneš, who nodded eagerly. "You may have noticed, Milan, that the Prime Minister's view of the situation is still far from ours. What is essential is that he has received us. Now it would be excellent if Monsieur Deschanel, President of the Chamber of Deputies, also received us."

"I'm doing all I can to achieve it. The fact that we've been received by the French Prime Minister will increase our chances, I am convinced of it," Štefánik nodded firmly sitting in his chair and breathing hard.

Masaryk carefully put his hand on his forehead. It was hot.

"You really have to relax, we'd better go. We'll send the doctor to you."

"We'll relax after we achieve our goal. It doesn't matter whether the target is in the sky or on earth, we have to fight for it."

"Yes, Milanko, our goal leads us, but we need to go after it with understanding, not at the price of self-destruction," said Masaryk.

"Illness is just one of the many obstacles that discourage the average but not the strong. Destruction is a possibility, victory is a certainty... Maybe you bumped into an interesting young man when you came in."

"The tall man?" asked Beneš.

"Yes. It was an Italian, Colonel Garibaldi, called Peppino. I met him two months ago when I was recovering in Rome after the Serbian front had broken. I spoke to him about Italian claims to the Adriatic territories occupied by the Slavs; that there might be a new Alsace-Lorraine. I don't think the Italians need it. Among other things, he agreed on it with me. He's an excellent fellow, a grandson of the famous General Garibaldi. We met shortly after his unit had conquered Col di Lana from the Austrians. He's a real warrior, an Italian patriot. He's already a Colonel but only a year older than me... He created an Italian unit here with his brother, which has gradually grown into a regiment and is now fighting on the French side as part of their Foreign Legion. At the beginning there were just a few of them, but now he has his fourth infantry regiment of 2,120 men and 57 officers. Imagine – the entire regiment is composed exclusively of Italians living in France. While the Italian government is neutral towards the Germans, they've long since understood where their place is."

"I've heard of them. They're the great brothers who fought at Belle Étoile in December 1914, where their brother Bruno died."

"Yes, they are. Their example of establishing a foreign Italian army is very inspiring," Beneš said.

"If we want the Allied governments to take us seriously, we should follow a similar path. It's only by action that they'll think that we're serious about our freedom," Masaryk nodded.

"Garibaldi first asked the English for agreement to establish an Italian legion. Since the English didn't allow him to do so, he persuaded the French. If we want to get support for our goal, we mustn't just follow them as empty-handed petitioners but also offer them something. And our offer will be Czecho-Slovak foreign legions that will fight on their side. It would be wonderful," Štefánik said.

Masaryk and Beneš warmly agreed with him.

"It would. As soon as you get out of hospital, we'll do it. Many obstacles await us, friends."

"The Germans have been supplying their front at full flow for some weeks now," Beneš said solemnly. "They've even built new railway lines to Verdun. They're transporting modern reinforced concrete mobile bunkers by train and, according to unofficial information, have dispatched more than a thousand ammunition trains. Can you imagine it? A thousand trains! They say they're concentrating half a million soldiers."

"What about the French?" asked Masaryk.

"I'm afraid they underestimate the danger. Some newspapers have already pointed that out."

"Yes, I read that the strengthening of the defence of the key fortress of Douaumont was minimal. If Douaumont falls, then maybe Verdun will follow and the Germans will have the route to Paris open..." Štefánik shook his head. "At the moment, there are just under sixty men in Douaumont... unbelievable, the French have probably fallen asleep..."

"Still Petain has quickly expanded and strengthened the single supply route to Verdun," Beneš said encouragingly. "I've heard that American veterans of the French Foreign Legion are creating an American unit that is going to Verdun."

At these words, Štefánik sat down.

"So you see! Neutral Americans help them from across the ocean while we, in Europe, fully depend on the success of the Allies while we lie in hospital! We need our legions and we'll have them! Only people willing to make sacrifices for it deserve freedom. And none of the obstacles that come our way will weaken us, but will strengthen us instead. As obstacles increase so must our energy in overcoming them!"

CHAPTER 8
The Dead Pile Up

Louise Weiss and Julius Sauerwein came to congratulate Štefánik on being received by Briand. Jules brought a large box from which he unpacked a special device: a case with a large trumpet, round plate on top, metal arm and a crank. On the side of the case was a gold logo, *Harmony type Great Northern Co. Chicago*. When Štefánik saw the miracle, his face lit up in a smile.

"My word, it is a phonograph!" With obvious excitement, he patted the device with a trembling hand.

"Exactly, Edison's phonograph. But listen first to the song we brought you," Louise smiled.

Sauerwein pulled the vinyl discs in their paper envelopes from a bag, put one of them on the plate, inserted a needle into the end of the arm, wound the crank several times and placed the needle on the turning plate. For a moment, all of it was screeching, but then his favourite song came out of the trumpet.

"*La Paloma*!" He exclaimed excitedly.

"It was your wish," Louise's hand touched Štefánik's.

"That's the most beautiful song I've ever heard. A song of hope and love. Wonderful, wonderful... Play it once more."

When the song finished, he couldn't hold back his feelings.

"My dear Louise, my dear Jules, you are doing a great job for us, but instead of my rewarding you, you bring me an incredible gift... Thank you, thank you... on behalf of Professor Masaryk. You did a wonderful job. Your interview with Professor Masaryk was excellent and we've had only the best response. Dear Louise, my thanks belong to you." He reached for a huge bouquet of roses he had prepared in a vase on the table, handed it to her, bowed and kissed her hand politely.

"You're doing amazing work for us."

"I have reason to - my mother also had Czech roots," she smiled, looking into the infinity of big blue eyes under which his eyelids flickered, tired from lack of sleep and pain.

"You're a noble woman. I bend before your courage to organize a field hospital for seriously injured frontline soldiers..."

"I'm just trying to make myself busy; I've used all my contacts to establish a hospital in Côtes du Nord. I have, thank God, enough of them. It's the duty of every decent person to do what they can to end this terrible war as soon as possible. Apparently the Germans are preparing an offensive on Verdun. As if there weren't enough dead in this war. In the newspaper, they write that in one of the trenches near Ypres a letter from one of our dead soldiers was found

– the dead man had written to his mother, unfortunately too late: "It's a horror, one crater next to another, in each of them three to four dead, Germans along with the French. The dead who died in October, under them those who died in March and below them the naked skeletons of January. All were fathers, sons, doctors, workers, bakers, peasants, people, each a real being with desires, hopes, love... Terrible," she put her head in her hands.

Štefánik stroked her arm tenderly.

"If we are united, it won't take long before... I'm sorry to be so pressing, but I need to reach the Chairman of the Senate, Monsieur Deschanel, as soon as possible. With Professor Masaryk I've told you about him."

"It won't be easy. The German offensive is expected every minute, they have other worries..."

"I would consider it unworthy of you to ask for simple things."

"I suggest you try it through Dr. Blondel, Deputy Chief Medical Officer at the Clignancourt Barracks," Louise smiled. "You know him."

"The one who gave me a confirmation of convalescence the day after I met the Prime Minister?" Štefánik looked at her disbelievingly.

"That's the one. You probably don't know that he's translated the text of your famous opera, *The Bartered Bride* from German to French. He greatly appreciated the excellent reception he received in Prague. He loves the Czechs because they've always had a love of music. He's Claude Deschanel's personal doctor."

"What! I didn't know that. I read his book on French interests in the Pacific Ocean, we've even met a few times, but I wouldn't dare approach him directly; it would be too forward," Štefánik said.

"Very well, I'll try it through the Senator."

She gazed into his eyes where she saw fatigue and pain.

"Now, my dear Milan, we have to go. It's only a few weeks since you had a major operation, you have to rest."

"I'm better than I've been for a long time," he tried to convince her.

"But, now, now, off to bed," she gently pushed him to the bed.

"So you don't believe me? Jules, be kind enough to play us the song again," he asked Sauerwein. He cranked the turntable from which captivating tones emerged.

"Shall we dance?"

Louise was so surprised she couldn't say no. But it was clear to Milan that her resistance was merely token.

Sauerwein rolled his cheerful eyes in disbelief as the door opened and Professor Hartmann stood there. He watched the dancing for a moment and said with a smile: "Lieutenant, you seem to be fine. We'll let you go home tomorrow."

After leaving the hospital, he barely looked around his apartment but headed straight to Rue Bonaparte 18, where a new body, the Conseil National des Pays Tchèques (The National Council of the Czech Country) had been established through transformation of the former Czech Foreign Committee. The activities of the Council were financially supported by American Slovaks who, through Štefan Osuský, asked Beneš to extend the name to the Czecho-Slovak Council. Therefore, from 1917, the name of the Czecho-Slovak National Council was used. This important event in Czecho-Slovak resistance took place on 13th February, ten days after their reception by Prime Minister Briand. The Chairman of the Council was Tomáš Garrigue Masaryk, Vice-Presidents Milan Štefánik and Josef Dürich, with Edvard Beneš appointed Secretary. The Council was a key body of the Czecho-Slovak foreign resistance movement and operated until 14th November 1918, when the first government of the new Czechoslovak Republic was established. Initially, it was intended to be just a propaganda body with the task of promoting the idea of Czecho-Slovakia visible; it quickly became a full-fledged political body, however. The Council's press outlets were *La Nation Tchèque* (the Czech Nation) and *Československá samostatnost*

(Czechoslovak Independence). One of its first resolutions was the creation of a Czecho-Slovak armed force in Russia, where most of their prisoners were held.

Štefánik and Professor Masaryk negotiated on 15th February in the Luxembourg Palace as representatives of the official body of their movement with the Chairman of the Chamber of Deputies, Paul Deschanel. As a typical official, Deschanel didn't hide his sympathy for preserving the Austro-Hungarian Empire. Masaryk reacted with annoyance, but was most put out that he couldn't speak with the Chairman of the Senate directly, as the Frenchman knew no English while Masaryk knew only the basics of French. The initiative, as with the meeting with Briand fell to Štefánik, who was so irritated that at some moments he had to walk around and calm himself down with various abrupt gestures.

"Sir, it is absolutely imperative that the independence of Bohemia be proclaimed in future peace treaties. On the day, Monsieur President, when you declare from the high tribune of the assembly that the Allies recognize the independence of Bohemia, 150,000 Czechs currently fighting against the Italians will switch their allegiances to the Allies."

Deschanel smiled, unconvinced, and tried to bring the exasperated Štefánik down to earth in various ways.

"I advise you to be prudent. The mass desertion of Czech regiments in the middle of the war would be a disaster especially for the deserters themselves, because the Germans would commit on them their characteristic atrocities. To weaken the monarchy too much would be rash. It would only eliminate the buffer state needed to stop German aggression in the Balkans. I believe the best would be a certain federation of Danubian states..."

He fiddled with his snuffbox and then to their surprise said, "I've got no influence on foreign policy. I am a prisoner of my work and have no power to prevent this muddle in the army and in diplomacy. There are still people in Quai d`Orsay who think, as they did in 1870, that it is better not to provoke Germany too much..."

The phone rang on the chairman's desk and with a gesture of apology to them he shook their hands and they left. On the way to the taxi, Štefánik told Masaryk exactly what Deschanel had said. They realized that the only way was through Prime Minister Briand, Philip Berthelot at the Ministry of Foreign Affairs and above all through the French General Staff.

CHAPTER 9
I Live Life in Seconds

After his discharge from hospital, Štefánik most often went to the Rue Bonaparte and the Quai d'Orsay, the site of the ostentatious building of the Ministry of Foreign Affairs. Fortunately, his apartment wasn't far from the Seine, so he had a pleasant and useful connection. His visits to Philip Berthelot were also a quick walk for him along Boulevard Raspail and back. Berthelot was an expert on the Balkans and Štefánik's views on the position of Slavic nations in the region were both interesting and inspiring for him. Štefánik's experience of fighting in Serbia and especially the ideal combination of his position as a French citizen and a Slav led the French government to entrust him with a special and delicate mission: to try and loosen the tensions between the two allies, Italy and Serbia, divided by territorial claims. Italy had received a pledge of post-war territorial acquisitions on the Adriatic at the expense of the Austro-Hungarian Empire and, as a result of these promises, came over to the side of the Entente, which also included Serbia, making similar claims to the region of Dalmatia. Štefánik learned that a certain Marchesa

Giuliana Benzoni had played a key role in mediation between the British and Italians.

In connection with this task, Štefánik was promoted to the rank of flight Lieutenant on 20th March, 1916. On 1st April, he travelled to Bologna to continue to the Italian headquarters in Udine, and then to Rome where he arrived on 12th April. He stayed in Italy for two months and worked there as a fighter pilot carrying out reconnaissance flights over the Austrian lines. At the same time, he dropped leaflets for Slavic soldiers in the Austro-Hungarian army, which he himself had formulated. "Whoever has honour in his soul and Slavic blood in his veins, remember that it is your sacred duty to use every circumstance to weaken those you serve today." During a risky flight in his Farman over the Tagliamento river basin, he dropped more than 20,000 leaflets. At the same time, Štefánik's Italian mission was his first diplomatic task as an official representative of the Czechoslovak National Council, a body responsible for exploring the possibilities of establishing Czechoslovak military units.

At the beginning of May, an event in Rome marked his life more than all his diplomatic and political successes. Again, he was invited to the palace of Giuseppe-Napoleon, Duke of Primoli, known to his friends as Gégé. The magnificent building dominated the Piazza di Ponte Umberto I and Via dell'Orso on the Tiber embankment opposite Castel Sant'Angelo. The Duke, a distant cousin of Napoleon Bonaparte, was a well-known philanthropist, intellectual, bibliographer and, above all, the owner of a splendid library of over 30,000 volumes. His hobby was photography. The young French Lieutenant and astronomer rose in his estimation as he showed him his exclusive Tahiti footage. The Duke liked the officer with the sensitive artistic soul and invited him to his palace. On that memorable evening, rain was pouring down, but a fire was burning in the hearth in the salon and the company present was listening to the passionate talk of the French Lieutenant. There was no need to translate, because in Europe at that time, French was the lingua franca in high society. The young man paced nervously in front of the sitting barons, ministerial officials, military dignitaries, and their wives, sipping an expensive *Malvasia*. When he noticed that someone wasn't paying due attention to him, he interrupted his speech and waited demonstratively until the inattentive listener looked at him again. A strange charisma emanated from the vital young man; his vigorous movements and gestures added persuasiveness to his words.

"We all realize that if this war is to be the last, it must result in one important thing: the right of every nation to a national life. This war has to solve the issue of the right of small nations and Central Europe is the place to solve it. It's the only way to stop German imperial ambitions forever."

"Perhaps you wouldn't want to claim that the Germans are the only nation with imperial ambitions. During Easter Week, just a few days ago, the British mercilessly crushed the Irish for wanting nothing but their freedom. These righteous English freedom fighters... they grant it to the subjugated peoples of Hungary, but if the Irish want to free themselves from the British yoke, their leaders execute them mercilessly..." the Duke said with a wry face.

"The British had no other choice because the Germans initiated and secretly supported the Northern Irish uprising," said Štefánik said.

"That's a very bold statement," said a young man furiously. "Remember that you're in Italy, which has a good relationship with Germany."

"Well... on the Italian front, German regiments come as reinforcements to the Austrian, so you are in fact at war with them..." Štefánik objected.

"Maybe there is an explanation why Britain will not support the Czech efforts to break away from the Austrians," Prince Colonna said.

"Excuse me, but I don't understand very well your... uh... beating the drum for the Germans..." Štefánik turned to the young man.

"I'm not beating the drum for the Germans. I'm just a journalist, I come from the Tyrol. In your place, dear sir, I would moderate my criticism of Germany. Von Berlin bis nach Bagdad, was the wollen sie damit sagen?"

Štefánik did not hesitate for a moment and passionately continued the discussion in German.

"Ich bin überzeugt, dass... Austria-Hungary is, in economic and military terms, only a bridgehead for Germany in the Balkans. I am thinking of the seizure of Bosnia and Herzegovina, intrigues in Albania, claims to Salonika... and the war against the Serbs is itself proof of German expansion!"

"Gentlemen, gentlemen... please, we are in a state of war with the Austrians, so it's certainly not a good idea to enjoy ourselves in this company using the language of the enemy," said the Duke. "And you, dear Abel, please restrain your German sympathies." Then he turned to Štefánik: "Excuse me, Lieutenant, I haven't introduced you, my son Abel, a writer and a little Germanophile. Sometimes he comes from Paris to visit his father," the Duke of Primoli smiled. The young men coldly shook hands. At that moment the huge glass doors opened and a servant announced the arrival of an unknown young lady.

"Oh, my dear Marchesa, what a wonderful surprise!" The lord of the house came over to the young woman, who had a shy expression and slightly damp hair that enhanced her charm, and kissed her hand politely. He gestured to a servant who brought a chair and put it next to Štefánik for the young lady to sit on.

"I apologize very much for having dropped in on you like this without announcement, but there is an incredible downpour outside, so I was looking for the nearest shelter," she explained.

"Such an apology, my dear Marchesa, it is an honour for us that you've visited my humble abode. Ladies and gentlemen, let me introduce you to the Marchesa Giuliana Benzoni, our family friend, the granddaughter of our dear Ferdinand Martini. You know most of us, honourable Marchesa. Perhaps it's time to introduce you to our new friend, Lieutenant Milan Štefánik."

Štefánik bowed and kissed the Marchesa's hand.

"My dear Lieutenant, I'm bringing this lady to your attention. Her famous grandfather is not only a writer but was also the Italian governor in Eritrea. He is currently the minister for colonies, a professor at the University of Pisa and a member of our parliament for forty years. I encourage you to devote your attention to Giuliana. It could be very beneficial to you," smiled Prince Colonna di Cesaro, the only man in the salon, whom Štefánik had known from previous meetings.

The young, twenty-year-old lady bowed her head to those present and ordered some hot tea to be poured for her.

"I'm sorry, Lieutenant, I interrupted your speech. It was rude, I apologize very much. Please do continue," said the Marchesa to Štefánik, who gazed at her quite stunned, as if something had just entered his head, but also gone straight to his heart. "Ah... yes... It is my honour to become acquainted with the marchesa of the famous Benzoni family... If you'd permit... um... I just wanted to say that the keener our mind... the more ardent is our relation to the world. For I sense that true understanding is the father of love. Only in true love is purpose, happiness and our eternity. Only in love boundless and unconditional. Sorry... Thank you for giving me your attention," and sat down. Those present rightly understood his sudden departure from the subject as his wish to attract the attention of a young lady. She drank in the gaze of his mesmerizing eyes, which had a special brightness in the candlelight. It had been a long time since he'd lowered his eyes under the gaze of a woman.

"Wait, sir, you won't get out of it easily. I don't want to be too political in this pleasant company, but you haven't explained to us who you are. I don't want to offend you in any way, but you say that you're a Slovak, but we haven't really heard of this nation so far," Abel teased him in French.

"We Slovaks have been living in the centre of Europe for time immemorial and are part of the Slavic group of nations, the largest ethnic and language group in Europe. We form the eastern part of the Czecho-Slovak nation, there are over three million of us, but almost a third have been forced to leave their country as a result of Hungarian oppression and material want. Czechoslovaks fight in the formations of the Austro-Hungarian army..." Štefánik returned to reality.

"So you are our enemies," he protested. "You're murdering our soldiers by Gorizia and in the Dolomites!"

"On the contrary, sir. Because Czechs and Slovaks have the same goal as the Italians, to break a hated monarchy, we're your friends. As you can see, I'm a French officer myself, I've had French citizenship since 1912. We're fighting for the liberation of Bohemia and Upper Hungary, just as you're fighting for liberation of Trieste. Our young men are coming over to the Italian and Russian sides.

"How many? Maybe a few individuals, but most are committed to fighting for their Emperor."

"They don't have it easy, they're being executed for coming over. Yet many are coming over. Personally, I'm doing everything I can to encourage them. The number of Czechs and Slovaks fighting with you is increasing every day. I've now come from the front where I flew to Gorizia, I've carried out reconnaissance flights in the areas of Salcano, Aisovizzo, Merna, Ranziani and Spacapani. I flew over Lago di Idro and Riva. I have dropped leaflets which I wrote for Czech and Slovak soldiers. I have one in my pocket." He pulled out a crumpled piece of paper and read slowly, translating the text into French. "Brothers, remember that the victory of Austria-Hungary means extinction for our nation, but its defeat is our liberation and a better future. Your friends at home, your fathers, mothers, brothers and sisters await your red-blooded action. Will you disappoint their hopes, will you go to die for those who have oppressed us? Don't do it! We await you with open arms." He put the paper back into his pocket and continued with enthusiasm: "From Caprone, we bombed

Austrian positions at Mattarelle, Val Sarca, Riva, Monte Palon. In the Farman I fought on the front at Cavazzo Carnico in the upper streams of the Tagliamanto. In the morning I flew over Sochi and in the afternoon, I dropped bombs on the enemy over Tolmin."

"Weren't you afraid of being shot down?" The Marchesa interrupted him.

"Well... Yes, afraid," he replied, for he didn't know how to wriggle out of her question. "Every soldier is afraid. I had strychnine pills all the time. If I'd fallen into captivity, it would have been certain death for me for treason..." He stopped talking and wiped his slightly perspiring forehead with his handkerchief. Due to the blazing fireplaces, it was hot in the salon, although this year's May was unusually cool for Rome.

"So you drop bombs on the heads of your compatriots, too," Abel said bitingly.

"I'm sorry I have to drop bombs on people at all," he said, taken aback for a moment. "But I didn't create this war and I believe that when an enemy has attacked us, it's the duty of everyone to defend their homeland and to help friends fighting for the same goals."

"What is your goal?" The Marchesa asked unexpectedly.

Štefánik looked at her with a penetrating stare under whose strength the young lady's gaze dropped and she blushed a little. "To free my homeland. I came to Rome not only to try to settle the dispute between the Italians and the Serbs, but also to help organize a Czechoslovak armed force out of our prisoners."

"If all the Czechs and Slovaks fight for their freedom with such enthusiasm, you'll certainly succeed. We heard you discovered the upcoming offensive of two Austrian Army Corps in the Upper Adige. Due to you, General Cadorna has successfully strengthened our defences. My grandfather knows how to appreciate courage, he'll be happy to help you," she said spontaneously.

For the rest of the evening he devoted himself only to Giuliana. He was so enchanted that he proposed another meeting. She agreed but was surprised by the pace the Lieutenant adopted. "I suggest we meet tomorrow. In ten days I return to Paris and I'd like to be with you as much as possible..." Without giving her the opportunity to refuse, he suggested a time and place for their meeting.

"It has stopped raining," she said with a slight blush on her face, shrugging her shoulders hesitantly, saying goodbye to her host and stealing out of the palace.

Štefánik didn't tarry and immediately after her departure, approached deputy Colonna to ask more about the Marchesa. The prince was a family friend of the noble Benzoni and gave the young man a lot of interesting information about her family and circle of friends. They sat in a separate drawing room.

"Giuliana is from a strictly Catholic, pro-papal family," the deputy said. "The Benzonis are very conservative; take care, she's young, she was born in 1895. Her father, Gaetano, married a lady from the Tuscan Martini-Marescotti family with a family mansion in Monsumman. She's a courageous young lady and smuggled under her petticoats dispatches from London to Paris and Rome at a time when Italy was an ally of Germany. At that time she also worked as a secret link between her grandfather Martini in the Palazzo Colonna and the French ambassador, Camilla Barrère in the Palazzo Farnese. She knew she was being watched by German secret agents, but she wasn't afraid. I'll keep my fingers crossed for you," said the deputy.

The next day a young man in the pale blue uniform of a French officer with a huge bouquet was impatiently walking in front of the magnificent Colonna Palace, home to the famous picture gallery, close to the smaller palace of Ferdinando Martini, where Giuliana lived. He'd gone several times through the Piazza Santi Apostoli, even going to the church of the same name and begging God to bring the young lady to him. Exactly at the stroke of three o'clock a coach pulled up in front of the palace, from which Giuliana got out escorted by a young lady. Štefánik bowed, politely helped both ladies to get out and with a little embarrassment gave Giuliana the bouquet. She thanked him and handed it to the coachman with an instruction to wait for a while.

"Dear Elsa, let me introduce you to Monsieur Štefánik, Lieutenant in the French Army."

"I'm Elsa Dallolio, a friend of the Marchesa," the young lady replied. "I'll leave and come for you in twenty minutes," she smiled and turned towards the coach.

"Elsa Dallolio? Daughter of the famous General Alfred Dallolio, Minister of Armaments?" Štefánik could barely control his surprise.

"Yes."

"The courageous nurse in the Red Cross?"

Elsa blushed a little once more.

"Excuse me," he apologized, jumping over a small hedge behind which were lawns and rose beds. He plucked one, walked to Elsa and knelt in front of her on one knee. Passers-by came up, but their wonderment didn't hinder the young man.

"Signorina, twenty minutes? I've no doubt that you know what it means to be in love, so it should also be clear to you that twenty minutes is pitifully short to confess one's love..."

Elsa glanced at the strangely silent Giuliana, smiled at Štefánik and commanded: "On your feet! Attention!"

The Lieutenant jumped to attention.

"How much time does a French officer need to confess his love?"

"For the French half an hour, but I'm a Slovak, we're shy, so at least two," said Štefánik.

"All right, a compromise! One and a half hours. She looked at Giuliana, who gratefully shrugged her shoulders. Elsa settled into the coach and it moved away.

For a while they walked silently through May-time Rome. The ice cream vendors were offering cold delicacies, from the cafés came the sound of conversation and the birds were flying through an azure sky as if the most amazing spring of peace had come.

"One and a half hours is not very much… I've brought you a small gift. It's a coral necklace from Tahiti."

"From Tahiti? How did you get it? "

"I spent the most beautiful moments of my life there…"

They walked, chatted, fell silent, listened, dreamed and little understood what was happening to them. He'd had a number of relationships before, had even been engaged and thought he'd truly loved, but now for the first time in his life he felt the constricting and at the same time liberating feeling he was afraid to call love.

"We all have only as much strength as fate has given us. And although we're different, we all have one thing in common; each of us would like a little piece of heaven for himself."

"What does heaven mean to you?"

"What is happening in me now. I've been in heaven since yesterday. I didn't know it would happen in Rome."

"You seem happy," she smiled.

"I'm not complaining. I live a beautiful life, I live it in seconds. Every second I spend with my beloved is eternity for me…"

"You're declaring your love for me but you don't know me at all."

"I feel I have known you for years, forever."

"Love… contains everything: purpose, happiness, our eternity. But only in unlimited love…" she repeated his words from the salon.

When the coach finally arrived, they could hardly believe their friendly chaperone had granted them almost three hours. They met every day until he left the Eternal City. He was involved in diplomatic negotiations the whole time but could barely concentrate on his official duties so much did she occupy his mind. When he was out of town, he tried to end his negotiations as soon as possible and urged his driver to hurry to Rome. Waiting until five o'clock, when he usually met the marchesa, took forever. He'd arrive at their meeting place half an hour early and walk impatiently through the adjoining streets. On the last day of his stay in Rome, on 30th May, at the Fontana di Trevi, a stone's throw from Colonna Palace, Giuliana grabbed his hands tightly and looked into his eyes:

"Oh, my God, Lieutenant, you've driven me completely mad."

"And you me."

He took her hand, pulled off a white glove, kissed it ceremonially and on her ring finger placed a ring with a pearl in it.

"The Tahitian pearl is a symbol of the soul in Polynesia. I've worn this ring for years, waiting for the right woman to give it to..."

They gazed into each other's eyes.

"When will you come to Rome again?"

"Do you want me to come?"

She nodded shyly.

"My dear Marchesa, as soon as I can."

CHAPTER 10
I'm Not Stefanik!

On the day of Štefánik's return to Paris on 5th June, Russian forces under the command of General Brusilov began an offensive on the eastern front, crushing the 5th Austrian army of Archduke Joseph Ferdinand in two days. When the offensive ended, the Austrian and German troops stood a hundred kilometres to the west and the Allied media wrote about a great Russian victory. The fact that the 100-kilometre shift was achieved at the cost of 800,000 fallen on the Russian and 614,000 on the Austrian and German sides was not mentioned.

North of Paris, on 1st July, 1916, a British and French offensive began on the River Somme. It was supposed to be a battle that would decide and end the war. The British had a seven-on-one advantage against the Germans, but despite the use of new weapons, the tanks didn't achieve a significant success. On the contrary, the battle became the biggest disaster in British military history. On the first day of the battle alone, German machine guns massacred nearly twenty thousand British, one of the German soldiers a Corporal Adolf Hitler. When fighting came to a halt on 18th November, the two armies found that they were in the same place they were at the beginning with the difference that the British had 420,000 men fewer, the French 350,000 and the Germans 500,000. Three out of four French soldiers had fallen.

Since the dead had to be replaced, the French government began to negotiate with Russia to send Russian troops to the Western Front. Štefánik, Masaryk and Beneš understood that their chance had come. This time they officially submitted a proposal to the French authorities to create a Czecho-Slovak army in Russia that would move to the Western Front. Together with Beneš, Štefánik spoke to important people who could influence the decision of the French government to obtain approval for this proposal. In London, Tomáš Masaryk regularly informed British ruling circles about the mood in Austria-Hungary. Štefánik was given the promise of financial, political and, in particular, material support for a future army from the highest French authorities if at least thirty thousand soldiers could be mustered. He applied himself to the task with vigour. As an officer of the French army, with full powers granted to him from Paris, allied doors were opened to him at the highest levels.

From the window of his apartment, he watched the hurrying people who in those cruel times of war were only interested in one thing, themselves. They were indifferent to the fates of Slavs and of unknown Slovaks. He'd have preferred to shout his feelings at this pampered yet beloved city from the windows of his cold flat. Yet he had friends here in whose studios he felt at home. Home. My God, where was his home? How was his Košariská, his native home, where none of the Štefániks now lived? For the Hungarian homeland, he was a deserter, an arch-enemy and he trusted that the powers would at least leave his relatives alone. He was strengthened by regular meditations in the silence and loneliness of Rue Leclerc and despite persistent pain, returned to the salons smiling. The work of the astronomer, philosopher and esotericist, Camille Flammarion, replenished his energy levels. He constantly returned to his books, *General Cosmogony, Real and Imaginary Worlds, God in Nature,* and the fantastic novels, *Stella, Heavenly Journey, The Mystery of Death.* He reminded himself of the sentence Victor Hugo had once said to Honoré de Balzac: "You desire to take a place among those whose world you demolish with an unapologetic pen. That is your misfortune."

"Monsieur Štefánik... the stories of your innumerable travels around the world are very engaging and I do not deny your great ability to present them. But your destiny reminds me a little of that self-proclaimed fraudulent nobleman, Monsieur Balzac... And he travelled a lot, especially when a dissatisfied creditor appeared on the horizon... But he was lucky because of a certain noblewoman... a Polish noblewoman..." Lacroix looked sideways at the Baroness de Jouvenel, who'd become a little pink at his words. She wanted to say something, but Štefánik forestalled her.

"Monsieur Le Baron, it is always better if charming baronesses take pity on us than grumpy barons..."

It was a public secret in the salon that Lacroix had shown interest in her since the Baroness's divorce. But Sarah was reserved in her response to the intense courtship of the eternally importunate aristocrat. At the same time, Lacroix had a sharp eye for her obliging and auspicious behaviour to the young officer.

"I don't get your point, Monsieur Stefanik...!" said the Baron.

"I'm sorry, I'm not Stefanik, but Štefánik... I'll repeat it to you again... Štefánik, Štefánik... sh is the sound... so, a Frenchman would never say 'sampagne'..." Most of the guests smiled encouragingly at Štefánik while the offended Lacroix could only frown.

"Monsieur Štefánik," Lacroix ironically put the emphasis on his surname. "You're perpetually repeating your vision of creating your armed force for our side, but that is patently nonsense, utopia, not to say provocation. Nobody will convince our public of the benefits of Austrian traitors fighting on our side," Lacroix began to grow heated again. "In this, Sonnino is absolutely right. Our public would be outraged. How could they behave otherwise? As far as I know, the Hague Convention permits the use of prisoners only for work unrelated to war operations. The fear that Austrians and Germans would engage in reprisals against our prisoners is very well founded. And then, you can never know how many spies they'll stick in among your prisoners. Deserters and traitors will help us..."

"Sir, I must categorically object. These aren't deserters and traitors, but Czech, Slovak, Serbian, Polish, Romanian and Croatian patriots who are fighting against their oppressors. I firmly believe that you are aware that in your glorious Declaration of the Rights of Man and Citizen there is also mention of foreigners who, taking their hearts in their hands, fought on the side of the French Revolution to help overthrow the tyrants!"

When the last guest had left the salon that evening, Sarah and Milan sat in their comfortable armchairs saying nothing for a long while.

"Some won't like you for that. You are rather too open and straightforward for the Parisian salons, though I won't deny you your diplomatic skills," she smiled.

"Madame, it's not important whether they like me or not, the important thing is that they hear my message and are not merely indifferent. And if we acknowledge that a word is an act, every act creates a variety of responses. It's therefore not possible for everyone to agree with me. But I have a feeling that I'm gaining sympathy for our idea."

"But not all people wish you well, you should be more careful..."

"I don't have anything to worry about, my jujitsu skills are rather good," he laughed.

"You are very clever and entertaining. I liked how you brought that opinionated Lacroix down to earth with your 'sh'!"

"Occasionally a person must be disrespectful."

"So far I have met with disrespect in my salon from other people than you... In contrast to some of my friends, you're the very model of a gentleman. To your health."

"To yours." They drank. Sarah gazed at him.

"It happens to me that when I listen to you, I don't notice how time passes. And I see how women devour you..."

"It's enough for me to be devoured by the women I care about..."

"Who are they?" She asked quietly.

Štefánik ran his eyes over her enticing curves. He realized how powerfully she attracted him. Ever since Anatole de Monzie had introduced her to him, he had always controlled himself in her presence, but now that they were alone, he felt he could be freer. He felt that his self-control was an unnecessary obstacle.

"For example, you," his smile spoke volumes.

"You're a little nervous," she returned his smile.

"Maybe because I've never been alone in the presence of a Baroness..."

"God only knows what virtue that has. They married me to a Baron, that's all," she replied laconically and took a drink.

"Baron Henri Bertrand Léon Robert de Jouvenel des Ursins. I'm just remembering your husband's full name... Once it would never have occurred to me that I would be in such company."

"My former husband... It was a problem for me at first. Although we have parted, our relationship has remained correct and Henri can help your cause considerably. Listen, Milan, we are equals, you aren't with me for the first time so why are we still on formal terms?"

"I have too great a respect for you," Štefánik shrugged.

"I'm Sarah," she held out his hand and leaned forward.

"Milan," he said, leaning forward. For a moment they looked closely into each other's eyes.

"It includes a kiss."

Not even waiting for an answer she put her lips to Milan's, holding his right hand firmly with hers and embracing him with her left. He didn't resist.

"I need to meet some of the influential members of the Foreign Committee very quickly..."

"Can you not think of anything else at the moment?" She clasped him firmly. "I don't know anyone in the Foreign Committee."

"You've got plenty of time till tomorrow to meet one of the deputies and invite him to your salon," he smiled slyly.

"Well, it won't just be like that..."

"I don't even want it to be... just like that."

CHAPTER 11
You're a Traitor to Slovaks

After agreement with the Allies, the Russian headquarters in Mogilev had to send 50,000 troops a month to the Western Front slaughterhouse. When Štefánik learned about it through his contacts, he understood it as both an opportunity and also duty of the Czechoslovak resistance. In his head he no longer entertained the idea of entering Czech and Slovak volunteers into the Allied armies; he wanted more, to create an independent Czechoslovak army as a sovereign allied army of prisoners and citizens in Russia, Romania, Italy and the USA. However, without the agreement of the governments of these countries, it wasn't possible to recruit soldiers, and so the efforts of the Czechoslovak National Council began to focus mainly on diplomacy. It was extremely difficult to persuade the governments of the negotiating powers to see the sense of building an army for a state that didn't exist and which few believed ever would. However, Masaryk, Štefánik and Beneš knew that the main argument in future peace negotiations would be the active participation of our soldiers in fighting on the side of the Entente. To accomplish this, it was necessary to acquire not only Czech and Slovak soldiers, but also allied governments. It was obvious that the road to a Republic was going to be through an army and the road to the army was through allied politicians. A huge diplomatic struggle began. Masaryk fought in London, Štefánik and Beneš in Paris, but then Štefánik moved to the most difficult section of foreign resistance, to Russia. The government in St. Petersburg was convinced that the building of a Czecho-Slovak army was just a pretext and that the main role of the representatives of the National Council was to promote English and French influence in Central Europe, in which Russia was also interested. In addition, disputes over the post-war direction of the new Czecho-Slovakia were growing among the Czechs and Slovaks living in Russia. Two directions of opinion were created: the pan-Slavs wanted to merge all Slavic nations into a large Slavic empire under the leadership of Russia, the other was for independent Slavic states that would be allies of Russia.

There were about 180,000 Czech and 70,000 Slovak soldiers in Russian prisoner-of-war camps. The position of the Czechs and Slovaks living in Russia was difficult after the outbreak of the war, with many having property confiscated or being sent to POW camps as citizens of a hostile state. The task of unifying the Czecho-Slovak resistance movement in Russia and forming legions that would gradually move to the Russian or Western front was initially commissioned by the deputy President of the National Council, Josef Dürich, who'd left in the summer of 1916 despite Štefánik's disagreement. He had been required to guarantee the subordination of Czech and Slovak associations in Russia to the Paris National Council. Dürich held to the idea of a post-war reconstruction of the Czech Kingdom with the support of the Russian Tsar, while Masaryk, Beneš and Štefánik focussed on the Western powers of the Entente. Dürich and his twelve-member board of the Russian branch of the National Council of the Czech Republic supported the Russian government financially in order to move the centre of foreign resistance from Paris to St. Petersburg. Dürich promoted Kramář's idea of a post-war connection of the Czech Republic and Slovakia to Tsarist Russia. He was the man for St. Petersburg who could guarantee Russian interests in post-war Central Europe and Štefánik's fears that Dürich wouldn't follow the instructions of the National Council proved to be justified. Therefore, in July 1916 he went to St. Petersburg, where he negotiated on behalf of the French government and the National Council in the Russian Ministry of Foreign Affairs. However, his position was complicated, as the President of the National Council, Masaryk, was known as a critic of Tsarist absolutism and the Russian authorities sought to limit Masaryk's influence on his compatriots in Russia. Moreover, the new Prime Minister and Minister of Foreign Affairs was the Germanophile and Hungarophile, Stürmer, to whom support of the Czechs and Slovaks was like a red rag to a bull. Like monarchist officers, he considered the voluntary passage to captivity a betrayal of his sovereign. That is why the Tsarist Ministry of Foreign Affairs had long refused to give Štefánik permission to travel to the Russian headquarters, the Stavka, in Mogilev, about five hundred kilometres north of Kiev. Finally, after the intervention of the Allied Commander in Russia, the French General Maurice Janin, Štefánik was granted permission to travel to the Stavka. Here he learned that on the day before his arrival, Italy had declared war on Germany. He arrived there on 24th August and the very next day met Janin for the first time, who took him to General Alexeyev. After Štefánik's brilliant arguments, the chief of the Russian General Staff agreed to the creation of a Czecho-Slovak armed force on condition that immediately after its establishment, part would move to the Russian front and part to the French front. Initially he had insisted on the troops being deployed on the Russian front alone.

At length, the tense situation in the Czecho-Slovak movement in Russia was temporarily alleviated when, on 29th August, Štefánik, along with Josef Dürich and representatives of the Czech and Slovak associations in Russia, after an 18-hour negotiation in Kiev, signed the so-called Kiev Report on the principles of Czechoslovak action. This managed to reduce the influence of Russia on Czechoslovak foreign resistance and agreed to subordinate expatriate organizations in Russia to the leadership of the Czechoslovak National Council (CSNR.) In the document, Czechs and Slovaks living in Russia agreed on the union of Czechs and Slovaks in a single postwar state. However, Slovak organizations in the USA rejected the Kiev accord because of some of its formulations regarding the exact nature of the union.

General Janin presented Štefánik on 3rd September at an audience with Tsar Nicholas II. To the Tsar's surprise, the French officer addressed him in Russian. After Štefánik explained to him that he was the vice-chairman of the Czechoslovak National Council, chaired by Professor Masaryk the Tsar gave Masaryk the unexpected approbation that he wished their work well. Štefánik realized that the Tsar had a different view from his ministry of foreign affairs; at that time, he had no idea that Dürich in St. Petersburg had weakened his position behind his back and even called him "Masaryk's pro-Western intriguer".

The French ambassador to the court of Nicholas II was a writer of Romanian origin, Maurice Paléologue. He had the confidence of President Raymond Poincaré, the brother of the astronomer with whom Štefánik had once collaborated. Like Štefánik he was a naturalized Frenchman and so the diplomats understood each other. The ambassador held a reception in late September in honor of the plenipotentiary of the French government, Lieutenant Štefánik. He also invited representatives of Czech and Slovak organizations operating in Russia. Among the guests was Štefánik's former professor of the Prešporok Lyceum, Ján Radomil Kvačala, who was working at the Estonian University of Yuryeva (now the University of Tartu.) Štefánik decided to talk to him confidentially as at the Mogilev Staff headquarters he'd learned about his Memorandum on the Slovak Question, which he submitted to the Russian government. In the Memorandum, Kvačala advocated Slovakia joining Russia, which was fundamentally opposed to what the National Council wanted. After a few formalities, he invited Professor Kvačala to a separate room which the Ambassador had provided. The servant served them and moved away discreetly.

"Professor, I'm a direct man, and that's why I have a lot of enemies. I don't know how to be otherwise. In Russia, I am not only the Plenipotentiary of the French government, but also of the National Council of Czechoslovakia. However, your action is not in line with its programme."

"It's not the National Council of Czechoslovakia but of the Czech Republic. The Conseil National des Payes Tchèques is the official name of your self-proclaimed authority," said Kvačala. Breathing hard, he added unconvincingly: "I'm not saying that we shouldn't associate with the Czechs, we just don't want the Czechs to swallow us. We may as well remain with the Hungarians."

"I read your Memorandum. You clearly ask the Tsar for a post-war joining of Slovakia to Russia."

"Just as you wish a member of the Orléans family to sit on a Czechoslovak throne..." Kvačala paused for a moment, but then continued quietly: "We want him to be a member of the Romanov family. Which is not only historically, but also emotionally much more acceptable. We are Slavs, we understand each other. Who of us understands French or English?"

"States aren't built on feelings but on purposefulness," responded Štefánik.

"But Slovak political leaders haven't expressed their support for coexistence with the Czechs," Kvačala said.

"They act with caution, taking into account the circumstances in which they find themselves. The most important thing today is to demonstrate that we deserve independence. And this is only possible with the Czechs. We won't survive by ourselves nor with the Hungarians. Without Czech hands, Czech intelligence, self-confidence and support, Slovakia cannot exist as a self-sustaining state; no-one will acknowledge us. The Western powers are concerned to create an anti-German barrier. A Czech republic is politically, strategically and geopolitically weak, but joined to Slovakia it becomes a serious player. And Slovakia will only get into the geopolitical game together with a Czecho republic, because we can only strengthen it, thus making it able to fulfill this task. A true Slovak patriot desiring Slovak sovereignty has to throw in his lot with the Czechs. The Hungarians are agitating for keeping Upper Hungary where they can. They wait for every signal of Czecho-Slovak tension and people like you hand them arguments on a tray. We don't emphasize that we're two nations because we don't want our Allies to question the internal political strength of our promised state. Why the devil don't you understand that?" Štefánik raised his voice.

"The Russians are also our allies, not just Masaryk's Westerners! We perceive the Czechs as equal, they perceive us as inferior. Finally understand that!"

"If you don't see that Russia is on the verge of revolution, you're blind!"

"You're a traitor to the Slavs and the Slovaks!" Kvačala finally exploded, breathing hard. "You're ready to help subdue your own nation! This is unacceptable! Better with the Russians than with the Czechs. Do you want us to be subordinated to them as we did to the Hungarians?"

"And you want us to fall under Russian hegemony like the Poles? The Finns? The Lithuanians? The Estonians, whom you yourself are helping to Russianize? So denation us!"

"You blame me for denationing? You who are making such a great contribution to the Slovaks, you who support Masaryk's and Beneš's ideology of a unified Czechoslovak nation? How are you a Slovak when you share in denationing your own people? Your father would turn in his grave! Rather Hungarian than Czech!"

Štefánik stood up in agitation and rubbed his temples with a troubled expression.

"I'm sorry, dear Jano, I've addressed you formally and politely all the time, because you were a teacher that I respected. I'm sorry but at this moment, in my eyes, you've lost your last shred of dignity. Goodbye."

He left the embassy and never met his former professor again.

CHAPTER 12
When I've Done What I Need I Will Die in Peace

General Janin promoted Štefánik to the rank of captain in Russia on 13th October, 1916, but his promotion didn't improve his mood. The situation in Russia was not yet ready for his mission. In the air there was a revolutionary explosion approaching which would fundamentally change the attitudes of Russian-oriented Czechs and Slovaks. In agreement with General Janin, he decided to use his time better and join General Berthelot's French mission in Romania and assist the Romanians in organizing military operations. At the same time, he tried to win over soldiers among the Czech and Slovak prisoners willing to fight for freedom. He travelled from Kiev to Bucharest on 16th October and four days later, King Ferdinand received him in an audience. The King, respecting the solidarity of monarchs, refused to let soldiers who had previously sworn loyalty to another ruler, fight alongside his army. However, he allowed Štefánik to recruit from Czech and Slovak prisoners and transfer them to the French front. The prisoners in the camps lived in appalling conditions, which was the decisive reason for them to report to the army. Štefánik created a contingent of 1,500 men. Before the occupation of Bucharest on 6th December by the Germans he travelled to the city of Iasi in the north-east of the country, which for two years became the country's temporary capital. Romania, after hesitating for a long time about which side to join, had declared war on Austro-Hungary in August and become an ally of the Entente. But the country was cut off from its Western Allies by the Central Powers, so Russia was the only power that could help Romania effectively. Despite their own supply problems, the Russians sent 350 food and gun wagons to Romania daily. Romania declared war on Germany the day before the war ended on 10th November, 1918. 305,000 Romanian men lost their lives on the battlefields.

Three days before Christmas Eve on 21st December 1916, near the town of Barlad, Štefánik witnessed the bullying and humiliation of captives by Romanian soldiers. Around a thousand impoverished men were moving westwards on foot. Tattered and torn, with no shoes, their legs wrapped in coarse rags, tied with string, in military trousers that had more patches than original fabric, their teeth chattered from cold and hunger. The ditches were strewn with frozen corpses, men dying like flies from frost and dysentery, their clothes and footwear having been taken by the Romanian soldiers who guarded them. They hated the prisoners who were enemies to them, not caring whether they were Hungarians, Czechs, Serbs or Slovaks. They were all 'Austrians' who needed to be beaten and left to die of hunger. When he was near them, Štefánik ordered his car to stop. The Romanian guards, seeing an Allied French officer, obligingly lined them up. Štefánik measured the men up for a long time and then spoke to them in a calm voice.

"Whoever is a Slav, take two steps forward!"

The soldiers didn't understand at first; they were afraid that it was some kind of aristocratic game in which they were finally going to be shot, so nobody stepped forward.

"I am Štefánik, a Slovak in the service of the French. I have permission from the King of Romania to save you. Who wants to may join our free legions in France! Who doesn't want to fight, can enter France and work in the arms factories."

At that moment, the faces of the men brightened: the Czechs, Slovaks and Serbs stepped forward as did some Hungarians with a command of Slovak. Only the Poles looked incredulously at Štefánik and continued their march. He called the commanding Romanian officer over, explained the situation to him and showed him some papers with the interpreter translating everything. The officer nodded and assigned a number of non-commissioned officers to form the soldiers who'd stepped forward into a line four abreast.

"Now you will return to Barlad barracks. The Captain has been ordered to have your guards treat you fairly. I'm going on ahead. You'll have new clothes, boots and good food."

The soldiers really got everything that Štefánik had promised. He came back to them on Christmas Eve. Some wanted to kiss his hands, but he refused them with emotion. The soldiers were given a special ration of tobacco, white bread, rolls and even some wine. The whole unit moved by train to Iași, from there to Odessa and by boat to Marseille.

In 1916 a wave of mass protests began, supported and funded by German banks and agents. General Janin told Štefánik that the British Ambassador, Buchanan, and the French Ambassador, Paléologue, were key figures in preparing a conspiracy against Tsar Nicholas II. The reason was clear: after initial problems, the Russian army had begun to consolidate. The favourite of the Tsar, General Brusilov had achieved great success, due to which Russian troops were approaching the territory of Central Europe, where France wanted to be influential in the future. In 1917, the Russians expected further success on the Eastern Front. A strong Russia was therefore a threat not only to Germany and Austria-Hungary, but also to French, British and Italian post-war ambitions. It was thus necessary to weaken Russia so it would still be able to tie down German forces on the eastern front, but unable to expand more significantly to the west.

At the end of 1916, a new player, US President Woodrow Wilson, appeared on the world scene, elected as President in December for the second time. On 12th December, the Central Powers submitted a proposal for peace to the Allied Powers which, if adopted, would have meant the collapse of the foreign Czecho-Slovak resistance. Emperor Franz Joseph I had died in Schönbrunn Palace on 21st November, 1916 at the age of 86. The new Emperor was the twenty-nine-year-old Charles I, who on 30th December accepted the Hungarian crown, which made him Charles IV and King of the Slovaks. The new Emperor aroused new hopes in the representatives of the entente powers that the fighting would soon end, a deadly threat to the anti-Austrian resistance. Masaryk began a feverish effort to reject this idea, although he realized that it would actually prolong the war. It was a devil's dilemma: either encourage mass murder on the fronts with the hope of establishing a republic or promote peace and with it the death of a dream of an independent Czecho-Slovakia. In an English newspaper he published a series of articles to persuade the public and politicians that peace without victory would mean the demoralization of Europe, while peace with victory would mean the democratization of Europe. Fortunately, US President Woodrow Wilson rejected German conditions and called on the states on both sides to declare the conditions under which peace could be negotiated. The Entente states responded to Wilson's note collectively on 10th January 1917, saying that the war must be brought to a victorious end.

A great diplomatic success for the foreign Czecho-Slovak resistance and personally for Štefánik was the fact that thanks to the French Prime Minister, Briand, the Allied statement spoke of "the liberation of Italians, Slavs, Romanians and Czechs and Slovaks". For the first time in an international forum, not only the Czechs, but also the Slovaks had been officially mentioned! The Entente announcement aroused bitterness in Poles and Southern Slavs, however, who'd only been mentioned under the common name, Slavs.

On 4th January 1917 Štefánik returned from Romania to Kiev and then to St. Petersburg, where an allied conference began, with Štefánik participating alongside General Janin. He stayed initially at the Hotel Dagmar on Sadova Street where he regained strength after the demanding negotiations. Again his health was affected: he coughed blood, drank only milk and coffee, ate mainly just bread.

One day, his adjutant, Baron Larienty de Tholozan, came to him with a strange look on his face.

"Has something happened?" Štefánik asked.

"I don't know how to explain it, but I feel like someone keeps putting a strange odour under my nose at night. I lose consciousness after breathing it in. In the morning, I always have a sharp headache and dizziness. I've never had such sensations before..."

"It is not possible!" Štefánik leaped to his feet in excitement. "I've had the same. In the morning my head hurts and my heart pounds. And in my mouth I can taste something sweet. I looked at the wardrobe where I keep the documents... They were mixed up somehow..."

"Unbelievable. I also felt that someone was searching my papers at night. However, I had the key inside the lock all the time..."

"That's no problem for a secret agent. I drew a faint line under the keyhole. In the morning, I found that somebody had moved the key..."

"So it's the same thing for us, the Tsarist secret police. I've talked to Dr. Pelican about this; he has a friend, the owner of the Europe Hotel on the Nevsky prospekt. We can move there."

One morning after they'd moved, the servant found Štefánik in the hall of the apartment unconscious with bruising over his left eye and face. Again, heart weakness had afflicted him. He was forced to stay in bed, but still received visitors and worked.

At the end of January, the Russian government approved the creation of the Czechoslovak National Council in Russia, which broke away from the Paris National Council. At the head of the St. Petersburg-supported council stood the Tsarophile, Josef Dürich. Between Štefánik and Dürich there was a sharp exchange of views on 9th February. Dürich called Štefánik an Austrian spy. Offended, Štefánik called him outside for a duel but General Janin forbade it. When Štefánik learned that Dürich was receiving financial support from the Russian government, he was angry and yelled at the top of his voice, even though he was bedridden: "The story of Dürich must be finished. If he doesn't listen to me, I'll shoot him like a dog!"

Continuous stress and disputes with Dürich undermined his health. A few minutes before the meeting with Chief of Staff Alexeyev on 6th March, he had a severe cough, put his handkerchief to his mouth and brought up a lot of blood with mucus. After a while he calmed down, threw the handkerchief into a waste bin, pulled another out of his briefcase and, as if nothing had happened, entered Alexeyev's office. Doctor Rudolf Pelikán, who cared for him, proposed an operation, but Štefánik rejected it.

"Doctor Štefánik, with so much energy expended you can't just live on coffee and dry rolls," Pelikan told him.

"That was what Dr. Girsa said in Kiev," Štefánik smiled.

"Losing so much blood while vomiting is especially dangerous. Stomach cramps cause intestinal adhesions. You need an operation."

"How long would it take?"

"You're very weak, so would need around a month to prepare and then at least two months for convalescence."

"I know my health is broken and I don't have much time ahead of me. So I must use the rest of my life the best I can. When I've done what I need, then I will die in peace. I can't afford to wait for three months..." He thought for a moment, adding softly: "But I'd be very grateful to you, Doctor, if you could sometimes stop in to see me... And I have another request... Please, in case of my death take care to conduct an exact autopsy... can you promise me?"

Dr. Pelikan stood by the bed and shook his head uncomprehendingly.

"Say, Mr. Captain, is stubbornness your usual way of solving problems?"

"It's how I am. But I do have other ways." He thought, then added, "First I try to go round them, but if I can't, I try to crawl under them. When that isn't possible, I try to jump over them, and when that isn't possible, I bite into them with relish... And when we do it together, by God, we will solve them..."

On International Women's Day on 8th March 1917 (according to the Gregorian calendar), about 90,000 women went into the streets of St. Petersburg to protest against hunger and war. The workers of Putilov and other enterprises gradually joined them and finally the protests grew into a general strike. The protests didn't have political leaders; the Bolsheviks followed the protesters more than they led them. The Tsar ordered a ruthless suppression of the rebellion with troops devoted to the Tsar initially killing about 150 people. But when, soon after, the Volinsky and the famous Preobrazhensky Regiment switched sides and joined the protesters, the Tsar's fate was decided. On the night of the 15th to 16th March 1917, Nicholas II wrote an abdication letter in the wagon of a train ceding the crown to his more decisive brother, Michael. However, the Duma appointed a government headed by the popular prince, George Lvov. Russia breathed a sigh of relief and the Allies welcomed this democratic change, especially when the new government declared that it would continue fighting on the Allies' side.

At the time of these dramatic changes, Štefánik was in St. Petersburg. Horrified, he watched the drunken crowds looting from shops and restaurants. The Tsar and his family had been gods for the Russians but suddenly were no longer. Soldiers and police were brothers with factory workers, especially female workers who teased the drunken boys with their so-called charms. Prison guards arbitrarily released inmates and the streets of St. Petersburg became an obscure film scene in which everything was allowed. A number of revolutionaries even invaded Štefánik's room in the Dagmar Hotel to carry out a search and try to get a gun from him. Štefánik refused, appealing to his rank and dual nationality. He urged them to calm down and told them, "You know, we had a revolution long before you." The fundamental purpose of his coming to Russia, to establish a Czecho-Slovak army, went unfulfilled due to the obstruction of the St. Petersburg Ministry of Foreign Affairs. In the prisoner-of-war camps, 20,000 Czechs and Slovaks remained ready to join the legions but there were serious disagreements between the Petrograd authorities and Russian headquarters, which supported his initiative. After the abdication of the Tsar, Štefánik decided not to waste time waiting for the appointment of new Russian authorities and responsible people to government posts. Instead he would continue recruiting Czechs and Slovaks in the USA. Before leaving, he discussed matters with Miljukov, the new Foreign Minister of the Revolutionary government, who agreed to recognize the Paris Czechoslovak National Council as the only representative of the Czechoslovak nation in Russia.

Dürich was finished, Masaryk excluding him from the National Council after the agreement and thus preventing a split between foreign resistance organizations.

CHAPTER 13

Our Cause Will Succeed!

Štefánik prepared the ground for the arrival of Masaryk in Russia and on 6th April 1917, the day of the declaration of war on Germany by the United States, he sailed in the English merchant ship *Umtali* from Romanov to Liverpool accompanied by Secretary Písecký and his assistant, Boucher. He met Masaryk on 17th April in Hampstead in London, where the professor lived with his daughter Olga. Despite his persistent health problems, he sought to bring optimism to Masaryk. The news from Prague wasn't good; Masaryk's daughter Alice was in prison for the eighth month and Charlotte's health was getting worse. At that time, articles about his traitorous activity on the side of the enemy with open threats to his family appeared in Czech newspapers. Masaryk drove off the bad news from home by working and decided to travel to Russia in the belief that the emergence of a democratic government would also provide a new impetus for the Russian army. But he found the Russian government in disarray with socialist elements demanding a share of power. The government of Lvov had been replaced by the left-wing government of Kerensky, listening to the voice of the people who demanded that Russia end the war. The Central Powers rejected his offer for a separate peace, so Kerensky decided to continue the war alongside the Allies.

On 6th May, a delegation of Czecho-Slovak troops, prisoners, Czechs and Slovaks living in Russia recognized Masaryk as the supreme representative of the Czechoslovak nation. On 31st May, Masaryk visited St. Petersburg's Basejna Street, where the editorial board of the weekly *Slovenské listy*, the newspaper of the Slovaks in Russia, was located. He was welcomed by the editor-in-chief, Vladimír Hurban, son of Svetozár Hurban Vajanský, who, despite his disputes with Masaryk, expressed his pleasure in his son's co-operation with the professor shortly before his death. Masaryk had brought Bohdan Pavlů with the intention of explaining to the Slovaks his attitudes to the future organization of Czecho-Slovak relations. It was a topic which sparked heated discussions. The guest gave a warm hand to Hurban, Jozef Gregor, Janko Jesenský and the other editors. Also present were the editors of *Bratský Čechoslovan, Švihovský, Žďárský, Dým* and others. He sensed that the Slovaks in particular were worried about future cooperation and thus initiated a debate on the subject.

"I want to inform you that the National Council is negotiating with the Russian military authorities to create a military force. Yes, our revolution has begun with our troops, who have moved to the Russian side, showing their opposition to the monarchy. Each of us knows what we want, everyone knows that this armed force will be the military foundation of the future Czechoslovak state. We have proved that we Czechs have been able to stand up to the Habsburgs; it's been evident throughout our history. I urge you to avenge the ancient injustices that the Habsburg dynasty has inflicted on the Czech nation... I have heard about the discussions that have been taking place between Czechs and Slovaks in Russia. It's natural and it's good. Two brothers of one family must have a clear relationship so they can help each other."

"Mr Chairman," one of the editors said after a moment of silence, "it is a serious worry that after the establishment of the Republic, you Czechs will be dominant in Slovakia... People are afraid that our Hungarian lords will merely be replaced by Czechs."

Most of the Slovaks nodded, others waited for Masaryk's response.

"How can you compare the Czechs and Hungarians at all? Have the Czechs ever hurt us, persecuted us, taken our speech or schools from us or forbidden us to speak our mother tongue in official matters?" said Gregor warmly.

"Well, no, but we haven't lived with them yet. How do you know what it'll be like in the new republic? After all, we have hardly any intelligentsia, officials, doctors, journalists; there are no Slovaks in county offices, post offices, railways, and judicial offices. Hungarian officials are in all the offices and I'm afraid that all of them will only be exchanged for Czechs."

"It'll all depend on us Slovaks," said Masaryk. "Yes, I'm deliberately saying us Slovaks, because I'm partly Slovak myself; my father was a Slovak from Kopčany, my mother a Moravian."

"Mr. Chairman," Jesensky turned directly towards their guest, "it isn't about you, we don't doubt your relationship with the Slovaks, but many of our Czech compatriots here in Russia simply ignore us. They're always talking about the Czech army, the Czech struggle, Czech politics, the Czech state, Czech culture, Czech history, as if we Slovaks didn't even exist."

"We want to create a Slovak regiment," brother Čipka said. "Let the world see the Slovaks better. This will impress our benighted, inhibited people in the prison camps. If there are only two to three hundred Slovaks now, two or three thousand may soon join them. Slovak companies will attract them. We're all ready to help and stand honourably alongside our Czech brothers."

"We request," said the lowlander, Janko Kutlík, joining the debate, "that the names and addresses of our birthplaces in Slovakia be published in *Slovenské hlasy*. And let our countrymen see this in the camps or wherever they are hidden, unawakened, intimidated... And when we are in an army of three thousand, five thousand, when we also in fact prove that we are men in the right place, we'll look into the eyes of those who would dominate us!" said Kutlík eloquently.

"I think it would be better to have a mixed Czecho-Slovak army, but in principle, if the Slovaks feel more confident in Slovak units, let the Slovak units be. They will be part of one army," said Masaryk.

"I'm in favour of us all being united," said the soldier, Holub. "The professor is right, we don't want separatism. And some zealots wear signs of separatism on their caps. White-blue-red ribbons on the peak of their caps."

"What do you have against them? Isn't that the tricolour of the Slovak nation?" Kutlík grew heated.

"Neither Slovak, nor Czech, I'm a Czechoslovak," said Holub.

"I studied and worked in Bohemia. I didn't meet a Czech who wasn't convinced that we were part of them, that we are just drops in the Czech Sea. Even here in the army, they are so sure. How much we argue with them but they won't listen. When you sincerely open-handedly tell them your feelings, they label you a separatist.

And we don't want anything else but to have a new common household organized properly and fairly right from the beginning. Finally, excuse me for saying so, but you always refer to we Czechs. What about the Slovaks?" And the editor looked reproachfully at Masaryk.

"But has the professor said that everything depends on us? We'll need Czechs until we raise our own intelligentsia," said Gregor calming the speaker.

"And you think that once the Czech directors are settled in their posts, they'll voluntarily give them up to Slovaks?" One of the soldiers shook his head.

"I believe we can come to an agreement," Gregor said, pausing.

"It's not in vain that you legionaries address each other as brothers. That means both Czech and Slovak brothers. You should be aware that as the Slovaks depend on the Czechs, so the Czechs depend on the Slovaks. When we imagine how the new republic will look, it must be dominated by its Czechoslovak and not German element. If we divide into Czechs and Slovaks, then there will be fewer Slovaks in the projected republic than the Germans. I understand the call for Slovak autonomy, but we would have to give it to the Germans first, because there may well turn out to be more of them than Slovaks. And also to the Hungarians of whom there will be many in the new republic. And it will actually be a small monarchy again. Do we want that? Do we want our allies to think we are at loggerheads about our future republic? If we were to declare this proposition to the world powers, they would ask us logically why we need to break Austria-Hungary and build a nationally mixed and therefore fragile state. But if we are united, then our state will be built on the dominance of Czechoslovakia." For a moment, Masaryk took a breath, tugged his moustache and continued.

"I admit that the Czech language was commonly used in my workplace and that Slovaks took it as a matter of course. It was an oversight of mine – I had no ulterior motive for doing so. However, I can imagine your feelings of injustice and therefore I promise you that I will now always use the word Czechoslovak and will impress this with my whole authority on our Czech brothers. If my language errs and I use the word Czech again, please don't hesitate to tell me as you have done now. I would like you to know that I've instructed the correction of the seal of our 'Conseil national des pays Tchèques' to the 'pays Tchéco-Slovaques'."

"That's good, we welcome it," said Gregor.

"Lads, keep your heads up, if we stick together, we will prosper."

The editors, both Czech and Slovak, nodded without demur. The atmosphere was now calm again.

"Do you know this one?"

To the surprise of everyone, the professor began to sing a Slovak song in a quiet, brooding voice: "When my heart hurts me, when distress bothers me, I go when evening falls to the green forest hills…"

The surprised editors, soldiers and printers gradually joined in. Their voices grew stronger, the song was carried out through the windows behind which the inconspicuous, but increasing determination of the dissatisfied masses would soon turn Masaryk's, Russian and allied expectations upside down.

CHAPTER 14
Lenin Cooperates

The cauldron of dissatisfaction was heating up in St. Petersburg, Moscow, Kazan, Samara, and other Russian cities, the hopes invested in the Kerensky government were fading and the war went on. Workers, peasants and soldiers followed the words of representatives of the emerging popular councils, the Soviets, more receptively than the instructions of politicians or their commanders. In society, the influence of radical Marxists, the Bolsheviks, advocating the dictatorship of the proletariat, was strengthened. They were headed by Vladimir Ilyich Ulyanov, who had adopted the revolutionary name Lenin, from the Russian river, the Lena, a protest against the founder of Russian Marxism, Plechanov, who used the name Volgin (the Lena flowed in the opposite direction to the Volga). But the dissatisfied masses did not know that the Bolshevik leader was working closely with the German secret service, collaboration proposed by Alexander Parvus, a former Russian revolutionary of 1905, an arms dealer and friend of Bronstein-Trotsky, born as Israel Lazarevich Helfand. Parvus made friends with the German Ambassador von Wangenheim in Istanbul, who said one winter evening in early 1915: "The interests of the German government are identical to those of the Russian revolutionaries: to defeat the Tsar. I have a plan to encourage a wave of mass demonstrations in Russia that will paralyze the country and lead to the fall of Nicholas II." In May 1915, Parvus secretly met Lenin in Zurich. After the meeting, he founded a trading company in Copenhagen specializing in illegal trade with Russia. Through Parvus's firm, the Germans secretly supplied drugs, surgical material, clothing and chemicals to Russia. The money earned that remained in Russia was available to the Bolsheviks. The Germans funded the publication of *Pravda* and another 27 newspapers and magazines. The threat of close US entry into the war forced Berlin to act quickly and their plan to use Lenin's Bolsheviks to dismantle Russia from within was brilliant. Highly educated, Lenin spoke perfect German and French, good English, read Aristotle in Greek and his favourite recreation was studying dictionaries.

In Zurich in Switzerland, a group of thirty-two men and women packed their suitcases on 9th April and gathered at the Central Station. The 263 express train to Schaffhausen was ready for departure. About a hundred Russian Tsarist exiled protesters screamed obscene insults and spat at the group of silent men and women. Some of the group on board the train looked frightened but their leader, a short, stocky man with a goatee beard in studded mountain boots and a cap on his head, didn't seem to be excited. He boarded last and the train moved off at 15.20.

"In six months we will be ministers or we will hang," remarked Vladimir Ulyanov Lenin. It was Easter Monday, the USA had declared war on Germany seventy-two hours before.

Border checks were not carried out as the competent authorities were informed of the group's transit but the hearts of the Russians were in their mouths at the border town of Gottmadingen, where they were required to disembark. However, as it turned out, this was only to move to a specially designed luxury wagon that would connect with the regular trains. At Lenin's request, the wagon was given the status of extraterritoriality and no German guide could enter it. Lenin, a stubborn non-smoker, generously allowed smokers to use the toilet at the other end of the wagon. They went through Frankfurt and Berlin; finally in the town of Sasnitz they took the Queen Victoria ferry to Trelleborg, where they continued by train and sledge to the Finnish town of Tornio. Shortly before midnight on 16th April, the train carrying the group of revolutionaries entered the Finnish station in St. Petersburg. When a stocky man in an elegant woollen coat stepped down from the train, the crowd of waiting sailors couldn't believe this was Lenin the revolutionary. He removed his top hat and exclaimed, "Comrades, you have had a revolution, but the traitors of the temporary government have deceived you and robbed you of its fruits!" The next day, an agent of German military intelligence from Stockholm sent a cipher to Berlin: "Lenin happily arrived in Russia, working together." But not everything went according to Berlin's instructions. After a failed coup attempt in July, Lenin escaped to Finland to escape arrest.

The Czecho-Slovak legionaries, whose number had grown to about 60,000 out of a total of 250,000 prisoners in Russia, had welcomed the democratic revolution. In the fighting at Zborov on 1st and 2nd July 1917, during what was known as Kerensky's offensive, the legionaries achieved a great victory over the Austrians. From the Austrian ranks, many Czechs and Slovaks crossed without a fight to the Russian side. In contrast, two Guards Regiments went over to the Austrians and one entire Division surrendered without a fight, as the disintegration of the Russian army went on apace. This contributed to the high losses among the legionaries as the Russians who were supposed to cover their flanks didn't enter their lines. The soldiers of the Czecho-Slovak Rifle Brigade captured 62 officers and 3,150 soldiers and thus ensured the battle of Zborov would be written in golden letters in the history of Czech-Slovak legions. On the second day after the battle, 3rd July, General Selivačov, commander of the Army Corps, cantered over to the legionaries and embraced them enthusiastically. "I have fought in three wars, but I have not seen such a brave battle as yours." After this victory, the Kerensky government finally allowed the formation of legions.

The July attempt to seize power by Lenin had been stopped by the interim government, but the Bolshevik promises, immediate peace, confiscation of land, surrender of power to the Soviets, and the right of non-Russian peoples to self-determination, were extremely attractive. The eruption of mass resistance in Russia came on 7th November, 1917 (25th October in the Julian calendar). Eighteen million workers, fifteen million soldiers and one hundred and thirty million peasants, overthrew the four million bourgeoisie, whose only concern, instead of carrying out the promised reforms and, in particular, ending Russian participation in the war, was to replace the expelled Tsarist officials and secure personal power and benefits in the new structures. On the day of the coup, which has entered history as the Great October Socialist Revolution, life in St. Petersburg was proceeding like any other day. The shops were open, the banks were lending devalued money, the opera was giving a performance of Verdi's *Don Carlos* and the trams were running regularly. On one of them was Lenin, who was travelling to the Bolshevik stronghold, the Smolny Palace, in the garb and wig of a white-haired old man without his characteristic goatee. His disguise was so good, in fact, that when he arrived at just before midnight, the guards didn't recognize him and didn't want to let him into Smolny. Only when Trotsky confirmed Lenin's identity did he take on his role as leader. After shots were fired from the *Aurora*, the Red Guards invaded the Winter Palace, but lost their way in its innumerable corridors under the influence of alcohol and so it took them a while to find the office of the Kerensky government (without Kerensky, who had managed to flee in a USA embassy car). A hundred and forty female troops, together with a hundred Cossacks and military cadets, face to face with masses of angry and drunken Red Guards surrendered, but many of them went over to their side. In protest against the coup, many of the delegates of the St. Petersburg Soviets left the hall and ceded space for Lenin's Bolsheviks, who did not let power slip from their hands. The number of members of the Bolshevik Party had grown incredibly: in the spring of 1917 they numbered ten thousand, now there were four hundred thousand of them.

Russia began to fall into chaos and civil war. Supplies to the population were restricted, industrial production fell and the masses of the new unemployed entered the revolutionary Red Guard, organized by Trotsky. Blame was put on the provisional government that had ruled with almost no army and had handed the Bolsheviks power without fighting. Political prisoners were released, the death penalty abolished and the dream of popular democracy seemed to be at hand. But it quickly disappeared as hopes were lost in the onset of violence and injustice. The masses realized bitterly that Trotsky (Bronstein), Kamenev (Rosenfeld), Zinoviev (Apfelbaum), Sverdlov (Movshevich), Rykov, Jugashvili-Stalin, Dzerzhinsky, Radek, Kaganovich and other revolutionaries were a group of utopian fanatics, Russian Jacobins who balked at no atrocities in pursuit of their ideals. Prisons under the command of mostly Poles and Latvians began to fill up with a new group of people, class enemies, who became virtually anyone who owned anything. One of Lenin's first pronouncements after taking power was: "The final struggle with the kulak is everywhere, exemplary action is needed against them. Therefore, I order: 1. Hang, in all cases hang, don't shoot, so that the people have the kulaks, rich men, leeches before their eyes. 2. Publish their names. 3. Seize all the grain from them. 4. Select hostages. Everything needs to be done so that people tremble from the horrors hundreds of kilometres around! We must organize violence on behalf of the workers. Anyone who is against us must be executed."

The legionaries perceived the revolution as betrayal, as the Bolsheviks concluded a ceasefire with the Central Powers on 3rd December, 1917 and began peace negotiations in Brest. Remarkably, on 8th January 1918, the director of Berlin's Reichsbank von Schansen wrote to Trotsky: "... 50 million roubles in gold have been put at the disposal of the People's Commissar."

One of the greatest risks to Czechoslovak foreign resistance was a domestic demonstration of loyalty to Austro-Hungary. The new Emperor Charles I tried to gain the trust of non-Austrian nations for their reform aims by a series of steps to weaken foreign resistance. On 2nd July, he signed an amnesty for 18,000 political prisoners, due to which resistance figures such as Kramář, Rašín, Klofáč and others were freed. They immediately joined the Maffie resistance movement. He appointed Count Clam-Martinic as Prime Minister and Count Czernin as Minister of Foreign Affairs, both of whom had Czech origins. Representatives of the Czech Union at an audience with Clam-Martinic in January 1917 publicly declared that the Czech nation saw its future only in union with Austria. In a letter to Minister Czernin, they wrote: "In view of the entente states' response to the USA's President Wilson, in which they declared the liberation of the Czechs from foreign dominion as one of their goals, the Presidium of the Czech Union rejects this goal as being based on completely wrong assumptions and decisively declares that the

Czech nation, as always in past, as well as in present times, sees its future under the Habsburg sceptre." This statement was in direct opposition to the goals of the Czech foreign resistance. Finally, under pressure from Czech intellectuals, deputies in Vienna's imperial assembly issued a statement which through an initiative of Vavro Šrobár also made mention of the Slovaks. "We request the Habsburg-Lorraine monarchy be transformed into a federal state of free and equal national states." They emphasized "the merging of all branches of the Czechoslovak nation into a democratic Czech state, not forgetting the Slovak branch."

Despite the efforts of the new Emperor, the monarchy was slowly entering its death throes and although censorship was still working, events of which ordinary people had known nothing were now being reported in the newspapers. News now reached towns and the countryside about the Czechoslovak National Council and the Czecho-Slovak foreign resistance. For the first time people heard names such as Masaryk, Štefánik and Beneš.

CHAPTER 15
Dubček Versus Štefánik

On the orders of the French Minister of War, Major Štefánik traveled to the USA on 2nd June on a "special mission". In addition to this mission, he also had a second task: to gain American compatriots to join the Czechoslovak army. An obstacle to recruitment was the fact that the United States was not yet at war with Austria-Hungary and hadn't been hurt by any hostile act. Wherever he went he spread optimism, hope and belief in the success of the Czecho-Slovak project, despite the fact that President Wilson didn't support the disintegration of the monarchy and that since the signing of the Cleveland Agreement in the Slovak League, the focus on Tsarist Russia had strengthened. The shift to a programme of uniting Czechs and Slovaks in a single state occurred only after the Bolshevik revolution.

Despite such setbacks, he worked tirelessly among his compatriots in American political, business, artistic and media circles. The French Ambassador, Jean Jules Jusserand, doyen of the diplomatic corps in Washington, who, at the time Štefánik arrived, had been in his post for fourteen years, became his protector and loyal supporter. He had great contacts with former presidents, Theodore Roosevelt and William Taft, as well as with the current President, Woodrow Wilson. Jusserand was an avid supporter of the entry of the USA into the war and strongly supported Štefánik's efforts to gain Czech and Slovak military reinforcements for France, all the more so because from top secret ciphers from home he learned of the growing unwillingness of the French to fight. Twenty thousand soldiers had deserted the army; those who remained in the trenches were willing to defend them but refused to attack. Jusserand acquainted Štefánik with Theodore Roosevelt, who still commanded great respect in society, even though he was no longer President. With Frank Polek, High Representative of the Ministry of Foreign Affairs and future minister, he achieved one of his most important diplomatic successes: the permission to recruit volunteers. He expected to convince at least twenty thousand in the United States. However, there was one problem that he hadn't counted on. After the USA declared war on Germany on 2nd April, 1917, the United States introduced general conscription, as exemplified by Britain. Washington needed troops for its own army, which it gradually moved to the French front. Štefánik was therefore only allowed to recruit Slovaks and Czechs who were below or above the age of recruitment, or who weren't yet American citizens.

On 16th September, New York's Carnegie Hall held a gathering of Czech and Slovak compatriots, with Štefánik as the main speaker alongside the mayor of New York, John P. Mitchel and the French minister, Franklin Bouillon.

"We will fight," roared the energetic Slovak from the podium in the sky-blue uniform of a French major, "until we gain freedom. We want peace, but it must be glorious, decided not on the grave of small nations. A nation that wants it to be regarded as a separate state-creating entity has the right and the duty to form an army and to release this army to fight alongside the Allies!"

His speech was published by all the major American dailies. Another success was achieved when he changed the position of the leading Slovak Catholic priests, who until then had remained loyal to Austro-Hungary. The Slovak banker, Michal Bosák, treasurer of the First Catholic Slovak Union, was the main organizer of the meeting with the priests and the spirit behind a million-dollar collection supporting a campaign for the Independence of Slovakia. One of the authors of the resolution in which Catholic priests confirmed their acceptance of Czechs and Slovaks having their own common state, was the priest and inventor, Jozef Murgaš.

After arriving in Washington on 24th September, Štefánik's health deteriorated sharply. Travelling, speaking, persuading, making statements and being under stress had once again had an effect on his health. He went into an emergency hospital, from where he was transferred to John Hopkins Hospital in Baltimore after three days. The celebrated Doctor Carrol urgently recommended surgery and at least three months in bed. He guaranteed that if he obeyed, his condition would improve significantly. But Štefánik refused to do so, as so often before.

"I can't lie in bed when our cause needs me most!"

But he did lie in bed though not in hospital, but in a hotel. He received many visits there, often holding a cold compress on his head, with his lips pulled back in pain. He also talked to Michal Bosák, who promised him financial and organizational assistance. During a friendly discussion, Bosák told him that one of his sons had enlisted in the US Air Force. Štefánik was in his element and spoke enthusiastically about the amazing possibilities offered by the new technical field of aviation. He urged Bosák to repeat to his son that air pockets low above the ground are most dangerous to airmen. Such areas of turbulence arose unexpectedly, but when an aviator rushed into them, he could plunge to the ground with almost no chance of saving himself. At a higher altitude an airman still had the opportunity to enter more stable air. At a low height above the ground, however, it always ended in disaster...

He embarked on formulating the Manifesto of the Czecho-Slovak National Council with the title of an anthem by Karel Kuzmány, "Who burns for the truth". It was a declaration of universal national mobilization. "Whatever happens, we swear we won't deal with our ancient murderer like cowards nor lay our weapons down until we gain full freedom! Forward, brethren, with heads held high and no gloom in your soul! We will triumph because our will is rock-like; a will of ten million, the nation's consciousness must at last be respected. We will win because our slogans are: Love, Work, Honesty – the slogans of the future, the God-given ages!" He signed it himself for the National Council, as Masaryk was in Russia at the time and Beneš in Paris. The *New Yorker Daily* published the Manifesto.

With a French major, the Count de Montal, and Karel Pergler, the organizer of Czechs in the USA, he travelled to Chicago on 13th October, where he was enthusiastically welcomed by masses of Czechs and Slovaks. At that time Chicago was the largest Czech and Slovak city in the world, with about 120,000 Czechs and 30,000 Slovaks. The weather in Chicago on 14th October, 1917 was unkind. Sharp winds blew through the streets, forcing people to rush into the first Chicago *Sokol* restaurant at the junction of South Lawndale and Avenue 27 to properly wrap up in their coats. The Military Committee, composed of representatives of the Czech National Association, *Sokol*, the National Union of Czech Catholics and representatives of the Slovak League, convened a public meeting in the Sokol Havlíček-Tyrš chamber. A huge poster, stuck on a brick wall, proclaimed in half-metre high letters: "Public meeting here. Dr. M. R. Štefánik speaks. On Sunday, 14th October, 1917, at 2 pm."

A poster depicting the Štefánik's Manifesto of the Czecho-Slovak National Council, 'Who Burns for the Truth', was hung on the wall above the chair. Hundreds of Czech and Slovak men and women, wondering about the Slovak Frenchman who had become so well-known and popular in expatriate circles, filled the hall to capacity. Ironworkers and smiths from the Strnad company, brewers, printers, tyre makers from the Western Wheel Company, car makers from Bugmobile, textile workers from Oxford Clothes, ironworkers from Armstrong Tools and many others eagerly awaited the appearance of the major whose reputation as a great speaker preceded him. *The Sun, the New York World, the New York Times* and *the New York Herald* had reported on the grand gathering of Czechs and Slovaks in Carnegie Hall and the great speech by Štefánik. Among the workers were also three men known for their left-wing opinions, Štefan Dubček with his brother Michal and his friend Jozef Griger. They were all members of the Slovak section of the American Socialist Party.

As the slender man stepped on the podium in a sky-blue uniform, as if to match his eyes, huge applause echoed through the hall. Štefánik bowed and on his weary face he conjured up his characteristic smile, disarming everyone.

"Please don't blame me for speaking Slovak, but my heart told me I should. I am Slovak in my body though my soul loves my Czech brother. I came to America to oblige the will of the nation. My main job has been in Washington in government circles where I worked for our cause. As a representative of the Czechoslovak National Council, I have worked to obtain the approval of the US government to form an independent Czecho-Slovak army. This has been successful, so I come here today to call on every Czech and

Slovak to take part in the fight for our freedom. Our goal is total self-determination."

His words were interrupted by applause, which then sounded after almost every sentence.

"The nation must pay for its freedom with its blood! A Czechoslovak union with its own flag will be the best guarantee that the victory of the Allies will be the victory of our cause as well! If we want to become independent, we must first show moral progress!"

"Bravo! Long live freedom! Long live Czechoslovakia! Down with the monarchy!" Enthusiastic chants resounded in the hall.

"As our boys in Russia, Italy and Romania are enlisting, so I also ask you, USA resident Slovaks and Czechs, to follow your brothers in Europe! We will fight as our men fought at Zborov!"

"It's fine enlisting when they're in prisoner-of-war camps and have only two options, to drop dead from hunger or typhoid in a camp, or to go to the front. But we're at home with our families and if we enlist, who will take care of them?"

His speech had been interrupted by a worker in a checked cap and threadbare jacket. Many nodded.

For Štefánik, it was unusual for someone to break into his speech, and he was momentarily caught off guard. But then he continued calmly: "It's difficult to say, but surely the truth is your brothers who have enlisted in their hundreds of thousands on the front have no-one to look after their families except their wives and parents. The struggle for freedom is a sacrifice, but looking at the fronts now that America has entered the war, it is obvious that it won't last long!"

"My brother is in the 35th Infantry Regiment in Pilsen. Am I supposed to go fight him?"

The hall fell silent, and Štefánik was again taken aback for a moment. Karel Pergler, sitting at the chair, was translating the content of the discussion to de Montal. The Baron watched Štefánik, who began to cough. He had to drink a glass of water and breathe deeply.

"I know that near Caporetto in Pijava there is about to be a serious battle between the Austrians, Germans and Hungary, including our Czech and Slovak boys. Against them is the second Italian army, which includes the legions we have created. Yes, my friend, brother stands against brother. It's a terrible situation. I'm also an enemy to my own brothers in Hungary. I can't go home because they would execute me immediately. Our leader, Professor Masaryk, our vice-chairman Eda Beneš, whose brother lives here with you, was sentenced to death for high treason. The son of our President Ján Masaryk fights on the opposite side of the front to his father. A tragic situation! But the time has come to decide whether the world will continue to endure the imperialism and aggression of the German, Austrian and Hungarian lords, or overthrow them. We have the advantage over our brothers fighting for the Austrians and Hungarians that while they are fighting from fear, we are fighting from conviction. It's our duty all the more to join the free army and liberate our brothers in arms from the yoke of Austrian corporals!"

"He's right, well said," declared various voices.

"But we don't want to fight our Russian brothers, either. Why are our soldiers in Russia fighting against workers and peasants?" A square man, who had so far watched the events in the hall in silence, stood up suddenly. "I'm Dubček Štefan, a carpenter. We want the Czecho-Slovak Republic, but we don't want to replace one oppressor with another. We want to replace the government of lords with a government of workers. We don't want war. We want peace and we want to put the land into the hands of the peasants, just as the Russian Bolsheviks want to! President Wilson has betrayed us. He argued that America would never go to war, but suddenly it was in up to its ears!" yelled the angry man from Uhrovec. With a questioning look, Štefánik gazed at the huge man who, with his voice, had electrified his countrymen. Some tried to shout him down, others applauded him.

"Well gentlemanly soldiering might appeal to you," the blacksmith Bernátek from Hodonín shouted angrily at the little major. "But what will our insurance associations pay from if we fall there like pears? Everyone is insured for a thousand dollars, so if only ten of us fall on the front, it will be ten thousand, if a hundred, a hundred thousand. There will be no money left to pay those who survive us!"

"Almost all of us are fathers of families. Who will take care of our women and children? Major, you have no family, so they say," Dubček's brother added.

"First we have to fight for independence, break the monarchy and then we can decide who will rule in a liberated Czecho-Slovakia!" said Štefánik.

"Well, who will rule? Regardless of the fact that Czecho-Slovakia doesn't even exist yet, you've already proposed for a Czecho-Slovak throne a Russian Grand Duke or the Prince of Orleans. Recently Queen Margherita has been wanting an Italian Prince to be on the Czech throne! But we don't want any kingdom, empire or monarchy. We want a socialist republic!"

"Our friends the French have suffered two million casualties. We didn't start the war, but must help terminate it as soon as possible so that Czechs and Slovaks emerge from it liberated and self-governing!" said an impassioned Štefánik. "Lenin is a German agent, I guess you know. He was sent to Russia by the German General Staff, also transported there in a sealed train! Do you know how much money the Germans gave Lenin and his gang? Fifty million gold marks. That's ten tons of gold! Just to create chaos in Russia!"

"Lenin is not a gangster, but a man who wants to remove the bourgeois and exploiters!" Dubček replied.

"Lenin and his adventurers are helping the Germans, Austrians, and Hungarians break Slavic unity. Only through the unity of Slavs with the French, English, Italian and Americans is our victory and freedom certain. The Russian Bolsheviks do not want freedom but a dictatorship. They want..." Štefánik coughed sharply, clutching his chest, and quickly drained his glass. His face flushed and he wiped his mouth with a tissue. After a while he calmed down.

"We would also like to go, but we cannot," Michal said more calmly. "We're American citizens and are subject to the United States Armed Forces. We must join the US Army."

"I know," said Štefánik. "Only those of you who aren't yet American citizens can apply to join our army. But you, American Czechs and Slovaks with citizenship, can and must fight for our cause in the US Army! The United States has been at war with Germany since April and is our ally. President Wilson is a great supporter of our cause!"

"Wilson wasn't supposed to drag the country into war! The Democrats said they were against the war. It was clearly promised in their 1916 election campaign. And we socialist workers are fundamentally against any war!"

"And how would you like to win independence from the Hungarians, if not through their defeat in the war?" said Štefánik.

"But if we go to the front, we'll be shooting at Czechs and Slovaks. They're in the Austro-Hungarian army, but I won't shoot at our brothers!" Dubček raised his voice.

Štefánik turned to the hall. He was shaking from nervousness.

"A person is worthy of freedom who fights for it alone! I tell you, Czecho-Slovak women, send a message to your men, those who crawl behind the oven, that we won't allow your children to live in slavery! I've already been on the Serbian and Italian fronts and after returning to Europe I'll go to the French front. If you don't go, I'm sorry, but I'll be there with the others and we'll fight for you! But I know you'll be there with me!" He sat down drained.

There was silence in the hall with people glaring at each other, and at the major, from whose mouth blood had splattered. He quickly put a handkerchief to his lips. As he composed himself, an old man who'd come to the chairman's table quietly interrupted in a trembling voice.

"I'm old and I sell newspapers. If I were capable, I'd come with you. In this way, please accept at least a little money for our boys... I have no more..." and he placed a few small coins on the table. Štefánik's eyes glistened. More and more men followed the old man. Suddenly Štefan Dubček also stood up. He walked to the table and stared firmly into Štefánik's eyes.

"I work in a musical instrument factory, I don't have much, but I'll give for the liberation of Slovakia from the Hungarians. Maybe I can help you again." He shook his hand firmly and returned to his place. Gradually, women, men, old and young came up, some giving money, others signing applications for the training camp in Stamford, Connecticut where they'd train for deployment on the French front.

After returning from Chicago, Štefánik recovered in Long Beach on Long Island. France's High Commissioner André Tardieu, a future three-term French Prime Minister, at the suggestion of Prime Minister and Minister of War, Paul Painlevé, appointed him on 20th October honorary officer of the legion for the extraordinary merits he demonstrated during the French mission in America.

Shortly before leaving he was visited in his hotel room by Jozef Dubnický, who fought his way despite the resistance of the attending physician. He walked over to Štefánik's bed, saluted and reported:

"Major, today the first expedition of Czecho-Slovak volunteers is leaving for France, and most of them are Slovaks. This is proof that the Slovak nation is not yet beaten!" Štefánik tried to shake his hand, but it remained limp on the duvet. Dubnický therefore pressed it firmly. Štefánik, much moved, whispered in tears: "May God go with you."

CHAPTER 16
The Woman of My Life

He left the USA on 3rd November. He was so weak that he was loaded on to the ship on a stretcher.

About 4,000 volunteers were recruited, with 1,500 men waiting in France. The formation of the legion in Italy had encountered problems, the greatest obstacles being raised by the Minister of Foreign Affairs, Baron Sonnino, although Czech and Slovak intelligence units had already been established. The Minister justified his position on humanitarian grounds and fear for the lives of prisoners. According to the Hague Convention of 1907, prisoners of war could only be used for work unrelated to war operations and could be executed for violation of the Convention. It was known that when the Austrians had captured Czech and Slovak soldiers fighting on the allied side, they had been brutally executed as traitors. The main reason, however, which Baron Sonnino couldn't openly declare was that Italy claimed Dalmatia, as did another ally, Serbia. This hard-tested nation, unlike the Italians, had been on the side of the Entente nations since the beginning; Serbia had been the first to be invaded by Austria, with huge casualties among its population. So France and Britain supported Italy's claim formally rather than genuinely. The Italians feared that the support of Czechs and Slovaks would revive the hopes of the Serbs.

On 16th November, 1917, a seventy-six-year-old fierce warrior, Georges Clemenceau, was reelected prime minister of France and declared total war on the Central Powers. This was great encouragement for the Czechoslovak resistance, who feared peace negotiations that would preserve Austro-Hungary. The very next day after taking office, President Poincaré signed a decree approving the establishment of the Czechoslovak army in France, subject to the ČSNR (The Czecho-Slovak National Council) and to be financed by

France. On 15th January 1918 Štefánik was promoted to the rank of Lieutenent Colonel and insisted that the Czechoslovak army be under one command, thereby ensuring that the Ministry of War approved General Janin, a Czech speaker, as the commander-in-chief of the Czechoslovak army. The first unit of our army was 2,200 soldiers concentrated in Cognac, which Štefánik had recruited in Romania and America. With Janin he convinced the chief commander of the French army, General Petain, that troops not fighting in the foreign legion as part of the French army, would be under the sovereign Czechoslovak flag. Thanks to Štefánik's continued effort at deployment in France, units with a strength of approximately 12,000 men gradually formed. Under an agreement between the government of France and the ČSNR, four rifle regiments were created. On 19th January Janin was appointed commander of the troops in Siberia. On 7th February, 1918, Masaryk declared the Army Corps in Russia part of the Czechoslovak army in France, subordinate to the Entente and, in agreement with the Soviet government, ordered it to begin preparations for its transfer through Vladivostok to France.

An unpleasant surprise was delivered by the ruling circles in Vienna on 6th January, 1918, when the Imperial Czech and German parliamentarians met in the Municipal House in Prague and adopted the Three-Kings Declaration; for the first time on domestic soil the desire for the union of Bohemia, Moravia, Silesia and Slovakia within one state was heard. Two days later, President Wilson submitted to the US Congress fourteen conditions under which the USA was willing to enter into peace negotiations. For the Czechs and Slovaks, the tenth point was a disappointment: in it the peoples of Austria-Hungary demanded the right to autonomous development while preserving the monarchy. For the Czechoslovak foreign resistance there was even more disappointment when a similar position was taken by British Prime Minister, Lloyd George and by Clemenceau.

Unexpected help to Czechoslovak resistance came from where nobody expected it: from Bolshevik Russia. After taking power, Lenin made an offer to end the war to all the governments of the countries involved in the war. The Entente powers rejected his offer, so the Bolsheviks negotiated with representatives of Germany, Austro-Hungary and Turkey. Negotiations were completed on 3rd March 1918 in Brest-Litovsk with the signing of a humiliating peace. Russia lost 780,000 square kilometres with 52 million inhabitants, a third of its railway network, 73 percent of its iron ore production and 89 percent of its coal production. Soviet Russia exited the war and became a neutral country. Due to the Brest-Litovsk Peace, the Germans could move their divisions to the Western Front, where they took the initiative. The number of German divisions increased from 129 to 192 while the Entente powers only had 173. Woodrow Wilson and the Allies were enraged. The Italians quickly felt increasing pressure from the Austro-Hungarian troops, escalating from their overwhelming defeat and huge losses at Caporetto. Every fighting man was needed. The experienced diplomat Štefánik knew that the time was right. Accompanied by his friend and secretary, Ludvík Strimpl, on 18th February he travelled to Rome and Padua, the site of Italian headquarters. For this mission alone he was promoted to the rank of Colonel.

He traditionally stayed at the Grand Hotel, where he set out to meet key Italian politicians. His main consultant and supporter was the French Ambassador, Barrère, and he was also a friend of the French Embassy counsellor, François Charles Roux. His friends included the American Ambassador, Nelson Page and the Russian diplomat, Anatoly Krupesky. Štefánik was like a chess player trying to guess every opponent's move. Giuliana Benzoni was excellent at helping him, gave him all her aristocratic contacts and took him to Luigi Aldrovani Marescotti, Head of the Office of the Foreign Minister, Sonnino. Thanks to Giuliana he entered into negotiations with the new prime minister, Orlando, and was received by King Victor Emmanuel III and also the Queen dowager Margherita of Savoy, the former queen. The King supported him, but finally shrugged his shoulders with the words: "Unfortunately, I'm not the government." Štefánik worked on a memorandum to allay the fears of the Italian government, arguing that Czechs and Slovaks weren't essentially prisoners of war because they hadn't been captured in battle, but had passed over to the enemy consciously and voluntarily and therefore the international Hague Convention on Prisoners of War didn't apply to them. He referred to the French government, which had already officially recognized the independence of Czechoslovak troops. At the end of the memorandum he called on the Italian government to take the initiative in building a post-war Central Europe. Unfortunately, he failed however. After consultation with the heads of the Italian military forces and political representatives of the Prime Minister, attended by Štefánik, it was stated that the Italian government maintained its opposition.

This decision disappointed him, but it didn't spoil his good mood throughout his stay in Rome. The source of his joy was the Marchesa Giuliana Benzoni and he used every spare moment to be with a woman who, it seemed, had touched his heart more than any woman he'd met before. Unlike his first two-month stay in the spring of 1916, which he spent mostly on reconnaissance flights behind the front, he now resided mainly in Rome. Two years had passed since their first meeting when he'd unexpectedly confessed his love to her in front of the Palazzo Colona. Two years before, Giuliana had introduced her fiancé to her aunt, Teresa di Venosa, a lady-in-waiting at the royal court. The aunt quickly became fond of the charming young officer and helped him establish contacts with influential politicians and journalists. It was less so with her parents, Teresa and Radaffo Benzoni, conservative Catholics, who could barely tolerate a Lutheran paying court to their daughter. He'd go to the Benzoni family, but each time he felt as though he were stepping on eggshells. Therefore, he enjoyed every moment he could spend with Giuliana alone or in the company of her discreet friends.

That May evening he'd enjoyed a concert at the Teatro Augusteo, where the famous Arturo Toscanini had conducted the symphony orchestra of the Accademia Nazionale di Santa Cecilia. He was in a good mood having a few days before inspected the 33rd Regiment in Foligno. After the concert, they walked for a long time in the evening streets, smelling the blossoming chestnuts, linden trees and beautiful flower beds. Milan was in a good mood and sang some melodies.

"Do you like Schubert?"

"Why?"

"Because you were singing him," she smiled and joined in. For a while they hummed Schubert's Serenade.

"That serenade of Schubert, for men eternally in puberty..."

"What did you say?"

"I was just poeticizing in my language," he translated for her the couplet which at that moment had come into his mind.

"That's nice... Do you like poetry?"

"I used to write poems, but, as you can see, even now, sometimes, the muse nudges me. I love poetry. It is the true essence of our soul, the secret to relative happiness. Poetry creates around us a kind of magic garden which absorbs our soul with dreams of beauty. Indeed, only in dreaming is life worth living, because only by dreaming do we approach the absolute. But we have to be wary of poetry if it changes into the amorous attire of love..."

"I don't understand you..."

"Love is a strong tree with its roots in two hearts. Only then is the tree strong, if both hearts nourish it..."

"I think that is how it is between you and me..."

He was silent and her eyes worriedly drank in his blue pupils. There were no words for him to express his contradictory feeling, but nevertheless at length he resolved to.

"With you there is no doubt, I'm just afraid I'm not yet quite mature enough for a solid and boundless love..."

"Only in true love is there purpose, happiness and eternity. Only in love limitless and unconditional," she said with a smile of nostalgia. "These are the words that you told me at the Palazzo Colonna."

He lowered his eyes and realized that his face was red.

"Oh, my little fable-making Slovak forever longing for perfection," she gently stroked his cheek with the back of her hand. In her gesture he felt a trembling uncertainty. Then she pulled a small oyster shell from her purse and opened it. The pearl shone there.

"A real Tahitian pearl. In Polynesia, it is a symbol of the soul. I've been carrying this ring with me, waiting for a woman to become my life partner... These are your words again."

It was as if something had suddenly broken somewhere inside him, he seized both her hands.

"I remember them precisely... and everything else I told you then. Everything is true. You're the woman of my life."

CHAPTER 17

I'll Continue When the Prince Returns!

After a brief consultation with General Foch in France, he returned to Rome at the end of March, where he continued his intense persuasion of Italian government circles. He cleverly argued that if a Czecho-Slovak government was formally created whose representative would be its National Council, the Hague Convention wouldn't apply to our troops, as Czecho-Slovakia hadn't signed it. The Italians were waiting for the start of the new Austro-Hungarian offensive at Piava. At the time of Štefánik's stay at Italian headquarters in Padua, where he negotiated with General Diaz, the Chief of General Staff, General Ludendorff launched an offensive on 21st March intended to bring a definitive victory to the Central Powers before the expected deployment of the Americans. Fifty German divisions broke the British defence, advanced sixty kilometres to approach Paris and began to fire on it with long-range guns. The French and British were forced to withdraw six divisions from the Italian front to defend Paris. These were crucial moments that ultimately influenced Rome's decision. Štefánik was a man whose enthusiasm reignited the declining morale of the Italians. They'd already begun to consider a separate peace with the Austrians, which would mean a complete collapse for the Czecho-Slovak cause.

"How can we accept an offer of a people who are fated for sacrifice and death if we can't guarantee anything in these circumstances?" Prime Minister Orlando confessed sincerely to Štefánik in the office of Zupelli, the Minister for War.

"'Sir, I don't request guarantees or obligations from you, I don't request anything. All I ask is to give this opportunity to people determined to die for their homeland," replied Štefánik.

After these words, the prime minister was moved to tears and finally promised his agreement. It was possible to formulate a treaty to create Czechoslovak troops in Italy. Štefánik's greatest diplomatic success had begun to take shape.

In Rome in the Capitol on 8th April 1918, a three-day congress began of the oppressed nations of Austro-Hungary, where Štefánik was joined by Beneš, Osuský, Sychrava and Gábriš. At the end of the congress, Prime Minister Orlando spoke of Štefánik's outstanding contribution and described it as an example of patriotism and moral power. "When I met him, a refugee stood in front of me, a vagrant with no homeland, no home. At that moment, I felt my spirit bend with appreciation in front of a man who emanated a tremendous moral force, the greatest force that could exist in the world – the power of thought." After that declaration, there was thunderous applause. The French Colonel was visibly moved as his incredible effort began to bear fruit. Štefánik's belief in the liberation of the Slavic peoples also impressed a professor of Slavonic studies in London and Oxford, Robert William Seton-Watson, a colleague of Masaryk's whom he met during the congress. After the congress on 21st April, the day Romans celebrate the founding of their city, Orlando, Zupelli and Spignardi signed the Convention between the CSNR and Italian government, which recognized an independent Czechoslovak state and consented to the founding of a Czecho-Slovak army in Italy, subject to the CSNR. It was a great success for Štefánik who signed the agreement for the Czecho-Slovak side, the first international document where the CSNR acted as an equal contractual partner and featured a hyphen in the Czecho-Slovak name in order to emphasize the equality of both nations. In cooperation with General Grazziani, appointed Commander-in-Chief of the Czecho-Slovak army, Štefánik created four regiments of legions in Italy.

Pope Benedict XV received Štefánik as the only representative of the foreign resistance. This success was all the more significant because Štefánik, as a French officer, represented a country that had severed diplomatic relations with the Vatican ten years before. Despite being a Lutheran, he saw relations with the supreme institution of Catholic Christianity as very important.

While Štefánik used his diplomatic skills in negotiations with Italian representatives, he had to use the hardness and vigour of command in negotiations with the representatives of the Czecho-Slovak volunteer corps. He removed the democratically elected command and replaced it with professional officers, changing a volunteer into a regular army. Only such troops could receive a combat flag and the Italians proposed he present the flag outside Rome in the usual military manner. But Štefánik needed a strong symbol and especially wanted to send to the world news of this significant event so took advantage of Italy's third anniversary of the war, at which the Italians organized a grand celebration on 24th May in front of the monumental memorial to Italian unification beneath the statue of King Victor Emmanuel II, located on the vast Piazza Venezia. Štefánik couldn't have gained a more dignified location than the Altare della Patria on the steps leading to the hundred-and-thirty-metre wide and seventy-metre high colonnade, all the more so because the celebration was attended by the King's son and heir to the throne. The participants were surprised to see the conservative Minister of Foreign Affairs, Sonnino present; he had never before been seen at a similar ceremony. Ministers Meda, Bissolati, Nitti, the Mayor of Rome, Colonna, senators, ambassadors and representatives of the Entente also came. Štefánik had cleverly persuaded Sonnino that if an army of a non-existent state is created that logically can't be a signatory to the Hague Convention, the countries of the Central Powers can't blame Italy. Štefánik understood the Minister's presence as a symbolic agreement with his argument. During the speech of Prime Minister Orlando, the engineer of this great diplomatic achievement shed tears.

"I see the baptism of a nation, its birth, or rather its resurrection in this pledge, because it was a free nation for centuries, before it was humbled and divided."

After that, the US ambassador, writer and lawyer, Thomas Nelson Page spoke. At the end of his speech, he turned to Štefánik and said: "Happy is a nation that has such a warrior." After his appearance the evidently moved Colonel Štefánik placed the war banner into the hands of General Grazziano, who then passed it to the flagbearer of the First Czecho-Slovak division. The next day the newspapers wrote: "Fu quello il giorno di Štefánik. Uno slovacco – quel giorno fu il re di Roma." (It was Štefánik's day. On that day this Slovak was king of Rome.) The CSNR declared war on Austro-Hungary and thus de facto became one of the countries of the Entente.

After the Czecho-Slovak ceremony, an Italian ceremony then took place in *Domus Augustea*, the seat of the Emperor Augustus. Prime Minister Orlando gave a speech, followed by Allied representatives, French Minister Simon, the American ambassador, Ambassador Page, the Belgian deputy, Lorand, the British heir to the throne and finally, to the surprise of all, Colonel Štefánik, Vice-President of the CSNR. He had claimed the right to speak from the Italian government, saying that by signing the convention Italy had recognized the new Czecho-Slovak army as its ally. What Štefánik said during his speech shocked the dignitaries present. When he noticed from behind the speaker that the British heir to the throne, the Prince of Wales, the future King of the United Kingdom of Great Britain and Northern Ireland and Emperor of India, Edward had risen and left his box he stopped speaking and said,

"I regret that our friend, the successor to the British throne, the Prince of Wales has left during a speech by a representative of the Allied army fighting alongside England. As this act could be politically misinterpreted, I cannot continue my speech."

The hall murmured, but the organizers maintained their presence of mind and persuaded the future King of England, who was somewhat uninformed, to return as Štefánik would also be making an address. The Košariská boy with a haughty calm waited for the next English ruler to take his place in his box again, and in perfect French he continued: "Penetrated by an unbroken faith, trusting in the victory of justice, the victory of law over violence, freedom over subjugation, democracy over privilege and truth over deceit, in this celebratory hour that opens a new epoch of human history, we lift our hands and for the dear memory of our ancestors before the eyes of a resurrected nation and over the graves of our fallen, in a massive harmony of souls, we confirm that we will fight until the day when we can hail an independent Czecho-Slovak state. We will be free and therefore we are free now!"

There was huge applause in the hall and calls shouting for the glory of Italy, Czecho-Slovakia, France, Britain and Štefánik. The first to come to shake his right hand after his brilliant address was the Prince of Wales. The calls for glory were then interrupted by tones that no one had heard before in Rome. At Štefánik's insistence, the military band of the Roman garrison had rehearsed the song, *Kde domov můj?* (Where Is My Home), which they introduced as the national anthem of the future Czecho-Slovakia. Those present treated it with the same respect as the anthems of the other countries.

CHAPTER 18
Masaryk: Support the Bolsheviks!

The representatives of France, England and the USA on 3rd December 1917 secretly agreed to a division of spheres of influence in Russia. The only way to achieve this goal, and thus maintain a hope of regaining money invested in Tsarist Russia, was direct military intervention. The French government had set up a commission to examine the possibilities of what forces could be used effectively to combat the Russian Bolsheviks, its members including General Janin, Beneš and Štefánik. The key force could have been the Czecho-Slovak legion. However, Masaryk, who was then in Russia, refused to deploy the legionaries in the anti-Bolshevik struggle and insisted on their transfer to the French front. After the peace between Lenin's Russia and the Central Powers, his argument was logical: the legionaries' role was to fight the Germans, Austrians, and Hungarians. He believed that when the Bolsheviks succeeded in forming a solid army, they would deploy it to fight the Germans and the Austrians. The Peace Treaty of Brest, which was a de facto surrender, obliged the Bolsheviks to immediately expel forces hostile to the Central Powers. This also applied to the Czecho-Slovak legion, whose position had been complicated since the Bolshevik Revolution. It was clear to the CSNR that after the Bolshevik coup, our legions had no reason to remain in Russia. A civil war had broken out and the Czechs and Slovaks had to maintain neutrality, which was not easy. However, most Czechs and Slovaks remained in the safety of the prison camps. Most of them were passive with a single desire; to wait until the end of the war and return home. The more courageous, determined to emerge from under the Austrian and Hungarian yokes, had entered the legion. Others, who were more intent on fighting capitalist exploitation and spreading proletarian revolution, entered the revolutionary Red Guards. Among them was the world-famous author of the novel, *The Good Soldier Švejk*, Jaroslav Hašek.

Since Masaryk had ordered the maintenance of strict neutrality in Russia, the main concerns were the question of the return to Europe, deployment on the French front or inclusion in the emerging legion in Italy. The road to Europe to the north through Archangelsk was considerably shorter, but eventually the Czechoslovak command, in agreement with the CSDNR, decided on the Siberian route to Vladivostok. In Finland, the Germans were operating and the possibility of their advance couldn't be ruled out, which would result in conflict with the legionaries as happened on 8th March at the Ukrainian railway junction, Bachmač, where Czechs and Slovaks supported by an unexpected ally, the Red Guards, defeated the Germans stopping their penetration of Ukraine. The way to the east was open and our troops began to move to Siberia.

Czechoslovak soldiers were deployed in 63 train echelons, with 40 wagons in each. The move to the east proceeded slowly because of a lack of coal and locomotives but was also hampered by the passage of trains with German and Austrian prisoners going in the opposite direction.

According to reports from Vladivostok, no Allied ships were in dock, which led the Legion to think they wanted to deploy them against the Soviets. In addition, due to legitimate fears of legionaries, the Bolsheviks demanded their full disarmament. This request became urgent after the events of 14th May 1918 at a station in Chelyabinsk in the Urals. An echelon with resting Czech and Slovak soldiers was standing in a railway siding. An echelon with Hungarian and Austrian prisoners was slowly passing alongside them travelling westwards, one of whom threw a piece of iron at our troops severely wounding one of them. The furious legionaries stopped the train and forced them to give up the perpetrator, who was shot on the spot. Then the local Soviets, who controlled the city, took several legionaries into custody. Another group tried to negotiate their liberation, but the Soviets also arrested them. Finally, a few hundred angry legionaries took out weapons from hiding places in the train, supplemented with rifles that had been taken off the rail militia, and with a song made off to the Soviet building. The locals were fed up with Soviet power and strongly supported our soldiers. About 8,400 of our troops invaded the city, of whom 1,500 were armed. They occupied key junctions and disarmed the local Red Army squad. About 3,600 of the Red Army took to their heels and the Czechoslovak prisoners were freed without a fight. The legionaries seized three thousand rifles and returned to the train. This event, which was reported by the world media, became the first significant military performance of Czecho-Slovak legions in Siberia. Following this incident, Trotsky's Military Commissioner issued an order that "... any Czechoslovak who is caught with a gun in his hand will be shot." Part of the army led by the rebel captain, Radola Gajda, rejected these requests, which was in breach of Masaryk's order not to interfere in Russia's internal affairs. In a dramatic atmosphere, a congress of Czechoslovak troops met in Chelyabinsk on 16th to 23rd May, where delegates refused the request of the Bolsheviks to hand over their weapons, which meant a de facto declaration of war on the Bolsheviks. Czechoslovak legionaries, thus, against their will became the first fighters in the planned Allied intervention against Soviet Russia and a key military element of the allies in Russia. After taking control of Chita on 31st August, General Gajda's troops met legionaries advancing from Vladivostok at the Olovjanna station, bringing the entire Trans-Siberian Highway into Czechoslovak hands; they had now occupied Chelyabinsk, Omsk, Samara and Irkutsk. After achieving this great success under the command of the twenty-six-year old General Radola Gajda, the American Consul General in Irkutsk, Ernest L. Harris, wrote to Secretary of State Lansing: "... a handful of Czechoslovak soldiers after fighting from Ukraine and subsequently disarmed in the city of Penza have performed a deed that will live in history as long as it is important to record human actions in its chronicle."

A portion of the legionaries were already in Vladivostok, but when they learned that the Bolsheviks were threatening their comrades by advancing to the east, 15,000 of them returned. They desperately needed aid, but President Wilson and the Allies still refused to help.

At the request of the American Ambassador, Masaryk drafted a memorandum for President Wilson on 8th April 1918 in Tokyo which shocked Americans so much that they began to suspect the author of spying for Moscow. It turned out, however, that Masaryk was right. In his visionary analysis, he urged the USA and the Allies to recognize the Bolshevik government and help revive their economy, reconstruct roads and railways, and avoid military intervention. In the memorandum he stated: "If the allies have a good relationship with the Bolsheviks, they'll be able to influence them. I know the weaknesses of the Bolsheviks, but I also know the weaknesses of the other parties, who are neither better nor more capable. The monarchist movement in Russia is weak, the Allies mustn't support it. The Bolsheviks will hold power longer than their opponents anticipate but will die like all other parties from political dilettantism. The Allies should support Russia at all costs and by all means. All the small nations in the east need a strong Russia, otherwise they'll be at the mercy of the Germans and Austrians. Breaking Russia means working directly for Prussia. If the Germans conquer the East, they will conquer the West."

After his arrival from Russia and Japan on 4th May, 1918, Masaryk was greeted triumphantly by a crowd of a hundred thousand in Chicago. On 31st May 1918 in Pittsburgh he signed an agreement between representatives of the Slovak League, the Czech National Association and the Union of Czech Catholics operating in the USA, formulated by Masaryk and based on a political programme seeking to unite the "Czech and Slovak territories" into one state. The agreement said: "Slovakia will have its own administration, its assembly and its courts. Slovak will be the official language in schools, offices and all public life. The Czechoslovak state will be a republic whose constitution will be democratic... Detailed provisions on the running of the Czechoslovak state will be left to liberated Czechs and Slovaks and their rightful representatives." In order to allay Slovak fears Masaryk assured them: "There will be a free Czech republic and a free Slovakia. In Slovakia, political leadership, schools and judiciary will be Slovak, in the Czech Republic they will be Czech. There is no need to worry about the Czech majority, it will be in the Czech Republic; in Slovakia the majority will be Slovak. Each branch will be master in his house. Slovakia will have its administration, its assembly and its courts." Masaryk signed the agreement first. Štefánik never signed this agreement, which later became a source of discord in the new republic. After proclamation of the Czecho-Slovak Republic, few promises made to the Slovaks were kept. Unlike the Cleveland Agreement of October 1915, there was no mention of a federal arrangement. Masaryk argued that they'd adhered to the agreement because the detailed provisions of the new state would be decided by its rightful representatives, among which were practically no Slovaks. None of the eighteen Slovak signatories to the Agreement returned permanently to the new republic. When one of them, Jozef Murgaš, holder of twelve patents in the field of wireless telegraphy, filed a request to return to his homeland where he wanted to teach physics, he received a negative reply.

For the Czechoslovak resistance, the American position to preserve the monarchy and give its peoples more rights was a major problem. Therefore, the main task of Masaryk, Štefánik and Czechs and Slovaks in the USA was to persuade Wilson to change his mind and agree to the collapse of Austria-Hungary. But since Wilson didn't appear open to the Czecho-Slovak solution, they sought to influence public opinion knowing that the President of the USA always respected it.

The leadership of the CSNR urged the Allies to recognize it as the Czecho-Slovak government and the legionaries as the Czecho-Slovak army. Štefánik therefore tried not to recruit soldiers into the army of an enemy state, but into the army of his own country. His argument that the convention could not apply to a country that did not exist yet convinced the allied governments in the face of increasing losses and demoralization of entente troops. On 29th June 1918 France officially recognized the National Council as the supreme body of the future Czecho-Slovak government, an important day for Czecho-Slovak foreign resistance and for its further influence on the US government. Several years of persistent efforts by Masaryk, Štefánik, Beneš and other Slovaks and Czechs living in France had paid off. On 9th August the British government issued an even more explicit statement and on 2nd September, the American government also recognized the Czecho-Slovak National Council (CSNR) as a de facto allied government and the legion as part of the Entente armies. When it was recognized as a de facto government by the Japanese government on 9th September, Italy also moved to do so, which it did on 3rd October 1918. All these documents of recognition by the allied countries emphasized that Czecho-Slovakia was a war ally. As a result, Czecho-Slovakia met at the peace conference alongside the victorious allies.

In July, the Czecho-Slovak National Committee was constituted from domestic resistance workers in Prague, which coordinated its resistance activities with the CSNR. The struggle for the liberation of Czechs and Slovaks had begun to culminate.

CHAPTER 19
My Dear Edušo, I Embrace You Warmly!

Štefánik ended his mission in Italy on 7th August 1918 and returned to Paris. Ambassador Barrère wrote to Foreign Minister Pichon: "Colonel Štefánik has accomplished the mission on which he came here in outstanding fashion." Pichon lost no time in putting a proposal of Barrère's to the prime minister: "In order to fulfill his expected tasks, I consider it necessary that Colonel Štefánik be promoted at least temporarily to a rank that would allow him to act with the authority of a general officer."

On 18th June, the Prime Minister and Minister of War Clemenceau promoted Štefánik to Brigadier General, "á titre de mission", a mission title. He explained the promotion by saying: "Colonel Štefánik is promoted to the rank of Brigadier General on a mission to the Czecho-Slovak Army, as long as the mission lasts where he acts as adjutant to the Commander of the Czecho-Slovak Army and member of the Czecho-Slovak National Council. The powers resulting from this rank entitle him to exercise them only in relation to the Czecho-Slovak sections and during his mission abroad in the service of the Czecho-Slovak cause." Ten days later, Czech and Slovak volunteers in Alsace, France, received a war banner from the hands of President Poincaré in the presence of Edvard Beneš.

On 25th July 1918, Généralissime Foch commissioned Štefánik together with the chief commander of the Czechoslovak army, Janin, to carry out a new mission in Siberia based on a decision of the Supreme Allied Council and the French government. The decision of the Supreme Allied Council was influenced by the work of Edvard Beneš, who convinced the Allies that the best candidate for the Supreme Commander of the planned massive anti-Bolshevik action in Russia would be Štefánik. By ensuring Štefánik's departure to Siberia, Beneš got rid of a key rival when the composition of the future Czecho-Slovak government was being considered.

Masaryk didn't know about Štefánik's appointment, so the new General went first to him in the USA in order to coordinate their joint activities. Accompanied by his ADC, Captain Ferdinand Písecký, and the French officers Fournier and Lévi, he sailed to New York from Brest on 22nd August on the *Mongolia*, a former merchant ship converted into a troop carrier and upon which 150 US wounded soldiers were returning to the USA. Štefánik was given the second captain Walker's cabin, where he spent most of his time in bed. The ten-day voyage was peaceful despite anxiety resulting from the threat of German submarines; Štefánik relaxed a little though wasn't happy about his health. They arrived in New York on 2nd September and, as was typical of him, he refused treatment, instead staying in bed for several days at the Hotel Plaza, from where he dictated instructions, appeals and newspaper articles. One of his first visitors was the chairman of the Slovak National Association, editor of the Slovak Sokol, Milan Getting, a keen supporter of Czecho-Slovak rapprochement. For three whole days, Masaryk, who had been in the US since the end of April, came to see him though didn't inform him of the letter he received from Paris on 28th July. In the letter, Beneš complained about Štefánik: "Frankly, nobody knows how much difficulty I have in getting along with him. He's sick, terribly touchy, amazingly thin-skinned, irritable, he reproaches me for a variety of things. Overall, it is petty, I try not to make too much fuss about it, but I admit that it isn't easy for me to work with him. Our basic philosophical views are completely different, his understanding of life and everything is different from mine and ultimately we can't hide it. I do everything I can to treat him well, to be friendly and fraternal. I have to make compromises all the time and do everything possible to conciliate him. But it is difficult and we have come close to conflict."

Štefánik during his forced stay in bed sketched a design for a new Czechoslovak flag, where he added the Slovak blue to the Czech white and red.

Masaryk, who was again received by President Wilson at the White House on 11th September, had been campaigning across the the US visiting the cities with the highest concentration of Czech and Slovak emigrants.

Janin and Štefánik met Secretary of State, Lansing and the American Army Chief of Staff, General March. Štefánik then continued via Pittsburgh to San Francisco, where he arrived on 21st September. To his surprise he was met at the station by city officials and enthusiastic countrymen. He calmly greeted them, but refused to attend the evening banquet, saying that there'd be enough time after the war for parades and celebrations. "No celebrations, no photography!" To the argument that the recent recognition of the Czecho-Slovak National Council by the United States government was a cause for celebration, he coldly replied that the American government had only rectified the injustice it had done when it looked on passively at the suffering of the Czechoslovak nation.

With Písecký, Fournier and Lévi, he boarded the Korea Maru on 24th September, sailing to Yokohama, Japan. They had a twelve-day voyage ahead of them, during which on 11th October he sent an unusually friendly letter from the post office in Honolulu to Beneš: *My dear Edušo! We came to New York on 2nd September as did our dear Chairman Masaryk. There was a lot of work, but little health. In San Francisco, on 17th September they wanted to welcome me to a banquet, but you know, celebrations are roses with cruel thorns that first prick the celebrated, sometimes painfully, sometimes fatally. We stopped one day in Honolulu on 30th September. I took the rare opportunity to go hiking with friends. It cheered my spirit but wore me out. But what of it! We can hold out until the end of the war, can't we, dear friend? You also know what it is to work when one has almost no energy. Greetings, please, to Strimpl, Markovič, Sychrava, Chalupa and all our good people. I shake your hand and embrace you warmly, Your Milan.*

He and his friends saw the Pearl Harbour military port west of Honolulu, which had been opened in August 1918 with the participation of the American Secretary for the Navy, Joseph Daniels. In a stationery shop he bought paper, coloured pencils, compasses and other supplies for work he now had time for and looked forward to doing. He designed a new Czecho-Slovak honour, the *Rad Sokola* (Order of the Falcon) with three classes; gold, silver and bronze with and without swords. On the cross he put a gold trim, an enamel white stripe, blue enamel arms with a metal centre and three hills above which four falcons fly. The degree of the order was indicated by a star. He proposed a high financial reward, as well as honorary and political rights, for the top tier. When the proposal was finished, he called Písecký.

"As soon as we arrive in Tokyo, you will as a matter of urgency have three sets of these awards made. I want them for our men in Siberia."

The initial war enthusiasm had long since faded, depression had spread throughout countries and diseases broken out. People were wracked by terrible hunger and grief for the fallen. The fatigue and exhaustion of nations had reached a stage where human will turned to resignation not only among the civilian population, but also, sometimes even faster, among the soldiers. Economies were collapsing, food was lacking and in Germany there was even an advertisement with these remarkable instructions: "Eat slowly, you will consume less food!"

The hungry had no desire to fight, the lists of the politically unreliable lengthened, police raids took place daily. The Ministry of the Interior created a photo album of Czech traitors for the needs of police authorities and gendarmerie. The first was a photograph of Tomáš Garrigue Masaryk. Internment camps in towns near the Czech border bulged at the seams. Ham, Raschala, Enzersdorf, Goellersdorf, Sitzendorf, Weyerburg, Mittergrabern, Hainburg, Drosendorf nad Dyje, Unterradelsberg, Katzenau, as well as the Hungarian fortresses of Arad and Komárno were the terror of Czech and Slovak patriots. Corruption had grown to a monstrous extent. Officials and military commanders in the background took bribes of food intended for front-line soldiers, functionaries in military offices absolved the sons of the rich from military service, so that only the poor kept the war going. But even they eventually devised ways out and so it was a common occurrence for closed cattle wagons carrying soldiers to the front to arrive at their destination empty. In the forests there were "green cadres" that the population supported. There were about eighty thousand war deserters in Vienna in the summer of 1918 and between then and the end of the war, 250,000 soldiers deserted the Austro-Hungarian army. The commanders motivated the Austrian soldiers on the Piava by promising that after the conquest of any village they could loot as much as they could; after a successful offensive, whole trains of looted property, including furniture, went to the rear of the battle front. But demoralization reached a peak with soldiers on both sides refusing to fight and civilians, politicians and journalists gradually resigning themselves to the hope that total exhaustion would end the murderous madness.

CHAPTER 20
Transforming Crashes into Take-Offs

On the basis of reports from Europe and Russia, Štefaník was feverishly thinking about how, upon his arrival in Russia, he could return to our soldiers the fighting spirit which had gained the sympathy and admiration of the democratic world. The endless waters of the Pacific Ocean, the calm, windless weather, the almost absolute silence and the clear night sky dotted with stars eased the tension that had bothered him in recent weeks and soothed his unceasing stomach pains. Having had a nap in the afternoon, he couldn't sleep at night, so he went on the deck of the steamer heading toward Japan at a standard speed of eighteen knots per hour. The nights were pleasantly cool, so he breathed in the sea air deeply. In these precious, almost meditative moments of absolute peace, memories, anxieties, fears and hopes flickered in his mind. He was concerned about his family, his homeland and especially his health.

"Not sleeping again?"

"Ferdinand, and why aren't you asleep?" Štefánik threw back the question.

"I'm thinking about a new verse drama. After the war I plan to write an epic about our revolution."

"Come on! Be sensible!" said Štefánik.

Disappointed and surprised Písecký fell silent. But he had needed somehow to give voice to his inner affliction.

"Verse, especially long verse, has had its day. People can't listen to it. Something new is needed, and therefore the exact form must be abandoned. Life is quite different now from the past. Dramatists may spread moral truths but whoever wants to preach should write sermons, not plays or a didactic novel! But now is hardly the time," Štefánik objected.

Písecký remained nonplussed by his objection, so changed the subject: "What was your last stool like?"

"A little bloody but not too bad. I feel better than in America. You know, the constant tensions, the necessity to make prompt decisions, to align French interests with ours while being alone for everything. Almost. I'm really glad people like you have stood by me."

"You can rest assured I will stay with you till we triumph," Písecky replied more optimistically.

"Thank you," Štefánik gave him a friendly pat on the arm. "Sit down... Do you remember our journey on the ship, the *Ice Sea*, from Romanov to England?"

"As if I could ever forget; it often comes to my mind. Incidentally, since the Bolshevik revolution, the city hasn't been called Romanov, but Murmansk. I remember very well what we were talking about at the time... How sorry I was about not seeing Elena and my children for so long..."

"I can tell you and I'm not ashamed of it. I miss my mother. She's somewhere far away... I wish I could see her sometime... To some extent, you've replaced my family..."

"Don't exaggerate."

"I like you. You've completed in me what Masaryk started. We attended his lectures in Prague together, after all. Occasionally Edo Beneš also came. Excellent man. He doesn't drink, smoke, look for women or society, doesn't play cards, works sixteen hours a day. A man worth following..."

Písecký listened to him with a frown.

"Don't you like what I said about Beneš."

"Not really..." Something seemed to be on his mind. "I would be warier about him..."

"I've heard all kinds of things, too, but I tend not to listen to rumours."

"Brother General, this is not about words, but about facts. I think today it's clear that Beneš would hardly have survived without Masaryk's protection. He's crafty and a master of intrigue... I'm sorry to say..."

"Despite all the slanders and occasional sparks between us, I want to believe that he's a decent man. He's one of ten children and from a family as poor as mine. He struggled with Parisian life just as I did."

"I don't know, it's said he lived the good life during his studies... And don't forget that he comes from a bigoted Catholic family. Isn't it strange that he's accepted by Masaryk, who has almost no time for Catholics."

"That hardly proves anything."

"Do you know any of his friends?"

"Well... um... he's not very social, that's true. In Madame's salon, most of the time he just sits and listens."

"Exactly, pricking up his ears and watching what's going on, whose opinion is what, that's him all over. Changing his mind and even his name was never a problem for him. You've always insisted on the correct pronunciation of your name, but he changed his name from Eduard to Edvard, from Beneš to Benesch when necessary. Rumour has it that he didn't complete his law studies in Dijon, so he transferred to the Sorbonne..."

"Yes, he studied law there."

"And finished his studies?"

"I know he switched to political science at the École libre des sciences politiques, but whether he finished..."

"Probably not."

"How do you know?"

"I only know this much, that when he returned from Paris to Prague after graduation, Charles University didn't recognize his diploma... You say he is happily married to Hanička... Have you seen any of his wedding pictures? And do you know who his witness was? Police President Olič!"

"The one who investigated the Omladina case so diligently that he was promoted to court counsellor?"

"Yes, that one."

Štefánik began to breathe deeply.

"Yet Olič was involved in the resistance movement, and it was he who organized the *Maffia* meetings. They even arrested him and sentenced him for it," Štefánik objected.

"Yes, that's right, maybe he was salving his conscience. But at the time Benes lived with him, he was a loyal government policeman."

"Please don't bother me with your conjectures," Štefánik was getting agitated.

"And did you know in 1910, he built a four-storey apartment building on Ruská třída in Vršovice as a 26-year-old?"

"You're joking..."

"I'm one hundred percent sure of it."

"How was it paid for?"

"Good question. The house went for eighty thousand, fifty borrowed. Where he got the remaining thirty is a mystery. Even stranger is that even though he owned several flats, he lived... hm... do you know where? In the house of Police President Olič..."

"What do you mean by that? That he was protected by the Austrian police president?"

"Your words not mine... Brother General, after the outbreak of the war, you fought for the French army to accept you despite your health problems, while he, as a league footballer, arranged "a blue book" classification... *Untauglich*, unfit!"

"Do you know what his health problem is?"

"No, but I know he performs well on his two tennis courts in Paris. I also know that since 1915 he's had his own account with the Swiss bank, Union des Banques Suisses."

"Please stop. Yes, I've had my doubts about that a few times but let's not get anxious now about Beneš..."

"We've all been anxious for a long time..." Písecký sighed resignedly.

"All right, a long time, but if we have held out this long, we'll endure somehow. We just need to work and work! Honestly! Not to look for recognition or even thanks. To stand alone! To feel the joy of action. Isn't it beautiful and satisfying when Masaryk tells you, 'You worked well'? Our father... I feel that he's already showing his age, everywhere they talk about him as the only candidate, but... um... I don't know if he will be sufficiently able to serve as President... Oh, we have so much work ahead of us..."

"Brother General, you say Masaryk is tired. And you? Why do you work so much? Tormenting your body and spirit!"

"And what is the meaning of human life? Yes, my body is sick..."

"Are you trying to teach me that the body is enough to push the spirit forward?"

"What can I teach you, dear Ferdinand? We are peers and we learn from each other. But you are right: if the body suffers, the spirit has two possibilities, to submit to suffering or to accept it and be strengthened. All the difficulties that I encounter are opportunities for me. I'll do everything I can to turn crashes into take-offs."

CHAPTER 21
The Republic has been Established but the Struggle for it is just Beginning

The steamship, *Korea Maru*, sailed on 12th October 1918 into the port of Yokohama. Štefánik was accompanied by his adjutants, Ferdinand Písecký and Gaston Fournier, his faithful servant Garreau and Lieutenant Daniel Lévis, the interpreter for the Japanese. They continued by tram to Tokyo, twenty kilometres away and stayed in the *Imperial*, one of the most luxurious hotels in the world, just a short walk from the Imperial Palace. In Tokyo, Štefánik learned about the Declaration of Independence of the Czecho-Slovak nation, under which he surprisingly found his signature, from a newspaper. Although Štefánik had asked him to, Masaryk hadn't sent the text of the Declaration to Tokyo before it was published. But Štefánik hadn't realized that time was crucial; Wilson had received a cease-fire request from Germany and Austria-Hungary from 5th October, in which both countries confirmed unreserved approval of his 14-point program. Emperor Charles I issued a manifesto on 16th October in which he promised significant autonomy for the peoples of Austro-Hungary. In the USA, Masaryk understood that he had to act and so he quickly drafted a text based on the US Declaration of Independence with his American colleagues. On Friday, 18th October from his home in Washington, he solemnly announced the formation of a temporary Czecho-Slovak government and the new country's flag was displayed. At the same time Masaryk read the Declaration before handing it over to Wilson that afternoon. On the evening of 18th October Wilson officially announced to Berlin and Vienna that he refused to discuss their proposals. The Declaration, later called the Washington Declaration, clearly stated the requirement to declare an independent Czecho-Slovak Republic. All the key American media carried this emotional statement.

On 25th October, Štefánik received a telegram from Beneš with a note announcing that on 14th October, a temporary Czecho-Slovak government was formed, headed by Masaryk, who also became Minister of Finance, Eduard Beneš the Minister for Foreign and Home Affairs and Milan Štefánik the Minister of War. His comments were minimally incorporated. Nevertheless, his name was also under the Declaration. In particular, he didn't agree that the form of the future state should be a republic in the American manner. He knew the United States well and feared that the stark contradiction between the magnificent wording of the Constitution and its sad implementation in real life could also be transferred to the new Czecho-Slovakia. "I've seen the republic up close and it is a hidden tyranny of the worst kind. I'm a fierce opponent of a republic that would imitate this. And I'll resist this idea to the end. I'm also against the monarchy, which for us today is an old garment. The Republic, a public affair, is a matter for the people and we have no right to replace or supersede their will." He also criticized Masaryk's proposal to separate church from state, arguing that "churches already exist, but the state as yet does not." Although he was an evangelist himself, he didn't like Masaryk's anti-Catholic campaign. He also disagreed with the proposed women's right to vote, arguing that politics should be the exclusive domain of men. On 2nd November, he sent a telegram to Masaryk, summarizing his criticisms and protesting that key decisions in the foreign resistance were being made without him and, worse still, in his name. Masaryk sent an explanatory telegram to conciliate him. Beneš in Paris and the Czech leadership of the domestic resistance led by Kramář had a similarly critical attitude to Masaryk's formulation.

Despite his disappointment that key activities of the emerging republic were happening without him, he continued the task for which he'd set out to Japan and Russia: mobilizing the legions and providing them with allied support. In Tokyo, he made his round of customary diplomatic visits, negotiating with the ambassadors of France, Britain,

Italy, the USA and, naturally, with representatives of Japan, who on 9th September declared their recognition of the CSNR and the rights of the Czecho-Slovak army. He met Prime Minister, Haro, Minister of Foreign Affairs, Uchid, explained the need to increase material assistance to Czechoslovak troops in Russia and also exhorted the Chief of General Staff, Ueharu. Yet everywhere he received only vague, general answers. The American ambassador, Morris even said that his government didn't agree with the presence of Czechoslovaks in Russia. He realized that our legions were starting to be an obstacle, especially to the American plan which conflicted with the Japanese. The Japanese, as a global power growing in strength, had the same interest in Russia's far-east mineral resources as the USA and had sent about 70,000 of their troops to Northern Manchuria. Neither the Americans nor the Japanese needed French competition in Siberia, embodied for them by Janin, Štefánik and the Czecho-Slovak army.

On 20th October, when he and Písecký were descending the stately staircase to the exit of the *Imperial*, a man walked into the lobby with an energetic stride and hurried over to Štefánik.

"Brother General, Lieutenant Miloslav Chyľo, diplomatic courier. Allow me to deliver to you mail from Vladivostok!" The soldier saluted and handed an envelope to Štefánik who passed it on to Písecký.

"Wait, wait... Okay... Why are you addressing me in such an official manner? We are all soldiers of the same army!" He looked at the soldier, and suddenly his face lit up. "Chyľo, Chyľo... the waiter from Turčianska stolica! Chyľo Miloslav. *The Mezey Café* in Bratislava," he recalled the encounter from his high school studies.

"Exactly," smiled Chyľo.

"Come to my room tonight. We can have a little get-together; I'd like to hear all about our soldiers. Seventeen hundred, all right?"

"As commanded, brother General."

At their meeting, Štefánik suddenly turned pale and seemed about to faint. At the last moment, however, he was caught and seated in his chair. Once again there was pain, this time stronger than his will to suppress it. He was forced to obey the doctor's advice. It turned out that he had caught the deadly Spanish flu virus, which at that time was mercilessly killing millions of people. There were no effective drugs, so he applied cold compresses and ice packs to his feverish body and after two days his fever subsided. He entrusted himself to the care of a Czech merchant family, the Trnožkovs, who took him to the Mianoshita mountain spa at the foot of Mount Fuji for a few days. However, he ended his stay there after learning that General Janin had come to Tokyo.

It was 29th October when he learned that in Prague a Czecho-Slovak Republic had been declared with a temporary government, in which he'd become the Minister of War. He'd got into a difficult situation, a French citizen becoming a minister in another country's government. The situation was solved, however, when General Janin wrote to Paris, "I propose to grant General Štefánik unlimited leave without pay and requisites dated from 11th November 1918, when he has been authorized by the French government, by letter from Minister Pichon, to accept the function of Minister of War from the state of Czechoslovakia. The emoluments he has received will end on that date." He asked his friend, Janin, for three golden stars and sewed them himself on to his brigadier's cap. This time they were Czecho-Slovak stars.

At the end of his stay he received an unusual honour when on 5th November he was received by the Mikado, the 123rd Japanese Emperor, Yoshihito, Štefánik's peer. According to Japanese protocol, the Czecho-Slovak Minister bowed slightly at the entrance to the Audience Room for the first time, deeper in the middle of the room for the second time, then greeted the Emperor with a deep bow just in front of him. The Mikado was dressed in a general's uniform, with dignitaries at his side dressed in black. On parting, the Emperor wished him success in inhospitable Siberia. With diplomatic charm, Štefánik replied: "The rays of the Japanese sun will warm us up there, too." With Janin,

Písecký and their entourage, they boarded a night train to Kyoto on 8th November. Again, his health was affected and on the day of his departure he'd taken three instead of one pill for stimulation, causing a sharp increase in his heart rate. He put his hands on his chest in pain and General Janin didn't leave his compartment all night to make sure, though by early morning his condition had improved and finally he slept. On the way to the port of Shimonoseiki they stopped in Kobe, where they learned of the surrender of Germany.

"It's hard to believe it's over, that we've won; somehow I can't fully take it in," said Janin.

"Yes, it's over," added Štefánik laconically, "but only there in Europe. In Siberia, however, we must and will continue to fight. The Republic has been established but the struggle for it is just beginning."

CHAPTER 22
How Isidor Declared the Republic

On 19th October, 1918, the Vienna government received a telegram from President Wilson announcing that as far as Czechoslovaks and Yugoslavs were concerned, he couldn't negotiate with the Austro-Hungarians but only with representatives of those nations. It was clear to Vienna that it was over. On 22nd October, Emperor Charles I asked the vice-chairman of the CSNR, Karel Klofáč, to enact a coup without bloodshed. Klofáč promised the Emperor and travelled from Vienna to Geneva, where representatives of the domestic resistance had been discussing with Edvard Beneš the composition of the future first government of Czecho-Slovakia. The Austrian-Hungarian Foreign Minister, Count Andrássy, announced on 27th October that his government accepted all President Wilson's terms, which meant a definitive capitulation. This news arrived in Prague on 28th October at approximately ten in the morning when a general strike had broken out across the country and masses of people were on the streets. A huge sign was posted on the *National Politics* newspaper building on Wenceslas Square: 'Truce'. Praguers assumed Vienna had surrendered and celebrations began immediately. People tore down Austrian symbols, the streets of Prague filled with thousands of enthusiastic citizens and the security forces dared not intervene. At that time, the chairman of the National Committee, Karel Kramář, was at a meeting in Geneva, to where the resigning authorities had surprisingly released him. The masses of Praguers passed from Příkopy to Václavské námestie, where a member of the National Committee, MP Isidor Záhradník, joined their procession. They put him on their shoulders and the deputy was carried, wrapped in the Slavonic tricolor, in the parade leading to the statue of St. Wenceslas. In spite of a strong rhotacism the crowds heard his clear message to the nation: "We are free. Here, at the steps of the monument to the Czech Prince, Saint Wenceslas, we swear that we want to become worthy of this freedom and defend it with our lives." The crowd greeted him enthusiastically. Then he got into a car driven by a local policeman who took him to the Franz Joseph Station. Here he announced that he would take over the management of the State Railways on behalf of the CSNR and had a telegraph message sent to all Czech railway stations: "The Czecho-Slovak state was declared at 11am today at the statue of St. Wenceslas on *Václavské námestie*. Remove all signs of the former state of Austro-Hungary immediately. Detain all goods to Vienna and Germany. Go well!! Dr. Záhradník." And thus it began.

Only a few hours after Záhradník, the once Catholic and later Orthodox priest, had been there, František Soukup and Jiří Stříbrný also appeared at the statue. At the evening meeting of the CSNR, one of the four Presidium members present in Prague, Alois Rašín, declared on behalf of presidium members, Antonín Švehla, František Soukup and Jiří Stříbrný, the first law on the creation of an independent Czechoslovak state which he'd written the previous night. It began with the words: "To the nation of Czechoslovakia! Your ancient dream has become law. Today, the Czechoslovak state joined the ranks of independent cultural states of the world. Czechoslovak people, everything you do, you do from now on as a new free citizen of the large family of independent free nations! With these deeds, your glorious new history is beginning!" For Slovakia, the law was signed by MUDr. Vavro Šrobár, who happened to be in Prague at that time. On the evening of 28th October, it was approved by a plenary of the CSNR, who declared the establishment of the Czecho-Slovak Republic and took over state power in the territory of Bohemia, Moravia and Silesia. In Czech towns, national committees began to form spontaneously and claim control.

Events in Prague weren't known in Slovakia as a consequence of disrupted railway and telegraph connections. Independent of developments in the Czechlands, on 30th October, two hundred prominent Slovaks gathered in Turčiansky Svätý Martin in the Tatra bank building, most of them Lutherans. The majority of the Catholic clergy had opposed the proclamation of the Republic and made it evident. The Assembly elected a twenty-member Slovak National Council and a twelve-member Executive Committee. In the future, the National Council would be the supreme body of Slovak politics. The Chairman of the Slovak National Party, Matúš Dula, announced the Declaration of the Slovak Nation abolishing the union with Hungary, claiming the right of the Slovak nation to self-determination and stating the wish to exist in union with the Czechs in a common state. When he thanked the American President, the people stood up and chanted: "Long live Wilson!" A platoon of the 15th Honved Regiment was transferred to Martin from Levice for any eventuality and the captain of the Martin Border Police, Beliczky, stood at the entrance to Tatra bank, with a notebook in his hands writing down the names of all those present. Only in the evening, when Milan Hodža arrived in Martin from Budapest, did members of the SNR Executive Committee learn that the Czecho-Slovak Republic had already been declared in Prague and that Austria-Hungary had surrendered unconditionally. The declaration was thus modified, the requirement for independent representation of Slovaks at the peace conference becoming nugatory.

The Chairman of the Slovak National Party, Matúš Dula, sent a telegram to Prague:

NATIONAL COMMITTEE PRAGUE
THE SLOVAK NATIONAL PARTY STANDS FOR UNCONDITIONAL AND UNLIMITED SELF-DETERMINATION RIGHTS OF THE SLOVAK NATION AND ON THIS BASIS APPLIES FOR THE RIGHT OF THE SLOVAK NATION TO TAKE PART IN THE ESTABLISHMENT OF A SEPARATE STATE CONSISTING OF SLOVAKIA – CZECHIA – MORAVIA AND SILESIA – MATUS DULA

Emperor Wilhelm II and the Crown Prince signed their abdication on 8th November and preserved themselves by fleeing to the Netherlands. The Plenipotentiary of the Entente, Marshal Foch, dictated to the German negotiators the conditions for ending the fighting, which they signed at Compiègnes, north-east of Paris, in a railway carriage at the Rethondes sewage plant on 11th November at 11 am. The First World War was over. It had killed 1.77 million Germans, 1.7 million Russians, 1.36 million Frenchmen, 1.2 million Austrian-Hungarian soldiers, 947,000 Italians, 908,371 British and Commonwealth citizens, 335,706 Romanians, 325,000 Turks, 126, 000 Americans, 87,500 Bulgarians, 130,000 Serbs and innumerable casualties from other nations. People in London, Berlin, Vienna, Paris, New York and around the world celebrated. A more than four-year-long hell, causing tremendous suffering to millions, had ended.

At that time, a soldier in a military hospital in the small Pomeranian town of Pasewalk lay temporarily blinded from a British gas attack. Later he wrote: "On the day of closing that humiliating peace I decided to be a politician to avenge for the humiliation." The soldier's name was Adolf Hitler.

In Austria-Hungary, on 13th November, Emperor Charles I abdicated and went to Switzerland. On the following day, the first meeting of the Revolutionary National Assembly, formed from the former National Committee, was held in Prague. Tomáš Garrigue Masaryk was unanimously elected President. When Chairman František Tomášek gave the floor to a member of the Slovak National Council, Metod Bella, the Gregor Hall of the Municipal House roared with applause. For the first time, the speech of the brotherly Slovak nation was heard in this land. Bella said at the outset: "Greatly Honoured National Assembly! This day, after a thousand years of suffering, the Slovak nation is entering history, joining our Slovaks with the Czechs... The nation of Slovakia expresses its deepest gratitude to the Czech nation and its great sons and great souls which our Slovak nation can only and exclusively thank. Our Slovak nation expresses our love for our brother the Czech nation, the love of a pure heart, emerging from a yoked thousand-year old soul, the pure love that has attained the highest ideal of its love in the Czech nation. We bring you that love, a sincere, heartfelt love!" After these words, enthusiastic shouts were heard. Slovak and Czech deputies embraced each other and the applause was unending. The National Committee of 254 delegates adopted a temporary constitution which Vavro Šrobár signed for the Slovaks. Later, in March 1919, the number of deputies was increased to 270, of whom 40 were Slovaks. Remarkably, thirty were evangelicals and only ten Catholics. Slovaks, being part of the majority nation of Czechoslovakia, couldn't claim minority rights.

On 7th December 1918, Štefánik sent a telegram from Vladivostok: *"Mr. Masaryk, President of the Czechoslovak Republic. With a son's feelings and with the great joy of the patriot, I greet you, venerable Master, as the first President of the Czechoslovak Republic."*

Gradually euphoria at the establishment of the republic subsided and citizens began to solve the ordinary problems of existence, eating, accommodation, heating, clothing and employment.

In December, mass protests broke out in Prague, ideal ground for bolshevizing the masses. The Prime Minister, Kramář, pleaded with Masaryk to return as soon as possible and to calm the masses with his almost divine authority. Indeed, the triumphant arrival of the President on 21st December brought the whole of Prague to boiling point. The writer, Alois Jirásek, greeted him in the hall of Wilson Railway Station and the ride between crowds of fervent Prague citizens led through Václavské náměstí to the ancient Assembly in Malá Strana, where Masaryk took his presidential oath in the afternoon. After the oath, he went to the sanatorium in Veleslavín to embrace his ailing wife, Charlotte, who'd been deprived of her legal capacity in May 1918 to protect her from the Austrian authorities.

The adored President was able to calm the situation partially, but not for long. His halo was not a magic wand and so pogroms and revolts continued. Corruption, typical of a society with scarcities, was widespread among civil servants, police and judges. The masses rebelled and the example of the Russian Revolution was tempting. The Bolshevik fire that Germany had fuelled in Russia spread not only to Germany, but also to Hungary, with workers' councils also established in other European countries. The war had ended, but in 1919 alone, twelve minor military conflicts between neighbouring countries with claims to each other's territories erupted on European soil. Even on the day of the Czechoslovakia's declaration of independence, Poland, under Wilson's right of nations to self-determination, officially laid claim to Těšínsko and later made claims to parts of Orava and Spiš. After the announcement that elections to the Warsaw Sejm would take place in Těšínsko, where they had also begun to recruit into the Polish army, the six-day Polish-Czech war broke out. In the summer of 1920, the Poles withdrew under pressure from the invading Russian Bolsheviks. Similarly, the Germans, referring to Wilson's program of self-determination of nations, declared Deutschböhmen in Northern Bohemia on 29th October should become part of Germany. In the west of Bohemia, the German Šumavská county was founded with the ambition of joining Bavaria and in the vicinity of Opava in the north of Moravia, Sudetenland was established while the Znojmo Germans wanted to join Austria. German revolts were suppressed only due to legionaries returning mainly from Italy.

CHAPTER 23
Traitor! Blackguard! String Him Up!

While, since the announcement of the Declaration of the General Assembly of the Czech Imperial Deputies on 6th January, 1918, an increasingly broader section of the population had joined the leaders of the domestic resistance, in Slovakia politicians and the masses had dozed or slept hard. The Upper Hungary deputies, Ferdiš Juriga and Vavro Šrobár had uncompromisingly called on the representatives of the Slovak National Party to shake themselves out of their passivity and start working vigorously to liberate the nation. "Turčianski Slovaks! The nationals are doing nothing, their patience comes from the feebleness of the Slovak intelligentsia. If they're doing nothing, the people themselves have to take matters into their own hands. He who lacks the boldness to stand up for his nation shouldn't speak on its behalf!" expostulated Ferdiš Juriga. Then, as ever, a Hungarian complex persisted in Slovak politics.

While the monarchy fomented strikes from the Czechlands to Serbia, Slovenia, Vojvodina, Transylvania, the masses in Slovakia waited in pious patience and humility for what fate would bring them. An important element in Slovak passivity was the Catholic Church, which, as usual, collaborated with the politically powerful. Almost all its priests were Hungarians or Hungarian Slovaks, and their words were of great importance for the common people. Andrej Hlinka, the most popular Slovak Catholic priest had declared: "I am a Catholic first and then a Slovak."

The most significant Slovak centre of resistance was Vienna, where Milan Hodža and Kornel Stodola worked illegally. They were in contact with the Maffia and Czech Imperial deputies. In the territory of Upper Hungary practically the only person courageous enough to act during the fall of the monarchy was the Ružomberok doctor, Vavro Šrobár. He was clearly aware that if there was no vote from Slovakia for joining the Czechs by the summer of 1918, the likelihood of a post-war separation from Hungary would be negligible. Therefore, in agreement with the Social Democrats, during the May Day celebrations in Liptovský Mikuláš he made a speech which was carefully concealed until the last minute, otherwise there'd have been a risk that the authorities wouldn't have allowed the demonstration. In the resolution he demanded, "unconditional recognition of the right of nations to self-determination not only beyond the borders of our monarchy, but also among the nations of Austria-Hungary, including the Hungarian branch of the Czechoslovak tribe". Although in the published text of the resolution, the words "Hungarian branch of the Czechoslovak tribe" were replaced by the word "Slovaks", which was an unknown term abroad, this statement was very well received in the Entente countries. For the first time the Slovaks had indicated clearly to the world that they wanted to go with the Czechs. The Hungarian propaganda lie about the desire of Slovaks to live in Hungary continued to lose traction, although there were no major displays of anti-Hungarian resistance among the Slovak masses. As a result of Šrobár's appearance, the Slovak National Party became more active and at a confidential meeting in Turčiansky Svätý Martin on 24th May, 1918, Andrej Hlinka managed to break away from his position on Czech anti-clericalism and proclaimed: "There is a time of action, we must make it clear whether we will go with the Hungarians or the Czechs. We are in favour of Czecho-Slovakia; the thousand-year marriage with the Hungarians is over, we have to break away."

More and more Slovak soldiers refused to fight for the hated monarchy and mutinies were increasingly common. The largest of them was the mutiny of the 71st Slovak Trenčín Infantry Regiment in the Serbian town of Kragujevac on 3rd June. Forty-four mutineers were publicly executed on 8th June. The next day mutiny erupted in the military garrison in the Vodné barracks in Bratislava.

On the day after the Washington Declaration, 19th October, the Slovak deputy, Ferdiš Juriga, gave a fiery speech in the Hungarian assembly which caused a storm of outrage from Hungarian deputies, not only because of its content, but also because for the first time in history, Slovak was heard in buildings of the Hungarian Assembly: "The Slovak nation calls out with its heart and soul, we speak the Word and the Word is Slovak. We are our own people, the nation of our language and we will not yield! We legitimately claim for ourselves, in accordance with King Charles' wishes, the rights of a separate nation and statehood in the territory in which we are established."

Juriga's performance was interrupted by insults and accusations, "Out with him, knock him down! Traitor! Blackguard! String him up!"

However, the courageous Catholic priest did not give up and went on: "It also responsibly demands for itself the right to fully establish the position of its constituted state and the nature of its relationship with other nations, freely and without foreign intervention. The Slovak nation does not recognize the legitimacy of this parliament and the government to consider themselves representatives of the Slovak nation as it has only two deputies, although it has the right to forty... Outside the bodies of its elected members, outside the Slovak National Council, no one is entitled to negotiate or decide against the Slovak nation on matters relating to its political position. *Itt az idö, most vagy soha!* The time has come, now or never! These are the words of our blood, the words of the son of Mária Hrúzová, the words of Alexander Petrovič – Petöfi Šándor, and these words fill our souls and strengthen us with the fire of our anthem. We stand firm like the walls of a castle! We demand our self-determined right to life and to death. With these we live, with these we die!" By quoting the powerful words of Petöfi, whom the Hungarian deputies considered their national icon, Juriga unleashed a hurricane in the building of the Assembly which the chairman managed to contain with the greatest difficulty.

Despite the resistance of the Hungarian deputies, the fate of the Slovaks had already been decided. Prime Minister István Tisza had no idea that he had only three days to live after the declaration of the Czecho-Slovak Republic. In the Aster revolution led by Count Mihály Károlyi, they blamed Hungary's loss of the war on Tisza and murdered him without trial.

On November 16th, King Charles IV. appointed Count Mihály Károlyi Prime Minister, later President of the Hungarian People's Republic. To the surprise of all, the first congratulatory telegram received by the new leadership of the Slovak National Council came from Károlyi. He acknowledged the injustices committed by the sinful politics of one class on the Slovak and Hungarian people and wished a happy future to the Slovaks. But Károlyi had no plans to give up Upper Hungary. He'd paid all state employees in Slovakia salaries for half a year in advance and thus ensured that they could rebel and strike against the emerging Czecho-Slovak authorities without fears for their survival.

The Slovak National Party chairman, Matúš Dula, said in his reply to Károlyi that "a free Czecho-Slovak nation wants to be a good neighbour and brother to the Hungarian nation". The Slovak National Council sent a delegation to Prague consisting of Ivan Dérer, Fedor Houdek and Jozef Honzalík. Houdek told Czech friends,

"We have brought a short report from Slovakia, namely that the Slovak National Council has agreed to Slovaks joyfully joining the Czecho-Slovak state, not wanting to live beside the Czechs as two nations, but as one nation because there lies our future and strength. The Czech nation has its past, the Slovak has merely suffered. We hope that coexistence will ensure freedom and bring glory to the Slovaks. Brothers, the Czecho-Slovak nation is alive!"

The Slovaks celebrated prematurely. On 16th November, 1918, the Prague National Assembly deprived the Slovak National Council of its powers despite the original Hodža proposal to create a regional committee from the Slovak National Council which, as the Slovak part of the National Assembly, would control state administration in Slovakia. Few people then realized that the abolition of the Slovak National Council and the creation of a ministry for Slovakia headed by Vavro Šrobár would prove a fatal mistake. Dr. Šrobár and his officials, appointed by Prague, could not, with the best will in the world, replace the Slovak National Council. If the Prague government had recognized the Slovak National Council as the representative body of Slovakia, it would undoubtedly have attracted the sympathy of most Slovaks, which was extremely important in a sensitive and tense situation. The abolition of the SNR was fuel to the flames of Hungarian anti-Czechoslovak propaganda, however, and raised the rivalry of the Czechoslovak Šrobár and the nationalist Hlinka from the Ružomberok environment to a national level.

In Slovakia, there was a catastrophic shortage of officials who could take over the administration of public affairs after the Hungarians. The only choice was to send Czech officials to Slovakia and Carpathian Ruthenia, many of whom were unqualified as the more competent were retained by the Czech authorities at home. Thus, people of varied intellectual and moral quality came to Slovakia, tempted by financial incentives.

Without the help of Czech and Moravians, Slovakia wouldn't have been able to provide vital work in the areas of railways, education, public administration, police, the army and post offices. The Czechs saved Slovakia from chaos in the first years of the Republic. Moreover, they also brought a functional system of trade unions that had been banned in Slovakia during Hungarian domination, as well as elements of a genuinely pluralistic political system. Many young Slovaks were sent to Bohemia and Moravia to train and acquire mainly administrative skills. Thanks to Czech aid, Slovakia had started to develop, but the price for that was the strengthening of Czech dominance.

CHAPTER 24
Above All I Love My Nation

After their takeover of power in St. Petersburg in October, the Bolsheviks extended power to other areas of Russia. Gradually, however, anti-Bolshevik forces became active, consisting of former army Tsar structures, liberal monarchist circles and Socialist Revolutionaries. Each of the three tendencies had its own interests, so there were three ideological clusters opposed to one another, increasingly plunging into the swirl of civil war. The monarchists and democrats were the main enemies of the Bolsheviks, but for the Democrats, the Bolsheviks and the monarchists were the same enemies. Conditions made for a merciless civil war...

The strongest anti-Bolshevik forces were concentrated in Siberia. However, there were two centres of power, the Temporary government in Omsk, oriented to the right and the Constituent Assembly Committee in Samara, oriented to the left. Before long, a temporary All-Russia government was established, headed by a five-member Directive based in Omsk, which began to operate in early November 1918. Soon, however, with secret support from the British it was overthrown by an excellent former Tsarist commander, the forty-four-year-old Alexander Kolchak, who was promoted to the rank of Admiral on 18th November 1918. He became the unlimited master of Siberia, introduced a cruel dictatorship and in Yekaterinburg alone had 25,000 political opponents tortured and executed. This senseless terror caused mass resistance and pushed desperate people into the Bolshevik forces, though they had no sympathy for them.

The key military factor in Siberia was the well-trained Czecho-Slovak legion, organized in twelve rifle (infantry) divisions, three artillery and two cavalry battalions, one strike battalion and several smaller units. Vladivostok harbour also hosted a smaller Czecho-Slovak naval unit, consisting of five tugs. They even had an air force. The legion consisted of predominantly young soldiers, ensigns about twenty years old, lieutenants twenty-two, captains twenty-five, staff officers under thirty and generals in their thirties, with many university graduates amongst them. The legionaries in Siberia resumed the mining of coal, gold, ammunition production, published books, newspapers, had a theatre and even a symphony orchestra, which also made several trips to Japan. Seven hospitals took care of their health, they ran mobile dental ambulances, established schools for children of compatriots, founded their own bank, the *Legiobanka*, issued postage stamps and organized a postal service along the entire main route. They had their own judiciary, regular sporting events and organized Sokol public music exercises. They talked to each other informally and used the word "brother."

28th October brought both joy and sadness to Štefánik with the establishment of the Republic. On this day, a forgotten and underrated Slovak scholar, the Lutheran pastor, Štefánik's friend from his youth and his fellow Parisian, Ján Lajčiak died in Vyšná Boca. Before midnight on 15th November 1918, Štefánik sailed aboard the *Taichi Maru* to Vladivostok. Two anthems were played in honor of the Czechoslovak Minister and the French General Janin, *Where Is*

My Home and the *Marseillaise*. For security reasons, he was privately housed in Dr. Girsa's apartment. His servant Garreau had set up a bedroom and the General fell into bed half-dead.

The next morning he invited Captain Písecký to see him. He offered him a seat and then the two men remained silent for a long time. Štefánik broke the silence. He tried to talk calmly, but he couldn't hide his trembling; the time to say goodbye had come.

"We'll talk a while until you leave me, you absconder," he tried to smile. "Here's money, the power of attorney and Czech and French service orders. It should be enough for you to start your mission in Japan. Professor Masaryk places great hopes in you. The task of setting up a branch of the National Council, now our official body, won't be easy, but you can manage it. You can go to the French Embassy in Tokyo as a home, they've promised to give you maximum support." He paused for a moment and looked into Písecký's eyes. "How are your wife and children?"

"Well, I think... They say hello."

"I hope you will introduce me to your great and self-sacrificing wife on my return."

"It will be a great honour."

"I hope I can come... I have a great liking for you, Ferdinand, there is no treachery in you... But today we part, you're going east today and I west. But wherever we find ourselves, it's our duty to support Masaryk with all our might. He's lifted the nation from moral decline, given it a moral goal, a fixed point."

"I believe that when you return to your homeland," he patted Písecký on his shoulder, "you and your family will go to Slovakia and organize the education system. I don't know a better person than you for this task."

"You talk as if you have no intention of going back..."

"Everything is in the hands of God. I'm not well, in fact I've never felt so bad before. At the moment, I'm under immense mental strain and I feel exhausted, extinguished. I don't think I can last another year. This is not life... I have terrible pains, but though you won't believe me, I am grateful to the Almighty for them and thank God that he gave me the opportunity to work for my nation. I love it with the same instinct as good spouses love. They don't have to tell each other every day how they love each other, they just know it." He paused again, clutching his heart. Písecký watched with concern.

"Thank you for all those chess games. You gave me the most precious thing a man has, his time," he took his hand.

"Brother Minister, your time is more precious, but you gave it to me in the same way, so I thank you," replied Písecký quietly.

"Remember when you read Cyrano to me in Umt in the cabin by the bed? Rostand is a brilliant poet. Some of his thoughts are amazing. You'll no longer read to me from my beloved books. I won't take them with me to Siberia, the road will be long and space needs to be saved in my trunks. I'd be pleased if you accepted my books as a gift. Here's Pascal, Joubert, Musset, Aucassin and Nicoletta, it's a wonderful story of love... I don't know, dear Captain, what is happening to me today, but something tells me I need to talk. So please don't think ill of me... I'll tell you something I don't even have the right to say, but I'll confide in you. Something amazing has happened... I've fallen in love with a girl... young, beautiful, very bright morally and intellectually. When we met, we spoke together like children, not even knowing each other's names. No one knew, except her and her mother. Her name is Guiliana Benzoni, she is an Italian Marchesa and grand-niece of the most beautiful woman in Europe, Teresa Marescotti, Princess of Venosa. It is a beautiful, pure, infinite love; it has something of the scent of the spring breeze about it..."

"Brother General, I greatly appreciate your trust. I want to thank you for everything you have taught me, especially your absolute honesty in everything," Písecký smiled.

"Honesty is a matter of course for me; you now know why I think so long about every word when writing a speech. Honesty, however, is not a word, but the logical consequence of life. And if it doesn't become mystical, it becomes a force. A dishonest person can't do a great deed – it's impossible. He may achieve a favourable outcome for a moment, but he cannot work consistently, unwaveringly..."

"It isn't appropriate, but let me give you some advice, after all, I am eight months older than you," Písecký smiled. "Please don't open your heart and soul to everyone."

"Whom do you mean?"

"You know..."

"Yes, yes..."

His voice weakened, fatigue overwhelming him. The Captain helped his combat companion make the bed and put on his pyjamas. The two men embraced and Štefánik closed his eyes. Písecký stared at him for a long time, gazing at the General in farewell, as if he knew he'd never see him again.

CHAPTER 25
We've Had Enough!

The next day on a short walk, Štefánik couldn't help but wonder at how bustling and dynamic Vladivostok was. The boulevards were full of people, cafés, cinemas and theatres; bars burst at the seams, as if a few hundred kilometres west of the city the White and Red Guards weren't fighting. Five days later he was in Charbin, where Russian military officials completely ignored his arrival. Štefánik, however, surprised the civilian staff when he arrived at the telegraph office and went up to a soldier and greeted him with a handshake. The locals weren't accustomed to such familiarity between General and soldier. He made an official visit to the Governor General of the three provinces of Manchuria, the Chinese official categorically protesting against some of the errors of General Gajda. After finding out that General Chia-ao Li was also an astronomer, Štefánik won him over not only with his expertise but also with his knowledge of Chinese vocabulary and the zodiac. A scandal was averted and Štefánik was given the gift not only of a photograph of the General, but also of an impressive military parade held in his honour before he arrived for a theatre performance in the evening. He had to cancel the evening ride through the city, however, due to stomach cramps.

In Charbin, he received a report on the monarchist coup d'état of Admiral Kolchak which took place on the night of Štefánik's arrival in Siberia, 17th November. Worst of all, the legion was divided at the time, especially as the division under General Gajda supported Kolchak.

Unlike in post-war Europe starved by hunger, there was enough food in Siberia. Nevertheless, the soldiers expected their minister to come and give them hope that they would soon start moving home. However, from Vladivostok to Yekaterinburg and Chelyabinsk, he had to explain to them why they had to stay in Russia, trying to convince them with all his authority but feeling an increasing loss of faith and determination. In the station vestibule in Irkutsk on 28th November he embarked on a discussion with embittered soldiers of the emergent Slovak regiment. Most often he had to answer the question that one of the Lieutenants formulated thus: "Why are we still fighting here when we have achieved what we were striving for, our state? The Allies haven't come to our aid and the Russians leave the burden of fighting the Bolsheviks to us. We are tired, hungry and exhausted, freezing and dying, but we don't know why. We want to go home!"

"We're exhausted. I've been away from home for three years. We are fed up to the teeth with it. I don't even know what my children look like," another Lieutenant added.

"I was at the birth of the legions, and I came to take you home. But before..." Štefánik excitedly but vigorously explained: "I'll convince the Allies that under these circumstances our army should have been at home a long time ago." He unfastened the warm fur coat once given to him by the furrier, Benko, then added with less conviction: "We're fighting against a Bolshevik anarchy that also threatens our state. Unless normal conditions are established in Russia, the sparks of anarchy from Russia will spread to Europe. If a fire breaks out, we shouldn't wait for it to reach our building and engulf it but put it out first... We're a member of the army of allies today and we must pursue our common interests."

"What are they? Why are we mixed up in this? If the Russians want Bolshevism, let them have it!"

"Bolshevism is a negation of democracy, a sign of disease and an apocalyptic chaos in which the gross, lowest instincts are displayed. I'm telling you this from the depths of my soul. Flirting with the Bolsheviks is tantamount to abandoning the path of honour and common sense. In our ethics, the struggle against Bolshevism must prevail in everything."

"The Bolsheviks are the same workers and peasants as us. There are no sons of the gentry among us for whom we have to fight. Where are they?" declared another soldier.

"Remember, we are grateful to the Russians, whether Tsarist or Kerensky troops, for the fact that since the beginning of the war Russia has been the only force with a sincere interest in breaking Austro-Hungary..." he thought and added more quietly: "Unlike the other allies..."

"Brother General, the Whites don't want to fight. Their troops are primarily youngsters, forced to join the army under the threat of capital punishment but people are volunteering for the Red Army. This is the reason for the differences in the morale of the two armies."

"There is no time to explain to you all the complexities of the international context. In the first place, we care for our state which was created mainly thanks to our allies. Didn't President Wilson himself guarantee the right to self-determination? The steps he took, as well as those of our allies, are clear proof that they've been honest with us."

"Vladimir Lenin guaranteed nations the right to self-determination long before Wilson. In addition, he promised to end the war and divide the land among those who work on it. And he's keeping his word. What do your allies guarantee? Nothing but a battle against our Russian brothers for their threatened money."

"Our allies were the guarantors of a freedom which we finally saw happen. Isn't it enough that we have our own state?" Štefánik tried to emphasize the idea with his voice, but he felt his strength leave him. The station commander, Warrant Officer Weiss, and Warrant Officer Blahož in the meantime tried to mollify the troops but with little success. The soldiers had verbalized what their commanders were thinking.

"Fair enough. We've had a state for a good month and our friends, who weren't fooled into entering the legion, are going home. But you're sending us west to fight again. They want us to fight for them, but don't even send us any damn blankets! So let them fight the Reds all by themselves! Besides in a thirty-degree frost, you can't even get out of your wagon. Can you imagine what it means being stuck for almost a year in wagons full of lice? Like chickens in cages and when you go to a latrine, your piss freezes as it comes out," said an exasperated Slovak soldier with a hole in his left cheek.

Štefánik, with a sweeping gesture, tried to calm the upset soldiers.

"Friends, our state already exists, but the favourable conditions for its development, such as border adjustment, waterways, trade agreements, will all be managed by the peace conference soon to begin in Paris. The world's most powerful statesmen will look at us carefully and follow our movements. If we lose the respect of the Allies, they will not curse us, but won't consider us as equals either and will lose interest in us. The consequence would be that we have a state that doesn't live but scrapes by. If we want Šopron, Prešporok, if we want Romania as a neighbour, if we want the Allies to support our claims, we must move ahead in unity and in line with them.

It's not enough to fight for freedom, it has to be maintained! We've become famous once and we'll become famous again. We'll defeat Bolshevism and the world will be grateful to us forever!"

"Ok, we have freedom! But they write from home that the Germans and the Hungarians are threatening us. Instead of going to fight them, though, we stay here fighting for the English, the French and the Italians."

"They'll help us back home."

"Let them come here instead; we can manage at home without them. Those crapheads of Kolchak are just boozing and snoring in the warm. The local people would have laid down their lives for the Siberian democratic government that Kolchak trashed. They were people like us. They got up the noses of those Kolchak tsarist generals and English advisors and were killed for it!"

"Indeed, people didn't even have to be recruited, they themselves reported to the government to fight against the Bolsheviks. But then they realized. Now they all run to the taiga to escape forced conscription!"

"What do you mean, to the taiga!" expostulated another soldier. "Out of anger, they join the Bolsheviks. And we feel that for the ordinary people we're Kolchak's Czech bitches! We're called here Czecho-sobaki, Czech dogs! Kolchak has two thousand tosspots on his staff. They just stroll along Omsk's boulevards with call girls, draping them with gold from head to toe. There are no richer whores in the world than Kolchak's so much Tsar's gold do they have... Even the sparrows are chirping that our commander Gajda wants to go over to Kolchak!"

"Where do you know this from?" Štefánik asked nervously.

"People on Gajda's staff are saying it; he keeps asking how many are going with him!"

Štefánik wanted to react, but he only began to breathe hard and cramp up from pain. But the indignant soldiers continued to remonstrate.

"One day we dig graves for the victims of the Reds, the next day for the Whites, but it's the same ordinary people who are always hurt. We've had enough death! We look her in the eyes every day! We don't want any more! Give us a break from the front! Brother Minister, you understand, *uže nadjelos*! We've had enough! We want to go home!"

"Brothers, I know what it is to look death in the eye. I was on the front myself. France, Italy, Serbia. There my plane was shot down... You don't have to tell me about death."

"Nothing will change. The Hungarian gentry will be replaced by Czech and Slovak toffs. The ordinary man remain enslaved."

"How can you say that? This denies all the sacrifices we have made! The Czechoslovak state already has a government in which Slovaks are represented," said Štefánik.

"You're the only one," someone commented.

"It is only a temporary government, there will be other Slovaks in the permanent one. Isn't it a wonderful feeling that in Slovakia there are no longer Hungarian servants, Hungarian notaries, gendarmes, that on the railways, in schools, in cities, in short, everywhere our Slovak language is heard?"

"As far as I know, Hungarian is still the main language in Slovakia. And if you, Brother General, are so very interested in Slovak, why have you ordered that the official language of our troops in Siberia be Czech?"

"The military can't have ten official languages!"

"We understand Czech and Czechs us. Why can't we have a separate Slovak regiment? If they're against it, it means they don't trust us," said the soldier.

"Don't worry," he said gathering his strength, adding in a weak, tired voice: "The first Irkutsk Slovak regiment will defile in the streets of Bratislava. You'll see!"

He was asked to say something else, but he lost consciousness. The soldiers quickly put him on a stretcher and carried him to his wagon. The train moved westward to Omsk, the seat of the Kolchak government. Here, however, to protest against the dictatorship imposed by Kolchak, which disgusted him, he preferred not to get off the train. In his wagon he negotiated with the French high commissioner, Renault and the commander of the local Czechoslovak garrison Major Kroutil. Shortly after a debate with Slovak soldiers and prisoners in Irkutsk he issued military order number 122, which said: "The camp for Slovak prisoners in Irkutsk is now named the Czechoslovak camp for Slovaks in Irkutsk."

Thanks to Štefánik's speech and order, out of 1,400 prisoners in Irkutsk, three hundred joined the legion.

CHAPTER 26
Aim Properly at My Heart!

Štefánik met Czechoslovak soldiers in Petropavlovsk, Kurgan and Šumicha. On 5th December, the Czecho-Slovak Minister was welcomed in the festively decorated streets of Chelyabinsk where he spoke without a fur coat but only in his General's uniform. His entourage consisted of General Čeček, the British, General Bowes, the French Consul, Vergé and a member of the CSNR branch led by Bohdan Pavlů. After a brief military inspection and acceptance of a report, the Legion Commander, General Syrový read from the train the message of Štefánik, who merely listened because the doctor had forbidden him to speak.

"Soldiers of the Czechoslovak Republic, I come to you as a brother who stood by the cradle of our army and wants to share his fate until the last moment... I'm visiting our valiant army from regiment to regiment, listening to your wishes and explaining the tasks still awaiting us. When these tasks are accomplished, we'll go on the journey together to our free homeland."

His enthusiastic, emotional words, however, didn't make a great impression on the soldiers, all the more because their author stood silent, sick and weak, in no way reminiscent of a brave army commander. He hadn't heard the final words of the General: "Success to our Minister of National Defence, General Štefánik!"

Not even a friendly meeting with his old friends Ján Jesenský and Jozef Gregor from student times cheered him. They felt disillusioned with each other. In Bohdan Pavlů's conference room he tried to shake them out of their lethargy.

"We need a strong, great Russia. We're fighting against the Bolsheviks. The Allies won't help us on our way to the north and we'll fight for Arkhangelsk and Murmansk by ourselves. I can tell you in confidence that in Romania, Berthelot is preparing to fight the Bolsheviks with five tank divisions. We'll conquer Perm and from there we pull north. There the army can rest and then we'll head home with me at the head..." But he saw that his words were no longer well received by officers and political officials.

Between 10th and 14th December, he visited the front line on the Yekaterinburg to Perm route. At Šamara, Šalja, Kuzino and other nodal points on the highway, he spoke to soldiers of the 8th Regiment and the 5th Company of the 5th Regiment, to members of the Fifth Battery of the Artillery Brigade and to the Seventh Regiment's soldiers, gunners and cavalrymen. His impressions from his conversations with soldiers and officers were overwhelming; the combat morale of the famous Czecho-Slovak legions was at rock bottom. Despite his dismay, he didn't slacken his efforts, however, and received members of the second cavalry regiment in Tyumen on 16th December. Ten cavalrymen and two officers visited him in his salon on the train. He was, as usual, dressed in his General's uniform, which he'd slightly modified, having had a golden lion embroidered on the collar under his chin. In the salon, the delegation was received by his secretary Lakomý and political plenipotentiary, Bohdan Pavlů. He greeted everyone genially, inquiring of the soldiers where they'd come from. His face lit up when one of them told him in a hard Kopanice dialect that he was from Brezová and that he'd been with him at the funeral of the pastor, Pavel Štefánik in Košariská. The minister stood up and embraced his countryman with joy.

"Friends, there is not much space in here, but good people can fit everywhere," and he gestured around for everyone to find a place. "I've walked through Tyumen and I want to tell you a few words. I come to you in very difficult circumstances. I'm not talking about winter, fatigue and my health – these are beside the point. There isn't one of you who hasn't suffered. When I was deciding whether to come here, I hesitated a little because I was elected minister, so I could go to Prague and as a Knight of Blaník draw a sword at Hradčany and exclaim: 'Here I am, my nation, I have brought you your freedom'. But I've come here because I know how difficult it is for you and wanted to share your pains. Now my doubts are greater and of a different kind. I see that it's right that I came here, but I don't know if it's right for me stay. I'm telling you those terrible words because I've come from the front. The first Czechoslovak army minister in four hundred years must address a company that refuses to go into battle! Do you understand? It hurts me terribly not only as a minister and soldier, but as a human being. Towards the end of the war, when the garlands for the victors are visible, I see cowardice among us under the slogan of democracy! Unbelievable..."

Štefánik paused; only the crackling wood in the oven could be heard.

"My friends," he continued in a calmer tone. "Why am I here? I wanted to shake your hands and thank you very much! We weren't a factor the world counted on but have become one. I know, lads, you don't have it easy, but if we accomplish the tasks that still await us here, we'll go to our liberated homeland together. We'll complete the work of a selfless Slav and an honest ally. It would be rough justice if hostilities were to arise between the Russian and Czechoslovak nations. We see and feel how Russia and the Russian soul have been terribly shaken. It would be unjust of us if we didn't seek to correct with love what abnormal times have inflicted. We need a large, strong Russia. We fight the Bolsheviks and will not be asking them for anything; we will find our way home ourselves. You can be proud that our officers are aware that they command an army that is one of the best on earth."

In the moment of silence which followed, one of the cavalrymen raised his hand. Štefánik gave him the floor, the soldier spoke in a low, sad voice.

"Brother General, we greet you on behalf of the Second Cavalry Regiment. We're proud to have you among us. As we've begun the battle against evil, we'll finish it... it's just... I just want you to know how it was with Honzík..." he unconsciously lit a cigarette, but nobody reprimanded him. "When we retreated before the Reds at Glazovka, they had an entire battalion while we were down to just one company," he said slowly, his voice faltering. "They surrounded us, the only way back was the swamp. We were carrying three badly injured brothers. A grenade had torn off one's arm, a second his leg, the third had been shot through his belly. We didn't want to leave them to those angry shits. But we could barely wade through the marshes, let alone do it with limp bodies on our shoulders. It was impossible to move the wounded along the trail. Then Honzík said, 'Finish us off, just don't leave us alive...' Can you imagine such a situation? Honzík, your best friend, and you've got no other choice... just that... None of us wanted to do it, but the reds were within range. So I picked up my rifle and pointed it at him. But the gun failed. Then he gave me his, saying: 'Aim properly at my heart!' I was shaking like a leaf, I begged him and God to forgive me. I shot and Honzík, my Honzík..." The soldier burst into tears and couldn't control himself. "Honzík says... 'I'm still alive, give me one more'... you see... friends... you see, brother General... I killed my best friend... What do I tell his wife and children at home?"

There was silence in the hall as the Minister wiped away his tears with a handkerchief.

"My brother, I promise you that when we're home, when we're all healthy together, I'll personally go to his wife with you and tell her. And we'll build memorials to Honzík and all our heroes so that those who were afraid know who won their freedom."

Carefully and with emotion, he put his hand on the soldier's arm.

"God has heard you, God hears you. Lads, we're like a company unveiling a memorial. When the monument is finished, the company disperses. But the monument isn't yet finished. Our free state isn't yet secure!"

Štefánik turned yellow and touched his chest.

"Now I'm sick," he said barely audibly. "Sorry, I can't continue."

The moved soldiers stood up and promised from their soul to continue fighting. After their experience from the front, however, he wasn't sure how much soul they had left...

CHAPTER 27
The House of Horror

At the behest of supporters of intervention amongst Czechoslovak officers and representatives of the Entente to the Kolchak government, he finally decided to travel to Omsk, despite his worsening health. Štefánik and Janin met with Admiral Kolchak, but instead of a hero they saw only a debauched and arrogant dictator. As they had been persuaded, his general staff had actually two thousand Tsarist officers who'd made him their obedient puppet. The Czecho-Slovak legions thus found themselves between Kolchak's dictatorship and the dictatorship of the Bolsheviks, who fought ruthlessly against each other. Kolchak criticized Štefánik for the late payment of bills by the Czechoslovaks.

"You haven't sent us bills for the graves of Czechoslovaks who fell for your Russia! There will soon be more of them in Siberia than graves of your soldiers."

"We don't have money for weapons and equipment. I read in the newspaper that your Mr. Masaryk received a loan of several million dollars from the United States. Can't you arrange for us to get something like that?"

"The regiments of truly fighting soldiers would certainly receive credits for equipment. Guarantees for such loans are signed on the battlefields with blood and bayonets…"

"Vous êtes très dur, mon général" (You're very tough, General), Kolchak smiled sarcastically.

"C'est exactement vous qui me dites ça? (Is that you who is telling me?). Je ne suis pas dur, je suis seulement conséquent (I'm not tough, only consistent). We came here to fight against the Bolsheviks, but also against the thugs…"

Kolchak grinned and in reference to ignoring Štefánik's solemn arrival said: "I hope my soldiers have explained to you why I didn't send a guard of honour to greet you. Our regulations forbid it when the frosts are particularly severe…"

"Naturally, I understand. I also understand your care for the Russian soldiers who are now behind the lines, and believe that you'll understand it when we withdraw our troops from the Ural front, where our troops are fighting in such frost." He struggled to catch his breath for a moment, watching Kolchak's red face, with its pursed lips smelling of vodka, before adding in a more conciliatory fashion: "We must agree, otherwise the Reds will overwhelm us…"

"Despite that, we still have cause to thank your soldiers," said Kolchak.

"I have the habit of judging the merit of work after it is completed; so far nothing is finished and no one knows when it will be…"

"When are you leaving Omsk?" said Kolchak visibly ashamed.

"In a few days, but don't worry, it doesn't seem as if the frosts will ease off..."

The civil war in Russia was harsher in its ruthlessness than the war in Europe. Who dared not kill his fellow was shot as a troublemaker and a Bolshevik. There was also rioting among the population to whom Kolchak sent criminal Cossack expeditions, which set fire to many villages and burned them to the ground. Czechoslovak legionaries refused to fight on the same side as those bandits, and some went over to the Bolshevik regiments. About ten million people died of hunger, disease, terror and fighting. For the same reasons, two million people fled Russia, especially members of the intelligentsia. Industrial production was a fraction of what it had been in 1913.

The Red Army gained ever greater territory and Czechoslovak troops began flocking to the Red Guards. On behalf of the Soviet government, the Commissar for Foreign Affairs, Chicherin, sent a telegram to Prague: "Despite the victories, we are sorry for the blood that has been shed and we declare to the Temporary Czechoslovak government that we are willing to allow Czechoslovaks to return through Russia to their native region. The Soviet government wishes to start talks with the Prague government on the conditions of this transition." This offer was rejected and the Prague government insisted again on the continuation of the Siberian anabasis.

On Christmas Eve of the last year of the war, Štefánik and his adjutants Fournier, Lévi, the French consul Vergé, General Janin and Dr. Mandaus were sitting in armchairs in the ministerial carriage. He was still mentally recovering the previous day's slaughter of socialists by Kolchak's men and grieving thoughts swept through his head. He felt that something was wrong with his calculations, he saw the different interests of Allied diplomats and was reluctant to admit that each of them put their own national interests before the main task of defeating the Bolsheviks. He regretted that the Wilson administration was actually helping them through their inaction. On that day, however, he was heartened by a telegram from General Gajda, whose troops had conquered Perm and crushed the 3rd Red Army capturing 21,000 soldiers.

The sombre mood of Christmas Eve was interrupted by the laughing Pavlů with a few soldiers. They brought a gust of freezing air into the carriage and a frozen fir-tree set in an improvised stand. They'd decorated it with paper garlands, nuts, crab apples, cigarette ornaments and fir cones and placed it on a pedestal near the oven, as if they wanted to give a little warmth to that holy tree. Soldiers with accordions, violins and whistles entered the wagon. One carried a cello, others a tambourine, a clarinet, a trumpet; some even used combs and pieces of birch bark. Others brought pots full of steaming Christmas fare, cakes, plates, cutlery and naturally – vodka. The faces of those present brightened. One of the soldiers bowed and gave a blessing:

"I wish to you all on this Christmas holiday health, fortune and a heavenly blessing; may your cattle be increased, may your little ones bring you joy and may our dear Lord God grant you everything you wish for after your death in the kingdom of Heaven. Amen."

After the blessing, the musicians stood before the General and sang to the sound of the crackle of the burning wood in tones that broke the hearts of everyone. The music spread through the carriages until the whole train finally broke into song, some in Czech, some in Slovak, some singing a Catholic text, others evangelical. From hundreds of sad, longing throats, the song carried up to the heavens and from there perhaps as far as to their distant homes.

Silent night, holy night, all is calm, all is bright
Round yon Virgin...

Štefánik, with a tired, trembling voice, added:

Silent night, holy night, people at rest, in blessed peace
Only two hearts awake in Bethlehem...

The Siberian steppe carried the Czech chorale of the emotional soldiers:

Silent night, holy night, all in sleep, breathing the earth,
Midnight struck, and the city slept...

Even Lévis and Fournier sang:

Douce Nuit, Sainte Nuit, dans les cieux l'astre luit,
Le mystère annoncé s'accomplit...

Some didn't manage to finish singing and trembled into tears like children. Hard men who looked death in the eye every day, accustomed to burying the frozen corpses of their friends, and, as good Christians, their enemies, became as sentimental as innocent virgins. They were like children again, recalling the Christmases of their youth, shouting and outdoing each other with stories of who looked forward to a new ram, gloves or just an apple or mother's poppy-seed rolls with jam.

Talk, laughter, jokes, cries of joy over a small gift from a friend filled not only the minister's carriage, but the whole train, right along the whole Trans-Siberian railway. The soldiers crept into their wagons long after midnight, Štefánik shaking hands with every soldier and officer. Although he was only thirty-nine years old, he was the oldest of them.

"My boys, you know that if I breathe and live, it is only for you, I think only of you. I'll do my best to get you home as soon as possible."

"This is the fifth Christmas of the war... when will it be over?"

Frustrated and disappointed, the Minister decided on 28th December to openly inform the President and the government of the situation (assuming, as he did, that the contents of his telegram would reach Beneš and the French Ministry of Foreign Affairs). His pained soul could hardly put words to paper: "The Czechoslovak army is shaken morally and physically. The current moral depression is a consequence of continuous activity and long-term nervous strain. The soldiers who have had to endure forty degrees of frost in a hostile country, separated from the civilized world, crammed in goods wagons full of insects, numerically weakened by disease and losses in battle, until recently under the influence of the lack of resilience of Russian soldiers, away from their native land of whose freedom they have learned and in which they desire to become involved, do not fight with their former fire." But he didn't spare diplomatic criticism of the Allies: "They are inclined to hope that the Allies' policy is not unanimous, given that some representatives have promised real aid in Siberia."

General Janin rejected his utopian ideas to break through to Archangelsk or down to the Black Sea. He was sorry for Štefánik, seeing his pride and joy, the army he'd created with his own energy, crumbling before his eyes. He fell ill; during the course of discussions he had seizures that came more and more often and lasted longer. He was afraid to accept normal food, living only on tea, black coffee and soup.

He spent the start of 1919 in Ekaterinburg. He dealt with a number of practical issues of financing the army, the judiciary, the political representation of soldiers, the evacuation of the wounded, took a decision on the defensive role of his troops and also addressed an unexpected problem with the commander of the second division, the hero of Zborov, the most successful commander of the Czechoslovak legion, General Radola Gajda. The headstrong General invited Štefánik to the Ipatiev Palace, where he lived. From the moment Štefánik entered the house, he had an oppressive feeling. Although he sympathized with the energetic General, he told him that President Masaryk wanted his departure from Siberia, suggesting it was probably because of his strong anti-Bolshevik attitude (which, in fact, they shared). Understanding that he was unwanted, Gajda decided to accept Kolchak's appeal to take command of his army. He informed Štefánik, who initially tried to talk him out of it, but eventually he decided on 1st January to leave the Czecho-Slovak army and join Kolchak's. Štefánik finally signed an agreement to his working in the Russian army from 1st January 1919.

"If I may invite you," Gajda said a little mysteriously after the conversation, "I'll show you something that few in the world have seen."

They put on their cloaks; Štefánik, full of anticipation, followed him down the stairs. They walked into a cellar, about five to six metres in size, where Gajda took his General's cap off.

"Here on the night of the 16th to 17th July, the family of Nicholas II was shot. Vermin, they shot them like pigs. They killed the Tsar, his wife Alexandra, five children, a doctor, a maid, and three servants," Gajda almost whispered in a trembling voice. "Red swine!"

The shocked Štefánik looked wide-eyed at the musty dungeon.

"How do you know all this?"

"One of them, a certain Kaban, was talking about it in a boozer. They were afraid that we could liberate the Tsar and his family. We actually would have done so, but the Bolsheviks were ahead of us by a week. The legions did not arrive in Yekaterinburg until 25th July."

Štefánik was stunned.

"Why did you choose this dreadful house to live in?"

"The best way to learn to overcome fear is to live in terrible places, and if possible, the very worst. In time it'll become a museum of the Bolshevik terror. And I will tell my grandsons how I lived there and beat the Reds…"

CHAPTER 28
A Golden Treasure

At the time of Minister Štefánik's stay in Siberia, there was a treasure of the Russian tsars supposedly equal to the wealth of the pharaohs. After the coup in October 1917 the Bolsheviks gained it, part of which they spent. After signing the humiliating peace of Brest-Livotsk, Lenin's government, fearing the advancing German army, decided to take the treasure from St. Petersburg east to Kazan. The sumptuous building of the Russian State Bank, with its colonnaded front on Golden Square, concealed more than five hundred tons of gold worth 651,535,835 rubles, consisting of gold bars, bricks, jewelry, silver, platinum, gems, coins, banknotes and cash. Today the value of this treasure would be 26 billion dollars. These were the largest gold reserves that any state had at that time and, such a treasure would have aroused the interest of all states decimated by their war spending. Therefore, on 6th August 1918 Russian troops under the command of Lieutenant Colonel Vladimir Kappel and Czechoslovak troops under the command of Lieutenant Kutlvašra headed towards Kazan. Czechoslovak legionaries even broke off their evacuation to Vladivostok and returned to the Western Front to help the White creation of a Volga Front. They intended to occupy this large city on the Volga with its full military warehouses and to take the leadership of the emerging anti-Bolshevik resistance. The Czecho-Slovak legions occupied the outskirts of the city while the centre and the building of the bank were occupied by White Russians under the command of Kappel. The last Bolsheviks who held the city centre with the bank building were red Latvian snipers under the command of Janis Berzinja. After their retreat, there was a short period of lawlessness where the bank remained unguarded, which was used by the people of Kazan who began to loot. In the afternoon of 7th August, 1918, at about 3pm, Kappel's soldiers, whom the inhabitants commonly referred to as "White Czechs", arrived at the bank. Kappel wrote a telegram to headquarters: *"The amount of gold we found exceeded our expectations."* At the behest of the Samaria government's financial department, Kappel ordered that trams be driven to the state bank branch at night and the gold transported to the port on to a steamboat. One hundred students from the combat troops, one hundred soldiers from the Pioneer battalion, and one hundred members of the Samara Social Revolutionary organization were assigned to load the sacks of gold. They carried out the entire operation under the supervision of state bank officials. Carrying the bags of gold was laborious and some ripped open, but the soldiers allegedly carried them in disciplined fashion to the command table though we may wonder how many coins made their way into the soldiers' pockets. Before the arrival of the Bolsheviks, the *Suvorov* steamer took the entire treasure to Samara. The importance of the city of Kazan, and especially the treasure for the Bolsheviks, was also emphasized by the personal arrival of People's Commissar Trotsky in Sviyazhsk, 30 kilometres away. The USA Consul General in Irkutsk wrote to Washington: "Czech and Russian forces were forced to evacuate Kazan on the night of 9th September 1918; the most precious military and other material had moved away earlier."

In early October, through fear of advancing Bolsheviks, the treasure was transferred from Samara to Ufa. In Samara an anti-Bolshevik temporary all-Russian government was formed on 24th September 1918, which had to compete with the government of autonomous Siberia based in Omsk. The Samara government asked the command of the Czecho-Slovak legions for help in securing the treasure, but only through an external service, which prevented the legionary units from having direct contact with the gold. The wagons were guarded exclusively by soldiers from the Russian White Guardians and supervised by Russian bank officials. At the request of the Samara government, the treasure was transferred to Chelyabinsk at the end of October for fear that it might fall into the hands of the Omsk autonomous government. Chelyabinsk was also the location of the High Command of the Czecho-Slovak army in Siberia, led by General Jan Syrový. The treasure was deposited in the concrete cellars of a grain store. From there, in the absence of Syrový, the Russian General, Dieterichs, in Czechoslovak service and in accordance with the request of Minister Mihajlov of the Russian Omsk government, gave orders to transport the treasure in sealed wagons to the east. However, the wagons were in poor condition with their bearings often having been welded on. As a result, they had to reload the treasure from a broken wagon to a functional one several times. The treasure was carried in two trains, one guarded by twenty-one legionaries and ten Poles, the other guarded by Russian officers, was taken to Omsk, the seat of the Siberian government, on 14th October. Here the Russians took over the protection of the train, guarded by the legionaries, and transferred the treasure to trucks that took it to an Omsk bank. It's not known in what state the second train, guarded by Oman government officers, arrived; the legionaries were temporarily parted from the treasure. When Admiral Kolchak overthrew the Omsk government on 18th November 1918 and was declared unlimited ruler of Siberia, he gained access to the treasure, which funded not only his megalomaniacal luxury cravings, but also the purchase of weapons for his army, although tt has to be said that the prices of the Allies were extremely high and despite advance payments, the agreed quantity of military supplies was not delivered to Kolchak.

Coincidentally, just on the day of the Kolchak coup, a bank for Czecho-Slovak legions was established in Siberia which absorbed the former Czechoslovak military savings bank. With its number of employees reaching 245, the bank managed Czecho-Slovak assets which, due to the intensive economic activity of the legion, continuously increased. While only three plants were operating in the Urals in July, as a result of the activities of the Czechs and Slovaks, 69 were already working in December and in January 1919 as many as 95.

A Russian-Czechoslovak Chamber of Commerce was established, which ran trains deep into the Siberian interior carrying Ural steel and returning with food for factory workers and soldiers. Štefánik also significantly helped the development of the Chamber. Under pressure from the Bolsheviks in the summer of 1919, Kolchak retreated to the east and, of course, along the Trans-Siberian Railway, transported trains with gold, whose value in the meantime had shrunk to a third.

The legionaries again came into contact with the gold within a year when on 25th December 1919 the chief commander of the allied troops in Siberia, General Janin, commanded that Admiral Kolchak's train and treasure be placed under the protection of the Czechoslovak assault battalion in Nizhny-Udinsk. They guarded only 28 wagons, however; there were still 80 in Samara. On 27th December 1919, a coup took place in Nizhny-Udinsk with troops abandoning Kolchak in droves. In Irkutsk on 1st January 1920 the Allied High Commissioners held a meeting, which decided that the treasure would remain together. They were to take it to Vladivostok and return it to the Russian nation in agreement with the Russian government. However, in Irkutsk on 4th January, another anti-Kolchak uprising broke out. Power fell to Socialists, calling themselves the Political Centre. Kolchak abdicated and, giving up power to Denikin, retreated further east. His train was joined by 27 wagons of gold. Kolchak was promised a safe departure from Russia but General Janin refused to hand over the gold treasure and Kolchak to the Bolsheviks so the legionaries again came under pressure from the Bolsheviks, who were growing in strength, demanding their surrender with the threat of cutting them off from their retreat to Vladivostok. So in the end they were forced to hand the treasure and Kolchak over, to bring him to justice. For this, the Bolsheviks guaranteed the Legionaries a smooth transfer to Vladivostok and then to their homes. Meanwhile, the Whites concluded a ceasefire with the Bolsheviks, and the Bolshevik political commission condemned Kolchak in their own court, holding him responsible for the murder of over 110,000 people. He asked for beer before he was executed. His last words, which he spoke on 7th February, 1920, were: "Spasibo, Czecho-sobaki" (Thank you, Czech dogs).

The headquarters of the Czecho-Slovak legion in Russia brought to Prague 32 million dollars in gold, obtained by their economic activities.

CHAPTER 29

If I Die I Go on to the Majority

Just at the time when Štefánik complained to Janin that Masaryk and Beneš were no longer thinking of him, he received a letter in early January 1919 in which President Masaryk paternally recommended him: "Milan, take care of yourself. It would be better if I saw you in Paris. Ask Janin politely if he can't send you there." It seemed as if Masaryk knew that Štefánik was in trouble. In constant strain, the General's health was getting even worse and Doctor Mandaus ordered him to stay in bed. The cruel Siberian frosts, gales, darkness, seclusion and the hopeless situation in the army had ruined his nerves. His head ached constantly, he had to lie in the gloom. If someone even opened a window or lit a light, he was upset and sick. Even the small celebration at which Janin handed him the Commander Cross of the Legion of Honour in Omsk on 13th January in the presence of Czechoslovak and Allied commanders was almost too much for him. According to tradition, the award had to be presented outside and Štefánik had decided to take the honour without a military cloak. In thirty-five degrees of frost, it was an almost insane decision, but he wouldn't be dissuaded. General Janin, who was to give him the honour, said decisively: "You're probably insane, but I don't hope to convince you. It's in my power, however, whether I give you the cross or not. I can tell you that if you come without a cloak, I won't give it to you!" So Štefánik obeyed and was wise to. In the cruel frost Janin also shortened the ceremony to a minimum, a good decision because Štefánik was on the verge of collapse. He could barely drag himself into bed. As their wagons stood side by side at the station, Janin accepted Štefánik's invitation into the pleasant warmth.

The General sent his adjutant for a bottle of wine. Štefánik, however, drank only fortifying tea from cedar cone leaves. The pleasant warmth and the presence of an intimate friend brought peace to his soul. He settled deep into his armchair.

"So my France hasn't forgotten me," he said with a spark in his eyes. "For me it is the caress my second country sends to her adoptive son, working far from her. My dear Maurice, I want to tell you that it was very agreeable for me that it was you, dear friend, who gave me the distinction. I have a deep affection for you as a man of directness, honesty and purity, the characteristic qualities of France for which my love will end only when my life ends." He pressed Janin's hand warmly.

Suddenly, the General, moved by emotion, took the head of the fragile-looking Slovak into his hands and hugged it to his chest. It was as if something had broken. The two generals in their shirt-sleeves looked one another in the eye and couldn't hold back their tears.

"Dear Milan, the difference between us is eighteen years, which is why I have a more paternal than fraternal relationship with you. You became an adoptive son not only to France but also to me... My son, my son, where have we got to? I don't know if your adoptive homeland will appreciate us. We haven't succeeded in our mission. We failed to convince the soldiers to fight..."

"We didn't fail. Our politicians failed. Yours and mine. Masaryk is like a father to me, but just as I stopped understanding my real father, I'm afraid I can no longer understand my political father.

In fact, to give up to the Bolsheviks and call for their support, unfortunately, as he is doing, is unconscionable. As soon as I learned of the congress of our troops in May 1918 in Chelyabinsk, when they refused to go west through Arkhangelsk, but decided to go east, I understood it as a revolt. I admit that since that moment, I have increasingly doubted our Siberian mission. And Kolchak? He abuses us. Our army in Siberia can be compared to a maiden who wanted to sacrifice herself for love of the Russians, but they didn't understand her. They took her manifestations of love as a matter of course; they were serviced by her, they wanted to have a girl for everything." He drank his tea and shook his head in frustration. And then he calmed down enough to continue his confession, "But if I want the soldiers to obey me even when they disagree with me, I must obey the President even when I disagree with him... And you, dear Maurice, don't worry. The task of any good commander is to defend his soldiers. And you do it perfectly and fully."

Janin couldn't say a word.

"Do you have news of your family?" He turned away from the subject.

"Um... my family? When was the last time I saw them?" he thought. "At least you have a family, but I don't know if I do anymore. There are already strangers in the rectory in Košariska as my father is dead. But my mother and sisters and brothers are alive and I may see them soon... I guess... I hope... I believe... If I live..."

He drank hot tea and crunched a dry biscuit. It was the only food he'd consumed in days.

"If you led your army to Prague, it would be a wonderful day," Janin smiled.

"First I would need to have liberated my Slovakia. But yes, it would be nice if we defeated the Bolsheviks and brought the boys home... But I won't live to see it."

"The plan to try to get home through Russia is madness. I can't imagine anyone living to see it."

"It's not so much the plan which is unreal but my life. Since I got that wound in Serbia, my condition has only worsened. And there is no time for it to heal nor will there be. I'll do the essential things here, complete my orders and go to Paris and Prague. There I'll be of more benefit."

"You say that as if we were saying goodbye forever…"

Štefánik didn't respond to his comment but looked straight into his eyes.

"In you I've had the most loyal friend and combat comrade. Please be so good as to accept from me a gift I give only to those I really cherish." With a shaky hand he took from his breast pocket a small leather capsule and opened it. Little snow-white balls glistened there.

"They are real Tahitian pearls. Take them. To remind you."

"I can't, it's a very valuable gift."

Štefánik picked out three pearls, pressed them into Janin's palm and slid the capsule back into his breast pocket.

The Frenchman held them awkwardly and said in a trembling voice: "Very well, thank you. I'll guard them like the eyes in my head."

"My God," said Štefánik, "but time has flown by. It's as if I've lived five lives… You say I often talk about death. But what is death? When I die, it'll just happen that I go over to the side of the majority…"

"Do you know what was one of the most beautiful moments in my life?" Janin looked at him searchingly and drank his wine. "In Paris, a prostitute spoke to me once. It was a cold winter and she was shivering. I invited her for tea and inside she said she was pregnant. She was from a poor family. With the help of friends, we managed to get her a place in a laundry. One day when I was walking through the park, a little boy comes up to me suddenly and says: 'Merci, monsieur Milan.' Only then did I see that the former prostitute was standing and smiling…"

Inside was silence, a frosty wind whistled outside the windows, the thermometer was showing minus thirty.

"There is death outside," said Štefánik suddenly. "There is death all around us. Tell me, my dear Maurice, have you ever been in a situation where your spirit wanted, but your body couldn't? Have you ever experienced the hell of torment when your spirit wants to fly off, but your wings are weak, feeble..."

"No, I haven't. Fortunately. But as I get older, I'm preparing for it."

"It is natural at an older age, but at my age this contradiction between spirit, will and body is unnatural. Can you imagine what I could achieve in life if my body was stronger?"

"Dear Milan, I don't know any other person who at your age has achieved so much."

"When all this is over, when the work of liberation of my homeland is complete, when Czecho-Slovakia is as solid as a rock, then I'll return to my stars. You can't imagine how I long for them..."

Janin squeezed his shoulder.

"Dreaming in a war of faith, thousands of miles from home, in a frozen country and in a whirlwind of love is amazing. I always thought that the purpose of a soldier's life was to win. Now I have a feeling that the warrior's sense should be love... This is probably the greatest victory a soldier can achieve."

"I wanted, I wanted to..." Štefánik didn't speak. His face went pale, he doubled up in pain, beads of sweat were on his forehead and his heart was pounding. He clutched at his chest, breathing laboriously. His eyes bulged, staring at Janin, but he was unable to say a word. The General shouted for an adjutant, who jumped out of the wagon; within minutes Dr. Mandaus came running with his bag. He shook his head with concern as he measured Štefánik's pulse. They put him in bed on a raised pillow. The doctor gave him an injection and put medication on the nightstand.

"Just to make sure, I'll stay here for the night."

Janin looked at him gratefully. The minister fell asleep and it was clear to the two worried men sitting by his bed that he had to go home as soon as possible. His return to Europe was essential; no one could take responsibility for his life.

When he received information that a French ship was planning to sail to Europe from Shanghai, he decided to leave on 15th January. Before he left, he issued a key order which he'd been delaying for a long time but which his impending departure hastened. On 16th January in Omsk, before embarking on the return journey to Paris, he signed order number 588, which disbanded the Czecho-Slovak soldiers' assembly as no longer necessary in the ordinary allied army. "The regimental and sergeant councils are becoming unnecessary, the army does not need democracy, but discipline." The order triggered a storm of protests and after its release three thousand soldiers left the council of legionaries and joined the Siberian partisans or disappeared into Siberian villages and the taiga. This order meant a fundamental reorganization of the legions into a proper army and a radical change that the ordinary, mostly socialist-oriented soldiers didn't accept and disregarded. Štefánik didn't realize that although, theoretically, he may have been right, his order significantly threatened supplies to Czechoslovak troops who had been compelled to cooperate with local Soviets. These bodies fundamentally refused to cooperate with the Czecho-Slovak officers and communicated only with the soldiers; in this way, Bolshevik ideas infiltrated into our army. The elected military officials insisted that distant Prague was no longer effective in engaging in ordinary service matters while Štefánik uncompromisingly held that he was the representative of Prague.

However, it soon became apparent that the Czecho-Slovak forces had been saved from the growing anarchy by these orders. It was a surgical incision that hurt after the operation, but the minister believed it would heal quickly and the soldiers themselves would understand that the times of volunteering were gone and that they were becoming the legitimate army of a free state. Its subsequent fate could be decided only by the Allied command in Paris led by Marshal Foch and representatives of the Czecho-Slovak state in Prague. At these places Minister Štefánik would try to agree reinforcements for the Czecho-Slovak troops and in the case of refusal would seek approval for their definite return home. But he wasn't sure that he'd convince the Allies. He understood what allied politicians couldn't understand in the warmth and comfort of their European offices. The thinking of the soldiers fundamentally differed from the thinking of the politicians who'd broken away from them. Despite the fact that his reason didn't want to admit it, his heart told him that the role of the Czecho-Slovak legion, which had played a great role in Russia and was admired by the whole world, had ended.

"I am afraid that a moral infection under the influence of a difficult, epidemic, alien atmosphere is beginning to consume the limbs of our army's body," he said to Bohdan Pavlů, who was with him as he looked out at the inhospitable snowy plains of Siberia. "I wouldn't want to die in this wasteland. When I'm at sea, I usually feel better. However, if I find out that my condition isn't better even at sea, I'll shoot myself."

CHAPTER 30

Milan, Come and Help Us!

In Paris on 18th January 1919 the peace conference began with great pomp. It was officially chaired by France, but the decisive role was played by the United States, which had become the world's greatest power despite having been threatened by a recession before the war. In the words of President Wilson, the USA had waged war "For peace and human rights, for the ideals that have always been close to our hearts." While at the beginning of the war in 1914, the USA had a debt of $3.7 billion, by 1918 they were the largest creditors, the Allies owing them $3.8 billion for war supplies. The British Prime Minister, Lloyd George, dryly remarked that in the USA, unlike in

Europe, not even a dog kennel had been destroyed. The Americans had got rid of their most dynamically growing competitor, Germany. Other competitors, France and England, had come out of the war weakened despite being the victors.

In the park of the Trianon Palace, literally a few metres from Versailles, stood the limousines of prime ministers and diplomats from thirty-two countries, Russia excepted. Talks between recent enemies hadn't been planned; the negotiators were preparing for Germany a text of a diktat that representatives of the defeated power would be forced to accept. Hundreds of diplomats negotiated in 58 committees how to divide the three defeated empires, their rows creating the impression of a marketplace where the sale of quality goods for cheap money was being announced. Serbs and Romanians argued over the Banat, the Chinese argued with the Japanese about the German colony of Kiao Cau, the Poles wanted German Gdansk, the Greeks wanted the small port of Smyrna in Asia Minor, New Zealanders wanted to claim the German colonies of Nauru and Samoa, the Italians would have liked part of the Adriatic coast (Prime Minister Orlando even wept when he was told that the port of Rijeka would not fall to the Italians). The Belgians demanded reward for the deployment of their Congolese troops against German East Africa, the Arabs demanded independence in the fight against the Turks as did the Armenians and Kurds. The Ukraine requested self-determination along with the Czechs and the Slovaks. The booty was slippery; it paid to be a tough negotiator. The British came in a four-hundred-member formation and the USA at length negotiated with 1,300 diplomats and officials. However, the key location of the peace conference was not the Palace of Versailles, but President Wilson's apartment at No. 11 the Place d'États-Unis in Paris's 16th district. Twice a day it hosted Council of Four meetings, consisting of Wilson, Lloyd George, Clemenceau and the Italian Prime Minister, Orlando. They decided not only the fate of the losers, but also that of the winners. On the floor of Wilson's apartment lay a map of Europe on which the statesmen drew borders according to the results of expert discussions. One of the key issues was the border fought over by representatives of Czecho-Slovakia, formally led by Prime Minister Karel Kramář. The real leader, however, was the internationally seasoned and pro-west oriented Eduard Beneš.

He had written to Masaryk to say that the naturalized Frenchman Milan Štefánik with all his contacts among top French officials would be much more useful to him in Paris.

Štefánik, however, was travelling through the frozen wastes of Siberia and China to Shanghai, via Mukden and Beijing, accompanied by Major Fournier and Lieutenant Lévi, where he boarded the *Porthos* steamer which set sail on 1st February towards Marseille. Two hundred Czech and Slovak seriously wounded soldiers were also aboard, indeed, Štefánik himself was in need of support and care. So the man who had excellent contacts with the peace conference chair, Prime Minister Clemenceau, and with the Allied Army commander-in-chief, Marshal Foch, was counting seagulls, playing chess, and resting in his cabin rather than making effective use of his connections. He slept long under the influence of narcotics prescribed by Dr. Mandaus before he left. When they ceased working, he was tormented by severe trigeminal nerve pain along with sciatic pain; the left part of his body was so stricken with pain, he was seized by the fear of paralysis. Gradually, however, he got over the worst and spent time on deck whenever possible. He looked at the endless mass of water and wondered what would happen to him when he returned. "I am alone, terribly alone… Even those birds of God have nests and I have nothing… Everyone on this ship is returning home. And I…? My home is hotels. There is nothing more terrible than lying alone in a foreign hotel room and not looking forward to returning because you have nowhere to go."

Yet events in Europe rushed upon him one after the other and he consulted the ship's captain every day as well as his adjutants. The mood for battle returned to him, and at times he felt that the twelve-ton colossus was moving very slowly.

Prime Minister Károlyi's new Hungarian government impetuously agitated in Slovakia, where strong pro-Hungarian sentiment continued to mushroom. The country was flooded with agitators, leaflets and banners. In towns they called for a popular parliament and even delivered leaflets in euphonious Slovak to a Žilina meeting. "Folk from the Highlands! On the wings of the winds, all of Hungary sends you brotherly sympathy and greetings. From a distance we will make equal our brotherly rights, which have always worked with yours for the good of the country. What the politicians want to commit is a crime before the world and before God. As long as the Váh and the other rivers of Upper Hungary flow into the Danube, the Highlanders and the Lowlanders remain bound to each other and cannot be separated by human power."

In a bomb-blasted Belgrade, in a dark room, Count Károlyi, by the light of kerosene lamps, tried to convince the Eastern Army's chief commander, the French General Franchet d'Esperrey, on 4th November, 1918, that his country had entered war only under German pressure. "We accept responsibility for neither the legal nor moral acts of the past system. We don't even want to hear about the alliance with the old German imperialism. My delegation represents the free will of the Hungarian people..."

"You represent only the Magyars but in no way represent the other peoples of Hungary," the General interrupted. "Likewise, please do not talk about Hungary, but only about the regions inhabited by Hungarians!"

The prime minister was a little embarrassed, but kept to his script: "We confirm that Hungary accepts the agreement on an independent state in the Czech Republic..."

The General stood up and politely told him, "Try saying 'on the state of Czechoslovakia'!"

"Um... the state of Czechoslovakia... We further confirm that our government guarantees the neutrality of Hungary..."

"You are late with your neutrality! You went with Germany; with Germany you will be punished!"

Károlyi's government willfully exploited the busy schedules of the peace negotiators in Versailles to do everything possible to maintain the integrity of Hungary despite the decisions of the victorious powers. It planned a referendum in Slovakia, which would naturally be organized by Hungarian authorities who would guarantee its outcome.

Two days after Károlyi's meeting with d'Esperrey in Belgrade, a temporary Slovak government headed by Vavro Šrobár and its members Pavel Blaho, Ivan Dérer, Štefan Janšák and Anton Štefánek had arrived on 6th November in Skalica, West Slovakia. At the same time, Slovakia began to occupy the Czecho-Slovak army, Slovaks accepting without objections the fact that Czech-speaking soldiers had come to the country. However, the Hungarians sabotaged the arrival of the new government and Czech soldiers, dismantling technical equipment, exporting to Hungary the most modern production lines of many factories, including the famous Kremnicka Mint, carrying off historical artifacts of immense value and intimidating the population. The peace talks in Paris hadn't yet begun and in Upper Hungary, or the Felvidék, as they still called it, Hungarian authorities, teachers, priests, railwaymen and police officers calmly continued their work. Nem, nem, soha! (No, no, never!) was the central Hungarian idea. The Hungarian government declared mobilization and Hungarian troops came to Slovakia, taking advantage of the fact that the southern border of Czechoslovakia and the demarcation line had yet to be fixed. Hungarian troops advanced against the weakly armed Czechoslovak troops to Vrútky and Žilina. In Martin they even arrested the chairman of the Slovak National Council (SNR), Matúš Dula. On 9th November Marshal Foch called on Károlyi for Hungarian troops to leave the territory of Slovakia, but Károlyi ignored his appeal.

The National Assembly abolished Šrobár's interim government and in early December entrusted Šrobár with the management of a ministry with power of attorney for Slovakia. The Office consisted of fourteen government officials.

Vavro Šrobár and his ministers moved from Skalica to Žilina on 10th December. On the same day, the National Assembly in Prague passed a law on "emergency and transitional measures in Slovakia". Šrobár uncompromisingly removed those unwilling to accept his strong-minded Czechoslovak worldview and became almost the unlimited ruler of Slovakia. The Catholic priest Andrej Hlinka introduced a renewed Slovak People's Party on 19th December in Žilina, three hundred prominent Catholic personalities attending the inaugural meeting, among them the Nitra professor of theology, Jozef Tiso.

On 28th December, 1918, the Supreme Council of Military Agreements decided on the demarcation line between Hungary and Slovakia, including Bratislava. Five regiments were then sent from Budapest to protect Bratislava against the incoming Czecho-Slovak army, the military commander of the city saying that "the city will not be given up to Czechoslovakia, I would rather die with my soldiers first". Czecho-Slovak units didn't have the key means of communication, the telegraph and telephone, because the post offices and railways were in the hands of Hungarian personnel. The soldiers, indeed, didn't have enough ammunition and only old, worn-out Italian machine guns were available, while the enemy had modern German machine guns, the *Schwarzlose*, which were left over from the Hungarian army and the German Mackensen Corps.

From 30th December to 1st January, the city was attacked by the 33rd Czechoslovak Regiment of Italian Legions under the command of Colonel Riccardo Barecca and after fierce fighting occupied the city on 1st January. But on the night of 2nd January street fighting continued, soldiers of the Hungarian Red Guards began to loot shops and four were shot. On the same day, the Bratislava governor, Samuel Zoch, asked for reinforcements of at least 500 Czech men from Sokol. In spite of the fact that it was Sunday, it was organized within two days and 2,480 men, who left their families, jobs and went selflessly to Slovakia, arrived in Bratislava on 3rd February. The strength of troops in Bratislava was gradually added to with an infantry company of the 33rd Regiment occupying the demarcation line on the left side of the Danube from the Käsmacher (Sihoť) island. Zoch, convened a meeting of city officials with the rector of the University of Elizabeth refusing the invitation, stating that he remained loyal to Hungary, for which the university was closed, most if its professors moving to Budapest.

Bratislava was declared the capital of Slovakia on 18th January and the Slovak government, headed by Vavro Šrobár, moved there from Žilina on 4th February. The legionaries prepared a ceremony, which the majority of the German and Hungarian population ignored, instead organizing protest rallies against Šrobár's government. In shops and restaurants, Hungarian, Jewish and German owners refused to serve customers speaking Slovak or Czech. In front of the sculpture of Sándor Petöfi on the promenade in front of the Municipal Theatre, continual Hungarian demonstrations were held.

The regulations of the Šrobár government were very difficult to implement but the gradually arriving legionaries made it possible. The young state administration lacked officials, there was a shortage of Slovak teachers and priests, and all over Slovakia there were only five Slovak engineers willing to enter the service of the new state. All forms and documents were in Hungarian and of 2,646 judges in Upper Hungary, only one was Slovak! For whole months after the establishment of Czecho-Slovakia, the courts in Slovakia delivered judgments on behalf of the Republic of Hungary. Of the 12,447 Hungarian civil servants in Slovakia, only 35 of them were available to the new Czecho-Slovak government; out of 660 professors only ten were transferred to the services of the new state. Šrobár created a corps of speakers who went out to convince simple peasants, most of whom were illiterate, of the benefits of joining the Czech Republic. Of the eight hundred locomotives that operated in Slovakia before the coup, only 70 remained in Slovakia, most of which were clapped out.

On 12th February, a mass of protesters carrying Hungarian banners gathered at Trhové námestie aand when an unknown student tried to mount a Hungarian flag on a gaslamp, one of the legionary officers present fired at him. Though he didn't hit him, the gathered masses began to attack the soldiers, who then used their automatic weapons and killed six people and seriously injured twenty-three. The Commander-in-Chief of the Allied Forces for Slovakia, General Luigi Piccione, had settled in the secure Archbishop's Palace in Kroměříž, and when at Šrobár's urging he moved to Grassalkovič Palace at the end of February 1919, he came with his own cow who had grazed in the Archbishop's Gardens. The Italian commander of the city, Colonel Barrec, was known to go over the bridge secretly to Hungary, where he was entertained by Hungarian Counts. Šrobár had no confidence in him and needed a man on whom he could rely absolutely, who had experience, authority and, above all, was Slovak, a man who could intercede in conflicts of jurisdiction between the Italian and French commanders. The only such person was his old friend, the Minister for War, Štefánik, who was then thousands of kilometres away from his homeland. Šrobár's telegram, ending with the words "Milan, come help us!" was burning a hole in his pocket.

CHAPTER 31
A Will of Tempered Steel

He stayed at the *Hotel Lutetia* on the Boulevard Raspail in the popular Latin Quarter but there was a shortage of coal in France and no heating in apartments or hotels. In the late afternoon he set out for the streets of Paris, already redolent with the scents of spring. He went through the Luxembourg Gardens to Rue Toullier, where he'd met

Ján Lajčiak for the first time at the *Hotel Soufflot*. He walked past Saint-Sulpice to Rue des Écoles. He bought a postcard at the kiosk and entered the café of the Hotel des Nations. His heart trembled. Here he'd dreamed his first Parisian dream on 28th November, 1904. He ordered linden tea, pulled out a pen, and started writing on the same table from which he sent his first Paris postcard to his mother and father. Address, Alžbetína Štefániková, Ladislav Štefánik... his hand wanted to automatically write Igló, Hongrie – Hungary, but suddenly he stopped. It took a moment to realize that he wasn't dreaming that the long, magnificent dream of his father and mother, ancestors, countrymen, the dream for which he had gone and fought all his life was a reality. His mind ran over all his struggles, deprivations, loneliness, injuries, pains, sorrows, suffering, adversity, but above all hope, faith, love and victory. He struggled to keep his hand from shaking and wrote very slowly, Spišská Nová Ves, Republique Tchéco-Slovaque. His eyes were dewy, his heart fluttery and his hands slightly moist. The only word he had in his head and especially in his heart was HOMELAND. My homeland. Czecho-Slovakia. When the waitress arrived, she laid a tray on the table with embarrassment and looked the small, thin man up and down for a long time. He was crying, crying and smiling. He finished his tea, paid for it, pulled out his handkerchief, wiped away his tears, dropped the postcard in a postbox and returned to *Hotel Lutetia*.

    A moment later he came out of the hotel in his General's uniform with all his insignia and decorations. A cab took him to his superiors, Prime Minister Clemenceau, presiding over the peace conference, and Marshal Foch. He presented them with a proposal to move the Siberian troops to the rear, from where they would start their journey to Czechoslovakia. His information about the disintegration of the Czecho-Slovak, Russian and also allied armies in Russia disappointed Clemenceau and Foch. He told Marshal Foch: "I came to you to tell you face to face how the situation in Russia looks to those who aren't afraid to look truth in the eyes. I've found understanding with you but elsewhere only indifference and embarrassing misunderstanding. Our army in Russia was sent by the Allies to fight with promises of aid and is now in a deplorable state. Further retention of our troops in Siberia will lead to disintegration with tragic consequences for the whole Czechoslovak Republic."

A 100,000 strong French, English, and Greek army of intervention landed in the Crimea to join with the three-hundred-thousand Ukrainian Petliyur army and the Denikin and Kolchak armies, and to advance to Moscow and St. Petersburg along with the Czecho-Slovak legions. However, something happened which allied politicians and commanders hadn't reckoned on. On 20th March, 1919, red worker flags covered the French and English battleships and allied soldiers fraternized with the soldiers of the Red Army. The combination of interventionist troops from the south, north and east had failed, Europe called out "Hands off Soviet Russia!" and Clemenceau and Lloyd George abandoned intervention against the Russian Bolsheviks for fear of further Bolshevization of allied troops. In this situation, Štefánik insisted on the rapid departure of our legionaries from Russia. He also intervened with Foch directly regarding the still undecided southern borders of Slovakia.

"Time is running out and in a short time things can get out of the hands of the Czechoslovak government," he told Clemenceau: "Nervousness is evident in Prague and the whole country."

On 3rd February, while Štefánik was on the ship before Hong Kong, Beneš had written to Masaryk from Paris: "It would be best if Milan was the second representative at the peace conference. I prefer him a thousand times to Kramář. We can work together, despite various difficulties; he's excellent, loyal, successful. He'd be best because he'll have a very strong position, great connections and a real influence. I'd like to point out, however, that he remains a French citizen and we're obliged to raise this question if his appointment to the Congress were to be discussed or if he returned home and took a ministerial office. My opinion is that he should stay with me at the congress if he's interested. I'm of the opinion that, as far as possible, he should be completely free to decide these matters. The reports on his health are very disturbing, however, and I'm afraid Siberia has done him great harm."

From the very first moment of their meeting, Štefánik perceived the hostility that simmered between our two representatives. Although Kramář was Beneš's superior, the cunning minister of foreign affairs was more successful than the straightforward Kramář, who honestly tried to treat the chiefs of superpowers as equals, while Beneš understood that we were subordinate to them. So he chose a crafty but ultimately successful tactic. With the huge volume of papers, analyses and documents, it was clear that the Heads of Delegation had no time to study everything and had to rely on their subordinates. Therefore, Beneš mainly communicated with secretaries and advisors, who prepared briefs for their busy chiefs. Štefánik didn't bring good news from Russia. When he said that after Germany, Europe had a second enemy, the Bolsheviks, Kramář nodded in agreement, but Beneš did not react. After the meeting he wrote to Masaryk on 21st March: "After talks with him, it is clear that he is absolutely against the Bolsheviks. Either there will be major intervention, or our soldiers will come home. They're opposed to going home through Russia and are negotiating here for the Allies to take transport through Vladivostok. In the coming days he'll go to Prague and explain his point of view personally. He considers it right to tender his resignation and go back to Siberia to put an end to the question once and for all. He wouldn't oppose being ambassador to Paris, but would insist on having special powers. The situation with his health is not good. I'll try to agree with him on it before his departure to the Czech Republic; I wouldn't oppose it, on the contrary. Kramář had plans to replace Klofáč with Štefánik. Milan is against it though – quite rightly and sensibly."

Masaryk wrote to him on 31st March: "I wish I had Milan in Prague. Not only for the Italian-French dispute."

When he'd recovered a little at the hotel and his face had regained a healthy colour, he ordered a cab to the place he had longed most to go back to, taking with him the largest bouquet of roses he'd ever bought. People were already waiting for him at the palace on the nearby Boulevard Saint-Germaine. A servant opened the door for him and two chamberlains stood before the entrance to the drawing room, bowing low. Inside sat people who'd supported him all these years, helped him, encouraged him, believed and hoped with him. When the tired, sick, little man entered, they rose; Strimpl, Berthelot, de Monzie, Louise Weiss, Jules Sauerwein, Claude Blondel, Professor Hartmann, Senator Chautemps, the Duchess Féry d'Esclands, Count d'Aulby with his wife, Count Borghes and others. Everyone had been waiting for him. In the middle, in her most beautiful robe, stood the lady, his guardian angel, the woman who'd helped him the most, Sarah Claire Boas de Jouvenel. The General walked over, stopped two paces in front of her, and clicked his heels.

"Madame, je vous annonce ma bonne arrivée. La mission accomplie... Nous avons prouvé notre bon droit. C'est votre mérite. Au nom des Tchèques et des Slovaques, merci!" (Madam, I announce my arrival. My mission is accomplished. We have demonstrated our right. It is to your credit. I thank you on behalf of the Czechs and Slovaks!). My Dear Baroness, friends, we have won for a single reason because we have loved and love our nation. As long as we remain faithful to this holy love, we will be invincible. I used to say in this salon that my most beautiful day would be when a French General used the term Slovak. Now it has been fulfilled to the letter. Slovak is no longer a concept in a military archive, but a living fact."

He put the bouquet into her hands, knelt on one knee, removed his general cap, pulled his sword from its scabbard and laid it at her feet. The noble Sarah stood, unable to say a word. Tears rolled down her cheeks. At first tentative but then increasingly strong applause rolled through the hall. Champagne bottles were soon popping in the salon.

The party was full of glorious words, good food and wine. A virtuoso played a grand piano and abundantly happy laughter rang out long after midnight. Štefánik walked from table to table, sitting down at some, sometimes standing up to answer curious questions. He talked about his experiences in Siberia and made sure he wasn't alone with the lady most eagerly awaiting his return, Louise Weiss. How many times had he thought about the words he'd say to her upon his return in such a way that he wouldn't lose her and at the same time calm her soul. He respected her and liked her, but he loved another. In the end, he walked over to Louise, sitting in a lonely alcove of the back atrium.

"I want to thank you for a great article in the Revue de Paris," he smiled, pulling a newspaper out of his uniform and reading. "This pale man in whose emaciated face bright eyes radiate is a diplomat and a conqueror. He has a will of tempered steel. He judges people by their secret motives. There is something surprising and brilliant in his behavior. He has a charm and spirit both geometric and extraordinary; through his artistic interests he always made exceptional friends for his country, and his fierce, passionate and peculiar nature never tires their patient loyalty."

"Have I written something wrong?"

"No, quite the contrary. You've always been honest and helpful with me. I won't forget how you stood up for me at the hospital in Neuilly when the Catholic nurses kept reminding me of my Protestant faith."

"I'm Protestant. You'd have a harder time with a Catholic," she smiled.

It was clear from her speeches and letters that he had aroused more than sympathy for the determined liberator of his nation. She even sent him one letter that read like a marriage proposal. "I love you with the most fervent and simplest feeling that can be. For a long time it seems to me that I've lived only for the love I feel for you. I'd like to be one of the sources of your strength, one of the secrets of your glory. I humbly ask to be your fiancée."

He liked Louise for everything she did for him. For his taste and view of the world, however, she was too progressive, leftist and cosmopolitan; he preferred more conservative women with a stronger bond to tradition. Such was Giuliana for him. Quietly he revealed what he had in his heart.

"I'm going to Rome shortly... I want to be fair and have to confess that I've become engaged to the Marchesa Benzoni."

"And what about me?" she looked into his eyes, as if startled by the words she'd expected.

"I would be very grateful if you told me that I was free to decide... I know... I owe you a lot, too much... but I would never be your master... There was never anything you didn't know, nothing I could teach you... And moreover, you're not innocent... innocent like the pearl I gave the other as a sign of our engagement... And I want to introduce my people to a virgin; a virgin in body, but especially a virgin in spirit. Do you understand?"

He looked at Louise, seventeen years younger and saw tears rolling down her cheeks. She wiped them away them with the scarf he handed her. For a moment he was embarrassed but realized that it wouldn't be honest to comfort her with false hopes.

"You're an educated, immensely large-minded woman with great ambitions. Your experience is inborn and astonishing, I would almost go as far as to say that you behave like an experienced statesman. To such an extent that physical innocence has no value for you."

"I know, I know... I am the daughter of an ordinary mining engineer and can never be a descendant of the royal Savoy family. I know you need to elevate your legend and a beautiful aristocrat will help you do that more than I can..."

"No, Louise, it's not that..."

"I've always liked my friends for their shortcomings. Fortunately, you have plenty of them. I know you're a tombeur des femmes, a heartbreaker, but I'm afraid you're doing this in a very calculated and designing manner. I believe your Giuliana will find out and understand your authoritativeness and devotion, your cheerfulness and irony, selflessness and boundless ambition, your spontaneity and miraculous activity, untamed energy and infectious attraction, your need for luxury yet rejection of the secular world, your sympathy for the humiliated despite your mistrust toward all people. I wish her to understand your contempt for women and your warmth in love, your patience in studies, your meditation on the stars, to understand your desire for martyrdom, your authoritarianism, your contempt for your health, just so she understands your terrible nature... Goodbye, Milan. Despite everything, I love you, and if you need anything from me, remember that my affection for you persists, and I will always be happy to help you." And she kissed him lightly on both cheeks and left.

CHAPTER 32
Your Homeland Awaits You

The first peaceful spring day, 21st March, 1919, was unusually beautiful. Paris was dressed in the varied colours of carefully cultivated flower beds and the Parisian gardeners seemed to want to make up for what the war had denied, falling over themselves to use every piece of green for planting flowers. People swarmed through the bustling, sunlit streets and inhaled the scent of violets, tulips, crocuses, daisies, dandelions and snowdrops. The city revelled in the wonder of the first postwar spring.

The *Lutetia* was busier than usual. Part of the Czecho-Slovak delegation at the peace negotiations was preparing to return to its new homeland. In the advisory room next to Štefánik's apartment were detailed maps, tables and charts. State officials studied and compared them for the needs of the Supreme Council, which was discussing the demarcation of the Czechoslovak – Hungarian border. Advisors and officers prepared papers from which Beneš and Kramář gave speeches at the Council. Štefánik was a frequent guest there, but when he was tired, he slipped out to his room or for a cup of tea in the lobby. As he came downstairs one day to to enjoy his customary drink of chamomile, he noticed a fellow flipping through the pages of every possible world newspaper with extravagant gestures, brimming with energy, full of the joy of life. Sometimes he shook his head, smiled and nodded in agreement. He was sitting in the magnificent lobby of an even more magnificent hotel and had come there for the last meeting of the evening with Štefánik, with whom he'd talked the previous day. The pianist was picking out a nocturne of Chopin's on a white grand piano. The General in his azure uniform sat down, smiled at the elderly man and shook hands. The same moment, the pianist began playing a familiar melody. The two men looked at each other in amazement. The hotel hall was filled with tones of a chorale which they weren't allowed to sing at home. This time they suddenly got up, went over to the pianist and without a word started singing:

*"Yes Slovaks, our Slovak language lives on,
as long as our faithful hearts beat for our nation.
It lives, lives, the soul of Slovakia, lives forever,
thunder and hell, your anger is futile against us!"*

The pianist joined them and the hotel staff and guests looked on in astonishment at the behaviour of three men singing a foreign song. The receptionist would have admonished the men, but like everyone around, he sensed that for the three singers, this moment was something special. Moreover, who would dare to admonish a French General?
"Are you a Slovak?" Štefánik asked the amazed pianist.
"Yes, but I've lived in Paris for twenty years. I came here from Budapest. I couldn't stand it there anymore, so I make music here in hotels and bars. Kovač is my name. I'm sorry, General, I was indiscreet, but rarely does a person have such a precious opportunity..."

"You were excellently indiscreet," said Štefánik. "But I'm not precious here. This man, however, is an ornament of Slovakia," he pointed to his jovial co-singer with the walrus moustache and narrow goatee. "Mr. Jozef Škultéty, journalist, writer, national revivalist."

The pianist bowed and began playing the song *Na Kráľovej holi*. Škultéty smiled, Štefánik started singing again. Then the receptionist came to him and politely addressed him.

"General Stefanik, s'il vous plaît..."

Štefánik stopped singing, the pianist stopped. Štefánik glared at the receptionist and corrected him firmly: "Non Stefanik, mais Štefánik! Štefánik! Comprenez? Essayez cela encore une fois... Not Stefanik, but Štefánik, Štefánik! Do you understand? Try again..."

The receptionist's face turned red.

"Excusez-moi... General Štefánik. Sorry... General Štefánik."

"Ça va bien... that's all right," he smiled, and all three of them went to their table. Kováč continued with preludes of Smetana, Dvořák, Chopin and Tchaikovsky.

"So we're going to finish tomorrow," said Škultéty, taking a sip of his morning coffee. "I would never have thought, my dear sir, that I would have the honour of having such excellent conversation with you during a peace conference."

"And I would never have thought that during the peace conference I would have the honour of having discussions with one of the most remarkable Slovaks," Štefánik returned.

"I appreciate your words," Škultéty replied a little embarrassed. "As you know my attitude to you at the time you were connected with *Hlas*... Well... I guessed a kinsman of the Šulek family and the son of Pavel Štefánik, brought up in the spirit of the Hlboké and Košariská manse couldn't act against Slovak patriotism..."

"I know that you changed the text of the Mikuláš Resolution of May 1918 in *Národný noviny* and instead of writing the 'Upper Hungarian branch of the Czecho-Slovak tribe' you wrote 'Slovaks'..."

"I had to! Otherwise, I'd have risked being censored," Škultéty heatedly began to explain.

"I understand," said Štefánik calmly. "It's well known that you warmly welcomed the Czech legionaries as part of a united Czechoslovak nation in November in Turčiansky Svätý Martin. The war has changed many viewpoints."

"Well, we are more experienced, wiser. Congratulations on your promotion to Commander of the Légion d'honneur."

"You know that?" asked Štefánik, pleasantly surprised.

"Every decision by Prime Minister Clemenceau is reported by the Government Gazette. I read there of your new rank. Indeed, your hierarchy of honours is admirable. We are all, dear minister, proud of you."

"Thank you, but... You're talking about the hierarchy of honours, but I only know the hierarchy of work and sacrifice. I have to tell you again that you have pleasantly surprised me. From my father's accounts, I had the feeling that Jozef Škultéty was a disguised Russophile, and lo and behold, you're a supporter of modern, European Russia, in which I would agree with you from the depths of my soul."

"From the time I and my valued friends, Fedor Houdek and Igor Hrušovský came here on 11th January, we have been working at full stretch. Mr. Beneš, asked us to come help as experts in the field of Slovak-Hungarian relations... so here we are. But we're leaving tonight."

"I am glad that you came to help our common cause... Sorry, I felt, even feared, that you weren't very happy with Czecho-Slovakia..."

"How could you feel that? At home everyone must help who can. Šrobár is under incredible pressure, Rašín doesn't want to give him money, he doesn't have enough loyal people. Prešporok is in a particularly difficult situation, the Hungarians will drag their heels to persuade the Allies over declaring a referendum and I am afraid it will turn out badly with other parts of Slovakia. Hungarian crooks smuggle sugar, coal and other goods into Slovakia, although they themselves are lacking. Twenty thousand railroad workers and postal operators have declared a strike, refusing to swear to the new republic. Hungarian propaganda terrifies them with the threat that when the Hungarians take over public administration again, they will be treated as traitors. For this reason, Šrobár cannot even find new governors. The coup in Prague ended on 28th October, but only started then in Slovakia. The situation is serious there. The Italians cannot be trusted, and even the French seem to be looking out for their own interests," Škultéty thought aloud.

"The British Prime Minister, Lloyd George at a secret meeting of the Council of Four described Czechoslovak demands as outrageous," said Štefánik. "He says it isn't possible to put German and Hungarian minorities under the power of a nation that has yet to demonstrate the ability to rule... It's just as well that Clemenceau supported us by clearly saying that a strong Czecho-Slovakia would be the only barrier preventing the union of Russian and German Bolsheviks."

"The British are still indulging the Hungarians. and want both Bratislava and Košice to stay in Hungary. It's as if they don't understand what danger the Hungarian Bolshevik dictatorship poses not only to us but to the whole of Europe."

"Minister," considered Škultéty, "for our soldiers you are a General with great authority. You should come home as soon as possible and try to save what you can, otherwise they will tear us to shreds!"

"I'm going to Prague as soon as I can; I promised President Masaryk to report in person on the bad situation in Russia. I just have to go to Rome first to try and settle the Italian-French dispute..." said Štefánik.

"When I say home, General, I mean Slovakia. In the Czech part it isn't easy, but in Slovakia the situation is critical. Surprisingly, after the revolution and the resignation of Károlyi, the Bolshevik mob has thrived. Kun is a capable organizer and personal friend of Lenin, on whom he relies. He's gone straight from prison to the Prime Minister's chair! Even though the Hungarian Bolsheviks have official internationalist slogans, they are primarily nationalists."

"I know what the Bolsheviks are, I have seen what barbarities they are capable of doing in the name of a worldwide revolution. According to Lenin's thesis, every square metre that the Bolsheviks conquer is the territory of the future empire of a world proletariat. This must be prevented at all costs. Their ideas have already caught on in Europe. And yet the slogan of the English dockers – Hands off Russia! – has spread across the continent! And we are not only not in a state to help the Russian Democrats, but I'm afraid that Bolshevism will overcome Europe!"

"The fear of them is great and the calls to stop Kun are like peas thrown against a wall. You have a unique opportunity... And from what you've been telling me, I know that your disappointment about the way they circumvented you in Prague is great. You deserved more than the humiliating post of Minister of War at a time when the war, thank God, was over. You, dear General, are the man who deserved to ride on a white horse at the head of your army into a liberated homeland. After all, you can ride a horse," he laughed. Štefánik paused thoughtfully.

"But the chance is still there. Czecho-Slovakia may already exist, but only on paper," Škultéty added another log to the fire.

"Masaryk calls me to Prague, Beneš, too..." Štefánik defended himself unconvincingly.

"If you're needed somewhere at the moment, it's in Slovakia. If the Czechs lose Slovakia, Masaryk and Beneš are also lost. Czecho-Slovakia without Slovakia will be a fraction of the old Czech Kingdom, in which there would be almost as many Germans as Czechs. It'll only be a matter of time before Germans in the Reich and in Austria gather to devour the Czechs. That's why your chance, my dear General, is here and now. The fate of Czecho-Slovakia is on thin ice. And it is you who can and must save it. Šrobár has forgotten our disputes and begs me to help him. In particular, however, he's begging you. You're the one who has authority and word among our legionaries, volunteers and Sokol."

"I'm afraid I don't. You should have seen how soldiers behaved towards me in Russia."

"I don't mean ours in Russia, but in Italy. They're gradually returning to Slovakia and they're angry that the soldiers of a sovereign country are being led by the Italian or French. And Catholic Italian officers don't love Czech Hussite soldiers very much. And the highest, most respected, most beloved General Štefánik sits at the *Hotel Lutetia* and fumes over a cup of tea. Šrobár begged me to call on you to come home as soon as possible. After their defeat the Hungarian army should have been demobilized, but the command and supply structures, light and heavy weapons, military industry, officer corps, aviation, medical service, barracks and field hospitals have remained intact. They have six armoured monitors and eight armoured trains on the Danube, one of which is on the rails on their half of the Bratislava bridge. Moreover, they have the armaments and equipment of hundreds of thousands of Mackensen's German army, which after the surrender of Germany was demobilized in Hungary. You have great moral authority among the legionaries, they'll follow you to the last man! By engaging in anti-Bolshevik and anti-Hungarian warfare, you'll gain undying merit. Isn't this an appealing challenge for you? He who stops the Bolsheviks in Slovakia will save Europe. And then he deals the cards!"

Štefánik's teeth were clenched as were his fists, his jaw trembled. Škultéty's arguments were inexorably clear and logical.

"Do you know what Prime Minister Kramář whispered privately to me? Masaryk said that Štefánik may give up the Ministry of War, that there would be a place for him in Slovakia, but he does not know if he is capable of doing detailed administrative work... So count on the fact that the President intends to offer to the French General a little administrative work..."

Štefánik listened and drummed the table nervously with his fingers.

"Dear General," said Škultéty striking while the iron was hot. "Wasn't it you that wanted to march to Prague at the head of your army? Unfortunately, it hasn't happened, but now there is a real chance to do something like that. Can you imagine a more beautiful picture than when, after the expulsion of the Hungarian Bolsheviks, an army led by its main commander, the victor, General Milan Rastislav Štefánik, marches into a free Bratislava! Only after that will Czecho-Slovakia really be free. Pack your stuff and go to Slovakia as soon as possible. Your homeland awaits you!"

Štefánik continued to think, nodding his head, frowning and clenching his teeth. Škultéty watched him closely and was pleased to feel that similar ideas had already gone through the General's head long before.

CHAPTER 33
I'm Tired to Death

In Central Europe, attention was attracted mainly by a returning superpower: Poland with its population of thirty million. Under the leadership of the national hero, Jozef Pilsudský, the country could serve as a solid buffer zone between the Russians and the Germans. After Poland, the interest of the great powers in the region focused on gaining influence in the Czecho-Slovak Republic, for which the Italians and the French competed. Piccione after his arrival with Masaryk in Prague before Christmas 1918 assumed that together with an Italian general staff they would be entrusted with the building of the Czecho-Slovak army, by which Italy would secure powerful influence. As a result of an agreement signed by Beneš with the French without the knowledge of the government, where it was stated that all Czecho-Slovak troops would be subject to the command of the French mission in Prague, the Italians financing the Czecho-Slovak legions crossed swords with the French. In February 1919 a French military mission led by the Chief of General Staff, General Pellé, came to Prague. He quickly began to fill key positions in the army with French officers and it was not until February 17th that Piccione became aware of his subordination to the French in the newspapers. It became apparent that the promised Dalmatia and Dubrovnik were lost to the Italians and so the Italians didn't agree that the troops which they'd trained and financed should be commanded by their de facto competitors, the French. For this reason, the military command in Slovakia was divided into two parts: the western, commanded by General Luigi Piccione and the eastern command, including Carpathian Ruthenia, commanded by the French General Edmond Hennocque.

In mid-March 1919, the newly drawn demarcation line was moved to the Danube with Czecho-Slovakia gaining the strategic areas of the Novohradské hills, Matra and Bukové mountains. According to the decisions of the Great Council (USA, France, Great Britain, Italy and initially Japan), the demarcation line ran through the centre of the Danube and not until the Trianon Treaty of 4th June 1920 was Czechoslovakia assigned a section of 10.5 kilometres (Petržalka and its boundaries) on the other side, the original border in Bratislava having run along the Danube and started at the level of the eastern arm of the Karloveský island where there was a triangulation point. The border between Hungary and Austria had run along the right bank of the Danube in the Hirschhaufen forest area, which was at the same time the border of the municipalities of Wolfsthal in Austria and Ligetfal (Petržalka) in Hungary.

The moderate Republican regime, headed by the Prime Minister and, from January 1919, President Karolyi, handed over power to the Socialists who joined the Bolsheviks on 21st March and proclaimed the Hungarian Soviet Republic. The proletarian government, under the leadership of Bela Kohn, Magyarized to Kun, rejected the decision of the peace conference. Although French Prime Minister Clemenceau twice warned the Bolsheviks, they refused to recognize the boundaries and fought on. Kun declared: "There is no border for us until the proletarian revolution wins everywhere." The Bolsheviks expropriated banks, factories, farms and, most importantly, quickly formed a Red Army. The educated and rhetorically proficient Kun cleverly linked Hungarian nationalism to Bolshevik internationalism. Creation of the army proceeded quickly, because in dualistic Hungary the Hungarians had the Honvéd home defence militia units, while the Czechs had nothing similar. These units made up eight divisions of the Hungarian Red Army with especial support coming from working class soldiers keen on establishing a proletariat dictatorship both in Russia and Europe. The Prague journalist Egon Erwin Kisch, known as the "Raging Reporter", was co-organizer in Vienna of 1,300 Red Guard fighters, criminal police units who came to help Bela Kun. The aim of his troops was to fight for the Polish border and destroy Czecho-Slovakia, which would be put to the peace negotiations in Paris as a fait accompli. The Poles duly attacked Slovak Spiš from the north creating a situation which forced Šrobár to declare martial law in Slovakia on 25th March, 1919. On the same day, Šrobár ordered the office of the Minister with the power of attorney to rename Pozsony (alternatively Pressburg, Prešporok even Wilsonstadt for a brief while) against the will of the majority of its inhabitants (Slovaks accounting for only about 15 percent of the population) to Bratislava. Since mid-December, five trains had arrived in Slovakia every day, gradually bringing in 25,000 legionaries. The legions of General Piccione finally occupied Slovakia at the end of January.

Štefánik was determined to come and help in the fight against the Hungarian Bolsheviks as soon as possible. First, however, he had to resolve the serious dispute between the Italians and the French. As a French citizen, who was at the same time a minister of the

Czecho-Slovak government, he tried to dispel the suspicions of the Italians, who, naturally, knew that the approval for him to act as a Czecho-Slovak minister had been given to Štefánik by his French superiors.

In Paris, Štefánik negotiated not only with Foch, but also with the chief commander of the Italian army, General Diaz. Talks with him after the treaty signed by Beneš with France, of course, weren't pleasant. However, they both honoured and respected each other. After the official talks ended Štefánik asked Diaz for one more thing: to ensure his flight from Italy to Bratislava was kept absolutely secret.

After agreement with Beneš and Kramář, Štefánik decided to travel to Rome on 20th April in order to resolve the issue of the Italian military mission in the Czechlands and Slovakia. On 3rd April, he had written his last letter to Prague, planning to start it with the usual: "Beloved Mr. President!" When it came to putting pen to paper, however, he hesitated. He wasn't sure if the word 'beloved' was still valid. He knew that the President was building his "castle" line-up, and sensed he wasn't counting on him. He tempered his affections and wrote:

"I will indeed see you again. That's my first thought. For the time being, however, I have to be in Paris because of:
1. The problem of our troops in Russia and the problem of Russia
2. The Pellé – Piccione conflict.
The Paris conference won't bring us what we might have expected. We're definitely weaker today than yesterday. Even proven friends are abandoning us. I do what I can, observing our people, observing the world. My soul misgives me. So much, so much is waiting for us and the world seems blind. I'll do what I can. But I'm tired to death. I believe in you and love you as always, Yours Milan."

But there was another reason for going to Rome. He was eagerly awaited by his love, the Marchesa Benzoni, who had come to Paris for a few days as a member of the Italian delegation. However, amidst the endless negotiations, they had little time in Paris and thus both looked forward to a calmer atmosphere in the Eternal City. After her departure, he realized he was more in love with her than before he left for Russia. But the more intensely he admitted his love for Giuliana, the greater he wavered with uncertainty stemming from his ill health. "It wouldn't be right for me to marry in such a terrible condition and soon leave a widow. As soon as possible, I have to be sure that I will live…"

He had to convince himself of the meaningfulness of their relationship. In Paris they had agreed to marry in June; he believed that the congenial Italian climate together with the power of love would help him recover from his illness and begin a new life. But he wasn't sure.

CHAPTER 34
It's Over Between Us!

Shortly after the departure of Marchesa Benzoni from Paris, it came to Štefánik's ears that in the circles of the Czecho-Slovak delegation her stay in Paris was being commented on sardonically. Several members of the delegation confirmed to him that Beneš had spoken contemptuously of the "Little Italian". Regardless of the feelings Štefánik held for her, he demanded that everyone treat her with the respect and honour given to every lady: she was a lady from aristocratic circles and had had a significant share in the foreign policy successes of allied resistance. Beneš knew that very well.

Differences of opinion between the ambitious peers had first appeared in the summer of 1918, when Štefánik and Marshal Foch negotiated at headquarters and the Slovak was subsequently promoted to the rank of Brigadier General by Clemenceau. Since he was almost constantly travelling, his place in Paris had been taken over by Beneš, although it was initially thought that he'd go to Siberia rather than Štefánik. Among other things, however, he declared that he hated travelling by ship.

After his return from Siberia, Štefánik became aware of the situation at home and increasingly expressed his dissatisfaction with the development of Czecho-Slovak relations. He was critical that Slovakia would not have its own assembly, which he considered a violation of the Pittsburgh Agreement. It was undignified for him that Slovakia was to be run as a province by a single official appointed by the central government and thought there should be a Vice-President for Slovakia. Beneš, like those in Prague political circles, didn't understand Slovak dissatisfaction, considering the liberation of the Slovaks sufficient. The Slovak intelligentsia, although not very numerous at the time, desired to be not only liberated, however, but also free.

Sometimes he was pained to hear information about Beneš acting behind his back. Since returning from Russia, he had felt Beneš's unwillingness, although their friendly relationship hadn't formally changed. He watched his colleague, three years younger, and was flabbergasted at how perfectly he could dissimulate. He often discussed Beneš with his aide, Ferdinand Písecký and learned from French friends that in front of one of the main negotiators, Philippe Berhelot, Beneš had expressed the opinion that Štefánik was an obstacle to a stronger French influence in Czecho-Slovakia because he was too attached to the Italians through his personal connection with the Marchesa Benzoni. So he decided to confront Beneš with this information. Their meetings in Štefánik's room at the *Lutetia* were commonplace, but this was to be their last. Initially, it seemed to be a normal meeting between two Czecho-Slovak ministers, but both felt the tension which separated them; at the time, they had no idea it would be their final separation.

When Štefánik thought aloud about the excessive pro-American orientation of President Masaryk, Beneš calmly, but with characteristic sarcasm protested.

"Milan, with all due respect, you really don't understand. Here we are focusing on the French and Italians, but they're already in the past. Don't you see that Americans are a new phenomenon; we have to respect Wilson's will, otherwise our entire project is doomed? The post-war cards are dealt in Washington, trust Masaryk."

"You accuse me of being pro-Italian because of the Marchesa, but what about Masaryk? Isn't he exclusively pro-American because of his wife's influence?"

"It's curious. It wasn't so long ago that you stood to attention next to me for our President and now... you impugn him. It isn't good to say this about our beloved President, a man who sacrificed his health and family for the liberation of his homeland," said Beneš reprovingly.

"I know for sure that if anybody has lost their health in the fight for our cause, it's me!"

"Sorry, I know you aren't at your best; we all appreciated your commitment to Siberia, you know... but I feel strongly that your relationship with the President is no longer as it used to be."

Štefánik felt that under the pressure of Beneš's hypocrisy he was losing control of himself.

"How could it be? He was in breach of the Pittsburgh agreement and practically nothing agreed has been held to. And I know you've had a share in that."

"So now you refer to an agreement which you refused to sign..."

"I didn't sign it not because of its content, but because US citizens have no business making such decisions for us."

"What Americans? The signatories were all Czechs!"

"If so, Czechs and Slovaks! But all of them with US citizenship! Edo, you're looking for excuses. You've always played games behind my back and also behind Masaryk's. You invented, without his knowledge, a three-man government for which he arbitrarily redesigned the National Council and you usurped the posts of Minister of Foreign Affairs and Home Affairs without asking me what I would say. You also put a done deal in front of Masaryk. You even wrote an official note about it and sent it to the French Foreign Ministry as well as to the friendly ambassadors. And how many Slovaks are in the new government? Three?"

"That's what a man tells me," Benes pursed his lips unconsciously, "who wouldn't even be in the National Council without my involvement?"

"You have always envied me being Masaryk's Vice-President, while you are just a secretary of state. And you put me in the government you cooked up with Kramář and his people in Geneva without asking me if I agree with the post of Minister of War, even after the war. And you made Klofáč the Minister of Defence. Was there any need to rush that through?"

"You were on your way to Russia."

"Firstly, you were supposed to go and secondly, the telegraph was working."

"There was a sentence in the statement that the names of T. G. Masaryk, Milan Štefánik and Edvard Beneš," Beneš ironically concluded, "are indelibly inscribed into the hearts of a grateful nation. Also without your consent. You didn't object there..."

"What is the practical meaning of such a formulation?"

Beneš opened his mouth but was silent.

"Why did you speculate with Masaryk about future cooperation with the Russian Bolsheviks? If you'd sent the promised help, Bolshevism could have been eradicated in Russia from the beginning. Now we have them under our noses in Slovakia! How could you, such educated people, underestimate the Bolsheviks? Can't you see that the Bolshevik Soviets are the seeds of a terror and dictatorship even worse than the Tsarists?"

Beneš was still silent and if the nervous shifting of his feet were anything to go by, he'd have liked to have been elsewhere. But he could not respond to Štefánik's attack.

"We were dealing with the dilemma of who was worse for us, the Bolsheviks or the Germans. Don't worry, Masaryk knows what he's doing. Didn't he tell you himself to warn our people in Siberia, especially Gajda, against saying anything anti-Semitic? In America, Jews have a tremendous influence. Jacob Shiff, the richest American banker, gave twenty million dollars to Russian revolutionaries through Trotsky's wife, the daughter of the banker Giwotoowski. That's why the Bolshevik soldiers received ten times more per month than our boys. Do I have to say anything more?"

"Where did you get this information?"

Beneš didn't answer Štefánik's question. However, Štefánik didn't let him take a breath.

"I don't believe it is true. It's nonsense for the Russian Bolsheviks to be supported by both Germans and Americans, two opposing parties! Quite stupid! And if this information is true, then it's outrageous that you're telling me now. My whole trip to Siberia was completely useless from the outset. I tried to persuade our soldiers like a little boy, made myself a complete idiot, while you entertained yourselves well here in the warmth! Remember that I'm a French citizen and general," Štefánik raised his voice.

"Then why are you playing for the Italians! And how dare you bring this Marchesa of yours to the Peace conference!"

"The Marchesa came as an advisor to Orlando, Sonnino and key Italian leaders whom she knows well. You can't accuse me…"

"Don't tell me that Miss Benzoni isn't behind your sympathy for Rome."

"Don't touch the Marchesa. She is a lady of great moral power and intellectual wealth, an exquisite person! And you know she's extremely dear to me! Therefore, I beg you not to speak of her as the little Italian!"

"Little Italian?… Well… I'm sorry, that slipped out… Who told you?"

"So you did say it."

Suddenly, a strange calm came over Štefánik, a moment of empowerment when one makes a decision.

"Eduard, doing good and fighting for truth are binding laws for all of us. Their violation must be strongly condemned by everyone for whom moral principles are a matter of life and death. In a society of decent people a person who hurts by spreading gossip about others cannot prosper. Only dishonest people practise subterfuge, deceit and intrigue. It hurts all the more if they plot behind your back."

Beneš looked at him like a chameleon before it strikes. Štefánik gazed intently into his eyes, for a while competing as to who would first look away. Finally, it was Beneš who couldn't stand Štefánik's gaze.

"You worked for our cause," he continued calmly saying what he truly had in his heart, "but underneath you always worked for yourself. In America, your notorious brother made such a cult of you, it was as if Masaryk and others didn't even exist. Everyone complained about your Vojta, there wasn't anyone with a good word to say about him."

"What about all the branches of the National Council he founded?" Beneš retorted.

"I'm not saying he wasn't valuable to us, but people complained that he usurped the right to information and made noisy speeches about how the Beneš family was destined to lead Czecho-Slovakia. And most of all, I heard that your brother in America interfered in financial matters..."

"What are you implying?"

"Only this; I was on the French, Italian, Serbian and Ural fronts; I lost my health there while you were playing tennis here in Paris and going around brothels with a blue book in your pocket. You have a great apartment with two tennis courts; I wonder where you got the funding. There are rumours about various commissions..."

"I beg your pardon. How dare you!" Beneš exclaimed.

"Do you think I don't know the money you made when the French concern Schneider-Creusot bought Pilsen Škoda?"

"What's wrong with that? Škoda after the war lost orders and French capital saved the company. After Austria had disappeared from the world map, they were left with debts of almost 250 million crowns. Škoda produced arms for an empire five times larger than our state, so it is perfectly legitimate," Beneš objected.

"It wouldn't bother me if the French had come in to save Škoda. But they came in to settle with us as a competitor. And there is also talk about the very handsome commission you received..."

"Milan, if we weren't friends, then I'd leave now!" It took him a moment to calm down. "I know we all have a lot on our plate and some degree of irritation is acceptable. But just so you know... I'm convinced that Škoda in the hands of our French friends is the best solution."

"Even without being a General, I know that the most effective armament production is the production of ammunition. We could have given it to the Italians."

"If we think like that, we'd give everything to our allies for their help." Beneš shook his head.

"I wouldn't have great illusions about the kind and brotherly hand of the Allies. As I think about it, I have the feeling that they only recognized our temporary government in order to give it loans to finance our legionaries in Russia. Not willing to finance them themselves, they lent to a sovereign government that would then have to repay the money! Now that we need every crown, it looks like we're paying not only reparations, but also bills for the legion! We fought alongside them, officially acknowledged as an allied government and now they treat us as losers. Why are you in Versailles? What nonsense is this "compensation for liberation"? Do they want us to pay them for liberation? Does freedom mean any commodity that is negotiated in the market? How are we the victorious side when we have to pay reparations just like the defeated Hungarians and the Austrians?"

Beneš bit his lips; he could hardly object.

"The total amount of Austrian reparations is estimated to be one and a half billion gold francs, half of which, 12,750 million crowns, we have to pay. It's outrageous!"

"The Hungarians will pay the reparations to us," Beneš argued unconvincingly.

"I'd take that, but it's unacceptable that they cynically demand another 4.2 million crowns for us to keep our legionaries freezing and dying in Siberia. Didn't they force us to stay on in Siberia? Now they're going to charge us for it. The legion is losing its purpose. By being forced to pay reparations, our new state has in fact sunk to the level of the defeated countries!"

"It's not the price for lives, but for weapons, ammunition, rifles, boots and tunics…"

"The Republic hasn't even begun, and we're already dependent on English, French, Italian and American money! And all because of your ineptitude. When Kolchak ran after me with a similar invoice in Omsk, I told him that we'd issue invoices for our graves! You should have told them! If I'd been at the negotiations in Versailles, it wouldn't have happened!"

Beneš blushed, his face showing his anger.

"Are you telling me something about money? And what can you tell me about the Tsar's treasure?"

"Sorry, but your question is outrageous. What do you mean? You, who built a house on Ruská třída from unknown money? You, a poor family boy, who led a bohemian life during his studies in Paris? You who have an account at a Swiss bank?"

"How dare you! I object to your allegations!"

"I object to such a tone from a man who can't explain where the money of our American countrymen which Jozef Murgaš gave you was lost."

"We used it effectively to help volunteers in America, Italy, Russia, France and we used it against Hungarian propaganda. We also gave it to Minister Šrobár, to the legions. Two hundred thousand was not so much money."

"Two hundred thousand? Masaryk himself spoke of $675,000! You'll have to explain!'"

Štefánik was breathing hard, his face burning.

"And while we are on the subject of Masaryk, I'd like to know who gave you the authority to deceive the American ambassador on behalf of the National Council when you claimed that the Decree of the National Council of 10th February 1916 established Masaryk's powers. How is it possible I know nothing about such a decree?"

Beneš lost control.

"Where do you know this from? It's provocation; you just want to discredit me?"

Štefánik calmly pulled out the *Petit Parisien*.

"You probably know that they call you here, 'le roi de roulette' and the author wonders where Mr. Beneš could have got the huge sums of money he lost in Monte Carlo..."

Beneš almost cried out in fury.

"Dear sir, if these were other times, I would challenge you."

"I've already been called out for one such duel... Don't worry, Minister, you'll have to explain this to the national court at home in the presence of the President. Let him know who has worked for the republic!" Štefánik's voice was trembling with indignation.

"There is no such institution as the national court," Beneš smiled sarcastically.

"Then we'll set it up!" After a while, Štefánik calmed down and added: "And you don't have to worry about the Italian-French dispute. I have resolved the dilemma of whether Piccione or Pellé will be the Commander-in-Chief of the Army in Slovakia."

"You don't say? And how?"

"The main commander will be a Slovak."

"For God's sake, who? You don't have a single Slovak senior officer..."

"But we do. A General. French, but Slovak."

Beneš swallowed.

"I guess... you don't mean that... You really think you're a soldier?"

"And you think you're a diplomat? You are a caricature of a diplomat! A paper revolutionary! My decision is final. I'll get things done in Rome and then I'll go home. I'm thinking of Slovakia! I'm the Minister of War and there is still a war in Slovakia."

"What about the French and Italians?" Beneš tried desperately.

"I don't need Italian consent and already have French consent. Personally, from Minister Pichon."

Beneš stared at him blankly, unable to utter a sound.

"And I have a request for you," Štefánik concluded in a calm voice. "The Hungarians will start the offensive in a few days, there'll be fierce fighting. I'll be with my boys on the front line. If I happen to…" his voice stuttered "die… please don't go to the funeral! Goodbye!"

Beneš stared at the door for a moment. He had to digest what had happened. Then he made contact with Šeba. At his suggestion, Masaryk had unexpectedly promoted a 1st Sergeant of the Sixth Rifle Regiment to Major, at that time a military attaché in Rome.

"He's going to Rome. I want to know every step he takes!" he said laconically into the phone.

On 9th April Beneš wrote in a confidential letter to Rudolf Markovič: "I had a conflict with Štefánik. You need to know. It's over between us, for good. But keep it to yourself."

CHAPTER 35
Amor, Roma

After arriving from Paris on 20th April, Štefánik stayed in Rome at the Grand Hotel. The next day he headed to the Ministry of War of Italy, where he negotiated with the Minister for Defence, Enrico Caviglio. He managed to overcome hostility towards the Czecho-Slovak government, whose efforts to dismiss the Italian mission were regarded by the Italians as an expression of ingratitude and disloyalty. On that day he told Masaryk that the Italian government had agreed to withdraw its mission from Czecho-Slovakia. It was his great success and the date of departure of the Italian command and soldiers from Czechoslovakia was set for 24th May. Minister Caviglio asked him to discuss this decision personally with General Piccione in Bratislava. Štefánik discussed the transfer of Czech and Slovak legionaries to his homeland not only at the Ministry, but also with Marshal Pietro Badoglio at the Italian General Staff headquarters in Padua. At the nearby spa of Abano Terme, he discussed with General Armando Diazo the question of preparing his flight to his homeland.

And then he rushed back to Rome. After an audience with King Victor Emmanuel II he met the grand master and sovereign commander of the Italian Masonic lodges, Raoul Palermi, who asked him to support the creation of pro-Italian lodges in Prague and other cities of Czecho-Slovakia. Then he had the meeting he'd been waiting for with the Marchesa. After a few wonderful moments spent with her in Paris, after their endless Siberian separation, he knew that for the first time in his life he felt a real desire to love a woman. Since his studies in Prague, when he had the feeling he was in love with the secondary school student, Emília Chovanová, later on Lidunka Bíla, Milada Vrchlická, Marie Neumannová, in Paris, Antoinette, the daughter of the astronomer, Jules Janssen, Mimi, the daughter of the furrier Benko, Yvonne, the daughter of Senator Chautemps and the journalist, Louise Weiss, he suddenly felt that for the first time in his life he wasn't looking at "pictures, but a living landscape".

It was as if nature favoured their relationship, conjuring up the best conditions for the loving couple. Fate directed their journeys so that they always met in the Eternal City in the spring, at a time when love fills the gloomiest souls with tenderness and beauty. They strolled through the gardens of the Quirinale, sat in the Piazza Scanderberg and wandered through the narrow streets around the Vicolo del Babuccio. They walked in silence, though they both felt they should open their hearts and commune as closely as possible. Unexpectedly, Milan took her hand and turned to her urgently.

"I know, you want to ask me why I'm not being more active with you when I love you so much... yes, that's what it is. It is my soul's greatest yearning... Truth versus love... To love means to be honest with the person you love and I'm afraid to tell you the truth... I'm afraid to think of it... Dear Giuliana, I... I am ill... seriously ill... The illness is not one I can shake off but is a permanent condition. Occasionally, when it takes pity and releases its grip, it seems to me that I am healthy, but I know that it is not so... Recently, during a conversation with the French ambassador my heart stopped beating for twenty-eight seconds... I came as close to death as I've ever come... and it didn't happen for the first time... on the contrary... That's why I'm not active... That's why I'm afraid to ask for the woman I love..."

The Marchesa seemed unsurprised by his words.

"But you have already asked me... And I take it seriously..."

"Giuliana, I take it seriously, too. I'm just afraid if I leave this world..."

"When you leave isn't in your hands. Even if you now know with absolute certainty that you'll leave tomorrow, you should live for today so that you can say at the last moment of your life that it was worth it!"

"Don't I live that way? Am I not living much more intensively than others? I feel as if I've had at least five lives."

"Yes, you've had an intense life, so why are you afraid to let love into it?"

"Love is a matter of two people, it's about responsibility... On my travels and battles I only risk my own life, but in love I risk two... That's why I didn't write to you from Russia..."

" You could've at least written a line..."

He felt the sting of her reproach.

"I was raised in such a way that when I do something, I give myself to it fully. When I love, perfectly, boundlessly..."

"And what's stopping you?"

"I've already told you..."

"I don't take disease as an argument. And finally, isn't love the best doctor? Or don't you really love me?"

"Don't torment me. I love you as I've never loved nor will ever love another woman. But I would wish to love you with no limitations... And only a healthy person can do that... Your family has had to take care of me at difficult moments... Such limitations pull us apart..."

"On the contrary, they bring us closer. My dear, my little fool, I know your work forces you away from me, but don't worry. Just think what you've done for me; you've given me a life of love. Thanks to you, my soul has been touched by a miraculous world of joy. I'm grateful to you with my whole being. Every time I think of you, I feel absolute joy despite all the upheaval of our lives. May God bless your work, *magnifico mio*."

Milan squeezed her hand tightly.

"Bless you for everything your eyes and words have given me. You've filled me with the good and beautiful, conjured in me joy, faith and hope. Bless you for being able to forgive without judgements and comments. For everything you've suffered in silence and understanding. For everything you've suffered for me, my shortcomings and for hardships."

"Oh, my beloved little Slovak," she involuntarily clung to him. "I'm what you want me to be. Do you understand, dear, what I want to say? Thanks to your passage through Italy, you've made history and a love that has enriched this earth."

He smiled.

"Do you remember the time we met during a funeral procession one morning. How it wove its way between the mass of people hurrying to work. We didn't say a word. You squeezed my hand as if you were saying farewell. Perhaps you'd seen my shadow walking among the living in the morning rush."

"Even though you won't be with me, as has happened many times, I'll watch over your work from a distance to make sure no-one destroys it. I'll care for your life with the purest love; you will always find me again and be happy."

"I'm grateful that you've watched over me so much, that you were so unexpectedly and powerfully attached to my fate, that you were always faithful to me even in the greatest pain. Forgive me for not being able to love you as I wished, for not always making you happy, even though I so wanted to. Don't be sad! Revive me; give me the strength to continue my work for the benefit of my nation."

His grip weakened a little. She looked at him with concern. "You know, Giuliana, I survived the war in every detail. I saw blood, wounds, frozen and maimed wretches. I go on asking myself: "Can you go on after all this? Do you have the right to joy and personal happiness when you send others into battle? My dear Marchesa, it's an enormous sacrifice for me, but I can't think of marrying just now. What will happen in the future, I don't know. The future belongs to no-one."

She was silent and bravely held back her tears. They barely noticed how they'd made their way down the square to the Fontana di Trevi, a place of lovers where they had been together two years before. They sat down on the pleasantly cool marble, silent together, ignoring the noisy crowd. Giuliana noticed that his face had somehow faded. It happened when in his thoughts he went somewhere to an ideal world which only he could unlock. He didn't end sentences, suddenly leaping from thought to thought, as if afraid of forgetting something vital.

"You know... then there's one more of my loves..."

She broke off her reverie, staring at his lips in tense anticipation.

"How can I... tell you the story of a famous Captain of Tahiti? He fell in love with a beautiful girl there and wanted to take her to Paris. She also loved him passionately but refused to leave with him. She claimed that if she left her homeland, she would lose her beauty. They lived together for two years and he returned alone. He wrote to her mother to persuade them, but the beautiful Tahitian remained at home. After another two years she died of grief. They buried her in the place where they had first met. When I went to Tahiti the second time, the captain asked me to put a precious diamond on the grave of his beloved girl, a family jewel... I did so. Symbolically, I got rid of the captain's most precious possessions. He no longer cared, because after the death of his love he decided to enter a Carthusian monastery..."

"A moving story, but I don't understand what you want to tell me."

"That I have a second love besides you: my country, my nation. Yes, I wear a French uniform, but I have a Slovak heart in it. We still have a lot of work to do. Above all, our souls need to be transformed. This will be a new victory, but we must win."

"*Amore mio*, don't worry, I understand your greatest love. Trust me, I'm not jealous of my rival. On the contrary, I'll always stand by her and help you both as I have done so far."

"I love you with all my heart, as a noble man can love a noble woman. I promise you that as soon as we finish the work and free my homeland, I'll be yours."

Water roared in the rocks of the Trevi Fountain. Just as it had for one hundred and fifty years since Pannini had completed it for lovers. Under the stern gaze of Neptune and his two prancing horses, Štefánik clasped Giuliana tightly to his chest.

"I'd like to give you this before you leave," she chose a chain from her purse saying "AMOR - ROMA".

"It's gold! I can't accept that," he was embarrassed.

"You gave me a precious pearl."

"No... it..." he tried to return her chain.

"All right, it's not a gift, it's just a loan. You will give it back to me when you come to Rome," she smiled.

"All right. As soon as I've done what I am obliged to do at home, I'll come."

"When will that be?"

"Not later than June. I'll come with a bouquet of the most beautiful flowers that are growing then."

CHAPTER 36
A Top Secret Flight

After their assumption of power, the Hungarian Bolsheviks declared a ruthless struggle against all representatives of the bourgeoisie, who they actually were being the decision of the local revolutionary commanders. The tone was set by the chief commander of the Hungarian Cheka, Tibor Szamuely, who regarded cruelty and ruthlessness, in the Leninist style as the main virtue of the Hungarian revolutionary soldier. Two weeks before Štefánik's arrival, on 20th April, 1919, he declared: "We have the power and anyone who wishes to restore the old regime will be hanged without mercy. The situation requires blood, streams of blood. We must not be afraid to shed the blood of our enemies; blood is the steel that hardens proletarian fists. Blood will make us strong. If necessary, we will liquidate the entire bourgeoisie." Szamuely, before whom the whole of Hungary trembled, had a car with a gallows instead of a licence plate. He gave orders from the armoured train in which he travelled across the country, sowing it with horror. Two luxury wagons belonged to him, in another two his protectors and executioners slept, and in the other two wagons he executed everyone who showed resistance. The floor of the two execution wagons was so bloody that they didn't even try to wash it and corpses were simply thrown out of the windows, as a warning. The Bolshevik terror in the coming days was about to spread its ominous wings in Slovakia.

The Hungarian army didn't have its own air force. Only Austrian aircraft, marked with black crosses, operated during the war in the territory of Hungary. Those that remained in Hungary after the declaration of the Republic of Hungary, had red-white-green stripes painted on and after the Bolshevik coup, the coats of arms were gradually repainted over with red stars.

Preparations for the departure of a man who had chosen to face the Bolshevik hordes face to face were being made at the North Italian Campo Formido Airport. He'd decided to fly of his own free will, without the consent of the government and without the consent of the President. At the command of General Diaz, the flight was top secret and a special cipher for all telegrams with Bratislava had been set up. The instructions for the Italian and French missions were to be sent to Bratislava only two hours after take-off! The mechanics uninstalled the radio. But they forgot the antenna wire.

The aircraft machine designer, Caproni, was ahead of his time when in 1913 he'd designed not a twin-engine, but a three-engine aircraft. From the autumn of 1916 it had been produced with the top Isotta Fraschini engines, increasing the range as well as the speed of the aircraft to 135 km per hour. The Caproni 450 with serial number 11 459, prepared for Štefánik, had been made in February 1918. It had a length of 11 metres, wingspan of 22 metres, height of three metres and weighed two and a half tons. The aircraft was wooden, the wings were covered with wax canvas and only the two longitudinal tail beams were metal. The performance of each engine was 150 horsepower with a range set at 450 kilometres and a maximum flight altitude of 4,100 metres with the aircraft climbing to 1,000 metres in eight minutes. It carried 300 kg of bombs and could mount up to four machine guns.

According to an order of the Italian Royal Air Force of 13th April 1919, a Caproni Ca3 type 450 was to fly originally from the airport

San Pelagio near Padua to Vienna. However, Štefánik visited the Eighth Army's crew on 30th April and asked that the flight's destination be changed from Vienna to Bratislava. They argued that it was risky given the aircraft's range. Štefánik, however, suggested that the aircraft take off from an airport closer to Bratislava. The airport in Campo Formido near Udine, which was 140 kilometres closer to Bratislava than the airport in San Pelagio, proved to be optimal. On 1st May Štefánik's plane was moved from San Pelagio Airport to Campo Formida. There they placed it in a hangar and checked all its functions even though the aircraft had been overhauled and its two towing engines were new.

In Slovakia, reports of Štefánik's arrival in his liberated homeland began to appear more frequently not only in military circles, but also in the media. The Spiš *Tatry* weekly newspaper on 29th March wrote about his 'imminent' arrival but said it was being delayed. Only professional soldiers knew that such delays reflected a regime of secrecy. Indeed, Štefánik's clandestine arrival had begun to be prepared on 13th April, when the Italian delegation's military section at the peace talks in Paris gave to the headquarters of the Italian Air Force in Abano Terme a report on the departure of Štefánik to Rome, where he was to travel on 17th April. At the same time, they asked for the preparation and introduction of a standby for one of the best Caproni 450 aircraft.

Štefánik extended his stay in Paris for another three days, so went to Rome on 20th April. He was accompanied to the station by his faithful adjutant and combat companion, Captain Daniel Lévis, who soon travelled to Bratislava together with Colonel Gaston Fournier, the head of his office. He showed unreserved confidence in the two men. He'd known Fournier since the summer of 1914, when he'd been admitted to his squadron. Both accompanied Štefánik on the most difficult trip of his life to Japan and Siberia, where theybecame close friends.

"Guard this for me and give it me back when I arrive in Bratislava," Štefánik told Lévis handing him a leather bag with documents shortly before boarding the train.

"If anything happens, what should I do about it?" Levi asked, surprised.

"Give the documents to Philip Berthelot to hand them over to the Prague government."

On 29th April, Fournier and Lévis were ordered by Štefánik to travel to Bratislava to prepare for his landing. On the way they stopped in Prague to meet President Masaryk.

On 30th April, the interim commander-in-chief, Colonel Lelio Gaviglio, sent an encrypted dispatch to the commander of Western Slovakia, General Piccione, "The Czecho-Slovak Minister of War, General Štefánik, weather permitting, will depart from Campoformida to Bratislava on 2nd May, or the days following, by Caproni 450. For that day I order that a landing sign be prepared at the airport of that city and that it is positioned in the direction of the prevailing wind. In addition, have petrol supplies available for the aircraft, oil and two experienced Caproni aircraft mechanics, who, if necessary, can be requested from the Italian air mission in Vienna. I request an urgent announcement by radio of landing field conditions in Bratislava, in particular the location of the terrain, its length and width as well as its location in relation to the city."

After receiving the cipher from the headquarters, informing him on 2nd May of the Minister's arrival within days, General Piccione gave orders to prepare the airfield near Szöllös or Vajnory. Major Fournier and Lieutenant Lévis were to be personally responsible for the task in accordance with Štefánik's request. The day before on 1st May, Piccione issued order no. 2278, distributed to all army units in the city by telephone strictly banning firing on any aircraft that would fly over Bratislava in the coming days. The ban would continue until the order was revoked.

Piccione replied: "Chief Air Force Commander at the Supreme Headquarters. Protocol 5996. Secret. The landing area is located eight kilometres north of Bratislava. It has a larger landing area than

Prague. The basic terrain is solid and excellent." However, Major Fournier, in his telegram to Štefánik on 2nd May, reported via Piccione a second landing area: "According to your instructions, I had the landing area near Bratislava repaired immediately after my arrival. This area is very large and flat, located 12 kilometres north-east of the city at the entrance to Vajnory (Weinern). It is marked with a white base and every day a landing T is laid out. Very respectfully – Major Fournier." According to the recorded measurements of rainfall, there was enormous rainfall that day, 37.2 litres per square metre, the day before there had been only 0.1 litres and 3rd May added 8.5 litres per square metre, meaning that the terrain was thoroughly soaked. In Bratislava they knew only what the sparrows on the roofs had already chirped: that Štefánik would arrive, but not exactly when. Originally he was expected on 1st May, then the next day. And then there was speculation about Saturday 3rd May...

His mother and close relatives had been alerted to his expected arrival. His mother now lived with her daughter on Jakubovo Square in Bratislava and was waiting patiently for news of his final date of arrival. Milan, however, didn't come.

After the visit to the headquarters of the 2nd Czecho-Slovak Army in Gallarate, under the command of General Graziani, Štefánik gave his last order to the Czecho-Slovak troops concentrated in Gallarate, Foligno and Avezzano.

"*Militia battalion! I have come from Siberia and am now going to Prague to take up the office there which the nation has entrusted to me. Though driven by impatience to enter our liberated homeland, I've come to Italy to greet you... It is a great thrill to me that instead of a bunch of prisoners I now see ranks of a properly organized army – upright as our slender firs and with a falcon's stare. We have risen from Austro-Hungarian slavery to become citizens of a free state... Soon you'll return home to a free Czecho-Slovak Republic. The nation is waiting for you. Goodbye!*"

In Padua he said goodbye to Major Šeba.

"You can't imagine my longing for my mother, my brothers and sisters, my friends, my Košariská Kopanice... My God, Janko, I'm going home... You understand?" Stirred with emotion he approached the Major and embraced him warmly.

"Here, lad, stay healthy. If I'm killed on the journey, send a message home that I loved our nation, our land."

Šeba couldn't say a word and got into his car. Štefánik smiled and returned to the *Hotel Savoia* on the Piazza Cavour next to the Perdocchi café. He read the newspaper, wandered around the city, saw the famous Basilica of St. Antony of Padua and Donatella's equestrian statue of the condottiere, Gattamelat. In the afternoon, his driver drove him to the Italian headquarters, where his friend, the Chief of Staff, General Armando Diaz, was already waiting to inform him about the state of preparation for the flight.

He returned to the hotel in the evening. In Paris, he had again agreed with Lieutenant Daniel Lévis and Major Gaston Fournier that they would receive an encrypted telegram in Bratislava just before his arrival. Only a small circle of trusted persons would report the arrival of the aircraft, including Štefánik's friend, Count Hanuš Kolowrat, who would be expecting him with his cameraman at the airport from where they would be driven together to Skalica. Štefánik ordered his driver to head towards Campo Formido, an airport near Udine. He didn't go to Portogruaro airport, as he'd told Major Šeba. From 30th April to the day of his departure, he disappeared for three days, probably spent in Padua with Giuliana.

CHAPTER 37
The Fall

On the morning of 4th May, after six o'clock, Štefánik arrived at the airport at the intersection of Udine with Campoformido and Vecchia Postale. He had had a light breakfast at Savoia and wore a general's uniform. In a special leather pouch he'd put eight thousand francs in cash and in a small briefcase had carefully stored several important documents and letters together with a cheque for 183,207 francs, issued by the Russian-French bank *Banque Russo Asiatique* (equivalent to about 800,000 euros today). It was Sunday, so the 100-kilometre route took a good hour. In the cabin of one of the wooden military barracks located between the hangars, he greeted the mechanics and pilots waiting for him. He was informed about the weather on the flight. The young Lieutenant advised him to dress properly, as the highest point of flight crossing the Julian Alps west of Triglav between Tarvisio and Kranjska Gora would be about one thousand, five hundred metres, where the temperature would drop below freezing. Štefánik smiled and unloaded from the trunk that Benoni, his adjutant, had brought underwear, pyjamas and two warm sweaters for the cabin. The pilots nodded their approval.

"They report that the weather at Pressburg will worsen and a northwest wind will be blowing almost all the way, so cold and at least three and a half hours of flying can be expected." Then the Italian Lieutenant spoke.

"Excuse me, Minister, I'm Lieutenant Giotto Mancinelli Scotti and I have the honour to be the first pilot for you," he said to Štefánik. "Let me introduce you to the co-pilot, Sergeant Umbert Merlin and the mechanic Gabriella Aggiunti."

"Sir, it's an honour for me that your command has entrusted me to the noble Mancinelli, the great Neapolitan Merlin and, as I have heard, the excellent mechanic Aggiunti. They say you've had sixty combat flights," he turned to Merlin with a smile. The men shook hands and slowly dressed in their flight suits, under which they wore multiple layers of underwear, making them move like penguins. Štefánik was carrying a smaller leather bag, which he wouldn't trust even to his aides.

Lieutenant Mancinelli pulled out a military map and spread it on the table.

"We will fly on this route, Gemona – Resiutta – Tarvisio – Arnoldstein – Villach – Klagenfurt – Dreavograd – the Mur river valley – Graz – Brück an der Mur – the Murz valley – Mürzzuschlag – Wiener Neustadt – Pressburg. We have an excellent machine from the ninth bomber squadron, both front engines have been overhauled, I've flown thousands of kilometres in it. My friend Umberto and I have flown from here to our base in Vienna several times," Mancinelli reported with a confident smile.

"Yes, it's a really good machine, I know it a little. I flew on one as a navigator on 4th May, 1916 on a bombing raid on the Trento – Mattarello section of the front," said Štefánik airing his knowledge.

"We know, we heard about your flights on our front and in Serbia. Why don't you pilot yourself?"

"I've not had time to test one. I have never flown a Caproni, so I gladly put myself in your hands."

At that moment the engines started to roar.

"You see, our great mechanic Gabi has everything under control. We're going to check the machine too. Let's get dressed, we've still twenty minutes to go. We'll start around eight."

Both pilots went out, Štefánik stayed in the room with Benoni. "Please, adjutant, can you leave me alone for a moment?"

Benoni rose and saluted.

"Sir, I'm at your service."

Štefánik was wearing his flying suit and put on a brown helmet. He remained silent, looking at pictures of smiling pilots and various aviation victory certificates hanging on the walls. The airport had been in operation since July 1913.

It came to his mind that he might have been too tough on Giuliana in Rome. Rather than expressing to her his serious interest in them living together, he felt he had sown seeds of doubt in her mind. The cruel words he had spoken about their uncertain future kept returning to his mind. He decided to write to her other, more beautiful, encouraging words that would better express what he felt about her. He took a piece of paper he'd stored in his breast pocket and sat down at the table. Before he wrote a word, he thought long and hard:

"My friend, my beloved friend! Farewell! Oh, what a terrible word to divide our lives! Sometimes, I grumble at a fate that submits our love to such trials. Farewell! But I'll be back. I'll return to stay, I hope, and continue to be with You, my warmly beloved. The engine is humming. We need to go. To go and keep going... I have circles in front of my eyes, in my heart unrest, but this time my frailty is completely human. Should I not leave you, Giuliana, withdraw and not seek out after years my family, my homeland? I'll see my country again. I have a country! What joy, what distress. The plane is calling me... Farewell, but don't be grieved. High above the peaks of mountains and the clouds, amidst the rays of the sun and the loving waves of azure, my soul will not find peace, and my lips will whisper to You with fidelity: Farewell, Giuliana! Farewell, my adored woman!"

He folded the letter and placed it in an envelope on which he wrote, Giuliana Benzoni, Roma, Palazzo Taverna, 85 Via Panico, and added "La mia amata" (My beloved).

"General, sir, I'm sorry to interrupt, but it's time to board!" Benoni interrupted his daydream.

Štefánik, however, didn't react, he felt that the letter did not express his feelings accurately. He needed a moment to think about the words he had written to his love in French.

"Mon General, please," Benoni and the mechanic urged.

"Coming!" Hastily he took a clean sheet of paper and wrote only the words: *"I love you! Forever Your Milan."* He took the original letter from its envelope and slipped it into his flying suit. In its place he tucked the new sheet into the envelope and sealed it. He handed the envelope to Benoni, requesting that the letter be delivered to the Marchesa Benzoni, then walked towards the aircraft. The propeller of the bomber Caproni 450 with a lily insignia had already been fully twisted. He said good-bye to the mechanics with a handshake, had his photograph taken together with them, and climbed a short ladder on to the wing. But then his sabre got caught as he crawled into his cockpit so the mechanic held it for him as he climbed through the side of the fuselage, about a metre high. In a similar way, the mechanic also helped the first pilot Mancinelli who sat behind Štefánik on the right, while the co-pilot, Merlino took the left seat and the mechanic-radio operator, Aggiunti, stood in the tower in front of the rear third engine. The sky was overcast, the morning chill pierced through to the skin, but the "onion skins" of clothing protected the crew.

At 8:07, the Caproni Ca3 aircraft of type 450 with matriculation number 11495 took off in the direction of Pressburg – Bratislava. Two hours after departure, at 10:07 an order was issued to send the cipher of the aircraft's take-off start to Bratislava. It took some time to encrypt and decrypt it in Bratislava.

Since the morning Minister Šrobár had been busy on a long-term planned event, planting a linden of freedom in Skalica. At eleven in the morning, employees of offices, schools, legal and social facilities gathered in Skalica Square. The ceremony started with the song *Kto za pravdu horí* performed by the Skalická peasant youth choir and the national anthem performed by the 72nd Czechoslovak Regiment from Bratislava. There was a speech by government advisor, Pavol Blaho, Maria Bellayová recited a poem by Hviezdoslav, *Nehaňte ľud môj*, and the songs *Hej, Slováci* and *Ktož jsú Boží bojovníci* were sung. People danced, applauded, speeches were given by Šrobár, General Luigi Piccione, the Skalica mayor, Štefan Mandík, the governor of Nitra, Ľudovít Okánik, the governor of Bratislava, Samuel Zoch, the Prague editor, Jan Erben, Ivan Krasko and others. Around half past eleven, the guests sat convivially at a festive table. In the event that Štefánik would arrive, several officials remained in the government building in Bratislava, led by the head of the administrative department, Dr. Ivanko. When he received the notice of the arrival, he immediately tried to contact Skalica by telephone, but they were cheerfully celebrating. As he was phoning the aircraft was seen over the Danube. He took his colleagues and raced toward Vajnory.

At the same time, the Minister of National Defence, Václav Klofáč was speaking at the Pištěk Theatre in Královské Vinohrady near Prague. He emphasized the role of the Czecho-Slovak legions in the establishment of the Republic and named three men who were most involved abroad in establishing the Republic, Masaryk, Beneš and Osuský.

He didn't mention Štefánik...

After take-off, the aircraft headed north. When flying over the Alps, Štefánik felt unusually good. It was as if the snowy heights had energized him. He turned several times to the crew and smiled encouragingly at the boys. He wondered what was awaiting him at home. He'd been called by President Masaryk, but Vavro in Slovakia needed him even more urgently, so he was going there first.

It seemed ridiculous that people had tried to persuade him not to fly: the Deputy Chief of Staff of the Italian Army, Badoglio; General Graziani; Šeba. Apparently spending four hours at three thousand feet could be fatal for his heart. But hadn't he endured the Siberian frosts?

He barely realized they were already above the town of Wiener Neustadt. Lieutenant Mancinelli noticed that the multi-metre tow wire had torn and got entangled with the elevator control. He wrote it in the on-board logbook and showed it to the passengers. For a while, the crew wondered if such a disruption would force them to land in Vienna, but after checking the manoeuverability of the elevator, they decided to continue the flight to Bratislava. The Danube was the safest indicator to navigate by and it was enough to fly comfortably over the river.

Pilots who had never flown on this route before reliably arrived at the city of their destination. The plane was descending, flying at a height of about a thousand metres, when the silhouette of Bratislava Castle appeared far in front of it. East of the village of Wolfsthal it flew over the Czechoslovak-Austrian border and continued at a height of about five hundred metres over the left bank of the Danube towards Bratislava.

Štefánik was happy to see the Franz Joseph Bridge, the opening of which he'd attended as a twenty-year-old. How could he guess that the bridge would soon bear his name?

Moved by the view of the capital of Slovakia, he glimpsed the hills of the Small and White Carpathians, which hid on the far horizon his Kopanice with the sacred Bradlo. Against the roar of wind and propellers he began singing:

Košariská meadows are rolling mounds,
my eyes roam to their very bounds.
I look for rest in their groves and fields,
This beloved homeland my heart heals...

When an enemy bombing aircraft with the Italian coat of arms and a typical double-hull appeared unexpectedly at 11:30 am over the Danube, the commander of the Red Guards, deployed on the right bank, was immediately clear what command to issue. Soldiers with loaded rifles, aimed at the plane and stared at him eagerly. They waited for one word: " Tüz!" (Fire!) The captain certainly wouldn't have hesitated a minute had he not read an encrypted command from headquarters where the War Minister, József Pogányi-Schwartz, warned against any clashes with the Czech army at the time of preparation of the general attack of the Hungarian Red Army against Slovakia, which was to begin in days. The commander wasn't allowed to give the command. The Hungarian soldiers could only watch in disappointment as the aircraft with the Italian coat of arms moved away from the Danube and turned northeast. As it had flown almost all the time against the wind, the hands indicating the contents of the gasoline tank had dropped towards zero; the plane couldn't afford any circuits above the city, but had to head as straight as possible to the landing area near the village of Vajnory. The co-pilot had a detailed map of Bratislava and its surroundings on his knees. The meteorological station at the Dynamit Nobel factory showed five degrees above zero and visibility was eight on a ten-degree scale.

In anticipation of an early landing, Štefánik undid his safety straps in his impatience to best watch the approaching ground. As they flew over the artillery barracks someone fired, perhaps thinking that it was an enemy aircraft. The soldier who fired, Meško, later confessed to the shot, but said that he wasn't informed about the ban on shooting and that he fired only in the air, not aiming at the aircraft. So although he was arrested, he was released the next day after his error was explained. The shot was one of three shots that each soldier had at his disposal. Due to lack of copper, Pilsner Škoda wasn't making bullets at that time; the bullets available were made of lower quality material and had a reduced accuracy and range. The crew didn't hear anything suspicious in the hum of the engines and the whistle of the wind and continued in the direction of Vajnory, where building of a field airport had started, located as the crow flies eight kilometres from the city centre. Workers and soldiers were gradually draining the swampy area, which the locals called the Lake. Wind gusts were frequent in this area at lower levels.

Major Fournier and Lieutenant Lévis had checked at the airport on the state of preparations for the landing; a specialist arrived in Bratislava from the Italian air mission in Vienna. However, they hadn't received any information about the arrival and noticed the plane only when it flew over the city. Quickly they returned to the runway and ordered the barrels of pitch to be lit to show the pilots the start of the runway and the wind direction. Present at the airport was an Italian Lieutenant from headquarters, an Italian mechanic and a driver, Jindřich Skořepa, who was supposed to take Štefánik to Skalica. Hanuš Kolowrat and the cameraman, Emanuel Procházka, had been at the airport in the morning. When he obtained information from the main headquarters that Štefánik wouldn't be flying due to bad weather conditions, he went to Skalica. Here in a purely Slovak town there should have been a celebratory welcome. Smoke, however, began to be seen as the aircraft searched for the designated area for landing. The man seated at the navigator's cockpit stared at the people on the field, waving cheerfully at them, a gold coin bracelet with the letters AMOR-ROMA gleaming on his wrist. They waved back at him. According to the direction of the canvas arrow at the airport, the pilot realized that he would be landing downwind. The aircraft therefore had to make a right turn over the village of Vajnory at a radius of about one and a half kilometres so that it could land against the wind according to standard rules. However, a second turn over the village of Farná at a radius of about two kilometres had to be made with the north-west wind blowing from the left. The increased radius resulted in the pilot failing to turn the aircraft in the desired direction. The only solution was a sharp arc at a height of about a hundred metres at flight speed, which through the previous manoeuvres had decreased significantly. Štefánik noticed that the pilots were nervous. The aircraft tilted sharply to the right to reduce the radius of the arc. For a heavy bomber, a sharp roll was extremely risky but perhaps the airmen would have managed it if the aircraft hadn't dropped a good twenty metres at that moment. The words "air pocket" surely passed through Štefánik's mind, an empty space in which the propellers have nothing to do. Then the propellers worked, but the wind was blowing from the right at almost a right angle to the aircraft. In addition, due to its inclination and sharp rotation, the difference in velocity of the right and left wings had increased significantly, causing an uneven buoyancy. The aircraft was at a height of 68 metres and the loss of height and speed could not be compensated for. A nearly three-ton machine with centre of gravity in the front third had no chance, dropping its nose perpendicular to the ground, causing unattached things to fall from the plane. In three seconds it was over. The plane crashed to the ground after freefall, ejecting the bodies of the crew as the aircraft turned over on to its back. It happened on Sunday 4th May 1919 shortly before midday near the village of Ivanka. The layer of turbulence behind the Little Carpathians, which Štefánik once told Bosák about in America, proved fatal for the crew. The warning for Bosák's son, a pilot, which he told the Slovak banker in New York on 29th September 1917, had overtaken him. "Emphasize to your son that the most dangerous thing for pilots are so-called air pockets low above ground level."

Hardly had the toasts been made in the Great Hall of the Federal House in Skalica when Piccione's adjutant approached and handed him a telegram. The General turned as pale as a ghost and Vavro Šrobár, who received a telegram with similar content, likewise turned pale. At the Abano Terme spa near Padua, the Chief of Staff of the Italian Army, General Armando Diaz, received telephone message 548 from Bratislava three hours after the accident on 4th May, 1919 at 15:45:

"Caproni 11495 arrived at 11:30 over Bratislava. Subsequently destroyed in an accident near the airport. Crew and passenger all dead. Stop. Major Noveda."

CHAPTER 38
We'd Kill You if …

On Saturday, 10th May, at one in the afternoon, four coffins from the military hospital chapel were carried to Eszterházy Square (Freedom Square) in Bratislava and placed on gun carriages. At half past two, soldiers, civilian political leaders, relatives, clergy, and journalists gathered in front of the wreath-covered caskets. Štefánik's family took pride of place; in the middle sat his mother, Albertina, around her his sisters, Ľudmila Zmertychová, Olga Hajštová, Elena Izáková, Marienka Štefániková, and brothers Igor, Pavel, Ladislav, Kazimír, his brothers-in-law, sisters-in-law, nieces and nephews. The guard of honour, composed of officers and non-commissioned officers from the Italian, Russian and French legions, stood at attention in double ranks. The funeral song was performed by the Bratislava choir, followed by a Lutheran and Catholic liturgy. The Choir of Moravian Teachers sang the chorale, *Ktož jsú Boží bojovníci* and both denominations sang the Czech and Slovak anthem. Funeral orations were delivered by Minister of National Defence, Václav Klofáč, President of the National Assembly, František Tomášek, French Ambassador Clémet Simon, General Luigi Piccione, General Maurice Pellé, Minister of Justice František Soukup. Vavro Šrobár, Štefánik's dearest friend, said with tears in his eyes: "An unpredictable destiny destroyed the life of a man, a hero at the moment he was about to enter his homeland, the land he loved above all, for which he made so many sacrifices so often in danger of his life. You rose to a height of world significance without foreign help. Throughout your journey, you never forgot that you were the son of a small, enslaved nation attaining power and glory. You set us an example of unprecedented love for one's country and ideal understanding of the higher meaning of life. Being a warrior indeed in the service of the supreme idea of humanity, you fought for your people in all conditions to live as a free, civilized nation, to contribute its humble talents to humanity's common treasure. Who is to replace you, who so peerless, self-reliant in deeds, thinking, diligence and love for his nation? The example of your life, your spirit, your idea of how the sun in the sky will shine for us and our descendants and will ignite your brothers and future generations of the Czechoslovak nation in our love for our nation and on our journey to the highest goal of humanity – may these inspire each of us to be better today than we were yesterday and make our homeland great and glorious. This is your message to us and our future. Live eternally in the memory of your nation, and the Slovak land you loved so warmly, may the earth rest lightly on you."

Those who loved and respected him came to Bratislava. Vice-Presidents of the National Assembly, representatives of the political parties in the National Assembly, Vlastimil Tusar, Gustav Habrmann, Colonel Otakar Husák, Professor of Astronomy, František Nušl, diplomatic representatives of France, Great Britain, Italy, Yugoslavia, Belgium, USA, Ukraine, Romania, Switzerland, the English writer and scholar, Seton-Watson, Slovak deputies and governors. The Prime Minister Karel Kramář didn't come, nor did his closest friends from the foreign resistance, Eduard Beneš and President Tomáš Garrigue Masaryk, who sent the head of his office, Přemysl Šámal, in his place. His lovers, friends, supporters, Louise Weiss, Sarah Claire Boas de Jouvenel, Marie Neumannová,

Yvonne Chautemps, Antoinette Janssen and even the one to whom he wrote his last letter four hours before his death, the Marchesa Giuliana Benzoni, didn't come. She couldn't, but soon visited his grave and her fiance's family herself. She addressed Milan's mother in Slovak and donated the dress she was going to wear for her June marriage to Milan to his niece, who later married in it.

The Bratislava Workers' Choir sang the hymn song, *Kto za pravdu horí*. Members of Sokol took the wreaths and the parade moved off. A whole legion marched in the procession, followed by garrison musicians, a flag bearer, and his family. Then the gun carriages flanked by legionaries in double rows advanced. On the first was the General, followed by Lieutenant Giotto Mancinelli Scotti, Sergeant Umberto Merlini and last of all, the radio operator Gabrielle Aggiusti. This was followed by representatives of the clergy, a Moravian Teachers' Choir in folk costume and black sashes and the wreath bearers. A company of legionaries waiting on the vast area of the square in front of the garrison hospital joined the procession together with Italian *carabinieri*, engineers, the Freedom Guard, a company of sailors, French and Russian legionaries, musicians of the 33rd Regiment and more cavalry at the rear. Slowly, with dignity, they walked down the route of Esterházyho námestie (Námestie slobody), Város utca (Námestie slobody), Széna tér (Námestie 1. mája, Kollárovo námestie), Maria utca (Mariánska ulica), Korház utca (Špitálska ulica), Vilmos császár tér (Námestie SNP), Frigyes Föhercég Utca (Suché mýto) and Stefánia utca (Štefánikova ulica) before proceeding to the main station. Their commander was accompanied on this last journey by his troops; cavalry, the 72nd Infantry Regiment, the 3rd Rifle Regiment, the 33rd Infantry Regiment, Italian, French, American soldiers, sailors, airmen and especially citizens, standing on the pavements. His Hungarian opponents also bowed their heads in acknowledgement of the importance of the man riding on the bier. The moment the soldiers carried the coffins to the station, the guns sounded, followed by an honorary salvo from the infantry, after which the flags of the individual military units were lowered and the national anthems of Czecho-Slovakia and Italy were heard.

On a special train, the coffins of the deceased were escorted by French, Russian and Italian legionaries, the Freedom Guards and members of Sokol. Štefánik went on his last journey along his usual route Trnava – Jablonica – Brezová, where the train brought him at ten in the evening. At eleven they placed Štefánik's coffin in the Evangelical church, the coffins with the Italians in the Catholic. The next day, 11th May 1919, there were mourning ceremonies. Martin Braxatoris, Jur Janoška, Alois Kolísek, Karol Medvecký and Slovakia's greatest poet, who disagreed with him in his youth, Pavol Országh Hviezdoslav, came to Brezová to say goodbye to their friend. After the requiem, delivered by a dignified Medvecký, they brought the Italian pilots before the evangelical temple and together with thousands of people went on the journey to Košariská. The majesty of death had reunited Catholic and Protestant priests. After centuries, Catholics entered a Protestant temple and Protestants entered a Catholic temple. Milan did not return home on the wagon of the driver, Štefan Žídek, but on a gun carriage. On the right were Roveň, Ševcova skala, Vysoká hora, Kopec, his beloved Lopušná dolina and Úboč, on the left the ridge of the massive Bradlo. And the meadows in glorious spring weather, in the month of love, as if to greet their son, gleamed with the most beautiful colours and emitted the most fragrant scents. Pink cherry blossomed on the same trees Štefánik had once climbed as a boy. For a few days until the day before, a gale had swept through the surrounding hills, but on Sunday morning it was calm and sunny. The head of the procession was already in front of the Košariská rectory but crowds of people were still coming in from Brezová. Around thirty thousand arrived not only from nearby but also by special trains from

Košice, Prague, Ostrava, Brno and Žilina. Pastor Michal Valášek was waiting for them in front of the church. After unloading Štefánik's coffin in front of the altar, more speeches were made. His faithful adjutant, Major Fournier said: "His only thought was Slovakia." Outside, moved by sorrow, were Catholics and Protestants, Czechs, Moravians, Slovaks, French, Italians and Russians, people rich and poor, brave and timid. In his sermon, the priest, politician and professor Michal Bodický likened Štefánik's fate to that of Moses.

"A boy from the most straitened manse of the Nitra seniorate brought his people into the promised land but did not enter himself. He will only look at it from above."

At the urging of the architect, Dušan Jurkovič, the governor Zoch, Vavro Šrobár and Štefánik's family agreed with his bold suggestion not to bury Štefánik in Košariská cemetery, but on Bradlo. The government sent a platoon of engineers to Bradlo on 7th May, brought there personally by Jurkovič. They prepared a burial place in three days and four nights in extremely bad weather, without a break. Dynamite broke the hard rock for the last resting place of the four Icaruses. They built temporary wooden obelisks. Dozens of civilian and military workers were deployed to work on the road to Bradlo, provisionally widening it so that cars could pass along it. On 11th May on the eastern slope of the Bradlo massif, thirty thousand people followed the vehicles with caskets. Behind them came soldiers, politicians and his family. At noon, at an altitude of 543 metres on Bradlo, Milan Rastislav Štefánik, Giotto Mancinelli Scotti, Umberto Merlini, Gabrielle Aggiusti found their final resting place. The evangelical bishop, Samuel Zoch, said farewell to a great son of the Slovak, Czech, and French people: *"We would kill your memory if we didn't have the strength to follow your path of truth, goodness and work. We would kill you if we were to seek our own advantage through self-love, if we were to seek the meaning of life in material wealth, in money, in food, in savage enjoyments that kill the spirit. We would kill you if we loved a lie more than the truth, if we did not cleanse our lives, both private and public, of evil and thievery. We would kill you if we lost our national awareness and national pride."*

Epilogue

Years ago, when I stated my intention to write a novel about our national hero, I had no idea what a difficult task I was undertaking. From the very first moment, some called on me to write how they had killed him, while, conversely, others raised a warning finger not to succumb to emotions and not to write about his alleged killing. I didn't intend to succumb to anything except the truth and my author's right to search for it. I don't think I succumbed. I spent long, exciting hours, days, weeks studying and examining French, German, Russian, English, Hungarian, Czech, Slovak documents and discussing things with experts. Perhaps the most time I spent was on the most frequently discussed topic in connection with Štefánik, his tragic death. Like my consultants, I am of the opinion that the failure of the aircraft due to weather conditions was the cause of the aircraft crash. Attributing the cause of Štefánik's death to Beneš is irresponsible and populist. I see the fundamental difference in character between Beneš and Štefánik in the fact that Beneš looked first at himself and then at the "cause", while Štefánik looked exclusively at the "cause" to the point of self-sacrifice. The "cause" that connected them was the Czechoslovak Republic. Unfortunately, the dispute between these two men grew to hatred, but with all reservations about Beneš, this cautious politician logically would not take the most fatal risk; the fatal risk being possible disclosure. If he gave orders to shoot down Štefánik, several dozen people would have known about it. Those who would like to see the death of Štefánik attributed to Beneš ignore that the flight was a secret and until the last minute it wasn't known when it would take place. Moreover, even if Beneš had learned about the exact arrival at the last minute, it can be ruled out that he would have been able to organize an assassination operatively, within a few hours. If that actually were the case right, a basic question would have to be asked: why would he do that? If he wanted to get rid of Štefánik, he had a number of ways and options after his return. Whoever intends to murder, however, will do so with as few witnesses as possible and won't give orders through intermediaries. At the moment of Štefánik's return, the struggle to join Slovakia to the Czech Republic was raging and Štefánik was essential in this situation: for the legionaries he had credit as their recognized authority. Otherwise Šrobár wouldn't have desperately called him to Slovakia. Beneš therefore also needed Štefánik so that his work on the establishment of the Republic could be successfully completed. Without Czecho-Slovakia, there would have been no Beneš. They signed a ceasefire with Hungary in Reduta on 1st July, 1919 and a peace treaty with Hungary at the Palace of Trianon in Versailles on 4th June, 1920. It is unthinkable that Beneš would have risked the total collapse of relations with France and Italy and thus the support of these countries for a still very fragile republic. Let us not forget that Štefánik was a French citizen and a General and that there were three Italian citizens flying on the aircraft. And as for considering it an act of suicide: it is undignified to suspect him of the murder of three innocent people with the principles and values that Štefánik professed.

Jozef Banáš, Košariská, May 2018

Literature Consulted

Baer, Josette: A life dedicated to the Republic, Ibidem Stuttgart 2017
Baláž, Anton: Prehovor Ezechiel, LIC Bratislava 2012
Bandrowski, Jiří: Bilý lev, Antonín Hajn, Praha 1919
Bassi, Roberto: Campoformido 100, Aviani, Udine 2013
Bareš, Arnošt: Štefánikův memoriál, Památník odboje, Praha 1929
Bartůšek, Josef: Štefánik II. L.Mazáč, Praha – Bratislava, 1938
Beneš, Eduard: Světová válka a naše revoluce, Orbis a čin, Praha 1928
Benzoni, Giuliana: La vita ribelle, Il Mulino, Bologna 1985 Berend Ivan T.: Decades of Crisis, University of California Press, Berkeley 1998
Bertin, Célia: Louise Weiss, Éditions Albin Michel, Paris 1999
Butvin, J. – Havránek, J.: Dějiny Československa, SPN Praha 1970 1929
Bodnár, Július: Dr. Milan Rastislav Štefánik – československý národný hrdina, Internet – Zlatý fond SME, 2017 (digitalizované)
Castleden, Rodney: The Concise Encyklopedia of World History, Parragon, Bristol 1994
Čapek, Karel: Hovory s T. G. Masarykem, Fr., Borový, Praha 1937
Čaplovič, M. – Ferenčuhová, B. – Stanová, M.: Štefánik v zrkadle historiografie, Vojenský historický ústav, Bratislava 2010
Čelko, Vojtech: Milan Rastislav Štefánik, Zborník k 125. výročiu narodenia, Slovenský literárny klub ČR, Praha 2005
Čulen, Konštantín: Slovenské študentské tragédie, Slovenská liga, Bratislava 1935
Čulen, Konštantín: Boj Slovákov o slobodu, Slovenská knižnica HSĽS, Bratislava, 1944
Deary, Terry: Prvá svetová vojna, Slovart, Bratislava 2008

Denis, Arnošt: Otázka Rakúska a Slováci, Ján Párička, Ružomberok 1922
Ditrych, Břetislav: V jiném světle, Veduta 2017
Dresler, Jaroslav: Masarykova abeceda, Melantrich Praha 1990
Dvořák, Pavel: Piata kniha o Bratislave, Rak Budmerice 2012
Duffack, J. J.: Štefánik a Československo, Naše vojsko Praha 2007
Ďurica, Milan: Dejiny Slovenska a Slovákov, SPN Bratislava 1995
Ďurica, Milan: Milan Rastislav Štefánik vo svetle talianskych dokumentov, THB Bratislava 1998
Ďuriš, Rudolf: Nepoznaná história, Eko konzult, Bratislava 1992
Eliáš, Rudolf: Bohatýr Štefánik, Moravská Ostrava 1922
Fabian, Juraj: Posledné dni Uhorska, Smena Bratislava 1990
Fuska, Ján a kol: M. R. Štefánik v myšlienkach a obrazoch, Elán, Bratislava 1999
Gacek, Mikuláš: Sibírske zápisky, Matica slovenská, Martin 2015
Geoepoche, Kollektion Nr. 10
Gunther, John: Evropa jaká je, Fr. Borový, Praha 1938
Hellwig, Linne: Daten der Weltgeschichte, Orbis Verlag, München 1989
Husár, Jozef: Musel generál M. R. Štefánik zahynúť?, Bratislava 2000
Chronik der Deutschen, Chronik Verlag, Dortmund 1983
Janin, Maurice: Pád carismu a konec ruské armády, J. Růžička Praha 1931
Joris, Pauline: Milan R. Stefanik: Figure (tchéco)slovaque, Nouvelle Europe 2009
Jung, Kurt M.: Weltgeschichte in einem Grif, Ullstein, Frankfurt am Main 1985
Juriga, Ferdiš Dr.: Blahozvesť kriesenia slovenského národa, Urbánek, Trnava
Juríček, Ján: M. R. Štefánik, životopisný náčrt, Mladé letá, Bratislava 1968
Kálal, Karel: Unterdrückung der Slowaken durch die Magyaren, Eko konzult, Bratislava, 2009
Kautský, Emil Karol: Kauza Štefánik, Vydavateľstvo Matice slovenskej, Martin 2007

Kele, František: Milan Rastislav Štefánik: Významný cestovateľ, RGT Press, Banská Bystrica 2010

Kele, Musil: Návraty do Polynézie, Po Štefánikových stopách, Print Servis, Bratislava 1996

Klimek, Antonín: Vitejte v první republice, Havran, Praha, 2003

Klempa, Jozef: Moje skúsenosti zo svetovej vojny, Slovart, Bratislava 2014

Kolektív: Na začiatku storočia 1901 – 1914, Veda, Bratislava 2004

Kolektív: Slováci v prvej svetovej vojne, LIC, Bratislava 2010

Kormošová Ružena: Po stopách rodiny M. R. Štefánika na Spiši, ABC Studio, Sp. N. Ves 2015

Kováč, Dušan: Štefánik a Janin, príbeh priateľstva, Dilema, Bratislava 2001

Kováč, Dušan: Milan Rastislav Štefánik, Rak, Budmerice 1996

Kováč, Dušan: Dejiny Slovenska, Lidové noviny, Praha 1998

Králiková, E. – Kováč, D. – Pauer, M.: Obrazopis sveta, Osveta, Martin 2004

Kšiňan, Michal: Milan Rastislav Štefánik, Albatros Media, Praha 2012

Kudela, Josef: Aksakovská tragedie, Moravský legionář, Brno 1932

Kulhánek, F. prof: Česi a Slováci cestou slávy a utrpenia, Náš domov, Banská Bystrica 1934

Lacko, Dušan: Milan Rastislav Štefánik, Gloria, Rosice 2014

Liška, Vladimír: Tomáš Garrigue Masaryk známý a neznámý, Nakladatelství XYZ, Praha 2017

Magenschab Hans: Die Welt der Großväter, Edition S, Wien 1990

Markovič, Ivan Dr.: Slováci v zahraničnej revolúcii, Pamätník odboja Praha, Praha 1923

Martinický, Pavel: Oslobodenie Slovenska, Vydavateľstvo Michala Vaška, Prešov 2010

Masaryk, T. G.: Světová revoluce, Orbis a čin Praha 1930

Matějovská, Marie: Milan Rastislav Štefánik, Melantrich, Praha

Miko, Václav: Eduard Beneš milován i nenáviděn, Petrklíč 2017

Milan Rastislav Stefanik, Ville de Papeete 2009

Monzie de, Anatole: Destins hors de série, Les Éditions de France, Paris 1927

Musil, Miroslav, Antonello, Biagiani: Milan Rastislav Štefánik vo svetle talianskych archívov, Bratislava 2012
Olach, Ľubo: Vavro Šrobár, Marenčin, Bratislava 2017
Osuský, Paulů: Štefánik I., L. Mazáč, Praha – Bratislava 1938
Palmowski, Jan: Contemporary World History, Oxford University Press 2004
Petrus, Ján: Od piky, Akademia, Bratislava 1933
Písecký, Ferdinand: M. R. Štefánik v mém deníku, EOS, Bratislava 1934
Podhorský, Dušan: Štefánikov svet, VEDA, Bratislava 2013
Polívka, Vladimír: Korespondence Dr. Milana Rastislava Štefánika, RECO 2003
Portisch, Emil: Geschichte der Stadt Pressburg II., Comissionsverlag S. Steiner, Pressburg 1933
Portisch, Hugo: Die unterschätzte Republik, Kremayr und Scheriau, Wien 1989
Rotnágl, Bulgakov: S Tolstým památce Dušana Makovického, Tranoscius, Liptovský Mikuláš 1944
Roy, Vladimír: Národný hrdina generál M. R. Štefánik, Daniel Pažický, Myjava 1932
Rušin, Vojtech: M. R. Štefánik slovenský astronóm, Alfa, Bratislava 1991
Seton Watson, R. W.: Nové Slovensko, Fr. Borový, Praha 1924
Sidor, Karol: Andrej Hlinka, Sv. Andrej, Bratislava 1934
Šaver, Ladislav: Bratři, Česká ročenka, Plzeň 1928
Šolc, Emil: Slovenská čítanka, Praha 1912
Štefan, Josef: Persekuce národa českého za světové války, Moravský legionář, Brno 1927
Štefánik, M. R.: Ekvádorský zápisník, Vydavateľstvo SSS, Bratislava 2005
Štvrtecký, Štefan: Náš Milan Rastislav Štefánik, Smena, Bratislava 1990
Šuja, Juraj: Milan Rastislav Štefánik – vek mladosti, Mazáč, Praha 1929
Teichman, Josef: Maďaři ve válce a po válce, Melantrich, Praha 1937
Tigrid, Pavel: Kapesní průvodce inteligentní ženy, Odeon, Praha 1992
Tkáč, Marian: Pravdivý slovenský príbeh, Post Scriptum, Bratislava 2009
Uhlík, Peter: V siločiarach ducha, Brezová pod Bradlom 2004

Valihora, Matúš: Brezová, Polleo Partners, Bratislava 2011
Varga, Ladislav: Hviezdny generál, Knižné centrum, Žilina 2005
Vároš, Milan: Posledný let generála Štefánika, Obzor, Bratislava 1991
Vencel, Pavol, MUDr: Koho majú bohovia radi, umiera mladý... Vlastný náklad
Zbavitel, Alojz: Milan Rastislav Štefánik, Státní nakladateľství, Praha 1929
Časopisy: P. M. History, Historická revue, History, Živá historie, Extra Historie
Internet

Words of Gratitude

After completing the work, especially one this demanding, it's beholden on the author to thank those who helped, those who encouraged him in moments of doubt and reined in him in moments of fleeting pride. First of all, I would like to thank the readers who reach for this book with confidence. Of the fifteen books that have come from my pen so far, this was the hardest to write. But I managed it thanks to the help of people who volunteered themselves and those I contacted, because they know Štefánik not only because of their encyclopedic and internet knowledge, but also because he is close to their hearts. First of all, I thank two precious men, devotees and connoisseurs of Štefánik: Pavol Kanis and Miro Musil. Both responded with enthusiasm to my approaches and offered me a selfless arm. Paľo was pleased to provide me with all the necessary information from his archive, in excess of his author's or filmmaking needs. He could have acted selfishly as he was working on a film documentary about Štefánik, but he acted like a knight, and with typical enthusiasm he advised, contradicted, and pushed me. Mirko Musil is a connoisseur of Štefánik to his fingertips, and like Paľo, has been to almost every corner of the globe where Štefánik appeared on his blessed journeys. When we encountered the mystery of Štefánik's first encounter with the fatal love of the Marchesa Benzoni, he didn't hesitate to call the most able, the Marchesa's nephew, former Senator Albert Benzoni. His phone number was kindly obtained by Mrs. Miroslava Vallová. Mr. Alberto was clearly pleased with the news that a documentary novel about Štefánik was being written. He confirmed that the love between Štefánik and her relatives really did exist... But let's not get ahead of ourselves. Miro translated the relevant parts of Benzoni's memoir, La vita ribelle, from Italian and selflessly supplied me with rare documents. Both deserve my deepest thanks. The long time chairman of the Štefánik Society, Mr. Peter Uhlík from Brezová, helped with many facts. Interesting documents and time was given to me by the parish priest, Zuzana Durcová from Košariská. I also thank the other wonderful people who had a hand in the work: Jana Matloňová-Klein, Ivan Šesták, Marek Eštok, Alexander Halvoník, Igor Chlebík, Ingrid and Peter Polačkovci, Danka Janovičková, Ernest Bagi (†), Blanka Ušiaková, Ruzena Kormosova, Bohumil Hanzel, Juraj Štaffa, Valéria Malíková, Miroslava Vallová, Vladimír Mistrík, Ivica Gavlasová, Anton Baláž and Slavomír Podmajerský. I would also like to thank Laco Kollár, a farmer, Radek Nižňanský, a cook, and Mrs. Elena Strihová, a housekeeper who created excellent working conditions during my creative stays at the House of Slovak Writers in Piešťany.

Contents

Zuzana Palovic & Gabriela Bereghazyova: The Man Who Made Us Proud to Be Slovak	VI
Kevin J. McNamara: A Slovak Unbound - The Global Impact of Štefánik's Brief Life	VIII
Michael J. Kopanic, Jr.: A Tragic End to a Storied Life	XV
Miroslav Musil: Enjoy!	XXI
Pavol Kanis: Combining Fact and Fiction	XXIII

PART ONE: PEACE

Chapter 1: If I'm Killed...	13
Chapter 2: The Bell of Freedom Strikes	22
Chapter 3: Spread the Glory of Your Nation	33
Chapter 4: Neither Obstacle Nor Illness Will Overcome Me	43
Chapter 5: A Defiance that Moves Mountains	48
Chapter 6: We Have Entered the Service of the Soul	51
Chapter 7: The Eighth Star	56
Chapter 8: Faith is Action	63
Chapter 9: Isten áldja meg – May God Bless You	71
Chapter 10: Not Humble in the Least!	75
Chapter 11: I'll Follow the Voice of My Heart	80
Chapter 12: Likewise in Times of Loss and Victory	90
Chapter 13: Always According to the Truth	100
Chapter 14: Thoughts, Words and Deeds in Harmony with Conscience	103
Chapter 15: It's the Meaning of Life That Counts	112
Chapter 16: Feet in the Mud, Head in the Stars	116
Chapter 17: I Will Break Through Because I Want to Break Through	120
Chapter 18: What You Give Comes Back to You	127

Chapter 19: Lack of Freedom is a Lack of Courage   130
Chapter 20: To believe, to love, to work!   135
Chapter 21: I Have Suffered for You   144
Chapter 22: A Miracle is the Consequence of Faith   151
Chapter 23: Serve Beauty, Spread Happiness!   157
Chapter 24: To Experience Eternity in Second   161
Chapter 25: Knock and the Door will Open   166
Chapter 26: Growing to the Stars   172
Chapter 27: You Can Do It!   177
Chapter 28: For a Person of Strong Resolve
    Nothing is Impossible   182
Chapter 29: Don't You Want to Triumph as well?   189
Chapter 30: If You Want It, You Already Have It   194
Chapter 31: My Soul Weeps, My Fist is Clenched   196
Chapter 32: Improve Yourself, You'll Improve the World   201
Chapter 33: The More I Learn, the Freer I Am   206
Chapter 34: Departing from Time   210
Chapter 35: Weaknesses are Stairs to the Heights   212
Chapter 36: Paradise in the Heart   217
Chapter 37: Pain is Suffering for the Weak,
    a Gift for the Strong   222
Chapter 38: The Shaman's Prophecy   227
Chapter 39: The Titanic Didn't Happen   232
Chapter 40: My Brother, You'll Be My Enemy   238
Chapter 41: A Prophecy Fulfilled   241

PART TWO: WAR

Chapter 1: Honneur et Patrie   251
Chapter 2: Father Against Son, Brother Against Brother   262
Chapter 3: The Weak Wait for an Opportunity,
    the Strong Create It   269
Chapter 4: I'll Give Up When I Die   272

Chapter 5: Whoever Dies Without Desires Has Lived a True Life	281
Chapter 6: Help me Liberate My Country!	285
Chapter 7: Obstacles Strengthen Us	295
Chapter 8: The Dead Pile Up	302
Chapter 9: I Live Life in Seconds	307
Chapter 10: I'm not Stefanik!	317
Chapter 11: You're a Traitor to Slovaks	322
Chapter 12: When I've Done What I Need I Will Die in Peace	328
Chapter 13: Our Cause Will Succeed!	335
Chapter 14: Lenin Cooperates	340
Chapter 15: Dubček Versus Štefánik	346
Chapter 16: The Woman of My Life	356
Chapter 17: I'll Continue When the Prince Returns	361
Chapter 18: Masaryk: Support the Bolsheviks!	366
Chapter 19: My Dear Edušo, I Embrace You Warmly	371
Chapter 20: Transforming Crashes into Take-Offs	376
Chapter 21: The Republic has been Established but the Struggle for it is just Beginning	381
Chapter 22: How Isidor Declared the Republic	385
Chapter 23: Traitor! Blackguard! String Him Up!	391
Chapter 24: Above All I Love My Nation	396
Chapter 25: We've Had Enough!	400
Chapter 26: Aim Properly at My Heart!	406
Chapter 27: The House of Horror	410
Chapter 28: A Golden Treasure	417
Chapter 29: If I Die I Go on to the Majority	421
Chapter 30: Milan, Come and Help Us!	427
Chapter 31: A Will of Tempered Steel	434
Chapter 32: The Country Awaits You	441
Chapter 33: I'm Tired to Death	448
Chapter 34: It's Over Between Us!	452

Chapter 35: Amor, Roma   461
Chapter 36: A Top Secret Flight   467
Chapter 37: The Fall   473
Chapter 38: We'd Kill You If...   482

Epilogue   489
Literature Consulted   491
Words of Gratitude   497

Jozef Banáš
PREBIJEM SA! ŠTEFÁNIK Muž železnej vôle

Jozef Banáš
Milan Rastislav Štefánik: A Man of Iron Will

Translated from the Slovak original Prebijem sa! Štefánik. Muž železnej vôle (an imprint of IKAR, a.s., 2018) by James Sutherland-Smith
Edited by Jonathan Gresty

First Edition Published by IKAR, a.s. in 2019 as its book number 6,306.
Typeset by ITEM, spol. s r. o., Bratislava

Second Edition Published by Hybrid Global Publishing, New York and co-published by Global Slovakia, Bratislava Slovakia, a.s. in 2020
Printed in the United States of America, or in the United Kingdom when distributed elsewhere

ISBN 978-1-951943-17-2
ISBN 978-1-951943-16-5

WWW.GLOBALSLOVAKIA.COM

The First Catholic Slovak Union of The United States of America and Canada (FCSU) is a non-profit fraternal organization headquartered in Independence, OH, USA. Founded in Cleveland in 1890 by 11 Slovak immigrants with the guidance of the Slovak immigrant priest the Rev. Štefan Furdek, the FCSU is also often called "Jednota" which in Slovak means "Union." This is the same name as its bilingual newspaper that has been published virtually throughout its history until today. During the communist era, the Jednota Press was one of the few places in the world that printed Slovak Catholic literature. The FCSU's original purpose was to help to immigrant Slovaks deepen their religious faith, protect their language and heritage, and provide an insurance fund for those working in and near Cleveland's dangerous factories. Today the FCSU offers very competitive annuities, wealth transfer, and life insurance products and services to 50,000+ members in communities throughout North America, and continues to support fraternal activities and events that preserve shared values of faith, family and heritage. More complete information can be found at www.fcsu.com.

ALSO BY GLOBAL SLOVAKIA

SLOVAKIA: THE LEGEND OF THE LINDEN

This book takes you on an emotional journey deep into the Slovak and Slavic inner world. Follow the trail that opens your eyes to the magical realm guarded by the Linden tree and its sacred heart-shaped leaf. It is a code that carries the story of the people born at the crossroads of worlds.

Available on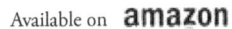

www.globalslovakia.com

SLOVENSKO: LEGENDA LIPY

Táto kniha pozýva na sentimentálnu cestu do hĺbky slovenskej a slovanskej duše. Otvára chodníček do čarovného sveta, ktorého vstup chráni lipa. Jej posvätný srdcovitý list je šifrou nesúcou príbeh ľudí, ktorí sa zrodili na križovatke svetov.

www.globalslovakia.com

THE GREAT RETURN

In the beginning of the 21st century, Europe opened its borders to the countries from behind the Iron Curtain. Since then, over 100 million citizens, including Slovaks gained the freedom to move West without a visa. Now, a decade after the East-West exodus, our pioneers are returning home.

Telling the stories of international Slovaks who left, learned and returned, 58 voices including government, business and society share their views on the transformation of a nation. The 59th voice is that of the author, who reveals a personal tale of loss, lessons and reconnection through a rite of passage shared by millions of people across the planet.

Time-travellers to culture-shifters, Slovakia's lost daughters and sons come home, proving that return is not just a possibility, but an opportunity.

Available on amazon

www.globalslovakia.com

VEĽKÝ NÁVRAT

Na začiatku 21. storočia otvorila Európa svoje hranice krajinám spoza bývalej železnej opony. Víza na západ sa stali minulosťou a viac ako 100 miliónov občanov vrátane Slovákov získalo slobodu pohybu. Po viac ako dekáde hromadných odchodov sa mnoho priekopníkov vracia zo západu domov.

Táto kniha prináša 58 hlasov z politiky, biznisu a spoločenských organizácií. Medzinárodní Slováci, ktorí odišli, spoznali a prišli späť, sa delia o svoje pohľady na prerod svojho národa. Päťdesiaty deviaty hlas patrí samotnej autorke. Odhaľuje podmanivý osobný príbeh straty, uvedomenia a znovu nájdenia.

Dnes sa stratené dcéry a synovia Slovenska vracajú domov. Sú cestovateľmi v čase a nositeľmi zmien. Dokazujú, že návrat nie je len možnosťou, ale i nesmiernou príležitosťou.

www.globalslovakia.com

CZECHOSLOVAKIA: BEHIND THE IRON CURTAIN

Take a journey into the borderland of the Red Empire, during an ideological battle that saw the world ripped in half. Dare to step into communist Czecho-Slovakia, where the controlled 'East' and the free 'West' converged at their closest.

This is a story of ordinary people caught up in the midst of the 20th century's greatest political experiment. Through tales only told in whispers, glimpse into the everyday reality of those whose entire universe was ruled by the Hammer and Sickle.

Available on amazon

 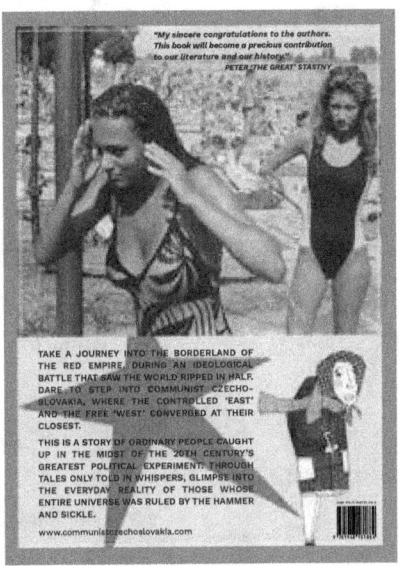

www.communistczechoslovakia.com

ČESKOSLOVENSKO: ZA ŽELEZNOU OPONOU

Preneste sa na pomedzie Červenej ríše v čase ideologickej vojny, ktorá rozštiepila svet vo dvoje. Odvážte sa vstúpiť na pôdu socialistického Československa. Práve tu sa komunistický Východ a slobodný Západ ocitli nebezpečne blízko seba. Toto je príbeh obyčajných ľudí, ktorí sa zachytili do siete najväčšieho politického experimentu 20-teho storočia. To, o čom píše táto kniha si mohli len šepkať. Nahliadnite do denno-dennej reality tých, ktorých svet sa točil okolo nekompromisnej vlády kladiva a kosáka.

www.communistczechoslovakia.com